This book is for my old
basketball buddy Pete Bennett.
Good luck and health —
Thad Stem, Jr.

Feby 7, 1970

This book belongs in the library of

James L. Bennett, Jr.

Durham, North Carolina

. . . seek ye out of the best books
words of wisdom; D & C 88:118

RANSACKING
WORDS AND CUSTOMS

FROM A TO IZZARD

THAD STEM, JR.

Moore Publishing Company

Durham, North Carolina

Library of Congress Catalog Card Number: 77-88204

ISBN 0-87716-086-4

To

my grandson,

William Thaddeus Anderson

and

Frank P. Ward, Jr.

PUBLISHER'S NOTE

What words can a mere publisher use in reference to the profound erudition of Thad Stem? To give words to Stem is carrying coals to Newcastle, as this book clearly shows. So I shall carry only a small bucket.

The most abstruse and arcane features of knowledge are within the detailed grasp of this Bard of Oxford. He reveals in each of his books and articles the personal mastery of knowledge that combines both learning and scholarship.

Book learning is not enough for Stem because he goes far beyond the understanding of other authors. Learning may be a proper word for Stem since it implies the sustained instruction and study that produces a rich and orderly background. The expression, He draws from a deep well, applies to Stem.

I wouldn't use pedantry even though it implies the grasp of knowledge. This word includes a negative meaning that suggests dogmatism rather than relevance. And this, of course, is not Thad Stem.

So, knowledge that comes from observation and experience, as well as learning and scholarship, forms the backdrop against which we see this literary giant. Maybe these are the words from which stem his unique literacy. I now wonder about the derivation of the verb, stem.

Eugene V. Grace, M.D.
Publisher

CONTENTS

Also by Thad Stem, Jr.

Picture Poems

The Jackknife Horse

The Perennial Almanac

The Animal Fair

Penny Whistles and Wild Plums

Spur Line

A Flagstone Walk

Light and Rest

Impact: 1919-1969

Journey Proud

Entries From Oxford

The Tar Heel Press

Senator Sam Ervin's Best Stories
(with Alan Butler)

Thad Stem's First Reader

FOREWORD

Insofar as I have the capacity to ascertain, the diverse material in this study-for-fun is accurate, but I do not intend the material to be authoritative or scholarly. I hope the manifold entries entertain, even instruct innocuously here and there. Scholars infinitely wiser and more diligent than I say etymology is likely to be matter of intelligent guessing, of giving credence to whatever seems to be supported by the greater weight of evidence.

The contents reflect interests that have fascinated me throughout my years of literacy. Someone else, just as easily, could compile a work of viable alternatives. And I do not agree that one picture is always worth a thousand words. Joseph Addison, writing in the *Spectator*, almost three centuries ago, spoke for me: "Words, when well chosen, have so great a force in them that a description often gives us more lively ideas than the sight of things themselves."

In focusing on words, phrases, customs, on the minutiae of history, and in telling some of the attending stories, I am exercising the older person's self-given privilege of personal selection, with the active hope that readers find rapport. Perhaps, Lord Byron had something of this sort in mind:

All who joy would win
Must share it,—Happiness was born a twin.

Here and there the reader will conclude that some assertion or anecdote is "without rhyme or reason," but that phrase may illustrate the paucity of absolutes in a study such as this.

Edmund Spenser (1552-1599) wrote the irrepressible phrase in "Lines on His Promised Pension." According to the story, Queen Elizabeth ordered Lord Burghley to tell Spenser she would pay Spenser one hundred pounds for a poem praising her. Burghley objected: "One hundred pounds is too much for a song." "Then pay Spenser what is reason," Elizabeth replied.

If Spenser wrote the paean, as he contended, he was not paid for it, and he sent these lines to Lord Burghley:

I was promised on a time
To have reason for my rhyme;
From that time unto this season,
I received nor rhyme or reason.

It's unromantic to question the authenticity of such a corking story, but Spenser may have versified on an established proverb. For his phrase occurs in a poem John Skelton wrote in 1529, twenty-three years before Edmund Spenser was born:

For reason can I non fynde
Nor good reason in your mater.

Even so, Spenser's "Lines on His Promised Pension" gives a twist to the common implication of "without rhyme or reason." Who knows, Spenser may have expressed the accumulated chagrins of countless bards and scriveners who have found promises and praises somewhat less nourishing than food and drink, less sustaining than hard cash.

In a couplet from his *Essay on Man*, Alexander Pope (1688-1744) published an aphorism:

Worth makes the man, and want of it the fellow:
The rest is all but leather and prunella.

For four centuries, "fellow" meant a man of small worth, often one of "mean parts," and "prunella," long worn out, was cloth material that served as uppers in women's shoes. (In this poem Pope makes the point that a drunken parson is no better than a drunken cobbler.)

"A to Izzard" implements the general fluctuations at which I have hinted. As I say in the text, many Englishmen, in the Elizabethan era, particularly, abhorred the letter "z," and this detestation produced many synonyms, such as Zed, Zod, Zard, Uzzard, Izzard and others.

And in telling some of the mores and customs that attend certain words, certain events, I have tried to remember, as best I understand them, the words of Joseph Wood Krutch: "Custom has furnished the only basis which ethics have ever had."

In poring, and pouring, over the diverse contents of this book I am happy and lucky to have the good offices of my wife, Marguerite L. Stem, Renee Buice, and Faye Apple. And, aside from the joy and comfort of their company, special thanks go to Lillian Dworsky, to Joy, Ben, and Ed Averett, and to Isabel, Royster, and Yancey Washington, and Dan Oldham and Mike and Myra, merely for existing and thinking of me.

RANSACKING
WORDS AND CUSTOMS

PART ONE
FOOD AND DRINK

"A loaf of bread, the Walrus said,
Is what we chiefly need:
Pepper and vinegar besides
Are very good indeed."

Lewis Carroll, from *Through the Looking Glass.*

"In wine there is truth." (In vino veritas).

Pliny, from *Natural History.*

"And what gave thee that jolly red nose?
Nutmeg and ginger, cinnamon and cloves,
That's what gave me this jolly red nose."

"Song No. 7" in *Deuteromelia*, perhaps, written and compiled by Thomas Ravenscroft.

"Then I commanded mirth, because a man hath no better thing under the sun, than to eat, than to drink, and to be merry."

From Ecclesiastes (8:15) and again from Luke (12:19).

"They drank with unbuttoned bellies."

Rabelais, from *Pantagruel.*

"You may tempt the upper classes
With your villianous demi tasses,
But Heaven will protect the Working Girl."

Edgar Smith, from the song, "Heaven Will Protect The Working Girl."

FOOD AND DRINK

Bread, the indispensable staff of life, is an ancient literary symbol. Various allusions appear in Ecclesiastes, Deuteronomy, Matthew, Luke, and elsewhere in the Writ. Today's basic human urgency is about as it was nineteen hundred years ago when Juvenal (60-140 A.D.) wrote that his fellow Romans longed most for "bread and circus games," and bread was not a semantical synonym for money in Rome.

Hlaf, Anglo-Saxon, gave us the English word "loaf," and for a considerable period "loaf" and "bread" were spoken interchangeably. Bread, long a symbol for friendship in several languages and dialects, came to denote the food, itself, while "loaf" fastened to the baked product that came from the oven.

"Bread," at first a "broken stick," to demonstrate one's disarming intentions, is common Teutonic. The Old English *bread* or *breat*, is derived from the Old High German *brot*, meaning a piece or a bit. Then for an extensive period, bread was used in the sense of broken bits of cooked dough, in the same connotation of breaking a loaf into smaller fragments to share with guests.

White, the simple opposite of black. is common in Teutonic languages, and the Anglo-Saxon *hwit* is cognate with the Anglo-Saxon *hwate* , or wheat, The ancient Chinese believed wheat was a direct gift from their gods, and the Greeks ascribed wheat to Demeter, who corresponded to Ceres, literally grain, the Roman goddess of growing vegetation.

The lake-dwellers of Sweden, the earliest known civilized inhabitants of Europe, cultivated several types of grain. Fragments of their bread, with portions of their primitive hand-mills, have been unearthed. Albeit, the Egyptians, believed to have been the first to brew beer, were the first to put yeast into bread. Around 450 B.C., Herodotus, "the father of history," wrote that the Egyptians of the fifth century B.C. kneaded clay with their hands and dough with their feet. The Egyptians made some white bread from bolted flour, but this was the ultimate luxury, available to nobles, exclusively. (Grain foods of the 12th and 25th dynasties—2,000-600 B.C.—found by archeologists in 1936, were astonishingly similar to modern light bread, eclairs, sweet crackers, and plum pudding.)

Diogenes (412-323 B.C.) is credited by several authorities with inventing the closed oven, and the ancient Greeks were supposed to have been excellent bakers. The building of communal ovens probably started sometime after Diogenes' era, and when the Romans conquered Macedonia in 170 B.C., Greek bakers were taken to Rome and the quality of Roman bread improved tremendously.

The Emperor Trajan established a college for bakers, and the Roman government passed strict laws pertaining to the weight and uniform quality of bread. Even so, there was one standard of bread for common people and a standard infinitely higher for members of the Roman Senate. And bread won a notable victory for the Romans. When the city was heavily beseiged by the Gauls, all food was severely limited, but the Roman general, Manius, had all of the remaining flour baked into bread *en masse* and then tossed over the ramparts to the attacking Gauls. The Gauls fled promptly because their leaders assumed that if the Romans had sufficient bread to throw away, there was no chance to starve the beleaguered garrison into surrender.

Many diverse inferences continue to be drawn from the curse placed on Adam in Genesis: "By the sweat of thy face will thou eat bread," and an erroneous, ultra-emotional rendering of a deathless passage in the *Rubaiyat of Omar Khayyam* befouled a love-nest projected in O.Henry's old story about the sagebrush miner who was courting an Eastern widow by mail. The semi-literate Lochinvar stumbled across a battered copy of the *Rubaiyat* around the mining-camp, and he copied out and mailed to his imminent mail-order bride the exhilarating invitation:

A Book of Verses underneath the Bough,
A Jug of Wine, a Loaf of Bread—and Thou
Beside me singing in the Wilderness.

The upright widow responded: "You can go on your lascivious picnics by yourself. The late husband never asked me to any such scandalous picnics and I ain't going with you."

Alas for romance, the testy widow didn't know that in Arabic, and some other eastern languages, bread is a symbol for wisdom and wine is a symbol for ecstasy.

Captain John White, leader of the "Lost Colony" on North Carolina's Roanoke Island, and grandfather of Virginia Dare (born August 18, 1587), the first white child born in North America, is supposed to have taken maize, Indian corn, from the Old Teutonic *Kurnom*, or grain, and the white potato, from the Old French *pomel*, from *pomum* the diminutive of the Latin, for apple, back to England as gifts to Queen Elizabeth I. But while corn continued to have verbal connections with the Indians of the New World, the white potato has come to be known universally as the "Irish potato."

And it's highly possible that the johnny-cake, irrepressible along much of the Atlantic seaboard until modern times, was here when the early colonists arrived. Some etymologists derive "johnny-cake" from "Shawnee cake," and there is evidence that the Shawnees, and some other tribes, made this standard, succulent fare from corn meal and water. Although many early colonists must have corrupted "Shawnee" into "johnny," the broader view is that johnny is a corruption of "journey" because "johnny-cake" has verbal viability in Australia, where the Shawnee are unknown.

It is an historical fact that Francis Asbury and some of the other circuit-riding ministers carried corn meal cakes in their saddlebags, on their missionary journeys, chiefly because the cakes did not spoil easily and retained their toothsome flavors. (Curiously enough, the word "rounder" has undergone acute transformation since Asbury's time (1745-1816). Asbury, and others who kept appointments by following a broad, diverse itinerary were called "rounders"; but by the end of the 19th century a rounder was a wastrel, a profligate, a big wheeler, as in the song "Casey Jones": "Come all you rounders if you want to hear.")

"Hoe-cake," spoken more often than eaten today, means about what it says. Colonists and some of the Indians made bread by the simple expedient of spreading watered meal, or dough, on the blade of a hoe over an open fire. Today's ubiquitous hush-puppy, corn meal and water, usually with the addition of egg and onion, rolled into balls and dropped into deep-fat, acquired its name from the old practice in which hunters, resting by the campfire at night, tossed corn-dodgers to placate restive dogs.

"Hoppinjohn," prepared slightly differently from section to section, is an outgrowth of the custom of eating black-eyed peas on January 1 to insure good luck the remainder of the year. The basic recipe, shorn of sectional appendages, is black-eyed peas cooked in flour dough or in some mixture of meal and water.

According to the Appalachian tradition, the name arose, simply enough, when some fellow named John came courting on January 1 and was enjoined to "Hop in John," to hop in and partake of the black-eyed peas.

While sundry reasons, many of them convoluted and contrived, have been advanced to account for the ritual of black-eyed peas on New Year's Day, the practice came in amid the harrowing days that followed the Civil War, when most of the American South was destitute, when all helpers and aids save the black-eyed pea seemed to have flown or faded. But the humble black-eyed, or cornfield, pea was always plentiful, and it is highly possible that the talisman for good luck began as a rough-hewn joke on post-war society, a joke self-inflicted. (This is almost in line with the old aphorism, "Too poor to paint and too proud to white-wash." *)

If the ritual alters slightly from area to area, one format subscribed to by many professional folklorists is that everyone in the family, and all the guests, must take a hand at stirring the pot of peas on the stove. Betimes, the eating plates on the table must be turned face down, with a new dime underneath each one. The peas are served on the plates straight from the pot, and the plates must be turned over carefully so as not to disturb the dime.

Subsequent activities seem predicated pretty generally upon regional caprices. Albeit, some communities adhere to the ritual that requires donation of the dime to the first needy person seen after the meal. And this is implemented by the tradition that requires all romantic girls to wear red garters. If, clad in red garters, a single girl bestows the dime, and then walks seven rails on a railroad track (about 240 feet), without falling off, and if she then looks over her left shoulder, she will be certain to see the man she's going to marry.

Curiously enough, "pease," as in "Pease porridge hot, . . ." is the old singular form. "Pea," as the singular, was coined much later in the word's history, simply because the final sibilant was misconstrued for the sign of the plural. "Pease," in the jingle means "pea." The rhyme's earliest known version was printed in 1797, but most experts believe it is much older. Not just incidentally, "Pease porridge hot, . . ." began

---

*In a post-war conversation in Lexington, Va., while he was President of Washington College, someone told General Lee that such and such a person had been "a good friend to the Confederate Army." Lee replied, apparently facetiously, "The only true friend the Confederate soldier ever had was the cornfield pea."

as a handclapping game by which children kept warm in cold weather, and the practical aspects of the game-chant continued until the present century.

Many black-eyed peas are cooked with that portion of the hog's carcass which we call "bacon," and fewer phrases in daily use have longer or wider viability than "Bring home the bacon," and countless other phrases involving the same symbolic use of bacon. Many students have encountered two somewhat enigmatic lines in Chaucer's "Prologue" to *The Wife of Bath's Tale*:

The bacon was not fat for them, I trow,
That some men have in Essex at Dunnmowe.

The allusion is to a flitch of bacon offered annually at Dunmow, a village of Sussex, England, to any couple who would kneel at the door of a church and swear that "for twelve months and a day he has never had a household brawl or wished himself unmarried." According to the story, records were kept between 1244 and 1772, and during this period of more than 500 years, the flitch, gammon, or side of bacon was awarded only eight times.

There is the theory that derives "Bring home the bacon," from the insular custom of awarding a greased pig at country fairs to the first blindfolded person who caught and held such a slick, elusive bundle. But this seems improbable in the light that "bacon" is applied to butchered pigs and hogs and not to those on the hoof.

("A pig in a poke," almost as irrepressible, dates from the same British period as "Bring home the bacon." Many unwary British farmers bought small pigs at country fairs. The pig was placed in a poke—sack—by the seller, but when many purchasers got home, a cat jumped from the bag. The complaints about this cruel ruse culminated in *caveat emptor*, or, "Let the buyer beware." Henceforth, if the buyer examined the poke at the time the sale was consummated, saw a pig inside, the seller was liable if anything untoward developed. But, if the purchaser did not examine the contents of the poke before quitting the fairgrounds, he was stuck. And, obviously, the ubiquitous, "let the cat out of the bag," emerged almost simultaneously.)

Historians say primitive man ate one enormous meal each day, and for the obvious, stultifying fact that he gorged until he could hold no more; in fact, he often threw up. Long before balanced meals and prior to any awareness of calories, Lucretius (96-55 B.C.) wrote, "What is food to one man may be sharp poison to others," and Germans like their ancient pun-aphorism *Der Mensch ist was er isst* or "Man is what he eats." Indeed, Americans have made inept and unfair ethnic characterizations on the basis of national dishes: Scottish haggis, Italian macaroni, French frogs, German wurst, English roast beef, Irish stew, and Australian steak and eggs.

But, strangely enough, the explicit format of three meals a day is so new it did not take hold until around 1890. The Anglo-Saxon tradition carried two meals, breakfast and dinner. And until the 16th century, breakfast seems to have been a furtive snack, something merely to break one's fast, as the word implies. But by the 18th century, breakfast was a sumptuous, leisurely spread, and guests were invited for breakfast as they are asked to dinner or supper, today. In the more fortunate British and American homes, the 18th-century breakfast often lasted for three hours, usually from ten until one.

However, by 1850 breakfast began about eight o'clock, and it became a skimpy meal, eaten hurriedly. And dinner or supper had an opposite history. During the era of the long, hefty breakfast, dinner was taken at five, and by 1850 at seven or eight o'clock. And lunch (dinner in the American South) is a recent innovation. It emerged as a snack merely to tide one over from breakfast to dinner. In his famous

Dictionary of 1755, Samuel Johnson defined "lunch": "As much food as one's hand can hold." And with a majority of Americans today, lunch retains its original implications of frugality, even paucity, of a "lump." From time to time lunch, or "dinner," has been a large meal, and it attained formidable proportions as the hours between breakfast and dinner increased.

Finally, during the latter portion of the Victorian era, it was the division of the working day into two definite periods—from eight until twelve, and from one until five, or from nine until one, and from two until six—that made lunch a regular institution and gave us our three daily meals.

"Soup (from the French *soupe*) to nuts (Anglo-Saxon *knula*) with fruit along the way," became an axiomatic cliche half a century back, but American inventiveness has given succulent, imaginative dimensions to various slum-gullions and stews. (Stew's first meaning was a hot bath, from the Anglo-Saxon *stofa* and this is probably from the Late Latin *extufare*, to steam out.)

"Julienne," applied to green salads today, is a chef's name for thick soup containing finely cut meats and vegetables, particularly onions and carrots. According to the legend it is named for one Julien, a refugee from the French Revolution, who opened a restaurant, the "Restorator," on Boston's Milk Street.

But whether or not "soupe julienne" originated in America, "julienne" and "julien" became generic names for an infinite variety of home-made vegetable soups throughout the 19th century. Slum-gullion was made of anything the housewife had left over, and, in the sense of a tasteless catchall, had long, derisive use in the military. Conversely, the making of the ultra-rich Brunswick Stew has long been a culinary art. It is believed that the name arose from the fact some of the early experts resided in Brunswick County, Virginia, and, perhaps in other American Brunswicks.

The various clam chowders ("clam," or "clamp," originally, and "chowder," meaning "hot," from the French word *chaudiere* for "cauldron") and oyster soups (from the Greek *ostreon*, through the Latin *ostreum*) are universal. Americans picked up avidly on the alleged aphrodisiac properties of oysters, especially raw oysters. (Despite King James I's being credited with saying, "He was a very valiant man who first adventured on eating oysters.") Richard Sheridan, Lord Byron and others wrote about the quirk that causes some species of oysters to contain two sexes in a single oyster. As Bergen Evans said, "This must lead to frustrations and complications of so remarkable a nature that human beings, considering the difficulties they have with a comparatively simple system, should charitably refrain from comment."

One of this writer's direct ancestors, in common with countless other Southern men of the insular era, drew up better than two foolscap sheets of foods he thought to be positively aphrodisiac; and raw oysters, heavily underscored, headed the list of foods to be eaten often and copiously. This man was unusually virile, but one suspects his stamina attached to the fact that he was well-nourished. (This writer has not encountered a single one of these old lists on which oysters weren't at the top.)

But if these sundry chowders and soups are international in scope, a few, sporadic geniuses along the coast of the Carolinas have come up with pristine art in their fish-muddles, the chief ingredients usually being whole, fairly small fish and whole tomatoes.

And, as is generally known, "fish," from the Anglo-Saxon *fisc*, has had religious connotations since early Christians wrote graffiti upon the walls of the catacombs. And, for a long time, one fishball was viable as a gastronomical widow's mite. George Martin Lane's poem of 1855, once well-known in America, puts the inconspicuous, almost anomolous fishball into perspective, and it conveys the appalling sense of intimidation which this writer, and thousands of others, feel in the presence of grandiose waiters:

The waiter he to him doth call,
And gently whispers—'One Fishball.'
The waiter roars it through the hall,
The guests, they start, at 'One Fishball.'
The guest then says, quite ill at ease,
'A piece of bread, sir, if you please,'
The waiter roars it through the hall:
'We don't give bread with one Fishball.'

An anonymous addendum to the poem has the waiter handing the harried guest his straw hat and telling him to eat it. Actually, "hat" is but a corruption of "hattes," a dish, according to the ancient recipe, made of "eggs, veal, dates, salt, safron, and so forth," and one that must have been almost as unpalatable as a felt hat.

Many of the edible nuts have Indian roots. The hickory nut comes from the Creek *pawcohiceora*, which seems to have meant food prepared from crushed hickory nuts, but chestnut is from the Middle English *chisten, chasteine*. The "chinapin," a modern spelling of "chinquapin," is from the Algonquin *chechinkamin*, and the same nation called the common pecan *pakan*. The several delicious varieties of walnut all stem from the Old English *wealthknutu*, a translation of the Latin *nux gallia*, a Gaulic or foreign nut.

At first all fruits were "apples," and not solely because of the Garden of Eden. The Greeks had one utility word, *melon*, and this was augmented later with *citron*, to include lemons and limes. The Romans had two words for fruits, *malum*, from the Greek, and *pomun*, from which the French obtained *pomme*. The Anglo-Saxon language had two words for fruits, *apple* and *berry*. (Thus, "quince" in Anglo-Saxon was *codapple*. "Potato" is still *pomme de terre* in French and

Erdapfel, or "earth-apple," in German. "Pineapple" was what the word says, originally—the cone or apple of the pine—but in the 18th century the word "pineapple" was transferred to the edible fruit solely because of appearance.)

"Orange" had and lost an initial "n." It is from the French *orange* from the Spanish *naranja*, from the Arabic *paranj*, from the Sanskrit *naranga*, and it was changed in Latin from *arangia* to *aurangia*, or the "golden apple." *Ranga*, used in a story by Kipling, calls up the dragon-guarded golden apples of the Hesperides.

"Banana" is tied to Spanish, but the Arabic *banana* means "finger," and *banan*, "fingers" and "toes." "Pear" comes from the Old French *piere*, through the Latin *pirum*, and "grape" is from the French *grappe*. A "bunch of grapes" is *grappes do raisins*. "Plumm," or "Green Gage," comes from Sir William Gage, who encouraged its cultivation in England in the 18th century. "Damson" is the plum of Damascus, and "cantaloupe" is from *Cantaloupo*, rural residence of the Holy See, to which the melon was brought from Armenia. And "fruit" comes from the Latin *fruii, fructi*, meaning "to enjoy," from which emerged the English word "fruition."

The "persimmon," from the Algonquin *passiminan*, and the "locust," from the French *loscusts*, or "lobster," have stigmatized in southern states as "hard times rations." Like the black-eyed pea and the rabbit, persimmons and locusts were available in parlous eras. But in astringent and in plush times, persimmon-and-locust beer used to be drunk in the old Confederacy as soft drinks are drunk today. And many people took a glass of beer with "heavy" meals, repasts at which much meat, especially game, was served.

The standard recipe is to place alternate layers of persimmons, locusts and dry broomstraw in a wooden barrel (Old French *baril*) of around thirty gallons' capacity, until the barrel is two-thirds filled, and then to fill the barrel with water. The mixture sits, sealed, for thirty days, but fermentation sets in, and if one wants "hard" beer, the brew will become patent in six weeks. In light of today's popular use of "small beer" to indicate the size of a glass or a mug, it is interesting to recall that many folks used to call persimmon-and-locust beer "small beer." Actually, "small beer" was prevalent in colonial society to mean "low alcoholic content," a brew "mildly alcoholic." In this context, Shakespeare mentioned "small beer" several times, and "double beer" to mean a more potent libation. Apparently, many colonial women, particularly wives of grandees, drank small beer regularly. William Byrd, of Westover, Virginia, the affluent, aristocratic planter who owned the largest library in the American colonies, had this entry in his secret diary, under the date of July 11, 1712: "My wife longed for small beer and I sent to Mrs. Harrison's for some but she had none, so that she (Mrs. Byrd) drank a bottle of strong almost herself."

George Washington kept a brew house for the manufacture of small beer at Mt. Vermon, and a notebook, in his own handwriting, contains this recipe, written in 1757:

To Make Small Beer

Take a large Siffer full of Bran. Hops to your Taste.
Boil these 3 hours, then strain out 30 Gallns into a Cooler.
Put in 3 Gallns Molasses while the Beer is Scalding hot or
rather draw the Molasses into the Cooler and Strain the Beer
on it while boiling Hot. Let this stand until it is little
more than Blood warm then put in a quart of Yeast. If the
Weather is very Cold cover it over with a blanket + let it
Work in the Coller 24 hours then put it into a Cask—leave
the Bung open until it is almost done Working. Bottle it
day Week it was Brewed.

"Drink," Anglo-Saxon *drincan*, is common Teutonic, and

14

Anglo-Saxon *waeter*; Old Slavic *voda*; seems equally as widely spread, but, otherwise, one must be specific in ordering libations. "Ale" and "beer" are common Teutonic words, and "wine" is also. (Spanish, *win*, from the Latin, *vinum*, meaning "wine" and "grape.") "Benedictine" was prepared by the monks of the order of St. Benedict, and "chartreuse" by the monks of La Grande Chartreuse. "Brandy," short for "brandywine," is from the Dutch *brendewjin*, or "burnt wine," and "champagne" takes its name from the French province. "Cordial" comes from the Latin *cordialis*, and it originated as a "heartening drink."

"Gin" is a diminutive of "geneva," from the Latin *juniperus*, whence *juniper,* the berries which flavor gin, and "julep" comes from the Arabic *julab*, through the Persian *gulab*, or "rose water." We obtained the irrepressible word "punch" from the Hindu *panch*, or "five," denoting alcohol, lemon, water, sugar, and spice. "Vermouth" is from the Anglo-Saxon *vermod,* and it seems to have meant "courage" in first context. The basic herb for vermouth was an early aphrodisiac.

"Rum," short for *rumbullion*, is a lengthy story. "Bullion" is the French *boullon*, a hot drink, from the Latin *bulire* ultimately "to boil." "Rum" comes from two slang sources: The Romany gypsy *rom* means "man," but *Rome* was an adjective for almost any superlative. In his *Dictionary of Slang* (1938) Eric Partridge lists five columns of words beginning with "rum," chiefly, in the sense of being "good."

"Sack" is from *Hippocras*, strained through a sac, and seltzer bubbled up in Selters, a German village with a mineral spring. "Sherbert" comes from the Arabic *sharbat*, a drink made of sugar and water. "Sherry" derives from the Spanish *vinode Xerxes*, made in Caesaris, now Jeres. "Soda," short for "soda water," comes down from the Arabic *suda*, or "headache," which the potion attempted to alleviate.

"Soda pop" originated in the United States. The first soda

is ascribed to Dr. Philip Syng Physick, of Philadelphia. In 1807 Dr. Physick asked one Townsend, a Philadelphia chemist, to prepare carbonated water for one of the doctor's patients, and Townsend flavored the carbonated water with fruit juice to make it palatable. Several experts hail this as the advent of the soft drink industry. Whether or not, Physick was real enough, and he used to be known as the "Father of American Surgery." In 1831 he removed almost one thousand stones, in a single operation, from Chief Justice John Marshall's bladder. Had Thomas Jefferson been alive, he might have added, ":I told you so."

Soda water became a popular commodity in 1832 when John Matthews, of New York City, invented an apparatus for preparing water charged with carbon dioxide gas. In New England, soda pop is called tonic, and this may be a logical survival of the original purpose of the drink.

We got "toddy" from the earlier *tarrie*, from the Arabic *tari*, from "tar," a species of palm. "Whiskey" is short for the aqua vitae, "water of life," which is the alchemist's phrase for "alcohol"; *eau-de-vie*, French for "water of life," or "brandy"; and the Russian *vodka*, diminutive of *voda*, or "water."

(Kill Devil Hill, a town on North Carolina's historic Roanoke Island, is supposed to have acquired its name from the unusually virulent brand of home-made molasses rum drunk by the inhabitants early in the 18th century, and called "Kill Devil" locally. "Booze" may have been introduced into the United States twice. "Booze" seems to have been popularized in and after the national election of 1840 when a Philadelphia distiller, E.C. Booz, got out a bottle, blown into the shape of a log cabin, at the Whitney Glass works in Philadelphia, and labeled "E.C. Booz's Log Cabin Whiskey.")

(While nothing is known about E. C. Booz's politics, there is every supposition that the bottle was designed to focus additional attention upon William Henry Harrison and John

Tyler, "Tippacanoe and Tyler, too," the famous, if puerile, "hard cider and log cabin" ticket. Actually, "booze," in varying forms, has appeared in English since the 14th century. It has appeared as *bouze, bousee, boose,* and *bowze,* and it is derived from the Middle Dutch *buyzen* or *buxen,* meaning to "guzzle liquor." Edmund Spenser, in his *Faerie Queen* (1590) writes of Gluttony's drinking wantonly from a "Bouzing can," of getting "Boozy," or drunk. And Washington Irving used "boozing" several years before E.C. Booz came up with his log cabin bottle. It is likely that "booze" was introduced, certainly as a verb if not as a noun, by the early English and the Dutch settlers, a long time prior to 1840, and then revitalized semantically during the log cabin and hard cider campaign.)

"Coffee" derives from the Turkish *gahreh,* but more basically from Coffa, Ethiopia, where coffee still grows wild. "Tea," pronounced "tay" at one point, is from the Mandarin Chinese *ch'a,* and "intoxicate" comes from the Late Latin *intoxicare intoxicat* as in poison, and when a man says, "Name your poison," he is always talking about whiskey and not some other toxic agent.

The explanations and the accompanying stories relative to the word "cocktail" are as interminable as the explanation of the word "highball" is brief. Whiskey, mixed with soda, or water, and ice, or a soft drink served with ice in a tall glass, obtained the name "highball" from railroad terminology. Early train signals were pointed metal globes hoisted to the crossarm of a tall pole that stood beside the track. "Highballing" meant a clear track, or a signal to start, to continue moving, or to increase speed.

Curiously enough, "highball," in the sense of whiskey and soda, was appropriated from American hoboes who spoke the word in the railroad sense. And, equally as curiously, "highball" seems to have denoted a soft drink before it became synonymous with whiskey and soda. While "highball" is hardly spoken today to mean a soft drink, the word was fairly vibrant in the 1890's around drug store fountains.

"Cocktail" must have been defined in literature first in 1806 in a forgotten book, *The Balance*: "A stimulating liquor composed of spirits of any kind." One brisk legend ascribes "cocktail" to a drink brewed by an Aztec nobleman from the spa of the cactus plant. The emperor came calling and he was served the drink by the lovely hand of Zochitl, the nobleman's daughter. The emperor married the girl, and to honor his bride he called the new drink Zochitl. Pronounced with the royal Aztec accent, the word came out "Octel." Then during the Mexican War, some of Zachary Taylor's men encountered the Octel, brought it home, and called it "cocktail."

The word has also been traced to Betsy Flanagan, a resolute patriot, who kept a tavern, "The Four Corners," near New York City during the Revolutionary War. Betsy's next-door neighbor, an Englishman and a loyalist, kept chickens. One day Betsy stole several chickens, cooked them, and to perpetuate her feat she adorned her jars and bottles with trophy feathers from the roasted fowls. An American soldier, needing a libation, asked for a glass "poured from those cocktails." Another diner is alleged to have raised a glass and shouted, "Long live the cocktails."

Yet another theory ties the word "cocktail" to the fact that some of the colonial physicians swobbed sore throats with potions applied by the tip of a long feather plucked from a cock. (The medications used by sundry doctors acquired the general name "gargle.")

Yet, there is a strong possibility that the dictionary supplies the logical answer for the elusive "cocktail." The "cocktail," or "cocked horse," the same one that still speeds down to Banbury Cross, never a thoroughbred, usually had its tail cocked, cut short, so that it stood up like a cock's tail. As the cocked tail horse was of several strains, so the "cocktail" contained several admixtures. As the old song had it:

Perhaps it's made of whiskey, and perhaps
      of gin?
Perhaps there's orange bitters and a lemon peel within.

Actually, it's entirely possible that the word "cocktail" comes from the "cocked horse," from Zochitl, from Betsy Flanagan, from the swob, as well as from other sources.

We clink our glasses because primitive man believed evil spirits might enter the body when he opened his mouth. So, glasses were clinked to frighten the devil away with the noise. There is the modern rationalization that to enjoy a drink fully one must taste it, smell it, touch it, see it, and hear it as well.

The custom in which the host pours a few drops of wine into his own glass before he serves his guest is related to the tradition of allaying suspicion of poison by taking the first sip. But before the introduction of corks, in Italy, wine was topped with oil, and the host wanted to be sure that he, not his guest, got the oil. After the advent of corks, the thoughtful host tried to make sure the guest didn't get any bits of cork in his glass.

The word "toast" referred to a piece of parched bread, originally, when a piece of toast served as an additive, and "toasting," as a social gesture, persisted after the additive-bread was determined to be almost valueless. And there is the story which is supposed to have occurred at Bath, during King Charles II's tenure. While a celebrated beauty was in one of the town's public baths, a roisterer dipped a glass of the water she was standing in and drank to her health. His companion offered to jump into the bath. He explained, "I don't like the liquor, but I'd like to have the toast."

Beer, the oldest of all alcoholic drinks, goes back at least 10,000 years, and crude brewing probably began when bread crumbs fell into water and started fermenting. Beer was a vital portion of the first diet, and it was poured on the earth to insure fertility. In some tribes, the job of brew-master was so sacred and sacrosanct, the brewer was not allowed any intercourse with mere mortals. (One of the most ancient of clay tablets depicts a crude Babylon beer-making machine, circa 6,000 B.C.) Beer-making spread from Egypt to Greece and Rome, but the people in northern Europe seem to have discovered it separately. (Roman invaders found and enjoyed beer in Britain at the time of Jesus Christ.) Medieval monasteries excelled in brewing, and churches sold beer to raise funds. Beer became the most popular drink at weddings, and it was poured on the bride's head to insure fertility. Since it was called "bride's ale," it accounts for the word "bridal."

The pilgrims had casks of beer on the *Mayflower,* and the rapidly diminishing supply of beer may have caused the skipper to seek a landing-place ahead of schedule. According to the *Mayflower's* log: "For we could not take time for further search and consideration, our victuals being much spent, especially beer." (Water became stagnant on long trips, but beer retained its taste and puissance.)

During some of the terrible plagues of the Middle Ages, beer was credited as a preventive and an anodyne for pestilence. Perhaps it did give buoyancy amid harrowing times, more especially when water was contaminated.

Although wine is not so old as beer, it was made in Mesopotamia prior to 3,000 B.C. Wine was a gift from the gods, and it came from the blood of the gods. Thus, when one drank it the gods entered his body. Drinking wine was a sacred ritual, and intoxication was merely the presence of the divine spirit in the human body.

The Persians ascribe wine to a remarkable error. Jam-Sheed, founder and ruler of the city of Persepolis, loved grapes so much he wanted them to eat out of the season. So he bottled some grapes to preserve the fruit, but a jar was broken and the grapes were crushed. Baffled by the forbidding-looking juice, Jam-Sheed rebottled it and labeled the container "Poison."

A female servant, despairing of life, decided to kill herself. She saw the bottle labeled "Poison" and drank deeply. She passed out, came to, and finished the jar. She thought she had died and come to life again. She told her master, and, ere long, "the delightful poison" was the toast of Persia.

The militant abstainer, the teetotaller, is fairly new, and the word dates, allegedly, from 1834 and Richard Turner, an English laborer who went around preaching total abstention, but who had an unfortunate stutter. Adversaries at Lancashire, watching and listening as Turner tried to put "t-t-total abstention" together, seized upon "t-t-t-total" for derision. The pro-whiskey people went around mocking Turner and his movement, but Turner's followers proudly called themselves "Teetotallers." (The word has been traced to the habit of serving nothing stronger than "tea" at early temperance meetings, and while this could reinforce "teetotaller," there is no doubt about Turner and his dramatic stutter.)

Not just incidentally, the ubiquituous bootlegger, the purveryor of illegal, illicit booze, takes his name from the tradition that those who peddled whiskey on Indian reservations secreted bottles, or flasks, in the legs of their high, leather boots. However, some authorities say the man with the bottles in the leg of his boots plied his traffic first among the mountain folks in Kentucky. But regardless of whether the first place was on Indian reservation or Kentucky hill country, there is no question about the origin of the word.

In the days before the court permitted public, legal sales of James Joyce's *Ulysses*, those who sold the verboten novel were called "bootleggers," and after national Prohibition had passed, sports writers resurrected bootleg to describe the deceptions of the T-quarter back who hides the football on his hip.

"Welsh rabbit," melted cheese and butter served on toast,

is corrupted often into "rarebit" on many imposing menus. The *Oxford Dictionary* calls "rarebit" an "etymologizing alteration of Welsh rabbit." And the late H.W. Fowler, in his *Modern English Usage*, wrote, "Welsh rabbit is amusing and right, and Welsh rarebit stupid and wrong."

Back when few people in Wales could afford a rabbit from a royal game perserve, melted cheese on toast was labeled "the poor man's rabbit," and in *The Merry Wives of Windsor* Shakespeare speaks of melted cheese and toast as a favorite dish of the Welsh. And for similar whimsical reasons, eggs on anchovy toast, sometimes garnished with sardines, are called "Scotish Woodchuck," or "Scotch Woodcock;" boiled Irish potatoes are "Munster plums"; many varieties of canned rabbit are "boned turkey"; red herrings are transformed into "Norfolk Capons"; and codfish becomes "Cape Cod Turkey," as are varieties of goose and duck, depending upon sectional vagaries; hogs' testicles, in a transition almost to rival water into wine, became "Mountain Oysters," although this transition was not predicated on whimsicality nearly so much as on decorum.

Melba toast, extremely thin and dry, seems to have been prepared by a chef at London's Savoy Hotel for Madame Melba, (1861-1931) (née Nellie Mitchell) the illustrious, Australian-born diva. And George Auguste Escoffier, "king of cooks," and officer of the Legion of Honor, is credited with preparing Peach Melba as a suitable reward for the prima donna's rendering of the most famous scene in Wagner's *Lohengrin*. (This is supposed to have occurred at the Savoy, also.) From a block of ice Escoffier fashioned two wings with icing sugar, and in between were peaches in a bed of vanilla ice cream. Ultimately, Escoffier added raspberry sauce.

The format in which the naked, or scantily-attired, girl emerges from an enormous cake is seen on some of the late television movies, often ones that depict the gangster era. If the hoods were ignorant of the history, this bit of ultra ostentation seems rooted in factual tradition:

Sing a song of sixpence,
A pocket full of rye;
Four and twenty blackbirds,
Baked into a pie.

When the pie was opened,
The birds began to sing;
Wasn't that a dainty dish
To set before a king?

The Opies, editors of the classic, *The Oxford Dictionary of Nursery Rhymes*, assert that the jingle merely celebrates a festive occasion in British antiquity when live birds were placed beneath a thin crust and opened at state banquets in deference to the guest-potentate. In fact, the Opies enumerate several "recipes" for the judicious placing of the birds within the pie so that live birds would fly out simultaneously, in a mighty swoosh, "to cause a diverting Hurley-Burley amongst the Guests."

Despite the abiding misconception, pork is not a forbidden food among the Jews, exclusively. Arabs subscribe to the same religious prohibition, and the Caribs did not eat pork because they feared eating the meat would give them tiny, hog-like eyes, and many Zulu maidens shunned pork because they thought their children would resemble small pigs. Few superstitions were more deeply ingrained than the primitive belief that man became whatever he ate. Several African tribes ate venison so that they could run faster, but they scorned bear meat* for fear that they would become clumsy. In ancient Hebrew tradition, and according to the Biblical injunction, an edible animal had to possess two requirements:

---

*Modern Africa is bereft of bears. Hence, the "bear" in the text may be some breed of wild boar, and even if the idea is valid, "bear" may be slightly faulty translation.

the animal had to chew its cud and to have cloven hooves.

And repugnance for pork emerged among the Hebrews because "lesser breeds beyond the law" ate pigs and sacrificed the animals to their idols. Any association of the pig with alien gods and rituals was sufficient of itself to cause the Jews, with their passion for monotheistic faith, to reject the animal in toto. The innate filthiness of the hog is a secondary factor in rejection. Too, some hogs ate their young, and any suggestion of infanticidal compulsions made the animal even more repulsive among a people with a high reverence for life.

Finally, although the ancient Egyptians raised and ate pigs, the Egyptians thought hogs unclean. Herodotus (5th century B.C.), the Greek, recalled that anyone who touched a pig had to dive into a river with his clothing on; and that swineherds, even when native-born Egyptians, were the only class barred from religious services; and swineherds were forced to marry within their own occupational class, to preclude conjugal contamination.

It was Samuel Butler (1612-1680) in *Hubibras*, once widely celebrated, who wrote, "As pigs are said to see the wind." Butler was merely repeating the very old belief that may have been predicated on the fact pigs have much more acute sense of hearing than humans. Thus, the ugly hog would display an awareness so keen it would appear to be profoundly mysterious.

The inadvertent genius who gave us "hamburger" has never been identified by name. Obviously, "hamburger" comes from Hamburg, Germany, but no one knows who put hamburger steak between two buns first. The generally accepted story is that in 1900 a customer, on the fly, went into a New Haven short-order cafe that specialized in hamburger steak, served on a plate. The customer, wishing to eat on the run, asked for a regular hamburger steak made into a sandwich.

And since then "hamburger" has had wide colloquial use to mean a prize fighter who is beaten badly often; a bum;

anyone who is destitute; an inferior race horse or racing dog (one that should be ground up for hamburger); fraudulent mixtures used for beauty treatments; and to make hamburger out of something means to trounce severely.

Two theories attempt to account for the origin of "hot dog," also prevalent since 1900. Hot dog has been tied to the older dachshund sausage, from the facetious implication that the sausage was made from ground dog meat. And, "hot dog" is supposed to have an accidental interjection yelled by a vendor at the Old Polo Ground, in the early years of this century. The weather was chilly, and the vendor had his dachshund sausages in a pan of hot water to keep them warm. The fire burned brighter as the vendor talked with a customer who wanted a frankfurter sandwich. Absent-mindedly, the vendor stuck his hand in the water, picked up a frankfurter, and exclaimed, "Hot dog."

While the original "hot dog" was a cry of pain, or shock, almost immediately "hot dog" became integral in the vernacular as an exclamation to denote excitement, delight, enthusiasm, or happy approval.

Slaw, served frequently with hamburgers, hot dogs, and barbecue, is advertized in American restaurants as "coleslaw" and as "coldslaw." If either spelling is acceptable, there is no etymological basis for coldslaw, save that much coleslaw is chilled. "Cole" is an Old English word for cabbage and other, plants of the same genus. "Cole," "kale," "caule" in "cauliflower," and "kohl" in 'kohl rabi'' all come from the Latin *caulis* or cabbage. New York's early Dutch settlers made a salad that consisted of finely cut cabbage leaves, dressed with vinegar, oil, pepper, and salt and called "kool-slaa." By the operation of the law of hobson-jobson, "kool-slaa" became "coleslaw" in American English. And folk etymology worked coleslaw into coldslaw, on menus and in some dictionaries.

Most of the restaurants that sell coleslaw have juke boxes.

"Jouk," meaning to dodge someone, to move swiftly, is an Elizabethan word that was preserved in the Appalachians after it had evaporated in England. "Jouk" corrupted into "juke," was applied to illicit liquor joints during Prohibition. When the automatic phonograph came to the jouk, or juke, joint, it was called the "juke box."

"Sandwich," as in frankfurter and other kinds of sandwiches, derives, as is generally known, from the fourth Earl of Sandwich, of George III's time, the very same nobleman after whom Captain James Cook named the Sandwich Islands, now the Hawaiian Islands. A notorious gambler, Sandwich became so engrossed in cards or dice he would not interrupt a game to go to the eating table. So, he had an attendant bring him meat between two pieces of bread, to eat as he gambled.

But while the Earl gave his name to the sandwich, meat between bread or biscuit halves was irrepressible among the Romans, who had called the concoction *offula*, diminutive of *offa*, meaning a morsel. Indeed, the invading Romans probably introduced the sandwich to Great Britain about 1800 years before Lord Sandwich's birth. And, not just incidentally, Charles Dickens (1812-1870) seems to be the first writer to use "sandwich man" to mean one who walks around carrying advertising placards on his back and chest.

"Barbecue," much older than one is likely to assume, is derived from *berbekot*, through the Spanish *brabacoa*. This is the name the Carib Indians of the West Indies gave to the wooden grill, or frame, on which fish and meat were dried, broiled, or smoked. Shortly before 1700 the word "barbecue" meaning a grill or an elevated bedstead, worked its way into the southern colonies of America. Within a few years "barbecue" meant the hog, or the ox, more often, that was cooked over a pit.

And by the 1750's "barbecue" was the social function, the gathering of clans, as well as roasted meat. The word must have been well-established as a verb by 1728 when Alexander

Pope wrote in one of his poems:

Oldfield, with more than happy throat subdued,
Cries, 'Send me, ye gods, a whole hog barbecued.'

George Washington, an inveterate party-giver and goer, recorded in his diary the happy fact that he had just attended "a Barbecue of my own giving at Accatinck."

The biggest barbecue in history probably took place in 1923 when John C. Walton was inaugurated governor of Oklahoma. In excess of a hundred thousand people were served barbecued pork, beef, mutton, rabbit, buffalo, bear, reindeer, antelope, squirrel, possum, coon, chicken and duck, all cooked across a solid mile of slit-trenches. Oceans of coffee were served from huge urns, each holding 10,000 gallons.

Today's inevitable salad comes through the French *salade*, from the Late Latin form *salata* or salted, from *salare*, to salt. (Roman soldiers were paid in salt, *salarium*, or salt-money, and this was the figurative for what we call salary today. How "with a grain of salt" acquired its traditional meaning of skepticism is obscure, unless, of course, it meant that a pinch of salt would enable one to get down something hard to swallow. The phrase appears in Pliny's *Natural History* as "a grain of salt added." Mithridates, fearing he would be poisoned, took small doses of poison daily to inure his body. Pliny says that when Pompey took Mithridates' palace he found the famous prescription for the antidote: "To be taken fasting, plus a grain of salt.")

"Salad days," the enduring synonym for innocent or naive youth, originated in *Anthony and Cleopatra*:

.....My salad days,
When I was green in judgment, cold in blood.

Ironically, Cleopatra, in praising Anthony, insists that she never loved Julius Caesar, by whom she had a baby. To twit Cleopatra, Charmian, her maid, puts together all the fulsome praise she heard Cleopatra lavish on Caesar. Cleopatra replies that her words meant nothing because she had been like a salad, green and cold.

In southern America "a milk cow and turnip sallit patch" has persistent durability for the basic means of subsistence. And hardly anything is more in evidence than turnip salad, the biennial cool weather crop. The turnip, native to Europe of the same genus as cabbage, appears in two American forms, the white, *Brassica rapa*, and the yellow, *Brassica napobrassica*, the rutabaga or Swedish turnip. Perhaps, it is more than mere coincidence that the late Carl Sandburg, son of Swedish immigrants, titled his famous book of tales for children, *Rutabaga Stories*.

Although it is unsupported by documentation, one of the most perennially pertinent tale-definitions relates to the origin of "giving him the cold shoulder." In medieval France it was customary to serve guests hot roasts, but if a guest out-stayed his welcome, or made himself odious, he was served a cold shoulder of mutton or beef. In a word, the cold meat indicated the guest was welcome no longer.

Fraudulent piety and legal chicanery accounted for the origin of the world-famous sundae. While some historians have Norfolk, Virginia, as the birth-place of the sundae and others have Evanston, Illinois, all accounts agree on the reason. Sunday bluelaws prohibited soda drinks on the Sabbath. (Some bluelaws even required that children's swings had to be chained tightly on Sunday.)

It occurred to a Norfolk druggist that if it was illegal to serve ice cream with soda, was not ice cream with syrup legal? This began as a "Sunday special," and sale was restricted to Sunday. But when customers asked for a "Sunday" on a Wednesday, the spelling was changed to "sundae."

And "Jerked meat," redolent in millions of homes via television's western movies, is a corruption of *charqui*, or *charki*, Spanish form of a Peruvian word meaning flesh cut into long, thick slices and hung up in air and sun to dry. (The Indians on the plains used this same format to cure buffalo meat.) When the meat was "jerked" fully it was folded and put into rawhide packs for eventual use.

Charqui became "jerked," and "jerky," common western name for meat, via hobson-jobson. (Here and there the adjective is spelled "jirked" and the noun "jirk.") A traveler in the west in 1800 wrote: "We jirked the lean, and fried the tallow out of the fat meat, which we kept to stew with our jirk as we needed it." In *The Voyage of the Beagle*, under the date of 1834, Charles Darwin tells of a visit to Chile: "When it was dark we make a fire beneath a little arbor of bamboos, fired our charqui, or dried strips of beef, took our maté, a native drink, and were quite comfortable."

Maté (may-tah) which the immortal Darwin refers to, is made by pouring hot water over the dried leaves of the maté plant, much as hot water is poured over dried tea leaves elsewhere. Maté is extremely popular with the South American cowboys, the gauchos of the pampas. In Argentina maté is taken straight, but since sugar is added in Chile, one assumes Darwin sweetened his. (A somewhat similar backwoods southern concoction, tansy tea, was medicinal and was used sometimes by unwed girl to debase themselves of "small pregnancies.")

Chow-chow (chou-chou), relish made of chipped vegetables, sometimes pickled in mustard, is pidgin English. In all probability, "chow-chow" is a reduplication of Mandarin Chinese *cha*, or mixed. ("Chow," now fairly prevalent to mean a meal, is pidgin English, also, and it is probably from the Mandarin Chinese *ch ao*, meaning to fry, cook, or stir. Chow, likely because of the various publicity given the military chow line, is more widespread today than grub.

"Grub," from the Middle English *grubben,* to dig laboriously, as for a root, came to mean food in the sense that one's power to purchase food was predicated on what he could "grub up," earn from physical labor.)

"Grub" attained tremendous vogue in the American west when "grubstake" meant the supplies furnished a prospector on his promise of a share in what he grubbed up. London's Grub Street (now Milton Street) was described by Samuel Johnson: "Much inhabitated by writers of small histories, dictionaries, and temporary poems, whence any mean production is called 'grubstreet.' "

Crawfish, probably spelled "crayfish" by a majority of moderns, is a culinary favorite of Cajans. In Cajan tall tales, crawfish are really lobsters, worn to a frazzle after following the Acadians from Canadian waters.

Similar tall tales of crawfish and other fish worn down to small size and to plebian status by the rigors of arduous, long travel abound in several localities. Here and there the channel bass, Old English *baers,* variant of the dialectical *barse,* became a creek perch, Latin *perca,* from the Greek *perke.* Tongue-in-cheek stories have been told about the crawfish and the perch at Ocracoke Island, N.C.

(Apparently, the first white settlers who comprised the famous "Lost Colony" on North Carolina's Roanoke Island, landed originally at Ocracoke, then called Wococoon, and went over-land to what became known as Fort Raleigh. There is the story that Blackbeard, the ruthless pirate, killed near Ocracoke in 1718, heard from his ship, a cock crowing on shore. Blackbeard is supposed to have yelled the mocking cry, "O crow cock, O crow cock," from whence the word Ocracoke evolved. However, the Indian word for the region seems to have been *waxkahkant,* meaning stockade; for , it is believed a fortified Indian village was in existence.)

While no such preposterously engaging tales attach to the sardine, the very name and the species have given experts considerable trouble. Scientists say that in the true sense "sardine" is not the name of a species of fish, that the real sardine is the cured species of young pilchard common in the waters of western Europe. The so-called New England Sardine is a young herring, and California sardine is a small pilchard.

While it isn't established beyond peradventure, it appears that the sardine acquired its name from Sardinia, the second largest of the Mediterranean Islands because the fish was plentiful there and because it was first caught and canned there. The species from which the tinned variety got its name is called *Clupia pilchard*, scientifically, and later on the British applied the name "sardine" to the young Cornish pilchard.

"Good wine needs no bush" appears in the Epilogue to *As You Like It*, but Shakespeare merely repeated a proverb established in the first century of the Christian era. Ancient wine shops were identified by a wisp of hay, hanging from the door. While some scholars have suggested this is an early variant of Emerson's "better mousetrap" analogy, much of Madison Avenue and television seem in sharp contrast. However, Samuel Johnson's barb, in *The Idler*, "Promise, large promise, is the soul of an advertisement," finds modern extension in Henderson Britt's quip of 1956: "Doing business without advertising is like winking at a girl in the dark. You know what you're doing but nobody else knows."

Many Protestants who are cavalier about eating fish on Friday forget that the fish preceded the cross as a Christian symbol by many years. The first Christians, ostracized and persecuted by the Romans, needed a means of sacrosanct recognition, and from the advent of the faith there were close associations, literally and symbolically, between Christianity and fish.

(Today most of us think of only one kind of cross, but the *Heraldic Encyclopedia* lists three hundred and eighty-five kinds, even if most of these are different solely in the variations of their limbs, forms, and extensions. The best known are probably: The Greek Tau Cross, which resembles the letter "T;" the Equilateral Cross, referred to also as the "Greek Cross," of which each limb is of identical length, a vertical line being bisected by a horizontal line of equal dimension; the Latin Cross, in which the lower branch is longer than the other three; the Looped Cross, which, like the Egyptian hieroglyphic, is a "T" with a circle on its top; the St. Andrews Cross, which takes the form of the capital "X:" and is so called because St. Andrew, patron saint of Scotland, was martyred on a cross similarly shaped; the Maltese Cross, formed of triangles joined at their apex, which represents the solar wheel turning darkness into light and night into day.)

Dandelion greens, virtually a gourmet dish today among certain segments of society, were fairly prevalent in the 18th and 19th centuries, as "hard times rations." Dandelion is a corruption of the 16th-century French *dent de lion*, literally lion's tooth, and the plant obtained its name from the jagged edges of its leaves. The plant was introduced into colonial America from Europe; and its roots, somewhat similar to chicory roots, have been used as a substitute for coffee, especially in the south during the Civil War.

Succotash and hominy, still popular, are Indian words, as are the much less known and eaten tuckahoe, edible elements of a fungus found on certain native trees, and samp, or corn porridge. All four were eaten, likely, at some of the early religious caucuses. Whether or not "caucus" is pure Algonquin or whether it is a corruption of "West-Corcus," a community near Boston now long abandoned, it is evident that George Whitefield, the eminent colonial divine, used "caucus" to mean a foregathering of worshippers. *Qughog* or *quahaug*, Indian for "hard clam," must have been served at some of the meetings with preaching by Whitefield or Francis Asbury. (Although the Indian "firewater" became derisive, principally, with settlers and their progeny, a dipper of local corn, or sugar mash, whiskey, chased with a chew of tobacco, a bite of apple, or a cigarette, ultimately had persistent use in isolated portions of the southern seacoast and mountains as a "Philadelphia cocktail," and later in history as a "Palm Beach cocktail.") Unfortunately, there have been some fatuous comparisons between the "Philadelphia cocktail" and the "Raines' sandwich." In 1897 a bill sponsored by a legislator named Raines prohibited the sale of whiskey on Sunday in any place in New York City except in hotels that were liscensed to serve meals. Almost instantaneously, saloon-keepers began renting hotel rooms on Sunday in which tables were set up as improvised bars. To circumvent the meals' provision, another table was stocked with bread and cheese, and reporters quickly hailed these as "Raines' sandwiches." Ere long, many men outside of New York City who were smitten with a Sabbath thirst walked out in search of a "Raines' sandwich" or merely for "cheese," as the subterfuge was known in many towns.

"Deviled" was associated in the early days of America with many of the delicacies eaten by the righteous, especially at camp meetings and dinners on church grounds. The first barbecue was laced with condiments said to be "hot as the devil himself." (But small credence attaches to the ancient legend that "deviled" arose, in general application to several foods, when early Catalan missionaries to what is now California said it was "hot as a furnace," or *calor de forni*, sometimes given as a source for the word "California."

Americans applied "deviled" to eggs, crabs, ham, and to other foods basted copiously with mustard, cayenne pepper, and Tabasco Sauce, made at New Iberia, Louisiana, where many of the Acadians, described in Longfellow's *Evangeline*, settled. Obviously, devil's food cake took its name simply because it was the colored antithesis of angel's food cake.

And the American Indians, who gave us names for many standard dishes, supplied the word "tuxedo," the garment worn by ritzy diners. The garment derived its name from the old Tuxedo Club, at Tuxedo Park, Orange County, N.Y. In 1814 Pierre Lorillard took possession of 13,000 acres around Tuxedo Lake, and his son developed the place as an exclusive resort for the wealthy.

In 1886 Griswold Lorillard, Pierre's descendant, suggested that the English dinner jacket, which resembled a skirtless dress, be worn in lieu of the full-dress suit for dinner. At first, the "tuxedo" as it came to be called, was worn as a dinner jacket, exclusively. Then it began to be worn as evening apparel on semi-formal occasions. But tuxedo derives from an Algonquin word which was applied to the Wold tribe of the Delawares. The word means, literally, "He has a round foot," a palpable allusion to the wolf. In some of the Revolutionary War maps the word is spelled "Took-seat" and on one of George Washington's maps the word "Taxeto" appears as a place name.

Many of the original home-remedies, especially those involving barks, roots, saps, and herbs, came from the Indians. The ginger root, from the Anglo-Saxon *gingiber*, was the base of crude medications, and, invariably, it was mixed with whiskey or with molasses rum. (Rachel Jackson swore smoking a pipe was the best medicine for her severe bronchial ailment, but tobacco was leavened with ginger and booze.)

If few verbatim remedies are extant, one, a "Guaranteed Cure for Rheumatism," survives precisely:

Hiera picra, powdered, 2 oz.
Cinamon bark, powdered 1 oz.
Gum gualicum powdered 2 ozs.
Good Holland gin 1 quart.

The mixture was put into a half-gallon bottle and allowed to "macerate (to soften by seeping into a liquid) for two weeks, with three vigorous shakings each day." A testimonial survives in the advertisement: "A lady was very much deformed for several years from rheumatism and could not walk a step without assistance. She took this medicine three times a day for two months, after which she walked about her room without letting her family know it. Then one day when they were seated at the table she walked downstairs, AND SHE IS WALKING YET, a thing she had not done for twenty years."

With that much gin abetted by the built-in chaser, it's a wonder the lady hadn't flown long before the Wright boys became bicycle mechanics in Dayton, Ohio.

"Strawberry acid," a home version of Kool-aid, was used for a variety of respiratory ailments. Strawberries were put in a pot on an open fire, or on a kitchen range, later, and cooked as though the housewife were making strawberry preserves, which were a natural by-product, often. The juice, acid was drained off, bottled and capped. While some folks kept the bottles of strawberry acid to mix with ice during summertime, it was indispensable during flu season.

But now that the strawberry is a paean to succulence* and not a panacea or anodyne, there is general agreement with Izaak Walton's (1593-1693) observation: "Doubtless God could have made a better berry than strawberries, but doubtless God never did." Alas, no etymologist is sure just how "straw" got into "strawberry." It's possible that "straw" comes from the Anglo-Saxon *streaw*, akin in origin to "strew." However, "straw" used to mean the stalks of several cereals, and there is always the theory that the name arose simply because the runners resemble straws.

Molasses, as aforementioned, was (is) the basic ingredient

---

*Succulent has a convoluted history. A succulent piece of meat is likely to be juicy, from the Latin *sucus* or sap, whence the Anglo-Saxon *sucan*, to suck. And some etymologists suggest that *sewer* is aphetic for the Late Latin *exuccu* draining the juice, but the real origin may be observed in the Old French form, *esseveur*, a channel for water over-flowing from a fishpond. Sewer is from the Late Latin *exauguare*, to drain, and, thus, the contentions by many experts of the correlations between succulent and sewer.

in rum, and while it is now taken, pretty generally, with
bread at breakfast, it has been high on the list of supper
desserts, especially during parlous times. ("Dessert,"from the
Old French *desservin*, means, literally, "to clear the table.")
Curiously enough, sorghum, or black molasses, seems to be a
Chinese importation, and in the south its uses are well-nigh
innumerable, including being distilled into alcohol and other
medicinal purposes, and to sweeten coffee in tight times.

An inexpensive crop to plant and harvest, an acre of good
cane used to produce about one hundred gallons of molasses.
The cane was cut before frost, and the thin fodder knocked
from the stalk with a stick. Some farmers left the green
fodder to enrich the soil and others fed it to horses, but most
mules spurned it. The heads of the stalks were cut and fed to
hogs and chickens.

Then the cane was fed into a "mill" located between two
rollers. A horse hitched to a long pole walked around and
around in a short circle grinding the cane into green juice, and
the juice ran from the "mill" into an evaporator, and fire
cooked the juice until it was as rich and sweet as the honey
in Beulah Land. But few people compared the aroma of
cooking molasses to a perfumed girl. It exuded a robust,
manly odor. It was as if perfumery had sprouted enormous
biceps. There was a stopper at the bottom of the evaporator,
pulled by a lever at the top. The cooked molasses ran into
pans, even as more was being cooked. The pans were dumped
into barrels, usually barrels "rived" from oak, made of stout
oak staves and smoothed to a fine finish by a lath.*

*Somehow, any recitation about molasses seems hollow unattended by the poem
composed by the late Dr. Samuel F. Mordecai, Dean of the Duke University Law
School:
Mary had a little lamb,
Its fleece was white as snow.
And every where that Mary went,
That lamb was sure to go.
Richard had a rakish ram,
As black as black molases,
He butted Richard in the rear
And gun him psoriassis.

If molasses and home-made bread was deluxe dessert, oftentimes it was a meal within itself. As late as the 16th century, "cake" meant any kind of bread baked into small, regularly-shaped pieces. And "You can't eat your cake and have it, too" is one of our most frequently quoted bromides.

The saying may have been printed first in 1546 in one of John Heywood's "Proverbs," although the saying was proverbial before Heywood. George Herbert, the British versifier and churchman, who died in 1633 used Heywood's aphorism in a poem called, curiously enough, "The Temple: Sacred Poems and Private Ejaculations":

To be in both worlds full
Is more than God was, who was hungry here.
Wouldst thou his laws of fasting disannul?
Enact good cheer?
Lay out their joy, yet hope to save it?
Wouldst thou both eat thy cake and save it?

And it was John Heywood, and also in 1546, who wrote: "I know on which side my bread is buttered."

Today the banquet is subjected to considerable derision, especially that kind described as the "rubber chicken circuit." But the "banquet," French from an Italian diminutive of *banco*, meaning "a bench," was not invented by Americans. The art of deluxe feasting was contemporaneous with the Hebrews and the Egyptians, and the Hebrew may have learned the secular art during their Egyptian captivity. Anyway, the Jews were having ritualistic feasts when the Greeks and Romans were subsisting on the humblest fare.

Banquets were held after the working day, and invitations were sent at least twice. An invitation was dispatched several days in advance, and on the feast·day special messengers repeated the invitation. Upon arriving, the guests were annointed with special oils and perfumes, and adorned in richly embroidered garments, cut in flowing fashion. Before the advent of spoons, guests wiped their hands on special pieces of bread between courses, and the pieces were ultimately fed to the dogs.

Bread was dipped into many dishes, and guests lay with their faces to the table, the left arm resting on a cushion, as servants went around sprinkling the guests' bare feet with special perfumes. The menu consisted of "flesh, melted butter, honey, and fruit." The Greeks and Persians seem to have initiated the custom of beginning and ending meals with wine.

Cooking declined tragically during the Middle Ages, and it seems to have been revitalized by the merchant-princes of Florence, from whom the celebrated French chefs learned the secret of gourmet cooking. But England made little progress in its cuisine until Henry VIII's tenure. Even so, emphasis was on the preparation of game, capon particularly. When someone gave Henry a hot pudding, he was so entranced with the flavor that he gave his benefactor a manor house and large estate.

Although America has made few savory contributions to the banquet, this nation has to take the blame for the introduction of that form of acute indigestion called the "after-dinner speech."

Many beleaguered folks who feel that they have suffered through aeons of after-dinner verbal torture still say that they "dined with Duke Humphrey"; that is, that they went without dinner. Facetiously, they explain that the period between the meal and the last speech is so enormous they can't remember having eaten.

Some authorities attach "dining with Duke Humphrey" to the erroneous report that Humphrey Plantagenet (1391-1447) was starved to death in prison. The nebulous phrase probably owes its existence to the misconception that Duke Humphrey was buried in St. Paul's Cathedral. (His bones lie in St. Albans Abbey.) An aisle, near the alleged burial spot of Duke

Humphrey, usually quick with beggars and tramps, was called "Duke Humphrey's Walk."

Thus, "to dine with Duke Humphrey" originated to mean the dinnerless vagrants who congregated in the aisle near his alleged tomb in St. Paul's Cathedral. And there is this bizarre reference to him in *Richard III*. The Duchess of York, Richard's mother, asks,

What comfortable hour canst thou name
That ever grac'd me in thy company?

Richard answers:

Faith, none, but Humphrey Hour, that called your Grace
To breakfast once forth of my company.

No student has ever seemed to know Shakespeare's allusion to "Humphrey Hour," but the phrase is supposed to have the same source as "dine with Duke Humphrey."

Logically, perhaps, a notation about the word "etiquette" should appear in the section of this book called "Customs and Manners," but since the modern connotations of "etiquette" ascribe so often to foregatherings that involve food and drink, a brief explanation seems germane. This is a French word signifying a "label or card," or "ticket," in English.

The readiest explanation of the derivation is the custom in the French army of posting daily orders on numerous small sheets called "etiquettes." A Scotsman, who had been in the French army as a mercenary became the chief gardener at Versailles, under Louis XIV, but in his efforts to make the grounds beautiful he was frustrated constantly by careless visitors who walked across his grass and his flower beds, often killing young plants before they could take root.

He remembered the military "etiquettes," and he posted notices of instructions over the grounds to tell visitors where to walk. The word worked its way into British English, and at royal receptions "etiquettes," or "tickets," relative to conduct were given to guests. A widening application of the word led to the endless modern applications of it.

A crude knife was standard equipment during the Stone Age, and there are sporadic Biblical allusions to the fork. Indeed, excavations have revealed that the Anglo-Saxons used the fork as far back as 796 A.D. But the fork fell into disuse for a long time after that date. One of the first books (pamphlets) written on child care, in 1480, admonished: "Take your meat with three fingers only and don't put it into your mouth with both hands, and don't keep your hand too long in your plate." By the 11th century forks were fairly common in Italy, and Thomas Becket, Chancellor of England, under Henry II, introduced them to British royal society. Becket's innovation passed out quickly, and around 1620, or about 450 years after Becket, Thomas Coryate, an Englishman traveling in Italy, encountered the fork and re-introduced it to British society.

Even so, the fork had difficulty surviving among our ancestors. Working people downgraded forks as effeminate and users as reckless; and some of the clergy denounced the fork as "ungodly," arguing that "to eat meat with a fork is to declare impiously that God's creatures are not worthy to be touched by human hands." It was pointed out, collaterally, that South Sea Island "savages" used forks to devour human enemies.

It was only toward the end of the 18th century, when the four-pronged fork became standard, that the masses of Englishmen and Americans started using them. Indeed, iron forks were not prevalent until 1846, when German artisans mass-produced them.

Finally, that little lump in the throat formed by the thyroid cartilage and known everywhere as the "Adam's apple" is an appalling misnomer. But the name persisted even after early surgeons were enabled by law to examine corpses. Vastly perplexed by the elastic tissue these early anatomists continued to call the lump the "Adam's apple."

Folklore has it that a bit of the "forbidden fruit" stuck in Adam's throat, and ever since Adam's progeny have been afflicted similarly. But the Writ never identified the "forbidden fruit," and the Bible fails to say it was an apple. Today, most experts say that if Adam had lived and if he had eaten fruit, it was an apricot, most likely. However, a most unscientific phrase, predicated on a non-existent fruit that wasn't eaten, has become glued to daily speech as tightly as that piece of mythological apple in Adam's throat.

"What is food to one man is bitter poison to others" has come galloping down from Lucretius (Titus Lucretious Carus, 96?-55 B.C.) to take its place, amid many variations, in daily speech.* By 1709 Oswald Dukes, in *English Proverbs*, had it, "One man's meat is another man's poison," the most familiar form of Lucretius' adage. (Eugene Healy, in *Mr. Sandeman Loses His Life*, published in 1940, has this interesting play, derided sometimes as a "Reno-vation": "One man's mate is another man's passion.")

In his *The Devil's Dictionary*, Ambrose Bierce (1842-1914?) defined "edible": "Good to eat, and wholesome to digest, as a worm to a toad, a toad to a snake, a snake to a pig, a pig to a man, and a man to a worm."

But Chief Justice John Marshall, among others, is credited with this happy limerick:

---

*In *Othello*, Shakespeare says: "The food that to him now is as luscious as locusts, shall be to him shortly as bitter as coloquintida." It is believed that John the Baptist subsisted upon such locusts, and luscious may evolve from the Biblical association of locusts with wild honey. The Coloquintida is an intensely bitter herb.

There was an old man of Tobago,
Who lived on rice, gruel, and sago;
Till, much to his bliss,
His physician said this—
'To a leg, sir, of mutton, you may go.'*

In his long, prancing rhapsodic poem, "Food and Drink,"
Louis Untermeyer (1855-) enjoins mankind:

Let us give thanks before we turn
To other things of less concern. . . .

Untermeyer's lusty, infectious paean to hedonism takes off
from a question fixed within invisible, highly savory
parentheses:

Why has our poetry eschewed
The rapture and response of food?
What hymns are sung, what prayers are said
For home-made miracles of bread?
Since what we love has always found
Expression in enduring sound,
Music and verse should be competing
To match the transient joy of eating.
There should be present in our songs
As many tastes as there are tongues;
There should be humbly celebrated
One passion that is never sated.

*Edward Leer, in his immortal *Book of Nonsense* (1846), says he was turned to
the writing of humorous, nonsense verses after reading "The Old Man of Tobago."
But although Leer is credited with inventing the limerick, he never used that word,
and no one seems to know just how limerick came to be applied to the popular,
often ribald, verse-form denoted by the word.

Ecclesiastes (8:15) and Luke (12:19) contain the same two-fisted injunction: "Then I commended mirth, because a man hath no better thing under the sun, than to eat, than to drink, and to be merry."* And this is leavened or extended, or extended and leavened, simultaneously, in Corinthians (15:32): "Let us eat and drink; for tomorrow we die." In his "The House of Life," Dante Gabriel Rossetti (1828-1882) puts a fatalistic twist to the celebrated passages from Ecclesiastes and Corinthians:

Eat thou and drink; tomorrow thou shall die.
Surely the earth, that's wise being very old,
Needs not our help.

It is in *Henry IV* that Shakespeare gives enduring form to a proverb that was already established: "He hath eaten me out of house and home." The man of prodigious appetite is an early, minor American folk-hero, and virtually every colonial and early American community boasted a man who could "out-eat, out-drink, out-jump, and out-fight" all others.** Literature used to be savory with the unparalleled exploits of

*In "The Man Higher Up," O.Henry (1862-1910) has this, "Eat, drink, and be leary."

The late Dorothy Parker's "The Flaw in Paganism" puts a neat twist to Ecclesiastes:
Drink and dance and laugh and lie,
Love, the reeling midnight through,
For tomorrow we shall die!
(But, alas, we never do.)

Perhaps, George Ade's (1866-1944) impish refutation of Poor Richard has some facetious pertinence in any exercise in hedonism:
Early to bed and early to rise
Will make you miss all the regular guys.

**Herculean labors attached to some of the real-life models, such as Peter Francisco, the Revolutionary hero, who is supposed to have shouldered a cannon at the Battle of Monmouth.

enormous eaters. Examples are found in works as dissimilar as Lewis Carroll's "Father William," Clarence Buddington Kelland's numerous stories about Scattergood Baines, and Eastman Johnson's "The Great Pancake Record" and the other stories that featured the Tennessee Shad.

There is the hoary story of Jacke Tarre, probably a composite, a pirate of the West Indies of the early 1600's, who ate a mammoth mess of diced candles, served in the guise of hominy, and asked for more. The origin of "chewing the fat" has been traced to Tarre's feat. But one starting point, "Eating the fat of the land," occurs in Genesis.*

The trouble with Jack Tarre and the candles' story is that virtually all illumination in the Elizabethan era was furnished by rushes, gathered along creek banks, twisted and dried. The odoriferous rush was placed in a clamp, and when it had burned about halfway down, or down to the clamp, it was reversed and the opposite side was lighted. This may be the origin of "burning the candle at both ends."

In *Gill Blas*, René Le Sage (1688-1747) says, "To burn the candle at both ends," and Edna St. Vincent Millay (1892-1950) caught the feverish essence of the frantic 1920's almost suicidal nuances in:

My candle burns at both ends,
It will not last the night;
But, ah, my foes, and oh, my friends,
It gives a lovely light.**

*In *Knickerbocker's History of New York*, Washington Irving leaves this paean to corpulence: "Who ever heard of fat men heading a riot or herding together in turbulent mobs."

**Edna Millay's poem found inadvertent, sardonic extension in the anonymous story-song of the 1920's, chanted almost simultaneously with the poem but infinitely more vibrant:

Papa makes book on the corner,
Mamma sells home-made gin;
Sister makes love for a dollar,
My God, how the money rolls in.

"Blessing," from the Old English *blestian*, probably from the common Germanic *blothiosjan*, "to hallow with blood," was coeval with the earliest expressions of religious feelings. Among primitive peoples and in patriarchal times, the authority of the head of a family was equal to that of a priest, even if a father's blessing was not so encompassing. For, when priests emerged as a separate class, primarily to invoke the favor and protection of providence, whatever a priest blessed was supposed to receive favor with God. The priest added quasi-official celestial ties to the blessings invoked by heads of households, previously. And with the advent of the priest, the father, the parent, continued his role as a surrogate, but a surrogate without divine implications.

In rural and small-town America, "grace," in "to say grace," was much more prevalent than "blessing" (from the Old English through the Latin *gratis*, meaning "favorable," or "pleasing.") The protective covenant of the early parental blessing finds enduring expression amid the gathering of the clans when the man seated, or standing, at the head of the large eating table says, "I will say my grandfather's grace."

In the 18th and 19th centuries, the "grace cup," taken as a benediction at the conclusion of a meal, usually supper, or the chief family-meal, was ritualistic in many American homes. In many homes one large silver cup, filled with wine or cordial, was passed around the table, as a talisman. If this was a continuation of the initial "grace," the original invocation usually gave thanks for food and health and the latter was a psychological attempt to keep the family-group in protective custody.

"Stirrup-cup," originally wine given to one about to mount his horse on an important or hazardous mission, had fairly extensive use, particularly in the American south, until the 20th century. Sidney Lanier's poem, written in 1877, not only distills the original essence of the tradition but adds heroic, poetic defiance:

Death, thou'rt a cordial old and rare;
Look how compounded, with what care!
Time got his wrinkles reaping thee
Sweet herbs from all antiquity.

David to thy distillage went,
Keats, and Gotama* excellent,
Omar Khayyam, and Chaucer bright,
And Shakspere** for a king-delight,

Then Time, let not a drop be spilt;
Hand me the cup whene'evr thou wilt;
'Tis thy rich stirrup-cup to me;
I'll drink it down right smilingly.

The Mizpah Prayer, "The Lord watch between me and thee, when we are absent, one from another" (Genesis 31:49), was used as a grace-cup in many southern homes. Jacob and Laban, his father-in-law, erected a "cairn," or "watchtower." The prayer spoken by Laban is called the "Mizpah benediction," but this may have been spoken more as a testy admonition than as a protective covenant. Laban and Jacob disliked each other, distrusted each other, and Bergen Evans has suggested that "Mizpah malediction," probably had more original pertinence than "Mizpah benediction."

---

*Gotama-Buddha.

**In common with many 19th-century writers, Lanier (1842-1881) spells Shakespeare as "Shakespere," or "Shakspare." *Shakespere and his Forerunners* is one of Lanier's posthumous volumes.

In America's insular period, the extensiveness of the board was indicated, from home to home, by "long," "short," "middling," and "company graces." In other words, eloquent gratitude was determined by succulence, by the number of dishes. The old axiomatic "as poor as Abe's grace," synonymous with intransigent destitution, originated to mean a cursory blessing for pitifully short rations. Somewhere in between "company grace" and "short grace," mumbled with hasty incoherence, was the terse blessing ascribed to Dean Samuel F. Mordecai, aforementioned:

Good bread, good meat,
Good God, let's eat.

The word "grace" is borrowed from St. Paul's writings, and he uses "grace" in the sense of a gift which enables those who have "grace" to do what they could not do without "grace." For example, Paul's abbreviated autobiography: "By the grace of God I am what I am." The Anglican Church, the Protestant Episcopal Church in America, and the reform churches agree that grace is assistance given by God to those who believe in Him.

The Graces, the Greek *charites*, translated by the Romans as *Gratiae*, according to Pindar (518-438 B.C.), greatest of the Greek lyric poets, were the goddesses from whom everything beautiful and agreeable came, and through whom man became wise and glorious. According to Pindar, the Graces were goddesses of "heavenly light," closely related to bloom and fertility, and, hence, patrons of marriage.

Hesoid (8th century B.C.?), best known for his didactic *Work and Days*, has Zeus and Euroyonome as father and mother of the Graces. To them Hesoid gives the names *Anglaia*, "brilliancy,"; *Thalia*, "the blooming"; and *Euphrosyne*, "mirth." In the *Illiad*, Homer mentions the Graces as handmaids of Hera (Juno), but in the *Odyssey*, Homer says the Graces are handmaids of Aphrodite. In

Homer's conception, the Graces form a troop of attendant
goddesses, responsible for giving immortals happy days.

In his liltingly clever poem "Food and Drink," Untermeyer
has a lengthy catalogue of rhymed beverages, meats, fruits,
and vegetables. Even if the couplet strains a little, Untermeyer
gets a high grade in ingenuity for rhymes such as:

The sage compound of *Hasenpfeffer*
With dumplings born of flour and zephyr.

The poem ends on this bouyant, triumphant note:

Let us be thankful for the good
Beauty and benison of food;
Let us join chiming vowel with vowel
To rhapsodize fish, flesh, and fowl.
And let us thank God in our songs
There are as many tastes as tongues.

"Now good digestion wait on appetite,/And health on
both," from *MacBeth,* is called "the perfect pagan grace," by
Bergen Evans and others. Even so, Robert Herrick's
(1591-1674) "Grace for a Child" endures as a model of
unaffected poignance. Three centuries of erratic social and
sociological flapdoddles have not effaced unadorned humility:

Here a little child I stand,
Heaving up my either hand:
Cold as paddocks though they be,
Here I lift them up to thee.
For a benison to fall
On our meat and on us all.

The selective genius of the poet has rarely gone beyond
Herrick's care in picking the word "paddocks," those small
hands, "cold as paddocks." Herrick means "toads," hands as

"cold as toads." That one word may have made Herrick's little grace-note immortal.

(In his *Life*, Boswell, quoting Samuel Johnson in May, 1776, says, "Every man of any education would rather be called a rascal than accused of deficiency in social graces." Curiously enough, in Milton's time, "buxom" was synonymous with "graceful": In "L'Allegro" the woman is described as "buxom, blithe, and debonair." And despite whatever descriptive advantages that accrue to the modern writer, unfettered by editorial or conventional restraints, two lines in *Paradise Lost* are unchallenged for sheer, pristine sensuality:

Grace was in all her steps. Heaven in her eye.
In every gesture dignity and love.)

Whether or not "Politics makes strange bedfellows,"* the election of Jimmy Carter has focused so much attention on grits, this addendum seems eminently appropriate. Just before Mr. Carter was inaugurated, a widespread argument developed over whether "grits" is singular or plural. Several newspapers ran editorials, to support the singular or the plural contention, and some, such as the Charlotte, N.C. *Observer* merely asked: "Is Grits Is Or Are They Are?"

Editorial disagreement is paralleled by dictionaries. *Webster's Third New International Dictionary* says "grits" can be "singular or plural in construction," but the *American Heritage Dictionary* says "grits" is plural. Many writers and talkers need the flexibility of either, although the plural has a better ring and makes more sense when one is asked: "Are your grits warm enough?"

*Usually, this is ascribed to Charles Dudley Warner (1829-1900), in *My Summer in a Garden.*

The word, from the Middle English *gryt*, meaning "bran," through the Old English *grytt*, supplied us with "grit" in the sense of "courage" or "perseverance," and with the old hobo phrase, "Hit the grit," popularized by Jack London in *On the Road* (1908). This phrase, suggested by the roadpath at the side of a railroad track, was popular for several years in the sense of starting or taking a trip.

And these spirited discussions of grits remind those who cherish the minutiae of folkways that on a normal ear of corn the rows of kernels on each ear are always an even number. And there is the story of the story of the slave in Granville County, North Carolina, who was promised his freedom by his master if the slave ever showed his master a normal ear of corn on which the rows of kernels were not an even number. This promise was made as a harsh, inflexible joke, but one summer, early in the growing season, the slave carefully cut a row of kernels from a young ear. When the ear was fully matured, he showed it to his master; and he was given his freedom.

And there is basis in fact for that indigenous Southernism, "He (a child) grows like corn at night." Scientists say that other things being equal, corn probably grows faster on warm nights. The rate of growth in plants is influenced by factors other than the formation of food materials through photosynthesis, and certain plants continue to elongate in darkness. A similar proverb must have been well-established during the Elizabethan era, for, in *Henry V*, Shakespeare has the Bishop of Ely to say that Prince Hal "no doubt grew like the summer grass fastest by night."

The grist-miller who ground corn into meal, grits, and hominy, may have been the first modern mechanic who was indispensable to society but who, traditionally, maintained his independence from organized religion, the guilds, and feudalism. A ballad current during Henry VIII's lifetime projected the monarch as envious of the resolute aloofness of the celebrated Miller of Dee. "The Miller of Dee's Song" is ascribed to Isac Bickerstaffe. It was sung in Bickerstaffe's opera of 1762, *Love in a Village*, but some scholars think the song is much older:

There was a jolly miller once
Lived on the river Dee;
He work'd and sung, from morn till night,
No lark more blythe than he.
And this the burden of his song,
For ever us'd to be,
'I care for nobody, not I,
If no one cares for me.'

In America each miller's garments, face, hair, and hands were so quick with the fragrant accumulations of corn meal he looked always as if he had just stepped from a driving blizzard. As aloof, independent, and meditative as Chaucer's famous miller, he was always "Dusty Miller" in southern America. A meticulous craftsman, his efforts couldn't be quickened by threats or bribes. His proverbial slowness in grinding corn furnished virtually every grist-mill community with some such lingering story as this one:

A customer had waited an interminable time for the garrulous miller to fill his sack with corn meal. Finally, in exasperation, he said: "Dusty, I got a bulldog can eat meal faster than you can grind it."

"Yeah? And how long could he do that?"

"Until he starved to death."

PART TWO
OF TIME AND SUPERSTITION

"There is a superstition in avoiding superstition."

Francis Bacon

*"Seize the day." (*Carpe diem*).*

Horace, from *Odes*.

"Time, you old gypsy man,
Will you not stay,
Put up your caravan
Just for a day?"

Ralph Hodgson, from "Time, You Old Gypsy Man."

"HURRY UP PLEASE, IT'S TIME."

T.S. Eliot, from *The Waste Land*. This is the standard warning of closing time in British pubs. In his poem Eliot used the phrase in its traditional meaning and, also, as a harrowing admonition.

OF TIME AND SUPERSTITION

In *Good-Bye Mr. Chips*, an enormously popular novel of the 1930's, the late James Hilton wrote: "*Anno domini*, that's the most fatal complaint of all in the end." One supposes that Chips, or Hilton, really meant that millions of humans suffer a fatal illness, old age. Hilton's dictum may have been a subconscious refurbishment of one of Herbert Spencer's "Devinations," written in the 19th century: "Time: that which man is always trying to kill, but which ends in killing him."

Ovid (43 B.C.-17 A.D.), who bridged the modern method of reckoning the beginning of time, or times, spoke of "Time that devours all things," but scholars say Ovid was thinking of Titan Kronos, in Greek mythology the father of the gods, who devoured his own children. Ovid also said "Time flies," or *Tempora asbunitur*, even though the traditional, popular rendering is *Tempus fugit*. But Browning is closer to the intention of this piece in "A Grammarian's Funeral":

Time goes, you say? Ah not!
Alas, Time stays, *we* go.

So little is known of Richard Grafton, including the date of his birth, one is not at all sure he died in 1572, as some aver. Yet, his "Abridgement of the Chronicles of England"is the most famous rhyming aid to memory in the English language:

Thirty days hath September,
April, June, and November;
All the rest have thirty-one,
Excepting February alone,
And that has twenty-eight years clear
And twenty-nine in each leap year.

Even so, Bergen Evans points out several Elizabethan variations, and Grafton's verse fails frequently because the chanter is confused by all the different versions he has heard, to say nothing of the fact that while there are only twelve months, there are twenty-eight words in Grafton's reminder.

And the calendar is not so ancient or fixed as many may assume. Originally, "calendar" wasn't something written down. It was a herald's blast. Grudgingly, one concedes there is some substance to Karl Marx's conjecture that economics is at the root of man's history, his goings-on, his doings. The English "calends," or the first of the month, is from the Latin *calare*.

Roman heralds proclaimed the days on which accounts were due, and the first meaning of *calendarium* was account-book. The day for reckoning and squaring accounts was proclaimed by the high priest, or a formidable surrogate. No one knew precisely when the new month would begin because it had to be coincident with the appearance of the new moon. Until the new moon was noted, officially, the beginning of a new month could not be announced. Hence, the calend referred merely to the first day of each month, and several authorities assume it was the acceleration of commerce which forced ancients to write down significant dates. As financial transactions multiplied, individuals began to make their own informal calendars. It was only by putting down the precise beginning date of a month that the neo-merchant-prince could know precisely when a specific account was due on the amount of accumulated interest on a debt.

So, regardless of Karl Marx, there is little question that the formal calendar was an outgrowth of the account-books kept by Roman merchants. Originally, a month was a "moonth," or the approximately 29 days it took the moon to revolve around the earth. Although methods of measuring time by sun were adopted, that classic misnomer, the formal designation "month," persisted.

Patently, ancient astronomy contributed to the early calendar because primitive man observed that the seasons—acute changes in weather, for considerable periods—came at the times stars had certain fixed positions. Primitive man had to know when to plant and when to reap, when drought or flood was likely to occur. Equally as vital, he had to know something about the perennial migrations of fish and animals. The enduring continuation of the phrase, "hunting season" bespeaks a shelf of reference books.

Undoubtedly, the first years were not reckoned continuously but were related to some bizarre, catastrophic, or episodic local event. (In the folk-lore of the American South: "It happened the year before the lightning burnt up John Turner's barn.") The first calendars depended upon the accession of rulers as the focal point, as the Bible has it, and even when continuous numbering of the years began, the process varied from nation to nation, and the various starting points for these calendars tell much about the ideologies and predilections of specific people.

The Hebrews, feeling, apparently, that they had strong emotional, cultural, and historical motivations for the grandiose claim, dated their calendar back to the creation of the world. Their scholars calculated that the universe was created 3660 years and three months before the birth of Jesus, and even today this fiction determines the calendar of orthodox Jews on the occasion of specific holy holidays such as Rosh-Hashanah and Passover. The athletic Greeks began their calendar with the advent of the Olympic Games, which they said occurred in 776 B.C.

The Romans started their calendar in 753 B.C., the year in which they said Rome was founded; but when Julius Caesar revised this, "brought it up to date," in 46 B.C., the Julian calendar emerged, and it was in use when Christianity began. The church adhered to the Julian calendar for the first five centuries of its existence. But the calendar of the modern Christian era, with the years counted from the date of the "Incarnation of Jesus," was adopted as late, as 530 A.D. It came into existence because Dionysius Exiguus, a scholarly monk of Rome, based the starting time of the new era on the tradition that Jesus was "born in the 28th year of the reign of Augustus." The new manner of numbering the years was slow in attaining acceptance; and it was not until 664 A.D., more than a century after Dionysius Exiguus, that the Christian era was instituted in England. This took place at the Synod of Whitby.

The Gregorian calendar, introduced in 1582 by Pope Gregory, is a modification of the Julian calendar. It was adopted by Great Britain and the American colonies in 1752, and it is responsible, indirectly, for at least two singularities, leap year and frivolities on April 1.

Caesar's Roman astronomers determined the solar year to be 365 days and six hours. These six hours were allowed to accumulate and to be added to the calendar as a 366th day, every four years. The *bissextile*, from *bis*, twice, and *sextux*, sixth, was so called because it followed February 24, the sixth day before the calends of March, and consequently, was counted as a second sixth day.

Under the Gregorian system the extra, or intercalary day is added after February 28, but years ago it was determined that the addition of a whole day each four years is a few minutes too much to enable the calendar to come out evenly; and this was adjusted by omitting the extra day, February 29, in each of the concluding years of the centuries except when a specific year, i.e., 2000, is divisible by four. To complicate this even more, "leap year," the English term for the *bissextile* year, antedates the Gregorian calendar by several centuries. In the 13th century the phrase "leap year" was suggested by the fact that in leap years any fixed date after February "leaps" over a day of the week "and falls on the next week day but one to that on which it fell before."

Most people born on February 29 celebrate their birthdays on February 28, in non-leap years. Rossini, the operatic composer, born February 29, 1792, had a facetious celebration of what he called his "eighteenth birthday," on February 29, 1864, when he was actually 72. He promised his friends: "I will turn over a new leaf and disregard the frivolities of youth, and the indiscretions of youth." Albeit, the composer overlooked the fact 1800 was not a leap year, that even according to his own flippant reckoning he was seventeen, not eighteen, in 1864.

According to the calendar used today, every leap year is represented by a number divisible by four, except those represented by numbers divisible by one hundred but not by four hundred. (1700, 1800, and 1900 were not leap years but 1600 was, and, as stated, 2000 will be a leap year. This attaches to the old fact that the addition of a whole day every fourth year produces a few minutes too many to make the calendar come out evenly.)

A person born on February 29 in a leap year would be one year old a year later, precisely, and his real birthday would begin then and last for 24 hours, regardless of the calendar. By custom, though, those born on February 29 have the option of observing their anniversaries on February 28 or on March 1. Not so long ago, an English barrister tried to determine, legally, the birthday status of his son, born on February 29; and he found that Parliament, under Henry VIII, provided that people born on February 29 could claim February 28 for their birthdays in all save leap years.

The perpetuation of April Fools' Day may be predicated on a joke infinitely more far-reaching than any that will be perpetrated the first day of next April. Throughout the Middle Ages, New Year came on March 25, but the merriment was postponed to April 1 because March 25 often coincided with Holy Week. But many Frenchmen could not adjust to the New Year when France adopted the Gregorian calendar in

1564 and January 1 was established as New Year's Day. Still others pretended to be confused and claimed a holiday on April 1.

Yet, even when January 1 attained full official recognition and deference, many Frenchmen continued to play pranks on April 1, to "goof off," in today's parlance. And while April 1 did not become a red-letter day on the calendar, it was given the privileges and latitudes accorded some of the official holidays. (For some years, "red-letter day," in American terminology, has been, more often than not, a date that has had particular importance or pertinence to an individual, a family, or a group. But the red-letter day, provocative of completely worldly implications, had just the opposite denotation, originally.

Saint's Days and Holy Days used to appear on calendars in bold red print, to distinguish them from other days, and to imply that special services could be found in the *Book of Common Prayer*. The visual contrast was strong because the other days were shown in black. And red was chosen to suggest the blood of the martyrs, and not merely for flamboyance.

There was nothing coincidental about the choice of the moon as an enduring division for time. As the moon appeared to revolve around the earth it was worshipped by virtually all primitive people, and primitive people equated the phases of the moon with their physical sagas: birth, maturity, deterioration, and death. And the advent of the new moon, to have deathless rhetorical pertinence in literature, was not merely the beginning of a new month but a holy day, with most nations and tribes.

We are indebted to the Romans for the names of our months. The Romans started their year with "March," named for *Mars*, the war god, but linked earlier with fertility. "April," *aprilis*, means to open, and at this juncture the Roman country side was permeated with buds and blossoms; "May" honors *Maia*, goddess of increase; and it's possible that some thought was given to honor the *Majores*, the senate in the first Roman constitution.

"June" perpetuates *Juno*, personification of womanhood and queen of heaven; and some thought may have gone to the *Juniores*, the lower house of the national assembly; "July," named for Julius Caesar, is said to have been Caesar's birth-month, and it's possible that Mark Anthony named the month the very year of Caesar's assassination; "August," for Augustus, Julius Caesar's nephew who followed him on the throne; apparently, Augustus named the month for himself, ostensibly to commemmorate some of his achievements and as a time of feasting and rejoicing because the Civil War had ended.

Perhaps, interest in political leaders and gods declined after the Romans had named the first six months of their year. For, "September," "October," "November," and "December" (seventh, eighth, ninth, and tenth) are banal, comparatively. There was a sort of twilight zone during winter on the Roman calendar of ten months, and there is the supposition that Numa Pompilius put in the two missing months, in 713 B.C.

"January" is for *Janus*, Roman god of beginnings, also the deity of gates and doors. Janus had a two-faced head and he could look backward and forward, simultaneously, a good symbol for the new year since Janus could see the past and future; "February," from the Latin *februare*, meaning to cleanse or purify; women who had not borne children were whipped with thongs cut from the hides of two sacrificial goats, on this occasion, in the belief that this sadistic ritual made them fertile.

If months and years arose from primitive man's observa-

tions of sundry natural phenomena, abetted by his superstitions, the week is the result of basic need and imagination.
The seven-day week is based upon the sacred and magical
elements ascribed to the figure 7, plus the fact that
Babylonian astrologers linked each day with one of the seven
known planets.

The Hebrews seem to have adopted the format of dividing
time into units of seven days in the 6th century, B.C., during
their Babylonian exile. The Hebrews brought the seven-day
week to Egypt where, some authorities assert, Egyptian priests
actually named the days after the planets. The Egyptians
thought that "the heavenly body which was in charge of the
first hour of a particular day controlled the day as a whole."
So, the Egyptians used the days and "regents": Saturn, Sun,
Moon, Mars, Mercury, Jupiter, and Venus. The seven-day
week worked its way into Rome, where, apparently, it had
been unknown in the pre-Christian era. When the seven-day
week spread onto Europe and into England, an inexplicable
development occurred.

Only three of the Roman names were retained. Four were
replaced in England by their Nordic counterparts to give
moderns a weird admixture of pagan deities, both of Roman
and Nordic extraction. "Saturday," honored *Saturn*, the
Roman god (substituted for the earlier Greek god) of time.
Since Saturn devoured all of his numerous children but three,
his star was unlucky, and for a long time bad luck was the lot
of those born on Saturday. "Sunday" is obvious, but it was
not until the 4th century A.D. that the Church declared it to
be a holy day. "Monday," the moon's day, is equally obvious.

Then, as stated, the British turned to Norse mythology.
"Tuesday" commemorated *Tiw*, Scandinavian god of war,
who lost a hand in a battle. "Wednesday" conjured *Woden*,
Anglo-Saxon word for the much better known *Odin*, god of
storms who welcomed warriors to Valhalla and gave them the

luxuries they had desired most on earth. "Thursday" was for *Thor*, Woden's son, and god of thunder and lightning, typified by his infamous hammer, and the iron glove by which he threw the hammer.

"Friday" came from *Frigga*, Woden's wife, and goddess of marriage, love and fertility. At one time, Frigga was a moon goddess who traveled in a chariot pulled by two cats.

Prior to the clock, time was kept by the sun. "Orient" means "the rising sun," and in many places the word for evening is derived from a phrase meaning "west." The Babylonians used moving shadows as somewhat erratic timepieces, prior to their invention of the sundial (*dial*, Latin for day) about the second millennium B.C. By using something so rudimentary as a stick, stuck into the ground vertically, the Babylonians kept track of the passage of hours. The stake's shadow described a curve, and the curve was divided into parts, for practical purposes. To identify the segments, each was given a number called an *hour*, from the Greek meaning "time of day." Since the figure 12 had practical and religious connotations, the day was divided into twelve hours.

But, of course, the sun-dial worked by day only, to say nothing of the fact that time could not be kept on rainy or cloudy days, and since the speed of shadows was irregular, some hours were longer than other hours. Inevitably, the precise geographical location of a sun-dial and the season of the year caused variations in the lengths of certain hours.

The Egyptians invented the water-clock to enable mankind to be independent of the sun and to clarify the division of time into regular periods. Basically, this was a tub or pot with a hole in its bottom. Since the same length of time was required to empty the pot, anyone could determine the time of day merely by looking at the water level. As the new timepiece spread from Egypt across. the Mediterranean area, improvements were added.

A floater, hooked to a gear which moved a pointer that

went around in a circle, was placed on the water. Behind the floater, or "hand," a dial, marked off with the sun-dial's figures from 1 to 12, was placed. Hence, the face of the modern clock made its original appearance, but despite these improvements, the water-clock had some of the restrictions of the sun-dial. When the water froze, time came to an icy halt.

The hourglass, invented around 250 B.C., was a progressive development. Time was measured by the passage of dry sand through a narrow neck between two bulbs. But even experts argue the origin of this notable invention, and the precise motivating impulse. Some contend the sand-clock originated on sailing ships, but others believe the Roman military devised it to measure "watches" during the night. Others contend a glass-blowing monk of Chartres gave the sand-clock its final shape, around the 8th century B.C.

But it, too, had severe limitations. In damp weather the sand became stuck, and when it wasn't stuck in damp weather, inclemency slowed it perceptibly.

Betimes, the Chinese burned a candle and kept track of the hours by the simple expedient of marking a taper before it was lighted. But if this was effectively simple, the exorbitant cost of candles precluded wide use of this means.

If religion and science seem at odds throughout history, the mechanical clock may have been invented specifically to aid people in saying their prayers. Praying was done for the multitudes by priests, monks, and nuns, and a clock that sounded the precise hour was essential, particularly during the hours of darkness. The chiming of prayer bells was an essential function of the original mechanical clocks. (The French word for bell is *cloche*.)

The watch, likely to be an heirloom, an award, or a special gift to signify one's majority earlier in the 20th century, took its name from the early "watch," policemen, who walked a definite "beat." The invention of the drive-spring, during the Middle Ages, revolutionized the size of the watch, made it a portable timepiece. And the iron-cased "pocket clock" was made-to-order for the "watch," to enable it to adhere to a regular schedule on its beat. Since the first men to carry the portable time-clock were the "watch," the policemen, people identified the new time-piece as "the watch," and so it has remained.

One of the more reasonable of the myths advanced to explain Friday 13th as an unlucky day goes back to the time when the Norse became Christians. Frigga, the Norse goddess for whom Friday is named, was a neo-swinger, and the more reserved but equally as fertile, Freya, succeeded Frigga in Norse mythology.

Frigga, incompatible with the image of Christianity, was banished to the deep woods, where, forevermore, she fore-gathered each Friday with twelve devils to have a lascivious bash.

Albeit, the figure 13 was unlucky in Norse mythology in the pre-Christian era: Twelve gods were invited to a banquet at Valhalla, but Logi, god of evil, crashed the party, and Balder, darling of the gods, was killed at the table. Obviously, thirteen people attended the Last Supper. However, it is highly possible that even before the Last Supper it was not uncommon for sailors to refuse to begin a voyage upon what they counted as the 13th day of the month.

The superstition against 13 probably found its most intense persistence in France and Italy. In France 13 does not exist as a house number, and it is never used in the Italian lotteries.

But of course, one may negate the latent disasters of Friday 13th by knocking on wood, finding a four-leafed clover, carrying a rabbit's foot, drawing a circle and spitting squarely in the middle of it.

Knocking on wood, as a counter-charm, relates to Jesus' cross, and the church offered sanctuary in the era before

Christianity. Once a pagan man reached the church building and knocked on the wooden door he was safe from harm. There is, also, the legend that ancient men, dwelling in wooden huts, thought evil spirits often invested its walls. Hence, men knocked on the walls to drown out the sounds of their own voices. This was done to keep evil spirits from being privy to their plans or vagrant joys.

But pre-dating any of these explanations is primitive man's belief that trees were deified because lightning struck them so often. Many trees were identified with specific deities. (The god of lightning and thunder lived in the oak tree.) To touch a tree, and to repeat some tribal mumbo-jumbo, was to obtain magical results.

There is the ageless myth that Eve plucked a four-leaf clover in the Garden of Eden and carried it with her, as a memento, when she and Adam were expelled. Although logic enhances the contention that the four-leafed clover's magical qualities are inherent in its paucity, in the extreme difficulty of finding one, there is the theory that the four-leafed clover was substituted for the shamrock.

In 433 A.D., on Slane Hill, near Tarn, St. Patrick is supposed to have used a shamrock to explain the Trinity to a crowd of pagan chieftans and Druids. Trefoil plants have sacred and magical connotations in antiquity. In Greek mythology a golden, three-leafed plant, a general talisman, was fed to Zeus' horses, and plants said to resemble a shamrock have been found on Roman coins, in Egyptian temples and in the pyramids, and on Assyrian tablets. However, there is considerable speculation over what the Irish shamrock (from the Gaelic *seamrog*, diminutive of *seamur*, meaning trefoil) really was. Apparently, there is no extant plant called the shamrock, although many Irish are still firm in the opinion that the "true shamrock will not grow in English soil."

Infants were brushed with a rabbit's foot at birth. Actors

were given a rabbit's foot with which to apply make-up, and the beauty aid was retained for luck. Too, prior to Freud, the foot was a phallic symbol, and the rabbit was heralded for his incredible fecundity. And, the rabbit's propensity to burrow was construed as communication with dark forces below. Thus, a rabbit's foot might placate the Evil-Eye.

But it is highly possible that the charm of the rabbit's foot relates to totemism, ties to the pre-Darwin eras when primitive man thought he was descended from various animals-rabbits, lions, tigers et al. Primitive man's belief that he descended from animals accounts in part for the animalistic characteristics long ascribed to certain men, including the avalanche of animal nicknames, in the insular era, as well as the variety of animals as enduring regimental mascots. Indeed, some subconscious tie probably exists between the ancient belief and the enduring animal—identification of the athletic teams of so many American colleges, the Bulldogs, Lions, Golden Gophers, Tigers, Wildcats, Gamecocks and so on.

Ancient man was positive that spittle contained purifying powers, and spitting in a circle, peculiar to the American south, is likely a hangover from African tribal mores. In order to guarantee efficacy, one drew a circle with his right big toe, and spat squarely in the center of the circle, to erase a conjure placed upon the spitter. In time the custom became a utility method of equalizing any mojo, any ominous event such as Friday 13th.

"Spit," itself, has several origins for several meanings: The spit on which meat is cooked is from the Old English *spitu,* a rod, and hence a narrow projection of land into water. The Old English *spit,* (OE *spittan,*) means to dig up, with a spade, or a spadeful. Our "spittin' image" is a corruption of the "very *spit* and image of," originally an exact, undeviating likeness.

Actually, "spittle," is closely related to "hospital," from the Latin *hospitalis,* a haven for rest and entertainment.

"Hospital" became *spital* by aphesis. Sometimes this was spell-ed "spittle," and by association with another meaning, the Old English *spitua* a blob of saliva, "spital," came to be used for sick indigents; hence, a loathsome place.

Despite the presence of charms and despite repeated knockings on wood, Friday 13th could be devastating if one spilled salt, walked under a ladder, broke a mirror, had one's path crossed by a black cat, or got out of bed on the wrong side.

Salt was such a holy substance, no early sacrifice to the gods could be made without it. (The Catholics still use salt in the baptismal ritual.) The Bible uses "the covenant of salt" to emphasize God's bond with man, and Scots who brewed beer used to throw a little salt on the malt to purify the drink and drive the witches away.

From the practical, historical perspective the superstition of spilling salt probably began when Leonardo de Vinci's picture of the *Last Supper* showed the salt upset opposite Judas. Jesus has just announced one of the twelve will betray him. All faces save Judas' show pain and consternation, but when Judas raises his left hand, (as his right clasps the bag with the thirty pieces of silver) in a gesture of feigned horror, it upsets the salt.

Even so, because of the tremendous value of salt, spilling it was bad luck among the ancient Romans, and the Romans probably originated the counter-gesture of tossing a little salt over the left shoulder with the right hand.

However, experts are exasperated trying to figure out just how "with a grain of salt" emerged as an enduring synonym for doubt. Among the most reasonable conjectures is the obvious fact that salt makes so many kinds of food palatable, enables one to get down many things that are "hard to swallow."*

*Late in the 16th century "Salt to Dysart" was interchangeable with "Coals to Newcastle." Dysart, a town in Fifeshire, Scotland, was an important center in the salt industry, the same as Newcastle was to the coal industry. The French express this same superfluity with "To carry water to the river," and the Romans conveyed the idea with their "Carrying wood to the forest."

Aside from the practical dangers of an early carpenter's walking under a ladder occupied by a fellow-worker, the superstition ties to the pre-Christian era when a ladder, leaning against a wall, formed a triangle, and to pass through the symbol of the Trinity was to court disaster by sacrilege. And, the early Christians were abundantly aware that a ladder had been used in the crucifixion.

The first mirrors were bodies of water, and men looked into them not through vanity or curiosity but to read their own fate. For instance, a distortion, a face broken into many pieces, was an horrendous portent. Soon, foes learned to sneak up and harass their enemies by chunking pebbles onto the water, and after the advent of glass, mirrors were used in all sorts of divinations. Primitive man believed the picture he saw was of his soul, long thought to have an independent existence, that it could detach itself from the body and be reflected in the mirror. And to break a mirror was to smash the soul.

The black cat, perhaps, the most dreaded of today's ill omens, was not only lucky but holy in ancient Egypt. It was sacred to the goddess Isis, whose daughter, Pasht, was represented with the face of a cat. Indeed, archaeologists have unearthed cat cemeteries in Egypt in which embalmed cats are buried in handsome small boxes. But the image of the black cat changed completely during the Middle Ages with the surge of witchcraft. Any bona fide witch could disguise herself as a cat whenever she pleased.*

Primitive man thought it was disastrous to go to bed and to get up on the same side of the bed, and the left side was the "evil one." The Romans were sure one courted abject tragedy if one entered a house on the left foot, and a slave, who came to be called a *footman*, remained at the door to be sure guests entered the house right foot first, put the best

---

*Curiously enough, Sir Thomas Browne, Sir William Blackstone, John Wesley and many other eminent Englishmen believed in witches. Wesley (1703-1791) the famous Methodist divine, said "The idea of giving up on witchcraft is in effect giving up the Bible."

foot forward. (*Sinister* is the Latin word for left side.)

The only sure-fire way to circumvent disaster was to complete the   magic circle,   get in bed on the right side, and get up from the left side, but the right foot must be put down first, getting in and getting out.

Not just incidentally, almost anything colored red was extremely bad luck for many centuries. While no stigma or superstition devolves today, the massive prejudices against various conditions of red were slow to vanish.

When the Egyptians found reddish sand in drought-riddled deserts the color came to represent disaster, and one of the Egyptian's evil gods was given a reddish complexion. Scarlet and sin are synonymous in the Bible, and early artists gave Judas, Cain, and other murderous or treacherous types red hair. The fear of the Anglo-Saxons for their red-headed Danish invaders was so ominous that the color, itself, became anathema in Great Britain in the years that followed the Norman Conquest of 1066.

And a medical fallacy augmented the fear and prejudice: Back when unskilled physicians attempted to diagnose according to the various colors in a patient's face, a red complexion was axiomatic for "gross humor," a catch-all that entailed a multitude of physical and emotional maladies. But since redheads were in a severe minority, more especially in the period before dyes were used, innate jealousy may have impelled many irascible blondes and brunettes to perpetuate all sorts of libels and slanders.

However, "red" in the irrepressible opprobrious "red-tape" is coincidental, and it arose from the British custom of tying legal documents with a pinkish red tape. This practice was evident in the 17th century, but "red tape," in the sense of official inaction attended by maddeningly irrelevant delays, did not attain semantical popularity until the 19th century.

Many examples exist in 19th century literature: In *Vanity Fair,* Thackeray wrote of the "Tape and Sealing-Wax office in the reign of George II," and in the first of his *Latter-Day Pamphlets*, Carlyle described a man as "little other than a red-tape talking machine* and unhappy bag of parliamentary eloquence." Washington Irving derided a fellow New Yorker: "His brain was little better than red tape and parchment." And Dickens, in *Little Dorrit*, anticipated the disaffections of millions of 20th-century men and women who are sure the convolutions and tortoise-speed of the bureaucracy are designed by sadists expressly for their own distresses, by the literary creation of the "Circumlocution Office": "Whatever was required to be done, the Circumlocution Office was beforehand with all the public documents in the art of perceiving how NOT to do it."

*Carlyle seems to have anticipated the popular American name for the early model gramaphone and graphaphones which played cylinders rather than flat discs. In the early 1900's "talking machine" was used even more widely than "flying machine," although the latter attained tremendous publicity in Fred Fisher's infectious song, "Come Josephine in My Flying Machine." A vintage joke had the husband of an unusually garrulous woman buying the first gramaphone in town. Then, one little boy asks his buddy: "Have you heard Mr. Smith's talking-machine?" "Yeah, I seen her this morning."

PART THREE
CATCH-PHRASES BECOME CUSTOMS AND CUSTOMS BECOME CATCH-PHRASES

"The word is half his that speaks it and half his that hears it."

Montaigne, from *Essays.*

"What times! what customs! (O tempora, O mores.*)"*

Cicero, from *In Catilinam.*

"Custom has furnished the only basis which ethics have ever had."

Joseph Wood Krutch, from *The Modern Temper.*

CATCH-PHRASES BECOME CUSTOMS AND
CUSTOMS BECOME CATCH-PHRASES

If, as Proverbs has it, "A word fitly spoken is like apples of gold in pictures of silver," (Wendell Wilkie said "A good catchword can obscure analysis for fifty years."), countless words and phrases in daily use emanated from specific people, situations, and events. "Limelight," inseparable today from the spectacular, emerged in 1825 when Thomas Drummond, British army surveyor, learned of the unusual luminosity of lime when he heard Michael Faraday lecture in London. While surveying in northern Ireland Drummond decided surveying stations might be visible, one to the other, by use of the lime Faraday had described. By directing an oxhydrogen flame on a cylinder of lime, Drummond produced a steady, brilliant light that was clearly visible on two mountain tops sixty-seven miles apart.

In the absence of electricity, this new lighting was used by the theater almost immediately. By using a lens, a beam from the cylinder of lime could be focused at any point on the stage. That portion of the stage on which important drama occurred was soon called the "limelight," and actors of the 1830's gave the word to the English-speaking world.

If limelight was appropriated by the theater, "To steal one's thunder" is the result of a neo-Freudian slip and the exasperations and acerbities of a disappointed playwright. In 1709, John Dennis' (1957-1734) play, *Appius and Virginia*, was an artistic and financial failure at Drury Lane. Nonetheless, Dennis had devised a revolutionary method to simulate the stage sounds of thunder by using troughs of wood with stops in them. Shortly after his play folded, Dennis returned to Drury Lane to see a performance of *MacBeth*, and he was horrified to see his thunder-making device being employed. Furious, Dennis raced to the footlights, shook his fist, and exploded: "By God, that's my thunder. The villians will not play my play, but, by God, they rattle my thunder."

Few phrases in constant use are disputed more than "by the skin of the teeth." ("My bone cleaveth to my skin and to my flesh, and I am escaped with the skin of my teeth." Job: 19-20) Habitually, the phrase means escape by the narrowest, most harrowing of margins. (Thornton Wilder used the title for his popular dramatic triumph.) Some authorities believe the passage means that Job's teeth had fallen out, that Job was so emaciated he could gnaw his own bones. And there are those who think the allusion is to Nasmyth's Membrane, a cutaneous covering on the teeth of a foetus. The *Interpreter's Bible* seems to have the final word: "No certain interpretation seems to be possible." Even so, the long, historical connotation—safely attained by a tenuous margin is inviolable.

"Simon-Pure," kidnapped by sports writers for regular application to all sorts of athletes, originated in *A Bold Stroke For a Wife*, Susanna Centlivre's play of 1718. Simon Pure, a "Quaking preacher of Philadelphia," and one of the guardians of a young woman's large fortune, is impersonated, in London, by the underhanded Colonel Fainwell. At the end of the play the Philadelphia Quaker appears with witnesses to prove that he is the real Simon Pure.

Fifty years ago American sports writers began to tag many amateur athletes and college athletes as "Simon-pures" to distinguish them from professional athletes, and many of the inadvertent contretemps have been as ludicrous as the penitant at the revival who testified: "I've lied and cheated and debauched but through it all I never lost my religion."

And several extant explanations purport to account for the origin of "the real McCoy," unrivaled in American parlance to mean undeniably authentic. Perhaps, the explanation with widest currency devolves upon the old welterweight champion, Charles "Kid" McCoy (d. 1940). McCoy and a lady-friend were drinking in a saloon when an outsider made unseemly suggestions to the woman. McCoy warned the intruder, adding that he was Kid McCoy.

The interloper sneered, "Yeah, and I am George Washington." McCoy knocked the man cold, and when the fellow finally arose from the sawdust, he looked at the bartender and exclaimed, "Jeez, it really was *the real McCoy*."*

McCoy is credited with ten legal marriages, and all ten wives are alleged to have shown up for his funeral and for the probate of his estate. The clerk of the court, looking at the ten women seated around his desk, is supposed to have shaken his head and to have said, amid exasperation, "Will the real Mrs. McCoy please stand up."

But before Kid McCoy, "Mossie McCoy," one of the story-songs of the late 1870's, tells of a muscular Irish wife who wallops her husband unmercifully merely to prove to the neighbors that she is "a real McCoy." Finally, some credence ascribes to one McCoy, a New York bootlegger of the 1920's, who steadfastly refused to sell his customers diluted or ersatz booze. Thus, his name became the unwritten brand and trademark for his whiskey. Ere long, "the real McCoy" had wide circulation to mean genuine whiskey, and, ultimately, the phrase attained its universal connotations.

"O.K." is credited to Andrew Jackson's placing "O.K.," Jackson's initials for "Orl Kerrect," on sundry Presidential memos and directives. Whether or not Jackson spelled the words "Orl Kerrect," his political enemies taunted him with this spelling, "O.K.," is traced, also, to the presidential campaign of 1840. Martin Van Buren, candidate for reelection, was born in Old Kinderhook, N.Y., and his adherents opened some "O.K. Clubs" around the country. Although the "Old Fox of O.K." was not reelected, the colloquialism came

---

*Information about Charles McCoy comes, curiously enough, from *88 Men and Two Women*, a book written by Warden Duffy, of San Quentin. McCoy was given a term when he killed a girl-friend accidentally. While working with a road gang, McCoy rescued a pilot from a burning plane that crashed near the road-gang. Duffy hailed McCoy's heroism with a gift of boxing gloves and punching-bag. The title of Duffy's book relates to the ninety people executed while he was warden at St. Quentin. McCoy was paroled in 1932.

bounding down to semantical immortality.

One guesses however, that Andrew Jackson affixed "O.K." to memos because of the Choctaw *okeh,* long used by the tribe to enunciate the validity of a statement. The Choctaws spoke *okeh* with the same emotional fervor that white men used "amen." Each of the explanations enumerated has validity and pertinence, but the nation's first "O.K.'s" probably were corrupted imitations of *okeh.*

"Twenty-three (or 23) skidoo" almost attained epidemic proportions in the 1910's and 1920's, and it endures as an engaging chromo today. "Skidoo" emerged in colloquial speech after the Civil War, from "skedaddle," to mean hasty retreat or retirement. "Twenty-three," spoken thousands of times to everytime it was written, seems to have been added to "skiddoo" simply for good measure. So eminent a linguist as Bergen Evans gives credence to the theory that "twenty-three" arose from *The Only Way,* a dramatization of *A Tale of Two Cities,* enacted in New York in 1899.

It was noted that in the play's last act, Sydney Carton was the guillotine's twenty-third victim, and, as often occurs, the public reacted to this heavy-handed bestiality with laughter, if with nervous guffaws at first.* As a catchword it completely dwarfed "Tippecanoe and Tyler, too" and "Remember the Maine," combined, but implications of the original vastly over-wrought horror remain because the phrase usually denotes a grisly admonition: "Get out here immediately, or..."

Curiously enough, "Umpteen (umteen)" and "umpteenth (umteenth)" meant any unspecified cardinal number from 13 to 19, inclusive, when the two broke into speech around 1900. "Umteen," now any large, indeterminate ordinal number, produced "umpty," frequently cast as "umptyninth," to mean any number between 20 and 90. It swept into the classroom to indicate boredom or consternation. ("We've been over that umptynine times," and "After umptynine" times I still don't get it." Indeed, "umpty" and umptynine" anticipated many

*There is the persistent stage-note that an elderly woman in the audience arose amid horror to yell, "Syndey, you are twenty-three. Skiddoo."

of the current, multiple uses of "cotton-picking.")

During World War II, Bill Mauldin, who became the laureate of the frustrated GI by dint of his incisive cartoons of front-line service, popularized the maddening peregrinations of the"umpty-fifth regiment,"and the despair of eating Spam for the "umpty-fifth straight time." "Umpty-umpth," originally any unspecified ordinal number from the 24th to the 99th, inclusive, absorbed political connotations: "He has made that same speech for the umpty-umpth time." (Interminable, convoluted rhetoric was "ubble-gubble," for a considerable inning.)

"Forty ways from Sunday" meant in all directions, simultaneously, or rampant confusion; "forty-one" was lunch-counter talk for a small glass of milk or orange juice; "forty-eight" was (is?) military talk for a week-end pass; "forty-rod" was hastily made whiskey; and "forty-leven," with its innumerable uses, seems to have been coined by the late E.N. Wescott, in his once-celebrated novel, *David Harum.*

The "nine lives of the cat," springs, obviously, from the ancient mystical powers attributable to nine. The number has three threes, or a trinity of trinities. Egyptian astronomers believed in the existence of nine spheres. The Greek lunar year had nine months, and the Styx encircled Hades "nine-fold." Odin, in Nordic mythology, gave Freya dominion over nine worlds. Indeed, Jesus died on the ninth hour.

But almost as easily and as logically, a cat could have forty lives. Forty, the length of sanctuary, came to be the period of quarantine at the time of the Black Death, 1348. Venetians introduced the quarantine as a "magic shield" against plague, and England soon adopted it. Plague was induced by demons, but their diabolical powers were spent within forty days. And the choice of forty is not accidental. Moses spent forty days on Sinai; the Israelites were in the desert forty days; Elijah and Jesus fasted forty days, each, and Lent is forty days, precisely. (The Italians call Lent by that figure, *quarantena.*)

The omnipresent "two-bits" stems from "bit," ancient in England in the sense of small coins, and at one time thieves' jargon for almost any kind of money. But "two bits," expressly to mean a quarter, comes from the West Indies where, in the 17th century, it was applied to one-eighth of the Spanish silver dollar or "piece-of-eight." This dollar circulated freely in the American colonies (The American round dollar is an adaptation in size, shape, and value.), and it was a common colonial practice to cut the silver dollar into wedge-shaped pieces for use as change. Thus, a two-real piece was a quarter of the whole, our ubiquitous two-bits. The phrase has long use. William Byrd, in that portion of his secret diary written between 1790 and 1712, mentions two-bits repeatedly. With the Westover grandee, two-bits seems to have been the habitual tip, and "gentleman's wager" at billiards, cards, and cricket. (In some parts of the late 19th and early 20th century south, fifteen cents was a "long bit" and ten cents a "short bit.")

Some authorities ascribe William Byrd's word "tip," in the sense of gratuity for small services rendered, "To Insure Prompt Service," the injunction emblazoned on the boxes that were prominently positioned in the eating places that adhered to the American Plan. These boxes may have appeared first in the restaurants in late 19th-century railroad stations. Passengers with a limited time to eat between trains soon adjusted to the expedient of dropping money into the box, and in time "To Insure Prompt Service" was shortened to the initials, TIPS.

Although this theory has practical validity, simple consultation of the *Oxford Dictionary*, and others, reveals the prior existence of the old verb "to tip," meaning to give. And "Tip me that cheate (booty), give me that thing," appears in Samuel Rowlands' *Martin Mark-all, the Beadle of Bridewell* published in 1610. William Byrd, in *A Journey To The Land Of Eden*, 1733, declared: "I tipt our Landlady with what I imagined a full Reward." It has been suggested that "tip," and "dibbs," in the sense of money, both owe their origin to *diodol*, Greek coin of small value.

"Buck," came to mean a dollar in the days when the barter system was prevalent, simply because the skin of the male, or buck, deer was more valuable than the skin of the doe. "Young Buck," still viable to mean the effervescence and puissance of the muscular teen-aged boy, arose at the same time and from the same source.

Throughout the 19th century and through the relatively innocent years of the 20th century, Americans off to attend a fair, circus, or other notable entertainment, said they were "going to see the elephant." Indeed, "seeing the elephant" became almost axiomatic with any excitement produced by something out of the daily ordinary. Had the moon-landings occurred a few decades earlier, many Americans would have said that the astronauts "saw the elephant."

In the sense of having seen everything worth seeing, of knowing one's way around, the phrase galvanized common speech when the first live elephant was brought to New York from India in 1796. A female, purchased for $10,000.00, the elephant, six feet four inches tall, was brought over on the famous armed ship, *America*. The elephant was exhibited at various points between New York and Charleston, S.C., to the fascination, bewilderment, and incredulity of the populace.

Kendal's *Narrative of the Texan Santa Fe Expedition*, published in 1841, tells that "see the elephant" was commonplace among the the adventurers along the California, Oregon, and Santa Trails. And "see the elephant" was still magnetic at the time of the gold strike of 1849.

The nationally-known "The Elephant Hotel," burned in 1896, was a salient feature at Coney Island. The hotel, 122 feet high, was built in the shape of an enormous elephant. Aside from parlors and saloons, the hotel contained thirty-two bedrooms, and a "howdah" "on the beast's back end," functioned as a dining and observation room.

In insular days the child too big for his britches "cut a dido," and the phrase still has considerable use to mean extravagant action or an ingenious trick of dubious merit. (In the 1960's "dido," though much less familiar, became a synonym for "caper," in police and underworld jargon.) "Dido," apparently, is an Americanism of unknown origin. Baffling to etymologists, it is often ascribed to the cunning ruse perpetrated by Queen Dido, of Carthage, when she and her followers landed on the coast of Africa.

According to the legend, Dido asked the natives for only as much land as could be enclosed within a bull's hide. But when this was granted willingly, Dido had the hide cut into countless strips. Within the large area of the strips, she built a fort, around which the city of Carthage grew up. Even so, there is little plausible relationship between the story and the Americanism. In American context the logical assumption is that "dido" is of American Negro origin, possibly, echoic, and probably, used originally in relationship to the spontaneity or verve of one of that or a similar-sounding first name.

"As tight as Dick's hatband," as proverbial as "as tight as the bark on a tree," is said to refer to Richard Cromwell, Oliver's son, in his aborted effort to succeed to his father's role. He was derided as "King Dick" and the British crown, "Dick's hatband," was too tight for him to wear. Known also as "Tumble-down Dick," it was said of Richard, by his countrymen: "His hatband went around nine times and still wouldn't meet." The younger Cromwell escaped to Europe, where he lived under an assumed name.

Hardly any phrase in daily use to suggest worthlessness exceeds "not worth a rap," in extensiveness or in intensity.* Although the words usually suggest some sort of vacuous rapping with the knuckles, several reputable etymologists

---

*By 1976, some of the youngsters who encountered "Not worth a rap" for the first time concluded that the phrase refers to "rap" in the sense of talking. And it is highly possible that some exercise in fatuity may come to be equated with the worthlessness of a pointless, boring "rap session."

believe the origin was a small copper coin first circulated in Ireland under George I (1714-1727). While the "rap's" intrinsic value was half a farthing (quarter of a penny), it passed for a halfpenny. By 1755 there was an acute shortage of copper halfpence and farthings, and many counterfeits were passed as "raps." By 1755 the "rap" was worthless, virtually.

It is possible that there is an etymological tie with the German *rappe*, a counterfeit coin circulated on the Continent during the 14th century. Undoubtedly, many of the counterfeit *rappes* were brought to the British Isles by soldiers of fortune. And there is the intriguing theory that "rap" was applied to money from the letters that formed the initials of the names of Indian money, as recorded in British account-books. In these London account-books, *r.a.p.* stood for "rupees," "annas," and "pice." These were used in the same manner that *l.s.d.* is used for "pounds," "shillings," and "pence."

"Not worth a tinker's damn (or dam)" is interchangeable in the American south with "not worth a dried apple dam" and the two have similar histories. A tinker's dam was (is?) a wall of soft mud or clay raised around the spot a plumber wanted to cover with solder. The material that made the dam was used but once and was then abandoned.

Some other authorities think the word should be "damn," not "dam," and that it arose from the proverbial tendency of tinkers to swear. In *Henry IV*, Prince Hal tries his hand at being a drawer in the Boar's Head Tavern, and he explains to Poins: "To conclude, I am so good a proficient in one quarter of an hour that I can drink with any tinker in his own language during my life."

Literature of the 18th and 19th century was redolent with phrases such as one's not giving "three damns," or caring "a two-penny damn," or not regretting some action "the smallest part of a damn." But the old theory that "damn" and "dam" in such instances is derived from the ancient Hindu coin of that name has nothing to support it.

The "dried apple dam," usually spoken as "I wouldn't give a dried apple dam" for suchandsuch, was a wall of dough, the crust, to hold the fruit in an apple dumpling, or other small fruit dumpling. (Actually, the old apple dam was more the size of cobbler that is made for individual servings.) Once the dumpling or dam, became dry it became stale, lost its succulence, and in daily idiomatical language the "dried apple dam" was equated, in worthlessness, with the "tinker's dam" and with "last year's birds' nests."

The guinea pig, the short-tailed, short-eared, robust rodent around seven inches long, is widely used in various biological experiments because it reproduces five or six times annually in its life-span of four years. The name of this South American native is almost an etymological mystery. The most prevalent theory holds that "guinea" is merely a corruption of Guiana, the confusion among early writers of Guiana in South America with Guinea in Africa.

However, there is abundant evidence that this rodent was called "pig cony" ("Cony," or coney," "ko-ni" or "kun-i," the European rabbit) in the early 1600's. This produced the theory that "guinea" is a corruption of "cony," but a third theory relates to the animal's being from an unknown country. Again, the name is said to have arisen because the rodent resembles the guinea hog, and yet another has the animal's being carried to Europe by Guineamen who were slavers.

Eliss P. Butler's sensational *Pigs Is Pigs*, published in 1906, regaled the reading public with the rodent's amazing fecundity. Butler told how the babies acquire a second set of teeth at birth, are able to nibble corn when they are forty-eight hours old, that one will live as long without water as with water.

"The Tailors of Tooley Street" surfaces during each political year in limited references, usually loose, incoherent allusions. Late in the 18th century several London tailors assembled in a home, or shop, on Tooley Street to publish certain grievances. Their petition to the House of Commons began: "We the people of England..." Authorities say between five and nine tailors were involved. Shortly afterward, "The Tailors of Tooley Street" became synonymous with preposterous declarations, with any pettifogging group who feigned large constituencies. But, not just incidentally, Tooley is yet the name of a London thoroughfare. The word is a corruption of "St. Olaf," which in turn was corrupted, successively, into "t-olaf," "Tolay," and finally into Tooley.

Several London editors said the tailors "were as proud as peacocks" when they affixed their signatures to the ludicrous petition. Montaigne (Michel Eyquen, 1533-1592), prince of prose writers, succumbed to an ancient myth in one of his essays: "It is the foulness of the peacock's feet which abates his pride and stoops his gloating-tail." Montaigne's natural error has considerable extension today. Many people say that if a peacock happens to see his feet he drops his train in abject embarrassment, to hide his hideous feet.*

Actually, he has to hold his head high in order to advance his train. When his head is lowered, his train falls. And, as experts have pointed out repeatedly, his train isn't his tail. But no manner of correction by animal husbandry seems to alter the ageless ascription of the lowered head to injured vanity. The tail, proper, of the male peafowl, is comparatively short, and it rarely ever attains twenty inches. The peacock's train is composed of inordinately elongated feathers that grow on the lower back, above the tail, and extend far beyond the tail. Ornithologists call the long train feathers, "tail-converts." The peacock can cause his train to vibrate majestically when

*Ironically, for its majestic image, the peacock's tranquility and domesticity are sustained by a court of five or six common laying hens. And his repulsive feet have no relationship to his need for sex and sycophancy being requited by common, barnyard hens.

it jerks its tail, proper. But the myth that tail and train are
the same length was old in Shakespeare's day. In *King Henry
VI*, the Bard gives this speech to Joan of Arc:

Let frantic Talbot triumph for a while.
And like a peacock sweep along his tail;
We'll pull his feathers and take away his train,
If Dauphins and the rest will but be rul'd.

"Pea" is derived through Anglo-Saxon from the Latin *pavo*,
the scientific name of the genus of birds to which the peafowl
belongs. In common parlance, any peafowl is called a
peacock, but, strictly speaking, only the male is a proper
peacock. Native to the wooded hills of Ceylon and India, it is
yet found there in wild state. It is assumed that Macedonians
took the first peafowls to Europe about the time Alexander
the Great conquered India. The throne of Persia (Iran) is
known as the "Peacock Throne." The original Peacock Throne
was constructed at Delhi for Shah Jahan between 1628-1635.
It consisted of twelve pillars, each holding two gem-studded
peacocks. In 1739 the original throne was taken to Persia.
   Although moderns rightly see the peacock as a filthy bird,
ancients cherished peacock pie. During the Middle Ages
peacock pie, with the bird's head and tail protruding from the
crust, was a prime delicacy among England's nobility.
   "Redlight district" or "section," specifically some area
known for its whorehouses, or cribs, such as New Orleans' old
Storyville section, birthplace of jazz music, has declined
tremendously geographically but semantically it continues, especially among older people. Two theories seek to account for
the origin of the phrase: With the popular advent of
electricity some of the prostitutes placed red crepe paper
around the bulb in the front hall, for the same kind of
trade-identification that marked the wooden Indian in front

of the cigar store.*

The second theory, which predates the light bulb, stems from the pre-electric light era when railroad men, especially in the frontier towns of the American west, hung their red lanterns, still lighted, in the hall, or on the proch, when they entered a whorehouse. This was done, apparently, to signal to fellow workers the availability of paid sex inside, and as a fraternal tocsin, in case a ruckus developed. Indeed, both theories seem to have basis in actual fact.

"Tenderloin" began to mean the center of night life in a metropolis. Later it meant corruption and a redlight section. At the turn of the 20th century "tenderloin" had come to mean the metropolitan district which offered the most fertile opportunity for graft to policemen. In New York this was said to be the region of the old 29th police precinct, from 23rd to 42nd Street, west of Broadway, as is known to the fans of the late Samuel Hopkins Adams, author of the interesting, informative book, *Tenderloin*. The word became resilient when a New York City detective, newly-assigned to the old 29th precinct, said he had been subsisting on chopped steak, but henceforth "It'll be all tenderloin," an obvious allusion to implementing his salary with graft.

"Black Maria," the horse-drawn police van in which some of the denizens of redlight districts and tenderloins were transported to jails, was in use as early as 1843. And it was a synonym for some of the horse-drawn hearses.** The name is

---

*To "redlight" someone originated in carnival and circus parlance to mean pushing someone off or out of a moving train. Later it meant to eject someone from an automobile. In the sense of volatile ejection the phrase was used by the late Dashiell Hammet, Damon Runyan, and by James T. Farrell.

**Many American soldiers in World War I called shells, especially those as large as the famous French 75, "Black Marias." Application to high-explosive shells may have been more a product of Black Maria as a hearse than as a paddy-wagon. In *My Life In New Orleans*, the late Louis Armstrong used "Black Maria" in the multiple senses of a police van and horse-drawn hearse.

said to have attached to police vans in Boston around 1840 when a black Amazon named Maria, a woman of incredible physical strength, assisted the police in putting drunken, obstreperous sailors into paddy-wagons.* Interestingly enough, "Black Maria" seems to have occurred next, in order of time, in New Orleans, another seaport city. Although there does not appear to be any written, factual evidence, there is the persistent story that a woman called "Black Maria" was employed as a bouncer in one of Boston's water-front saloons.

"Hands joined for prayer" does not seem to have appeared in the Christian church prior to the 9th century. But primitive man accompanied his most fervent petitions with gestures and postures. This probably began with arms spread towards the sky, and later on this was abridged to hands folded or crossed on the chest, wrist resting on wrist.

The joining of the two hands in prayer is not mentioned in the Bible, and several authorities trace the custom to the primitive format of handcuffing someone to induce in him a spirit of abject subservience or servility. The theory is that the joined hands remained, as a token of total submission to constituted authority, after the handcuffs disappeared, for this specific use. It is contended that the joined hands demonstrated that one would not seize a weapon.

Tactius (great historian of the 1st and 2nd centuries A.D.) writes that the Semnomes, a Germanic tribe, so venerated a sacred woodland that no one entered unless bound, "as a sign of dependence and as public homage to the gods." The Greeks and Romans invoked joined hands as a way to bind the devil and other occult powers, to compel their obedience. And feudal lords required their vassals to join hands to indicate subjugation to the master's authority.

---

*"Paddy-wagon," obviously, received its name from the fact that so many Irishmen served as policemen in New York City, in Boston, and in other metropolitan areas.

The Christian church began the practice of joining the hands for supplication sometime in the 800's.

By similar token the clergyman's "dog-collar," worn back-to-front, is fairly recent and is not ecclesiastical in origin. Indeed, such a practice would have been inconsistent with the early church's passion for simplicity, its abhorrence for anything that suggested the pretentious.*

An outgrowth of the medieval Amice, a square of white linen worn by 11th-century priests while administering Mass, and modified in the Tudor period to become a white neck cloth with long ends, ultimately discontinued, the "dog-collar" began as a sweat-band. Roman orators wore a similar garb to protect the throat in cold weather, and to prevent the remainder of the garment from being stained by sweat in hot weather.

Around the 6th century laymen abandoned the old Roman practice of wearing flowing gowns. Laymen began wearing short tunics, trousers, and cloaks, but priests continued to adhere to the Roman toga and the long tunic, which survive today in the surplice, cassock, and frock. But by the 9th century, priests tried to embellish the Roman fashion with something akin to the priestly garments worn by the Aaronites in King Solomon's Temple. Thus, the clerical collar came in as a relic. Actually, the cloth attached to the collar, to protect the throat and to serve as a sweat-band, was worn by virtually all men after the 16th century until the introduction of the collar in the 19th century.

(In one of its earliest colloquialisms, "collar" was a noun, meaning a policeman, from the stiff, white collars formerly worn by metropolitan officers. Ultimately, "collar" came to mean an arrest, and it meant to understand something thoroughly. For instance, the hep-cat of 1935 was said "to collar the jive." This meant he was not merely an intelligent

*As late as 428 A.D. Pope Celestinus upbraided some priests for wearing costumes that distinguished them from laity.

devotee of swing music but one in a group who found instantaneous rapport with what was being said, to be in the know, to be hip. And "to collar a nod" meant to sleep, more especially to avail oneself of a short nap.)

Sporadic allusions to the once-famous "neck verse" bring consternation, or facetious rejoinders that run the gamut from the cruel to the ribald.* This appears, originally, in Chronicles (16:22): "Touch not my annointed ones, and do my prophets no harm." This then, is the alleged "neck verse," which, when invoked in court, entitled the defendant to "benefit of clergy." In other words, the defendant was exempted from capital punishment by dint of his literacy.

The "neck verse," seems to have started as a special dispensation for clergymen who were charged with a felony. The "neck verse" excluded clergymen from secular courts. Since the Ecclesiastical Court did not pronounce the death penalty, the verse was credited with saving the life of any minister charged with a felony.

Nonetheless, the guility person, be he clergyman or literate laymen, was branded in the hand, and one could not claim the privilege on a subsequent offense. "Rare" Ben Jonson (1573-1637) claimed the "neck verse" successfully when he was arraigned for killing a man in a duel. In 1691 the privilege of the "neck verse" was extended to British women, and the whole practice was abolished in 1827.

Legal hangings in England and in America were public spectacles, ones with much of the hoopla of county fairs. The victim elicited tremendous admiration if he approached the gallows with bravado. Indeed, Samuel Johnson (1709-1784) was certain that public hangings were infinitely preferable to private hangings because the victim was sustained and strengthened by the waves of admiration that permeated the spectators.

*"Necking," or active petting, attained national recognition after World War I, with the advent of Prohibition and with wide-spread availability of the automobile.

The condemned man was extended small favors, and the great Jonathan Swift (1667-1745) leaves this example, "On Tom Clinch Going To Be Hanged":

Clever Tom Clinch, while the rabble was bawling,
Rode stately through Holborn to die at his calling.
He stopt at the George for a bottle of sack,
And promis'd to pay for it when he came back.

Samuel Pepys, under date of October 13, 1660, wrote in his *Diary*: "I went out to Charing Cross to see Major General Harrison hanged, drawn, and quartered; which was done there, he looking as. cheerful as any man could do in that condition."

Trampass, in Owen Wister's (1860-1938) *The Virginian* (1902) is accosted by ranchers who prepare to hang him for rustling cattle. The ramrod launches a boring, garrulous speech about Trampass's alleged misdeeds, and Trampass interrupts the diatribe with: "You—are you going to hang me or talk me to death?"

In 1920 Carl Wanderer, of Chicago, World War I hero, was convicted of the murder of an anonymous indigent known to history only as "The Ragged Stranger."* Wanderer, not overly bright and an insufferable ham, was enamored of his singing voice. On death row, he sang interminably, his *piece de resistance* being "Old Pal, I Miss You Tonight." Wanderer sang the song as he was led to the gallows in the basement of the Cook County courthouse. As the noose was affixed he had reached that portion of the lyrics that laments, "My eyes embrace an empty space," and as his neck was cracked, he intoned, "Old pal, I miss you tonight."

*Wanderer entrapped the stranger by hiring him to rob Mrs. Wanderer, in the vestibule of the couple's apartment house. The stranger pulled a gun on Mrs. Wanderer. Wanderer killed her, and then the stranger, with his own pistol. He was acquitted of the murder of his wife, but later he was convicted of killing the transient. A Chicago newspaper took up a purse to bury the indigent and his marker reads: "Here Lies The Ragged Stranger."

A reporter in the crowd, perhaps, young Ben Hecht, said: "Son of a bitch ought to be hanged for his singing anyway."

"To pile ossa," often miscast as "to pile on ossa," is from Vergil's (70-19 B.C.) *Georgics*: "To pile Oassa on Pelion, and to roll wooded Olympus upon Ossa." The reference is to Ephialtes and Otus, whom Bergen Evans so properly and charmingly calls the juvenile delinquents of the Greek gods. According to Greek mythology, the youngsters piled Ossa on Olympus, the Pelion of Ossa, in their aborted effort to reach heaven and attack Juno.

Apparently from unvarnished ebullience, the two young gods caught Ares, god of war, and sealed him in a bronze jar for thirteen months. Zeus, failing to share the mirth, had the two destroyed.

The "mad hatter," or "mad as a hatter," encompasses several theories. The most probable is *atter*, Anglo-Saxon for adder or viper. The original person was meant to be described "as venomous as an adder." Even so, some experts think the phrase means precisely what it says, that it arose in the days when mercury was used in processing animal skins for hats. The dangerous properties of mercury were not known, and many hatters came down with the "shakes" from repeated handlings of mercury. It is likely that the phrase entered modern British English from hatters, and Lewis Carroll (1832-1898) and Thackeray (1811-1863), who popularized the phrase in literature, seem to have had the mercury-mad hatter in mind.

"As mad as a March (or marsh) hare" is closely allied. If "March" and "marsh" both seem highly appropriate, the greater weight of evidence supports "March" as the original word. Scientists of the Middle Ages supposed that rabbits underwent periods of excessive depression, from eating various plants, and humans who ate rabbit at such times .succumbed to profound melancholia, also.

March is the hare's favorite mating season, and the spell of sex accelerates the rabbit's inate aberations. But, then, again, such breeding is done in marshes, and a hare in a marsh finds itself bereft of the protection of trees and bushes. Hence, unable to hide from human and animal foes, it goes crazy.

Today,"the four hundred" is spoken often as derision or scorn, but the phrase, the inviolable open sesame to New York City's poshest* circle, was coined in 1889 by socialite Ward McAllister. McAllister, who had gravitated to New York from Virginia via California's gold coast, was regarded as an authority on social matters by New York's smart set. In 1892 McAllister boasted to the inner sanctum of the Union League Club that he had pruned the list for Mrs. William Astor's ball to "a mere four hundred." McAllister is alleged to have implemented this with the assertion that "not more than four hundred are capable of crossing a dance floor."

In the sense of the upper echelon of society, "the 400" stuck, although many outlanders used the phrase to mock those whom they thought to be pretentious and officious. In 1850, James Fenimore Cooper, in *Ways of the Hour*, had popularized "upper crust," modifying this with, "These families, you know, are our upper crust, not upper ten thousand." This ties in with the theory, prevalent throughout the middle of the 19th century, that the fashionable of New York City did not exceed ten thousand in number.

But of course, Cooper's "upper crust" came to be used sardonically and facetiously in common speech much more than it was used to convey any social accolades.

Although "make no bones about it" has been vital in daily British and American speech for several centuries in the context of showing no reluctance and of not making any ostentatious show, the phrase appeared in print, in its present form as recently as 1894. Robert Louis Stevenson (1850-1895)

*"Posh," now widely written and spoken to convey opulence in physical appointments, is supposed to owe its incubation to the policy of certain late 19th century luxury liners that sailed regularly between London and the Mediterranean. Special, rich passengers were assigned staterooms "Port, out" and "Starboard, home," to have the benefit of the sun both ways. Thus, "posh" emerged as a status-symbol.

has it in *St. Ives*, "Don't make any bones about it." The injunction appears to have been in the language around five hundred years before Stevenson used it.

In 1548, Nicholas Udall (1505-1556) praised Abraham by saying that when God commanded him to sacrifice Isaac, his son, Abraham "made no manner of bones nor sticking." It is usually agreed that the ancient expression referred to finding, or pretending to find, bones in stew or soup. A gracious guest ate his soup and he made no display if he found any small meat bones it it.

The old reference to "bones" may have produced, and certainly ties closely, to other phrases wherein acceptability is equated in terms of eating: "Too tough to chew;" "that's hard to swallow;" "that won't go down;" "it sticks in may craw;" and even "biting off more than one can chew." (C. Hugh Holman, distinguished author and professor of English at the University of North Carolina, Chapel Hill, said of Henry James: "He chews more than he can bite off.")

Nicholas Udall (or, perhaps, Uvedale) served a stint as headmaster at Eton, until he was booted out. His clumsy rhymed comedy, *Ralph Roister Doister*, seems to be the earliest of the English farce-comedies. This was produced and enacted first by the boys of Eton College.

Udall, or Uvedale, seems to have been enraptured with "no bones," and in *Ralph Roister Doister* he writes:

Sweet male maketh jolly good ale for the nones,
Which will slide down the lane without any bones.

(Nones," doesn't make abundant sense in Udall's couplet."Nones," from the Latin *nonae*, was the ninth hour, by the ancient, Roman reckoning, or three p.m. This was also an office recited at three p.m. but which is recited earlier now. And there are sporadic attempts to evolve "roisterer" from Ralph Roister. But it is more likely that "roister" is from the Old French *rustre*, a churl or a boor.)

Few people ever ask why the inevitable length of the pole one wouldn't touch an object with is always ten feet long, never nine or eleven, but, world without end, a "ten foot pole." This axiomatic phrase arose simply because the poles used to push, to pole, the flat boats on the Mississippi were cut to a standard length of ten feet.

In all probability, when young Abe Lincoln made his celebrated trip down the river on a flat-boat, this small, floating barge was impelled by ten foot poles.

"Peeping Tom," formerly used more often to characterize the snide habits of the morbidly inquisitive, now applies more often to prurient interferences, to various facets of voyeurism.*

Obviously, Tom, the tailor of Coventry, was the original "peeping Tom." The story, in circulation several centuries, tells that Leofric, Saxon Earl of Mercia and Lord of Coventry, imposed cruel taxes on his subjects. His wife, Lady Godiva, made numerous appeals for the beleaguered people of Coventry. Finally, to be done with her frequent harassments, Leofric agreed to remit the heavy tolls if Lady Godiva would ride a horse naked through the streets of Coventry.

The word went around, and everyone in Coventry remained indoors with closed shutters except Tom, the tailor. Tom bored a hole through his shutter, and he peeped. And, so it is said, for his crass impudence, God struck him blind. The legendary incident is commemorated by a stained glass window in St. Michael's Church, Coventry. This window is mentioned as early as 1690, and for several centuries an effigy of "Peeping Tom of Coventry" appeared in a niche of a public building.

St. Michael's, now restored, was almost demolished by Nazi bombs in the Second World War, but the famous stained glass window of the legendary incident survived the destruction.

---

*In June, 1976 several elements of the press carried an interesting Freudian slip: An alleged voyeur was called a "voyageur," and this word, meaning a traveler, means specifically, one who transports furs and men to and from remote stations in Canada.

For a period in local history there was an annual Lady Godiva pageant.

Inevitably, some demurrers entered the list, and there are those in Coventry who have averred that it was the horse, not the lady, that was naked. But others, stressing Leofric's intractible recalcitrance, say he would never have predicated his offer on a naked horse. Indeed, Isaac Disraeli (1766-1848) seems to make an accurate assessment in his book, *Curiosities of English Literature*: "This anecdote some have suspected to be fictitious, from its extreme barbarity, but the character of the Middle Ages will admit of any wanton barbarism.*

"Dead as a dodo" has declined somewhat as a workable simile, but it is still invoked by thousands of older Americans. The "dodo," a corruption of the Portuguese *duodo*, silly or foolish, inhabited Mauritius, a British Island in the Indian Ocean, east of Madagascar. The bird, larger than the average turkey, was excessively clumsy, with poorly developed wings. Because the dodo had great difficulty in flying and hiding, it is supposed to have been destroyed when hogs were introduced to Mauritius.

A Dutchman, van Neck, described the dodo in detail in 1598, and he dispatched a live specimen to Holland. (It died enroute, but it was preserved for many years at the British Museum.) Apparently, none has been seen since 1681. If there is no historical doubt about the extinction of the bird, "dead as a dodo," obviously, owes much of its continuity to simple alliteration.

---

*"Naked," is prevalent in Biblical and in secular literature: "Naked I came out of my mother's womb, and naked shall I return thither." (Job 1:21) "There syr launcelot toke the fayrest lady by the hand, and she was naked as a nedel." Thomas Malory (15th century), *Le Morte d'Arthur*.

And Robert Graves (1895-) makes this clever semantical distinction in his poem, "The Naked and the Nude":

For me, the naked and the nude
By lexicographers construed
(As synonyms that should express
The same deficiency of dress
Or shelter) stands as wide apart
As love from lies, or truth from art.

PART FOUR
BEING A SOMEWHAT LIMITED GUIDE
TO PODUNK, USA

"I've come to his fair city
To seek a mother dear,
And you wouldn't dare insult me sir,
If jack were only here."

> From "My Mother Was a Lady," song of 1896, by Edward B.
> Marks and Joseph W. Stern.

"All cities are mad; but the madness is gallant.
All cities are beautiful; but the beauty is grim."

> Christopher Morley, from *Where the Blue Begins.*

"The city is recruited from the country."

> Emerson, from "Essay on Manners."

"Fancy a novel about Chicago or Buffalo, let us say, or
Nashville, Tennessee! There are just three cities in the United
States that are 'story cities'—New York, of course, New
Orleans, and best of the lot, San Francisco." *Frank Norris.*

> Quoted by O. Henry (William Sydney Porter) as a preface to
> "Municipal Report," short story set in Nashville, Tennessee.

BEING A SOMEWHAT LIMITED GUIDE
TO PODUNK, USA

In this election year of 1976 one recalls the sardonic crack of Jonathan Daniels, brilliant American author and editor. Daniels, speaking of the massive reluctance of defeated Congressmen to return to their native bailiwicks and former occupations, wrote, "They don't go back to Poccotella." By similar token, few of the solons unhorsed in November, 1976 will go back to "Podunk," vibrant since 1846, and defined by *Webster's New International Dictionary* : "An imaginary town taken as typical of placid dullness and lack of contact with the progress of the world."

"Podunk" is not listed in the *United States Postal Guide*, but the word exists somewhat loosely as a place-name for two or three American communities. "Podunk," apparently, is of Indian origin, and a small tribe of that name lived in Hartford County, Connecticut until the end of King Philip's War, 1676, when they vanished from history. (The "Podunks" must have been absorbed by a larger tribe.)

A "Podunk" pond in Worcester County, Massachusetts is said by Worcester historians to mean "place of burning," an allusion to its having been the spot on which captives were put to the stake. But it seems more logical to relate "Podunk" to Potunk, Long Island place-name, which is supposed to have derived from the Algonquin, *P'tuk-ohke*, meaning "a neck of land."

As early as 1846, the American magazine *Vanity Fair* ran a series of "Letters From Podunk," and in 1861 this magazine had a fat, little man, a campaign worker, importuning Abraham Lincoln for the position of postmaster at Podunk.

In the great days of minor league baseball, when a ball player was demoted to a league of lower classification, "sold down the river,"* he said he had just been given "a one-way

---

*"Sold down the river" was popularized by Harriet Beecher Stowe in *Uncle Tom's Cabin*, published in 1852.

ticket to Podunk." The postage-stamp size of the Class D league baseball park in Podunk was known by all players and fans. Thus, fly balls that were routine outs elsewhere "would be a double in Podunk."

Vaudevillians added to the Podunk lore: The town was so small the public square was a man's Sunday hat; a woman in Podunk gave birth to Siamese twins, but the town was so small one of the twins had to live in another place; of course, the sidewalks were rolled up at night, and the annual Fourth of July parade was postponed because someone borrowed the balloon. According to the vaudevillians, the principal excitement came from watching flocks of jaybirds cross the main street of Podunk, while all human and vehicular traffic was suspended.

Indeed, there is a strong possibility that "jay-walking," the minor misdemeanor, obtained its legal designation from observations of jaybirds crossing the street of some Missouri village.

Many "bungalows" were built in Podunk especially around 1900. This is a corruption of the Hindustani *bangla*, meaning "of, or belonging to, Bengal," province of old British India. The original "bungalow" was the type of house lived in most frequently by Europeans sojourning in the interior of Malaysia. As the name implies the first of these "bungalows" resembled a type of architecture common in Bengal. In India a "bungalow" is a lightly-built, one-story cottage, with a pyramidal, thatched roof, and an extensive porch.

In common with small-town citizens everywhere, especially of a former era, those who live in Podunk's bungalows proclaim, "A man's house is his castle." This phrase, ancient and obscure, owes its present form to Sir Edward Coke (1552-1634), who in Sermayne's case (1605), said: "The house of everyone is to him his castle and fortress, as well for his defense against injury and violence as for his repose."

The legal principle in the Sermayne case is widely encompassing. According to the maxim, no officer of the law may force the door if the occupant is adamant. But despite this well-established theory, in actual practice this applies only to any civil process. In 1765 William Blackstone wrote: "No outdoor doors of a man's house can in general be broken, though in criminal cases the public safety supercedes the private."

The most dramatic of the "house-castle" declarations came in 1760 when the elder Pitt, speaking in Commons on the Excise Bill, thundered: "The poorest man may in his cottage bid defiance to all the force of the crown. It may be frail, its roof may shake; the wind may blow through; the storms may enter,—the rain may enter,—but the King of England cannot enter; all his forces dare not cross the threshold of the ruined tenement."

In 1831, an Irish lawyer, trying a case before Justice John Toler, quoting Pitt, said of his client's house, "The rain may enter but not the King."

"What," exclaimed Justice Toler, "Not even the reigning King?"

Curiously enough, in context of the disparity in time, many of Podunk's lovers, courting couples, including occupants of bungalows, are dubbed "Fair Helen" and "Lochinvar," both as accolades and facetiously. Helen, in Greek legendry, is the daughter of Zeus and Leda. Helen came as a swan, and thus, was born from an egg. Even as a child she was so beautiful she was stolen by Theseus, but Pollus and Castor, her half-brothers, brought her back.

As a young woman, all of Greece's nobles coveted and pursued her, but they made an inviolable pact to support the man who won Fair Helen. And, according to Homer, she married Menelaus. But when Paris decided to award the Apple of Discord to Aphrodite, the goddess had to make good on her promise to give Paris the fairest woman in the world, in exchange for the Apple. With Aphrodite's help, Paris abducted Helen to Troy, where they married.

But the Greek nobles and chiefs, true to their covenant, moved to avenge Menelaus, and, thus, began the Trojan War, the subject of the *Illiad* and several other legends. When the war ended, Helen returned to Sparta to live quietly with Menelaus. They had one child, Hermoine.

This is the story in the major legend, although Euripedes (5th century B.C.) adheres to the legend that Helen was taken captive to Egypt, until Menelaus came to reclaim her, that it was a phantom Helen who went to Troy. It is in his *Dr. Faustus* that Christopher Marlowe (1564-1593) posed his deathless question:

Was this the face that launched a thousand ships,
And burnt the topless towers of Ilium?

Some high school students continue to assume that Edgar Allan Poe's (1809-1849) exquisite, short poem, "To Helen," written in 1831, is inspired by the Homeric legend. Actually, Poe's poem was addressed to Mrs. Jane Stith Stanard, who died in 1824, and who was the mother of one of Poe's Richmond schoolmates. Mrs. Stanard had done young Poe some kindness.

No one seems to be sure of the meaning of the word "Nicean" in the celebrated first stanza of Poe's three-stanza poem. It may refer to Nice, France, or to Niceae, in Asia Minor. And Poe may have derived the word from "that Nyseian isle" in Milton's *Paradise Lost*:

Helen, thy beauty is to me
Like those Nicean barks of yore,
That gently o'er a perfumed sea,
The weary, way-worn wanderer bore
To his own native shore.

Lochinvar, curiously enough, often confused with Lothario, is the hero of Sir Walter Scott's (1771-1832) *Marmion*:

Oh, young Lochinvar is come out of the West.
Through all the wide Border his steed was the best;

So faithful in love, and so dauntless in war,
There never was knight like the young Lochinvar.

The verbal confusion with Lothario must be due to simple alliteration, but many Americans speak "gay Lotharia" and "young Lochinvar" synonymously, to mean exalted lovers, or to be facetious, to mean just the opposite. Actually, a "gay Lothario," never a homosexual, is a libertine, a debauchee, a master of avarice. Lothario is the main character, dastard in the story-songs of the 1890's, in *The Fair Penitent*, Nicholas Rowe's play of 1703.

In Rowe's tragedy, Lothario seduces Calista, and he is described as "Haughty, gallant, gay, and unscrupulous," in his deceptions of Calista. And Lothario appears much earlier, as a character in *The Cruel Brother*, written by Sir William Dunevant, reputed to be William Shakespeare's "natural son." It is possible that Nicholas Rowe* borrowed the name, "Lothario," from Dunevant, to popularize him as the "gay libertine."

Inevitably, several "Jacks" lived in Podunk, from the town's advent. And hardly any word in common usage has a more extensive or protracted history. "Jack" is a man's name, the name of several animals, such as the male mule, and it is a fellow. It is any one of several trades or specialities, such as lumberjack, bootjack, waterjack, and jack-of-all-trades.

A "jack" is a brace, or support, especially the iron cross-tree on a topgallant masthead. It is the popular designation for several fishes of the genus *Caranx*, and it is the piece of wood that holds the leather, or the quill puck, in a harpsichord, and it is the hammer in some other keyboard instruments, such as the piano. It is used in changing a tire, and it is a translation used surreptitiously by some students who take foreign languages. "Jacks" are several kinds of games, including the one played with a set of small six-pointed metal pieces. It is a small ball, a socket, and the card the British call

---

*Nicholas Rowe (1674-1718) succeeded Nahum Tate, another poetic non-entity, as Poet Laureate in 1715. And Dunevant (1606-1668) succeeded Ben Jonson as the laureate.

the "knave." It is a small flag, a sort of guidon, flown at the bow of a ship, to indicate nationality, usually, and the British flag is the "Union Jack," in popular parlance.

Some men hunt deer with jacklights, and every community has jack-rabbits, jack-o-lanterns, jacks-in-the-pulpit, jackknives, jackdaws, jackhammers, and all sorts of jackpots at gaming tables and raffles. "Jack Tar," "Jack Spratt," and the effervescent "Jack Frost" have almost as much resilience as the folks next door. And until fairly recently "jack" meant an ape, one who wore a suit of clothes.

"Jackanapes," once prevalent in British English and somewhat more restricted in American English, meant a cheeky fellow, a bounder, a monkey, or a mischievous child. Long ago Lord Chesterfield (Philip Stanhope, 1694-1773) described a youngster: "Dressing him out like a jackanapes and giving him the money to play the monkey." Apparently, "Jack Napes" was the sobriquet of William de la Pole, the third Duke of Suffolk, whose badge, or crest, depicted the figure of an ape's ball and chain.

"Jack" has been ubiquitous in the sense of money throughout the 20th century, and "applejack," usually local brandy, is a heady potation. "Every man Jack" is invoked to mean a crowd, and "jack" is the pin in several games such as bowling. "Jackeroo," probably from the Spanish *vaguero* has meant a cowboy, and the "jacker-upper" increases something. "Jack-roll" means to rob, to roll someone of his "jack," and "Jack," or "John Roscoe" is a pistol. "Jackleg" emerged in 1850 to mean an inferior lawyer, and it is yet applied to many sorts of unskilled workmen. (At one juncture the non-union worker who penetrated the strike line was a "jackleg," although "blackleg" and "scab" became more viable.) "Blackjack" is the weapon carried by policemen. It is "21" in the game blackjack, and some of the tougher varieties of oak trees are called "blackjack."

In 1913 the infectious song, "Balling the Jack," popularized by Eddie Leonard, first, and then by Eddie Cantor, come out with the force of a lyrical meteor to grab the nation by its coattail. The song prompted the ingenious dance, "Balling the Jack," and for a decade the American who "balled the jack" moved quickly and decisively. (If a father told a son to do something, and if he added, "And ball the jack," the boy did his chore with dispatch.) And for a fairly long inning, "balling the jack" had the same "in" relevance that "swinging" would have half a century later.

Any modern who has taken "French leave" from any Podunk probably left surreptitiously without paying his debts, if, indeed, he didn't leave several worthless checks bouncing around. However, the familiar "French leave" arose semantically in the 18th century when it was permissible for guests at a large French social gathering to leave mid-way the soiree without taking leave officially of their host and hostess.

The phrase was born among conservative Englishmen who abhorred the custom of precipitate leave-taking when this was introduced in the British Isles. Thus, "French leave" was a derogation during the phrase's incubation period. *The Oxford Dictionary* says the earliest use of the phrase was by Tobias Smollet (1721-1771), in 1771. (Curiously enough, to desert, in French *S'en aller (or filler) a l'anglaise,* is to "leave English fashion.")

The theory, often asserted, that "French" is merely a corruption of "frank," in the sense of free, as in franking mail, seems without foundation.

Tobias Smollet, Scottish author, benefited by the comparable wave of literacy that expanded about the time he commenced writing novels, and his were among the first novels read by comparably large audiences. Smollet came to London to get his *The Regicide* dramatized, and when it failed, he went to sea as surgeon's mate. He set up practice as a London surgeon in 1743, but that same year his *Roderick Random* became the first English novel of the sea. Still acclaimed critically for his *The Adventures of Peregrine Pickle,* Smollet was among the first of the long line of physician-authors, the list that includes Chekhov, Somerset Maugham, Robert Bridges, William Carlos Williams, Oliver St. John Gogarty, Frank Slaughter, Walker Percy and many others.

Smollet, always enamored of literary horseplay, got off a crack in *Humphrey Clinker* that has far more relevance to today's intellectual soirees than often occurs to us: "One wit, like a knuckle of ham in soup, gives a zest and a flavor to the dish, but more than one serves only to spoil the pottage." In *Roderick Random* he quoted a proverb: "Some folks are wise and some are otherwise." Whenever this is spoken today, the speaker usually pauses dramatically so that he and his auditors may contemplate his sterling wit.

Undoubtedly, Podunk's mythical population included some "grass widows," and several theories attempt to account for the origin of the phrase. The theory that this is a corruption of the French *grace* seems improbable. The *grace* widow is separated from her husband by the church, and the "grass widow's" husband is still her spouse. It is highly possible that this began as a social denigration to mean the unmarried mother of the old "hedge child." For, in 1528 Sir Thomas More wrote: "For then had wyuys ben in his time lytel better than grasse wydowes be noe."

However, two theories seem to be substantial: The prospector, off to dig for gold in the west, put his family to board and room in a private home during his absence, and this was called "out to grass." Again, British civil servants in India, late in the 19th century, sent their families to the much cooler hills, to "the grass lands," during the hot season.

Yet, a parallel seems to exist in several cultures. For instance, in German *Stohwifewe* means "straw widow."

Before streets and sidewalks were laid off, incipient Podunk consisted of a few relatively isolated "neighbors."

Neah, in Old English, meant dweller or farmer, and these two words were combined to form *nehgeber,* which meant, literally, " a nearby farmer." The meaning amplified amid the constant evolutions of society.*

Whether or not sporadic violence necessitated any "curfews" in Podunk, many American communities understood the harrowing legal proscriptions of "curfew" at some point during the tempestuous 1960's. During the Middle Ages British peasants were required by law to put out, or to cover, their fires when a bell rang each evening at a fixed hour. The ringing of the bell, called "cover-fire," is from the French *coorefew.* This word was used by the Norman French, and it was adopted in England as *corfew,* first, and finally as "curfew."

There would be a "chapel," or the equivalent, and school children, of a former era, would attend "chapel." The Late Latin *cappa* was a cloak, and a Medieval Latin diminutive form, *cappella,* meant a short cloak, or a hood or a cowl. The cloak worn by St. Martin of Tours (died in the 4th century A.D.) was preserved as a holy relic, and the shrine in which the sacred cloak was kept was a *cappella.* Ultimately, *cappella* came to mean any holy place. This was the meaning of the Old French form *chapele,* which was taken into British English as "chapel." The custodian of St. Martin's shrine was called *cappellanus,* the Medieval Latin, and this in turn gave us the Old French *chapelain* and the English "chaplain."

The "congregation" which assembled at Podunk's chapel evolved from the Latin *grex, gregis,* flock or herd, the basis for *congregare,* or to gather in a flock. *Congregatia,* derived from that, came into British English as "congregation."

---

*"Neighbor," as a salutation, especially when spoken to a stranger, has declined tremendously in the second half of the 20th century.

"Love your neighbor, yet pull not down your hedge," published in 1640 by George Herbert in *Jacula Prudentum,* seems to have been echoed subconsciously by Robert Frost as "Good fences make good neighbors," in "Mending Wall."

"Pastor," from the Latin *pascere*, to pasture, to feed, fulfills the same symbolism. The past participle, *pastus*, produces the Latin *pastor*, or the one who has care of the flocks.

The chapel had a "belfry" and some of Podunk's citizens were said to have "bats in their belfries." But the origin has no relationship to bells. The word traces from the Middle High German *bererit*, a moveable tower used by military forces attacking a place under seige. Subsequently, "belfry" acquired a collateral meaning as "bell-tower" when medieval cities erected "belfries" as portions of their defense systems, and the bell was sounded to spread the alarm in case of an attack. The Middle English word *belfray* contained both meanings, a seige tower and a bell tower.

Podunk's limited commerce necessitated some sort of broker or factor. "Broker" comes from the medieval French noun represented by the Old North French word *brokieres,* in turn from the verb represented by *broquier* a cask or to broach. Hence, it meant one who broached a cask to draw the liquid from it. Because the wine merchant's intercourses with his community were so numerous, "broker" came into English to mean an intermediary between other individuals in their various business arrangements and dealings.

Obviously, there were "candidates," such as the garrulous little man who importuned Abraham Lincoln for the appointment as postmaster. *Candidus*, in Latin means white, even glimmering, and in Rome the man who sought public office was required to wear a white toga, to be "white-robed," during his campaign. (This same Latin word supplied our English adjective "candid," first spoken in British English in its original, literal meaning of "white.")

The intention in Rome was not so much to electrify the office seeker's physical image as it was to make him easily and clearly identifiable. For a portion of each day he was required by law to take elevated position on a public square so that he could answer questions from his potential constituents. (It is interesting to note in this connection the interplay between the words "blackball" and "ballot." Ballot is from the French *ballotte*, or "little ball.") The candidate's peregrinations were denoted by the word *ambitieo*, "a going about." Because "going around" soliciting votes indicated a desire for power and status, the word *ambito* came to mean a desire for official honors. This was borrowed with broader provisions, as "ambition," in English.

Whether or not Podunk was ravaged by the devastating "flu" or "grippe" epidemic of 1918, many of its residents must have taken their Swine-flu shots in the autumn of 1976. During the 17th century Italian doctors named epidemic catarrh *influenza* because their astrologers attributed the disease to the "influence" of the stars or planets. This virulent infection, known since the 14th century, has been called *grippe* or *la grippe*, intermittently, and the word "grip," or "the grip," has been especially viable in the southern states.

There is a persistent story, not believed to be apocryphal, which accounts for the unusual popularity of the word "grippe" in America throughout the 19th century. A Bostonian, who had a White House appointment, was presented to John Tyler, President from 1841 to 1845. A few hours later when the man was running a fever and suffering chills, he told his Boston physician that he had caught cold shaking the icy hand of John Tyler. Thenceforth, for a considerable period, influenza went by the facetious name of "the Tyler grippe."

Finally, any massive "trip" in Podunk, any serious, protracted hallucination, probably came accidentally, or certainly coincidentally, from jimson weeds. This famous weed was seen first by English settlers in and around James-town, Virginia. The Jamestown-Weed (*Datura stramonium*) became the "jimson weed" because in colonial Virginia the habitual pronunciation of "James" was "jeems," the usage that English settlers brought from England.

The colonists were ignorant of the poison in the weed that flourished around them early in spring. Of the nightshade family, the "jimson weed's" leaves yield the drug start-monium. And in 1676 a group of British soldiers, assisting in the suppression of Nathaniel Bacon's Rebellion, boiled a large mess of the greens. Robert Beverly, in his *History of the Present State of Virginia*, published in 1705, describes the hallucinations that went on for eleven days.

The soldiers thought they were dogs and cats and monkeys, and they rolled and tumbled in mud. Beverly says that at times their antics were so volatile some would have been killed had they not been restrained. Beverly ends his graphic account: "A Thousand such simple Tricks they play'd, and after Eleven Days, return'd themselves again, not remembering anything that had pass'd.

Shortly afterwards, the settlers learned of the tocsin qualities from Indians. Some of the Indians, the Algonquins notably, had used the jimson weed as a pain killer for many years, and the Algonquins and the Aztecs of Mexico had used it as a ceremonial stimulant for centuries.

Thomas Jefferson in his *Notes on Virginia* writes of the narcotic properties of the weed that came to be used in many medicines and tonics.

The people of Podunk, along with a sizeable majority elsewhere, delight "to call a spade a spade." Obviously, and abundantly, this is a contradiction in terms.* No one in Podunk in his right mind objects to calling a spade a spade. Thus, what one really means by the ancient phrase is that many people have an innate tendency to gloss picayunes or minor offenses with assorted euphemisms.

The words seem to appear in print first in 1621 in Robert Burton's *The Anatomy of the Melancholy*: "A loose plain, rude fellow, I call a spade a spade." (Burton has Democritus make the speech to the Reader.) However, Plutarch (46-120 A.D.) used it first in his story about Philip of Macedonia father of Alexander the Great. Philip had an

---

*In line are Robert Frost's "Good fences make good neighbors," and Kipling's "Oh, East is East and West is West." Each phrase, written facetiously, in irony, is spoken often in the opposite context of the cynicism intended by Frost and Kipling.

official visit from several pseudo ambassadors whom he did not trust. These luminaries complained to Philip that they had been treated rudely and discourteously by some of Philip's staff. Whereupon, according to Plutarch, Philip explained that the ambassadors must pardon his offensive entourage because they were rough, unpretentious fellows who didn't know any better than to call a "tub a tub."

Apparently, Erasmus, who repeated the incident in his *Adagia*, in 1300, changed "tub" to "spade." And different cultures have used various objects as euphemisms for plain talk. For instance, the ancient Greeks spoke of calling "a fig a fig." The fig, in some manner now lost in the mists, was indecent among some of the Greeks.

Podunk continues to light tremendous "bonfires" to ignite political rallies, high school football pep rallies, and the like. Throughout the Middle Ages tremendous piles of human bodies were burned in times of plague and war, as an obvious necessity. These were called *bonefires*, "fires of bones." And a bit later in European history when heretics were put to the torch at the stake, the word *bonefires* attached to these inhuman burnings. Indeed, the same word was applied to the burning of books, and other articles, under proscription by the church.

Still later in European history the meaning and the practice was extended to encompass outdoor fires to celebrate sporting and athletic events. But at this juncture the infinitely less gruesome word, "bonfire" was spoken and written. Even so, it is interesting to contrast the relatively innocuous "bonfire" with its horrendous progenitor, "bonefire."

The murders of President Kennedy, Senator Kennedy, Martin Luther King, and the wounding of Governor George Wallace crystalized the ancient word "assassin" in Podunk. In Persia during the 11th century a secret order was established among the Ismailis, a Muslim sect. Hashish was taken as ceremonial stimulant, and under its influence the membership terrorized Christians and other enemies of the secret order with many acts of surreptitious murder.

The organization spread its clandestine terror from Persia across Syria and Asia Minor for two centuries. In their Arabic language these murderers were called *hashshaskin*, from which comes our popular, infamous English word, "assassin."

The people in Podunk who try to obviate colds and flu with various libations are likely to invoke the word "toddy" when speaking of medicinal alcohol. A man may take a "drink" before supper, have a "highball" or a "cocktail" before supper,* but any drink taken earlier in the day seems to warrant the extenuation of "toddy." This is true of any whiskey drunk before breakfast or any daytime potations taken on hunting and fishing junkets. Perhaps, the psychological and emotional implications tie to the fact that during the 18th and 19th centuries most toddies were made with sugar and water added. Indeed, many resolute church leaders and patriarchs gave the crystalized sugar in the bottom of their "toddy" cups to a child to suck.

"Toddy" and "dram" were prevalent semantically amid the rampant boozing of the 18th century. Apparently, almost all the early Americans drank whiskey, including clergymen, women, and older children. And most of the men seem to have begun the day with a before-breakfast nip, dram, or toddy, including even so temperate a man as John Adams.

"Toddy," Hindustani, attaches to the toddy-tree, close cousin of the palmrya, and the word comes to us as the juice or sap of the palmyra tree, called "toddy," which, when fermented, induces a fiery intoxication.

Podunk's art lovers castigate their cultural opposites as "Philistines." Matthew Arnold (1822-1888), taking his text from Judges (16·9): "The Philistines be upon thee, Samson," gave "Philistine" its anti-artistic meaning in his work of 1869, *Culture and Anarchy*: "The people who believe most that our greatness and welfare are proved by our being very rich, and

---

*Small town Americans, and, perhaps, some in metropolitan centers, invite their friends to homes for cocktail parties. In forty years of attendance, this author has never seen a cocktail, or a cocktail shaker, at one of these soirees. Highballs are drunk, often copiously, but the phrase "Cocktail Party" is so compulsive it is here to stay, apparently.

who most give their lives and thoughts to becoming rich, are just the people whom we call the Philistines."

In the Old Testament the Philistines are the principal foes of the Jews, "God's chosen people." Regardless of how Matthew Arnold felt, many modern aesthetes feel that they are the chosen of God. "Philistine" passed into German in this context as *Philister*, in universities a townsmen, the antithesis of the gownsman. Bergen Evans says that the text of the funeral service of a student killed at Jena in 1693 in an argument with a Philister was: "The Philistine be upon thee, Samson."

From the advent of the telegraph, the Western-Union Office, called "Western and Union" in many small communities, was one of Podunk's magnetic, perennial honey-holes. The telegrapher, wearing his sunshade and fancy, ornate garters to hold his sleeves up, was a man of mystery and awe. Via his magic key he abnegated time and distance, as the most sacrosanct secrets of the far-flung universe poured into his ears and out his finger-tips.

Radio knocked the operator's halo askew, but for a long time he posted deathless events on a bulletin board just outside his office. He was the community's entree to the World Series, to national elections, to all the dramatic disasters. The magic key was Pegasus shod in silver shoes, and when he took down a message on his pad everyone who saw him was obsessed by tremulous awe. It might be a message that someone's Cousin Lucy was coming visiting on the 10:12 train on Tuesday, but there was always the implication that the operator was talking to Buffalo Bill, or to John McGraw, or, perhaps, even to the President.

The telegraph is usually credited to the inventive genius of Samuel F.B. Morse (1791-1872), talented artist and the man who perfected a system of dots and dashes. However, "telegraphy," from the Greek *tele*, far off, and *graph*, to write, existed centuries before the magic key. When the Roman legions were defending against the fearsome Picts, in Great Britain, the Romans noticed puffs of smoke by which Pict units signaled one to another.

And in America mounds on certain hilltops tell us that the aborigines used a similar system of communication. Twenty such mounds have been traced between Chillicothe and Columbus, Ohio, and each relates to the next so that signal fires could be seen throughout the entire valley within a few minutes. But the Greeks probably had the first telegraph system, one described by Polybius around 300 B.C.

At each telegraph station there were two walls about seven feet long and six feet high, separated by a space of three feet. At night, from one to five torches were placed on each wall to represent certain combinations of the Greek alphabet. Each station had a tablet that depicted the various combinations. For instance, two torches on the right hand wall and three torches on the left represented "H." Five torches on the right and four on the left meant "Y." The tablet was divided into five vertical and five horizontal rows of squares, with each letter of the Greek alphabet's being allotted a certain square. For instance, "Y" was at the intersection of the square allotted to that letter. This code, in modified form, was used by the signal corps of many modern armies. (What is known as the Chafe semaphore system came in during the 18th century.)

Polybius was born in Arcadia around 250 B.C. and he died around 120 B.C. Trained as a soldier, he fought against the invading Romans in 169 B.C. Captured, he remained a sort of trustee in Rome for seventeen years. He entered the service of Scipio Aemilianus, and he was with him at the destruction of Carthage in 146 B.C. After the defeat of the Achaeans, Polybius was instrumental in arranging a satisfactory peace. For this, many statues were erected to Polybius in Greece.

He wrote thirty-eight books of military history, plus two introductory books that contain a sketch of Roman history from the capture of Rome by the Gauls. His military history ranges from the 140th Olympiad (220 B.C.) to the overthrow of Greek independence in 146 B.C. The first section of

Polybius' thirty-eight books run from the beginning of the Second Punic War to the over throw of Macedonia. The second section deals with the war in Spain against the Celtiberians and the Vaccaeans, and it ends with the destruction of Corinth.

While the affairs of Rome dominate the books, Polybius relates current events in other nations, and he introduced didactic politics into history—by intermingling his views of underlying causes and the effects; but he was indispensable to Livy (50 B.C.-17 A.D.) in recreating the Second Punic War, and Cicero cites Polybius' writing on the Numantion campaign.

Podunk's soiled doves, or "hookers," may have acquired their professional identification from the story that General Joseph, "Fighting Joe," Hooker's commands in the Civil War carried female camp-followers, and these came to be known as "hookers."

Maybe so, but "hook" has long, wide use in American slang. It has meant a crook, perhaps, from hook, or curve, in baseball jargon, and a hypodermic needle or a bent pin used by narcotics addicts. In sales banter, especially that employed by pitchmen, a "hook" is the promise of some free item, and in the sense of stealing this started with "hooking green apples" and came down to professional shoplifting.

Motorists who violated Podunk's traffic laws were "hooked" by policemen, and a crooked dealer "hooked" someone in a card game. The person put into an anomolous position unwittingly was "hooked," and the addict is "hooked" today. ("Hooked by horse" had become commonplace by the 1960's.) A "hooker," usually a fairly small quantity, got its impetus from "Give me a hooker of rye, bartender."

Conversely, to "get someone off the hook" means to rescue him, usually from trouble, and "on the hook" has meant in difficulty, throughout much of the 20th century. In baseball or football, the "hook arm," somewhat in decline now, means the right arm of a right-handed person, and " to go on the hook" still has limited use to mean into debt. The hands are yet "the hooks," and "to hook it" means to run from trouble. "Hooknose" is applied to whatever ethnic race one fancies one dislikes at the moment, and a brothel or a cheap hotel is a "hook shop." Yesterday, those kids who took one-day vacations from school played "hooky," and "pin-hooker," or independent tobacco buyer, came in during the era when such men were said to be so poor that they couldn't afford one fishing hook, that if they fished they had to hook a straight pin.

Portions of Podunk may have been enveloped by the waves of agnosticism that began with the disaffiliations of the 1950's, to encompass Vietnam, Kent State, and Watergate. *Agnostic*, from the Greek *agnostos*, unbelieving, was coined in modern context by Thomas H. Huxley (1825-1895), brilliant British biologist, tagged "Darwin's bulldog" for his militant, eloquent espousal of the revolutionary doctrine of the author of *Origin of Species* (1859).

Huxley, the anti-clerical Victorian rebel, coined "agnostic" to mean one who was not prepared to accept orthodox religion, or any dogmatic views on the origin and destiny of man in the absence of scientific evidence. But although, Huxley, the agnostic, refused to accept the existence of an omniscient God, religious miracles, or personal immortality, he rejected atheism for a comparable reason: The non-existence of God could not be proved by scientific evidence.

From the publication of *Origin of Species* until his death thirty-five years later, Huxley took on many of Darwin's opponents, seeking to expose mental errors, not human beings. These numerous adversaries ranged from Samuel Wilberforce, mathematician and Bishop of Oxford and his British Association for the Advancement of Science, which Huxley, or some wag, dubbed "the British Ass," to William E. Gladstone (1809-1898), Britain's "Grand Old Man" of politics, and resolute exponent of strict orthodoxy.

When a statue to Gladstone was unveiled at Liverpool, Huxley, though ill, gladly accepted the invitation to speak, "to pay tribute to my favorite enemy." The anecdote is illustrative of Huxley's true mettle.

In *A Liberal Education*, Huxley wrote, "For every man the world is as fresh as it was the first day, and as full of untold novelties for him who has the eyes to see them." And it was in *The Struggle for Existence in Human Society* that he trumpeted: "This may not be the best of all possible worlds but to say it is the worst is mere petulant nonsense."

Even if one believes, as this writer believes, that environment is vastly more formidable in shaping human personality than heredity, one cherishes such happy, fruitful exceptions as the Adams family, in America, and the Huxleys in England. (The family originated in Hod's lea (meadow) in medieval Cheshire, and, in time, Hod's lea was corrupted into Huxley.) Leonard (1860-1933), one of Thomas' several brilliant progeny, fathered Aldous (1894-1963) and Julian (1887-1975) two of the most creative minds of the 20th century. Aldous' novels such as *Come Yellow, Antic Hay, Point Counter Point, Brave New World* et al are too well known for additional elucidation, and Julian, biologist, professor, and author, strikes this author as one of the most civilized men of the modern era.

If Podunk had an institution of higher learning in its early years, it was likely a "normal school," known locally, as "the Normal." This is a literal translation of the French *ecole normale*. Actually the French and the English forms of *normal* derive from the Latin *norma*, which means a carpenter's rule, a model, or a pattern, such as seamstresses use. The French called teachers' training colleges *normals* because such institutions were supposed to be model schools whose methods of instruction for future teachers would be emulated by other training centers.

The first *ecole normale* was founded at Rhiems in 1685 by Abbe de la Salle, founder of "The Brothers of the Christian Schools." It was la Salle's declared intention to train teachers for the schools in his religious order, and these schools were designed to offer free primary education to poor children, to make primary education available to children of workingmen.

However the "normal" attained popularity in Germany, and from there this concept spread to England and to America. The first "normal" in America was established, privately, in 1823 at Concord, Vermont. The first headmaster was Samuel R. Hall, a teacher-minister, who accepted a call to the Congressional Church at Concord with the stipulation that he be permitted to conduct a seminary to train teachers.

The first state-supported "normal" was established in Lexington, Massachusetts in 1839. By 1857 the movement had spread to the Mississippi Valley, with the formation of the State Normal University in Normal, Illinois.

Podunk, of course, had a "little red schoolhouse," and the location of all such buildings is light years beyond the comprehension of all extant map-makers, topographical engineers, architects, and real estate tycoons. No such building, from the 18th century into the 20th century, seems to have been built within five miles of any known point of human habitation. This author cannot remember anyone born as early as 1900, or before, who doesn't swear that he had to walk ten miles, round-trip, to his "old field" school-house.

And in the era prior to such sissy innovations as school buses, one assumes snow and sleet fell everyday school was in session. The seeker after learning seems to remember his daily trek was always made through two feet of snow, in a blizzard. And it is unfortunate that those engineers who are entrusted with building interstate highways could not learn the secrets of those former wizards who managed, always, to build every schoolhouse precisely five miles from all other buildings. The savings in condemnation proceedings, alone, would be monumental.

But one recollection is accurate. This was "a little red schoolhouse," in all probability. "Red" had no relevance to artistry or to learning. Early in the 19th century, red paint was cheaper than other kinds of paint, and New Englanders painted their schoolhouses red. Much of the nation adhered to the format. In time, "the little red schoolhouse" became a national symbol for popular education in general.

The names of some of the flowers in Podunk's gardens tell many fascinating little stories, although civic pride probably induces considerable ambivalence over Abraham Cowley's (1618-1667) aphorism, "God the first garden made, and the first city Cain."

Even cursory exposure to a bed of iris reveals why the Latin word for "rainbow" (*iris*) was appropriated, and "pansy" ("That's for thoughts," said Ophelia) comes from the Middle French *pensee*, or thought. The Greeks must have cultivated the red varieties of phlox first because the Greek word *phlox* means flame, and *rhododendron* is a rose tree, literally, from the Greek words *rhodon*, rose, and *dendron*, or tree. Anyone in Podunk who bends low over a nasturtium understands that the flower is "nose-twist," from the Latin *nasus*, nose, and *torquere*, to twist. The pungency of the flower still causes sniffers to make wry faces.

Dandelion, "lion's tooth," derives from the Middle French *dent de lion*, and "delphinium's" from the Greek *delphis*, or dolphin. And the geranium's carpel or spore-bearing organ, suggests the bill of a crane, from the Greek *geranos*, crane. Ancient neo-botanists were sure the snapdragon conjured the visage of a mythical, ferocious dragon, and helianthus became a "sun-flower," from the Greek *helios*, and *antho* flower. This is balanced by aster, the "sun-flower.""Chrysanthemum" literally, is the "golden flower," by dint of the Greek words *chrysos,* gold, and *anthemom,* flower.

The Turks certainly thought the tulip resembles a turban since *tulbend* means turban, and the campanula's bell-shaped blossoms explain its name because the Late Latin *campana* means bell. Botanical historians say the carnation has been cultivated more than two thousand years. It must have been flesh-colored, originally, since its name stems from the Latin *caro* genitive *carnis,* or flesh. The "daisy," almost everyone's perennial darling, comes directly from the Anglo-Saxon *daegesage,* which meant "days' eye."

"Gladiolus" means "a small sword" in Latin, and this borrowing relates directly to the flower's sword-shaped leaves. Conversely, the hepatice, from the Latin *hepaticus,* suggests the Roman notion of the shape of the liver. The centanry acquired its name from Chiron, the *centaur* and Chiron is supposed to have discovered the plant's medicinal powers. *Paion,* Greek god of healing, supplied the name for peony, and "sage," from the Middle French *sauge,* through the Latin *salria,* from *salvus,* means safe or healthy.*

Whether or not Podunk's industrial planning commission ever talks about the etymology of business terms, "business," itself, arose solely from the sense of being busy at something. "Economics" is from the Greek word *Aidonomika,* meaning "the art of houskeeping." The word's present sense reflects the early importance of an intelligent budget in the operation of household affairs.

"Finance" evolved from the French word *fin,* or end, and this had the same source as the English word "final." Originally, "finance" denoted the settling of accounts between two parties, or "bring to an end" an indebtedness. This is intriguing since in today's operations, "financing," more often

---

*There are, of course, in Podunk and elsewhere, those men who make a fetish of bragging about their abysmal ignorance of the names of all flowers. The late Ogden Nash immortalized all such creatures in his "He Digs, He Dug, He Has Dug":
My garden will never make me famous.
I'm a horticultural ignoramus.
I can't tell a stringbean from a soybean,
Or even a girl bean from a boy bean.

than not indicates that one is getting into debt, not getting out of debt.

The noun "firm," in the meaning of a business concern, comes, finally, from the same source as the adjective that means fixed or secure. The Italian language appropriated the Latin *firmare*, to make firm, in the sense of confirming a business agreement by affixing one's signature. This formed the noun, *firma*, or signature. In German this was used, first, as the legal name of a partnership or a company as a signature in making contracts, rather than in an individual's name. Ultimately, it became the regular term for the partnership, or the company, itself. Thus, the English word "firm" retains both meanings, even if the former meaning is usually restricted to members of the legal profession.

Many of the people who visit and leave Podunk fly in and out, but many of these take taxis to and from the municipal airport. Obviously, "taxicab," is an abreviation of "taximeter cab." "Taximeter" means "tax meter," and "cab" is a shortening of "cabriolet." Prior to automobiles, a cabriolet was a light carriage, drawn by horses. This is a French noun diminutive of *cabriola*, or *capriole*, a leap. This, in turn, is from the Italian *capriola*, derivative of *capriola*, or roebuck, from the Latin *capreolus*, meaning roebuck or "wild goat." Such a carriage was called a "cabriolet" because it was light, and, hence, it bounced along rough, unpaved roads.

Many of the precious gems worn and owned in Podunk reflect interesting facts and fancy. "Amethyst," from the Greek *amethystos* (from *methgein*, to be drunk, from *methy*, wine) was a remedy for drunkenness. The ancients believed that this stone, consisting of a violet-blue variety of crystalline quartz, would keep the wearer sober. Drinking cups were fashioned from amethyst to prevent intoxication. The amethyst became known as the "bishop's stone" from its

---

In "Intimations of Immortality," Wordsworth (1770-1850) trumpeted:

To me the meanest flower that blows can give
Thoughts that do lie too deep for tears.

In "Peter Bell," he satirized the absence of such perception:

A primrose by a river's brim
A yellow primrose was to him,
And it was nothing more.

wide usage on the third finger of bishops. Such a ring on the third finger of the right hand symbolized the wedding of a bishop to his diocese. The "aquamarine" is taken from the Latin *aqua marina*, or seawater, which suggests its color. "Jade," borrowed from the French, was supposed to cure kidney pains, and the Spanish called it *piedra do la jaka*, or "stone of the loin," and, hence, the word *jade*. The Latin *rubeus*, red, is the origin of "ruby," and "turquoise" comes from the French, and its popular meaning is "Turkish." This was applied to the stone because it was brought through, or from, Turkey.

In the early spring of 1977 many dailies carried photographs of Miss America, 1976, and her wedding in "The Little Church Around the Corner." The story and photograph rekindled interest in the days when many of Podunk's, and the nations's brides and grooms sojourned to New York City just to be married in the famous "The Little Church Around the Corner."

This, the Church of the Transfiguration, acquired its deathless designation in 1870 when George Holland, a popular comedian, died. Joseph Jefferson, the famous dramatic actor, tried to make funeral arrangements for Holland at the Church of Atonement. The rector declined to bury an actor, but he added, implying Transfiguration, "There is a little church around the corner that might do it."

Actors across the nation joined Jefferson in exclaiming, "Thank God for the little church around the corner."

The church became the religious center for theatrical people, and it is still referred to as the "actor's church." Throughout the 20th century this church, located at No.1 East Twenty-ninth Street, has been noted for the large number of weddings conducted there.

When O.Henry (William Sydney Porter) died in New York City in 1910 a funeral service was scheduled at Transfiguration. But via a foul-up, a wedding was scheduled for the precise hour, and the undertaker and O.Henry's funeral party had to wait in the rear of the church until the wedding ceremony ended. Had Porter been living he would almost certainly have put this O.Henry-twist to a short story.*

---

*O.Henry is buried in Asheville, in a cemetery over-looking the French Broad River, and in the same soil that contains Thomas Wolfe's (1900-1938) remains.

118

PART FIVE
GRAB-BAG

*"The art which (Sir Francis) Bacon taught was
the art of inventing arts."*

Thomas Babington Macauley, from *Francis Bacon*.

"In times of calamity any rumor is believed."

Publius Syrus, from *Maxims*.

*"Oh, I would like to be a ghoul
And ruffle the poet's mound,
To dig up the rhymes he laid aside
For the sake of another sound.*

*"And otherwise, if that were vain,
A diver I would be,
To be pick the rings the doges dropped
Whenever they married the sea."*

Nathalia Crane, "Desire."

*" 'Tis not so deep as a well, nor so wide as
a church door; but 'tis enough, 'twill serve."*

Shakespeare, from *Romeo and Juliet*.

GRAB-BAG

Belief that amethyst induced sobriety was as realistic as the militant faith in "tattooing" as a magical antidote against various illnesses and many types of misfortune. And several cultures, including the Egyptians, used tattooing to designate status and rank. Conversely, special tattoos were pricked on slaves and criminals for purposes of identification. Tattooing has been found on Egyptian mummies interred as early as 20,000 B.C. In this sense, the word is of Polynesian origin, akin to the Tahitian *tataw*, pricking with a needle or pin.*

"Beyond the pale," more common today as "within" or "outside," was popular in the 14th century to mean a boundary or restriction. "Pale," from the Latin *palus*, a stake, means a place enclosed by a fence, within pales. In Shakespeare's *Comedy of Errors*, Adriana compares her husband to a "too unruly deer that breaks the pale and feeds from home." But "beyond the pale" came into use to designate the pales maintained by England in France and in Ireland.

In 1494 the British crown established a pale in the territory around Calais. From the 12th through the 17th centuries the area in Ireland controlled by England was known as "The Pale." (In 1786 Catherine II of Russia issued a ukase that required Jews to live in certain specified areas of Poland and southwestern Russia, and these places were designated as "the Jewish Pale.")

The authority of Great Britain prevailed within the pale,

*"Tattoo," originally *tap-too*, from the Dutch *taptoe*, the shutting off of taps in taverns at day's end, is a signal sounded on drum or bugle to summons soldiers or sailors to quarters at night; a display of military drills or exercises offered as entertainment; and it means to beat out a rhythm with the fingers.

but the crown was powerless beyond the pale, and thus it seems likely that "beyond the pale" was dramatized by Irishmen who slipped beyond the jurisdiction of British authority, although today the phrase usually applies to the person who is alleged to have committed some serious social or moral transgression.

"Pass and repass," long spoken in the American south, and elsewhere to more limited degree, as a high-blown type of unofficial permission, stems from the bluegowns, an order of paupers in Scotland. These paupers, known also as the "King's Bedesmen," were paid annual stipends upon the condition that they "pray for the Royal Welfare." The number of official bedesmen extant at any time was predicated on the number of years the king had lived. On the day of the king's birthday, each bedesman was given a blue gown, and a purse containing as many shillings Scots (pennies sterling) as the king's attained age. And each bedesman was given a badge that bore the words "Pass and Repass." This injunction protected the bedesman from all the various laws that pertained to begging and vagrancy.

Some of Sir Walter Scott's fans may recall that Edie Ochiltree, in *The Antiquary*, is a bedesman, a bluegown. But Scott's praying mendicant seems more intelligent and meritorious than his real-life counterparts. The official practice of appointing bedesmen was discontinued in 1833, although a few already fitted into blue gowns persisted. The last of the bedesmen, the last person endowed legally with the permission "to pass and repass," drew his final allowance from the exchequer in Edinburg in 1863.

"Nasby," in abeyance today, had synonymity for several generations with the most palpable of sinecures. Nasby originated as a generic name for postmasters from a humorous, facetious series of articles written by David Ross Locke (1833-1888) in 1861. Locke, writing as "The Rev. Petroleum V. Nasby, at Confedrit X Roads, Kentucky" published his 1861 series in the Findlay, Ohio *Jeffersonian.*

"By hook or crook" seems to have surfaced around 1380 in some of Wycliffe's tracts, in the persistent sense of by fair means or foul. Experts are not undeviatingly precise about the origin of the phrase, but the most intelligent and realistic surmises relate it to the early British forestry laws. On certain days the poor were allowed to enter the government's forest preserves to pull off all of the fire wood they could obtain by "hook or crook." "Hook" was a long, crooked pole, akin to a shepherd's staff, and "crook" was a sickle. Axes and saws were forbidden, and it is easy to picture the peasant slashing and hacking away as rapidly as strength and agility warranted.

"Jakes," often confusing when spoken or written today, is an old word for privy. In *King Lear*, Shakespeare says: "I will tread this unbolted (unrefined) villian into mortar, and daub the walls of a jakes with him." On balance, "jakes" strikes many students as infinitely preferable to "little girls' room," "head," "john" and many other modern synonyms.

(This entry about "jakes" conjures H.L. Mencken's famous, or infamous, bathtub hoax of 1917. Mencken wrote in the New York *Evening Mail* that the bathtub was invented in Cincinnati in 1840, that Millard Fillmore, President from 1850-1853, installed the first bathtub in the White House. Despite the fact that Mencken made repeated attempts to rectify his hoax, readers wouldn't have it, and the piece, as "factual material," made its way into some encyclopedias. For several years after 1917 Mencken did his best to demolish what he had intended as an innocuous whopper, but hardly anyone listened to him.)

The sign of the fish, which preceded the cross as a symbol, was an early form of "graffito." The immediate choice of the fish must have been due to simple expediency. The figure was easy to trace, and the meaning was patently clear. Many of Jesus' first disciples were fishermen, and the story of the miracle of the loaves and fishes was popular, and there was Jesus' injunction to become "fishers of men."

And the fish was a mysterious word as well as a picture. In
its Greek form, the original language of the *New Testament,
fish* contained a summary of the Christian faith in the form
of an acrostic. *Ichthus* spelled out the initial letters of the
new creed (in its English rendition) of *Jesus Christ, the Son
of God, the Savior of man.*

And fishes were sacred to Aphrodite, foam-born goddess of
beauty and fertility. Some of the Greek philosophers believed
a diet, with fish as the main ingredient, sharpened their
faculties, and there is the old legend that fish is an
aphrodisiac.

"Graffiti," found often on the walls of modern's rooms, is
as ancient as Pompeii and Rome. "Graffito" is from the Latin
graffio, a scratch, from the Greek *grapheim*, to scratch, then
to write. (Graph is an element in many English words.) In the
catacombs "graffiti" were religious signs and notations during
the era when Christians foregathered quietly and surreptitiously.

Bathing was integral in the ancient Egyptians' religion, and
the Hindus endowed the Ganges with spiritual significance.
Bathing pools, sheltered by porticoes, are mentioned in the
Bible, and wherever the Romans settled, they erected public
baths, forthwith. (The Romans, also, had a crude equivalent
of our sauna, and after the body was steamed until sweat
poured freely, a servant beat the dirt out and off with a
thong.) According to Seneca (4 B.C.-65 A.D.) the Romans
annointed their bodies with pomades, and in addition to hot
and cold water, they took vapor baths and baths of hot and
cold air. Virtually all the Roman baths were public, and all
bathing, in all stations, was sexually mixed.

Tubs of the crudest sort existed almost from the outset,
but, curiously enough, in America the public bath, much
more luxurious than anything available in the home, came
afterward. Philadelphia installed some public baths in 1829,

and these had the aura of the status-symbol. But the secular halo toppled when Boston put in public baths in 1866, and more than 300,000 people used them the first year.

Bath, the famous town 107 miles west of London, was established originally by Romans who called it *Aquae Solis*, or "waters of the sun." Similar therapeutic lithua waters found lively translation in America in endless spas, usually designated as "springs," around which summer and winter resorts emerged.

Finally, an epidemic of public bath laws passed in many states during the 1880's produced considerable editorial asperity, as well as some indignation from the pulpit, and the word "Draconian" was attached to this legislation, by opponents. Editors began to speak of "Draconian laws" in 1895 when New York passed a bill that required all towns of 50,000 people to build a certain number of public baths. Many other states followed with similar legislation.

Draco is supposed to have written Athens' first code of laws, in the seventh century B.C. Oppressively harsh, these laws became proverbial for their severity. Demandes, the orator, who lived three centuries later, said: "They were written not in ink, but in blood." Under Draco's code many trivial offenses such as laziness and vagrancy were punished as harshly as treason, sacrilege, and murder. (Apparently, every offense was subject to capital punishment.) Draco explained, "The smallest of them deserve death, and there is no greater punishment I can find for the greater crimes."

Draco's code was superseded by the more compassionate laws of Solon, one of the Seven Sages of Greece. There is the legend that Draco moved to Aegina, introduced a similar code, and that he was smothered to death accidentally in a theater by garments thrown upon him as tokens of admiration and esteem.

While our public bathing laws were anything but Draconian, the opprobrium attached for a while, in some of the papers.

PART SIX
A FEW TRADITIONS OF WEDDINGS, BIRTHS, LOVE,
AND ALL THAT

"Same old slippers,
Same old rice,
Same old glimpse
Of paradise."

William James Lampton, from *June Weddings.*

"Will you love me in December,
As you do in May?"

James J. Walker, from song of same title.

"Therefore shall a man leave his father, and his mother, and
shall cleave unto his wife and they shall be one flesh."

Genesis (2:23).

"No man is genuinely happy, married, who has to drink worse
whiskey than he used to drink when he was single."

H.L. Mencken, from *Prejudices: Fourth Series.*

"To church in the morning, and there saw a wedding in the
church, which I have not seen many a day; and the young
people so merry one with another! and strange to see what

delight we married people have to see these poor fools destroyed into our condition, every man and woman gazing and smiling at them.''

Samuel Pepys, from his *Diary*, December 25, 1665.

A FEW TRADITIONS OF WEDDINGS, BIRTHS, LOVE AND ALL THAT

The basic meaning of "wedlock" isn't precisely compassionate and passionate chains linking a man and a woman permanently with love: The original "lock" was the Anglo-Saxon word for gift, and "wed" meant a promise. If the semantical difference seems slight, a promise of continuing gifts of love is a bit more salutary.

For a long time, and in many cultures, marriages were arranged independently of the bride and groom, and the couple met for the first time on the day of their marriage. Rome maintained a famous lottery for lovers, and in many societies marriage brokers made arrangements, for a fee.

But the best man evolved from physical necessity during the times when boys stole their brides, frequently from unfriendly, or certainly adamant, tribes. In some places, the best man acted as surrogate during the wooing, in a manner almost to call up Longfellow's delightful *The Courtship of Miles Standish*. Hence, the enduring word "best." The best man was chosen for friendship, but also for strength, bravery, and agility. Often, the best man was an armed escort when the groom captured his bride, and after bride and groom were together, the best man enticed the bride's disputatious relatives into chasing him.

Primitive weddings could be hazardous even when arranged via parental consent because antagonists liked to pillage wedding parties and guests. For this reason, many of the early Scandinavian marriages were held at night, and lances and torches were stationed behind the High Altar. If an attack developed, the best man acted as ordinance dispenser and as commander of the repelling force.

But where the bride was stolen, where irate relatives chased the best man, the bride and groom sought sanctuary in a cave And the actual original meaning of "honeymoon" is predicated upon literal or figurative interpretation. From the ancient lunar interpretation, the honeymoon means the first month, or moon, of marriage. But the most likely beginning of the word is the old Scandinavian custom of drinking honey, wine, or some sort of fermented honey, as an aphrodisiac during the first month, or moon of marriage.

And there is the appalling theory that "honeymoon" is merely a cruel interlude of lambent-conjured ecstasy in a swiftly-changing life in which care is a steadier partner than passion. The theory that happiness is brief and capricious as the phases of the moon found support in a verse by waggish Tom Hood (1799-1845):

But of all the lunar things that change,
The one that shows most fickly and strange,
And takes the most eccentric range,
Is the moon—so-called—of-honey.

The bride's veil is ascribed frequently to the Biblical account of Rebecca's meeting with Isaac, whom she married: "She took a veil and covered herself with it," but the initial veil, a crude sheet, came in to placate evil spirits. Lovely brides were veiled, even disguised, to prevent capture by envious demons or other malevolent forces.

Superstition is likely to be most acute at times of tremendous anticipation. Moroccan brides shut their eyes throughout the service to conceal their identities from the "evil-eye," and in some oriental countries brides cover their eyes with the sleeve of their garments. Undoubtedly, the bride's veil has some relevance to her becoming a new person, at least in theory. Various candidates for sacrosanct orders, various people about to be initiated into some new order, are veiled. This must carry over to the "one flesh union" implicit in the wedding ceremony. And some historians see the bride's veil as the last of what the Anglo-Saxons called the "care-cloth," the thin covering that enveloped the couple, allowed them, simultaneously, to acknowledge and to be wary of mysterious higher forces.

The wedding ring, as an essential part of the ceremony, is only a thousand years old, and Christians seem to have appropriated it from pagan society. Apparently, the Greeks adopted the ring from the east. (In the Egyptian hieroglyphic script, eternity is represented by a circle.) The remainder of the civilized world takes the wedding ring from the Romans.

As such, the wedding ring developed from the engagement ring or the engagement token, both of which were mandatory in the days of bought and bartered brides. Unglamorously, the early engagement token had the same finality as today's "Sold" signs. The Romans used the engagement ring as a commercial pledge, and the Hebrew male handed the bride a coin as a sort of promissory note and as a visible token of his ability to provide for her, to be responsible for her obligations.

Primitive man bound a rope around his chosen woman because the "magic circle" transfused his spirit into hers. Thus, the two were consecrated by inviolable, inexorable supernatural forces. And almost from their advent, rings were amulets. Most of the early rings were signets, providing a seal with which orders and agreements were signed, or made official with a family-mark. The handing over of such a ring transferred authority. (When Pharaoh gave Joseph his ring, his signet, he made Joseph a judge and a ruler of the Egyptians.)

Several authorities say it was Pope Nicholas, in 800 A.D., who first mentioned the Christian use of wedding rings, and once sanctioned by the church it denoted a sacred covenant as well as a commercial transfer. Ultimately, and patently predictable, some of the early psychiatrists saw the finger and the ring as the union of the male and the female sex organs.

Wearing the wedding ring on the left hand must have denoted subservience, in the beginning, because the right hand is the old symbol for authority. Submission was enhanced when unskilled Greek and Roman anatomists "discovered" that a special vein ran from the third finger to the heart. This finger, actually the fourth when the thumb is counted as the first, became the lecheman, or "medical finger," in England.

It was supposed to give off an instantaneous signal when it touched poison, and doctors and leches used it to stir various medications.

The wedding ring was connected with the heart, and a ring on the third finger was (is) easy to see. There is even the theory that the third finger was consummated as the receptacle for the ring because it, unlike the others, cannot be stretched independently to its full length. (It was (is) harder for a ring to slip off the third finger.)

Until the 16th century the groom did not put the ring on the bride's third finger, directly. He began the ritual by placing the ring atop the bride's thumb, with the words, "In the name of the Father." He said "In the name of the Son," as he moved the ring to the forefinger, and "and of the Holy Spirit" when he moved it to the middle finger. He moved the ring to the third finger, and he left it there as the word "amen" was spoken.

The bride's position on the groom's left, and her right arm within his left arm, is not the culmination of some obsolete fetish of etiquette. The bride's unalterable positioning on the groom's left is an outgrowth of the days in which the groom had to keep his right hand, his sword arm, free to protect the bride, and himself.

Orange blossoms, frequently present, and always symbolic, came in because the white blossoms suggested innocence, to announce the bride's virginity. And the acknowledged fecundity of the orange tree symbolized the implied hope for many strong children. And since the orange tree produced fruit and flowers, simultaneously, its blossoms crystalized the wish that the bride, too, would be fruitful and lovely.

However, status was formidable in Europe. Because orange trees were rare, exotic, and costly, they were unknown in northern Europe, save to wealthy, who could import them. Inevitably, less affluent people obtained the blossoms on special occasions such as the marriage of the daughter. Apparently, the British obtained this custom from the French around 1820.

The French got orange blossoms from the Spaniards, who,

according to legend, got them from the Moors. In Spanish soil, the orange tree was revered, especially by reigning royalty, and there is this saccharine story to explain the origin of orange blossoms for brides:

A Spanish king almost deified one of his orange trees, a tree of inordinate exquisiteness. The French ambassador begged repeatedly for a shoot, but always vainly. Simultaneously, the king's gardener's daughter, desperate for a dowry, stole a slip and sold it to the French ambassador for a large amount of money. To show her indebtedness to the tree, she put some of its blossoms into her hair on her wedding day. Thus, simple gratitude started a universal tradition.

Innumerable legends attach to the prowess of shoes, albeit, more shoes are probably tied to the bumpers of honeymoon cars than are actually thrown at weddings today. The shoe is an ancient symbol for fertility. ("There was an old woman/ Who lived in a shoe.") Until fairly recently many Eskimo women carried a piece of a shoe to insure fertility. Some primitive people believed the soul resided in one's shoe. To throw one at newlyweds was to endow the lovers with one's best portion.

Too, the handing over of a shoe, or sandal, from seller to buyer, was the equivalent of a deed, a clear title. And when women were construed as chattels, when many marriages were arranged by parents, the woman's parents gave the groom a shoe, in view of witnesses, to signify they had relinquished all claims and all authority.

And there is the ancient legend that says that throughout marriage the woman had to supply the man with shoes. So, her friends threw shoes immediately after her wedding ceremony so she would have a large supply for her husband.

Today more confetti (Italian with the same root as "confectionary") is thrown than shoes, and the word, a reference to "sweet meats," rekindles the era when sweetened almonds were thrown at brides and grooms. Earlier, among so-called pagans, grain was thrown to repel evil spirits, and to insure proliferation. The fertility of the grain was transferred to the couple.

Ironically, confetti, a shredded paper substitute for grain, is thrown upon honeymooners protected by the pill, by ebullient friends, also on the pill, most likely.

Wedding cakes, of varying sorts, go back to antiquity, and these are axiomatic in many, many cultures. Here, again, the origin is fertility; but the affluent Romans, among whom a real cake may have appeared first, made one, called the *confarreatio* or "eating together," of flour, salt, and water. The bride and groom were given small portions. Then the cake was smashed over the bride's head. The guests scrambled for the broken pieces so that they could have the blessings insured by the marriage ritual. In order to be eligible for high Roman office, one had to be born of a marriage that was consummated with a cake, one smashed over the bride's head in the presence of ten witnesses.

At Anglo-Saxon weddings, the bride's mother handed round an enormous basket of biscuits. Each guest ate one and the remainder was given to the community's poor. Later, Anglo-Saxon guests brought sweet buns. These were raked into a huge pile, and if the bride and groom could kiss each other above the mound, happiness was guaranteed. Afterward, the couple and guests ate the buns. According to British legend a visiting Frenchman, in Charles II's reign, appalled by the trouble it took to rake all the buns into a huge pile, decided to ice all of the buns into a single, many-tiered cake.

The groom's carrying the bride across the threshold was popular among the Chinese, Abyssinians, and some of the Indians of Canada. The custom probably began when many brides were captured and entered their new dwellings unwillingly. But the fear of stumbling, one of primitive man's most enduring superstitions, is bound to be a factor. A nervous bride, unfamiliar with her new surroundings, might stumble, and thereby, in keeping with the tenets of the superstitions, not only impair her reproductivity, but call down the evil-eye.

The Roman threshold was sacred to Vesta, virgin goddess, and in Rome it was sacrilegious for a woman, about to change her maiden status, to touch the threshold. Some other peoples believed demons lurked beneath this piece of wood. To touch it with the feet was bad luck.

The kiss, such as grooms bestow on the bride, may be the final sensual development in a long process of evolution. Albeit, some authorities think the kiss began because primitive men thought the air they exhaled had magic powers. So, by kissing each other, men and women joined their souls.

Still others think kissing started as a subconscious evocation of the ancient custom in which some mothers prechewed, or warmed, food for infants and transferred it with a "kiss."

Although some of western civilizations' finest rhapsodies are paeans to kissing (Some of the Greeks called it "the key to Paradise."), the Chinese never kiss, save for parents kissing children, and the Japanese have no word for it. Some of the mothers in Indo-China frighten unruly children by threatening them with "the white man's kiss." (This is invoked by some of the Indo-China women in the harrowing sense that nurses in the American south threatened their small charge with the boogey-man.) Even today many Chinese equate kissing with cannibalism.

One of the most convoluted of the Victorian "purifications" came when Lord Nelson's "Kiss me, Hardy," was amended to "Kismet Hardy." The only trouble with this "purification" is that Lord Nelson, who spoke the words to his friend, Hardy, as he lay mortally wounded, was killed at Trafalgar in 1805. And as experts point out, "kismet," Turkish for destiny, or fate, did not reach England, via Arabic, until 1849.

The 19th century English were horrified that Lord Nelson, a national institution, would ask a man to kiss him, even amid the delusions that accompany shock and intense pain and dying. For, as the 19th century British put it, "That disgusting custom is done by foreigners."

Many married and unmarried swains used to affix copious "X's" to their love missives, and the old custom carries over to some of the current Valentines. This is an offshoot of the rampant illiteracy of the Middle Ages when many legal documents were signed with "X's." To make the "X" official, it was sealed with the maker's kiss. But, actually, the "X," St. Andrew's mark, signifying a sacred covenant or a promise, attained universal pertinence as a sort of short-hand for love.

"Spooning," almost as indispensable to Tin Pan Alley* as fried chicken was to protracted meeting dinners-on-the-grounds, tied to the old Welsh custom in which boys carved ornate, heavily-embossed wooden spoons for their sweethearts. Often the wooden spoon was given in lieu of the more expensive engagement ring, but, in any case, the exchange of the wooden spoon (usually the first item in a Welsh girl's hope chest) contained all of the tacit implications of an "understanding." When the girl accepted the spoon she had parental permission "to go walking out at night," sans chaperone. What they did when they went "walking out" came to be denoted as spooning. And, of course, there is the suggestion that when two people lie closely together they project the image of two spoons fitting into each other.

The "right" of women to propose marriage during leap-year is supposed to have legal precedent in a decree of 1288 which Queen Margaret of Scotland issued through her parliament. According to the story the man could not refuse unless he was already formally engaged to be married. Other-

*Until 1900 the center of the nation's music publishing was on New York's Union Square. Around 1900 the industry moved to 28th Street between 5th and 6th Avenues, and known for several decades as "the street of song." "Tin Pan Alley" emerged coincidentally from a piece written around 1903 by Monroe Rosenfeld, for the New York *Herald*. At the publishing house of Harry Von Tilzer, amazingly successful song publisher and tunesmith, Rosenfield was captivated by upright pianos into which Von Tilzer had stuffed strips of paper through the stings to produce the tinny effect Von Tilzer favored. From then on, until the advent of rock, 29th Street and the popular music industry were known, everywhere, as "Tin Pan Alley."

wise, if he refused he was fined 100 pounds, then a fortune. The Scottish rule is said to have been adopted in Florence, Genoa, and France. But the English did not adhere to the rule, and realism indicates that the adoption in Florence, Genoa, and France was based on legal fiction.

Other authorities ascribe the leap-year proposal to innate celibacy. Certainly, that is the clear implication. St. Patrick (5th century A.D.) was approached by a distraught St. Bridget who said the nuns in her charge were in revolt because women were precluded from taking the initiative in marriage proposals. To placate her, St. Patrick decreed that women might initiate proposals each seven years. Whereupon, St. Bridget wailed, "Make it four, make it four." And so the leap-year proposal was inaugurated.

The feast of love, or certainly the prodigious exchange of greetings, that occurs on February 14, St. Valentine's Day, probably has remote basis of fact since many birds began mating in the middle of February, and the period became propitious for all sorts of love. Too, a lottery attached to the perennial celebration of Juno, queen of heaven and Jupiter's "venerable ox-eyed wife." Juno, identified with Hera, the Greek goddess, although a goddess of war, was also the guardian of marriage and women. Young girls wrote their names on slips of paper. These were placed in a drum and drawn out by young men. The girl drawn by a boy became his sweetheart until the next annual lottery.

Early Christianity appropriated this pagan ritual and tied it to the martyrdom of St. Valentine, brutally murdered by order of the Roman Emperor Claudius on February 14, 269 A.D., insofar as one can tell. Apparently, Claudius prohibited Christian marriages, and Valentine, a pagan priest converted to Christianity, who became a bishop, was imprisoned because he continued to perform weddings. His execution is related to the legend that he restored the sight of his jailer's blind daughter.

At one point in history, and for what seems to have been a considerable period, names of saints were put into the drums, and during the ensuing year the recipient was supposed to adjust his daily conduct to the life-style of the saint whose name he had drawn. But some frustrated young women, neo-women libbers, complained that they were the objects of discrimination. So, they seized the lottery drums, and they took out the saints' names and inserted their own names.

This annual pairing continued for a while, but, ultimately, boys and girls insisted on doing their own selecting and the lottery was abandoned. And the picking of a valentine usually entailed some sort of written printed declaration, some effusive nosegay, and illiteracy, semi-literacy, and literary ineptitude were not barriers. Examples of prefabricated valentine greetings are evident from the outset. And in 1797 *The Young Man's Valentine Writer*, the prototype of the modern card embellished with syndicated verse, was published. Young men and women who had difficulty writing, or expressing their thoughts, could copy out an appropriate sentiment from *The Young Man's Valentine Writer*.

(In essence, this same format has had active ramifications in unusual ways in American life. For instance, Richard Walser in his *The Black Poet* (1966) tells how George Moses Horton, young black slave, became an integral member of the community of the young, small University of North Carolina, at Chapel Hill, in the early 1800's, and for many years afterward. When Horton became an unofficial, but vital, entity in the University community, he could read but he could not write.

(However, he had learned to "write" ringing poems in his head, and these rhymed poems were set, usually, to the music and swing of Charles Wesley's lively hymns, hymns the young black slave had heard sung at camp-meetings. He became the surrogate love-lyricist for the white students. For

a fee, sometimes a quarter and sometimes fifty cents, Horton
wrote in his head a love poem and a specific student took the
lines down in ink and dispatched the lyric to his sweetheart.

(Richard B. Creecy, class of 1835, leaves this foot-
note: "On Saturday evening he came up to the college from
the country with his week's poetical work in manuscript
which was ordered by the boys on the Saturday before. When
he (Horton) came he was a lion. His average budget of lyrics
was about a dozen number. They were mostly in the love line
and addressed to the girl at home. We usually invested a
quarter a week,* and generally to the tune of the girl we left
behind us."

(It is fascinating to consider the permanent romances that
may have come between landed white students and their
sweethearts on the wings of poems of the black slave such as:

When I have told my last fond tale
In lines of song to thee,
And for departure spread my sail,
Say, lovely princess, wilt thou fail
To drop a tear for me?

"O princess, should my votive strain
Salute thine ear no more,
Like one deserted on the main,
I shall gaze, alas! but vain,
On wedlock's flowery shore.)

In popular mythology, the stork, from the Greek *storge*,
meaning strong, natural affection, brought babies in its bill.
Ancients were cognizant of the stork's astonishing consi-

---

*A quarter for one of Horton's poems was hardly a picayune, Richard Walser
reckoned that a student's total expenditure for one year at the University averaged
$138.00.

deration of its fellow storks, especially the young and old ones. In popular lore, storks cared for enfeebled and blind parents, even to feeding them and to transporting them on their own wings. And it was common knowledge that the stork, to a degree greater than other birds, built its nest with meticulous care, and often rebuilt the nest in the same spot from year to year.

The presence of a stork, especially among Germanic peoples, was recognized as a sign of good luck, and many German farmers put wagon wheels atop their homes as permanent foundations for nests. The stork's being migratory at a time when little was known about the migratory habits of birds enhanced the baby-bringing legend. In a considerable body of European lore, the stork flew to Egypt during winter where it became a human being. Additional implications sprang from the stork's fondness for swamps and lakes because tradition said that the souls of unborn children dwelled in watery places. (Perhaps, this has some nebulous tie to the story of Pharoah's daughter finding Moses in the bull-rushes.)

For a long time Scandinavian, Dutch, and Germans said that when a stork brought a baby it always bit the mother in the leg, forcing her to take to her bed for a spell.

The birthday party emerged from a ritual that ensured health and prosperity for the twelve ensuing months. Our traditional "Many happy returns of the day," which goes back to antiquity, denoted that the observance of the birthday was a renewal, a magical process by which one repeated, or perpetuated, one's own life.

The birthday cake goes back to the Greeks. The adherents of Artemis, goddess of the moon and of the hunt, placed honey-cakes at the goddesses' temple on the sixth day of each month, to celebrate her nativity. The honey-cakes, always, moon-shaped, were lighted by tapers. This custom seems to have reappeared among German peasants during the Middle

Ages. The Germans lighted a cake to celebrate a child's birthday the very second the child awakened. Attained age was represented by candles, and one additional candle always symbolized the "light of life." The candles burned until the cake was eaten at the family's evening meal. If candles burned out during the day, replacements were added immediately.

Since the earliest periods the burning of tapers, and sacrificial fires, was endowed with magic. Hence, the blowing out of the candles came to be associated with the granting of the birthday child's unspoken wish. (The magic of illumination is evident in the timeless jingle, "Star light, star bright, first star I see tonight.")

Insofar as one can ascertain, the baby-carriage was invented in New York around 1848 by one Charles Burton, but it didn't sell because New Yorkers thought it was hazardous to pedestrians. (It is possible that a prohibitive ordinance was in effect, temporarily.) Undeterred, Burton began the manufacture of baby-carriages in London, and they caught on with the British public amazingly when Queen Victoria bought one for a grandchild. But the baby-carriage became the "pram" in England because the literal translation of "perambulator" described an instrument which measured walking distance. The shortened version, "pram," came along in 1857. While "pram" is sporadic and limited in American English, it is almost inevitable in British English.

Since most babies look alike, many authorities say decking boys in blue and girls in pink was done to identify babies by sex in hospitals. While this seems based on historical precedent, blue for baby boys goes back to primitive fear and superstition. Evil spirits, always around, were distressingly prevalent in the early equivalent of nurseries. But evil spirits were highly susceptible to certain colors, to blue, particularly. Blue, suggested the sky, thus heaven, and the color made evil spirits impotent and sent them scurrying in horror.

Because little girls were deemed incalculably inferior, evil spirits didn't waste their horrendous prowess on them. So, no preventive color was necessary, but, much later on in history, a type of E.R.A. came when baby girls were dressed in pink. But the best legend is the European story that boys were found under cabbage leaves, often blue on the continent, and that baby girls were born inside pink roses.

By the middle of the 20th century, divorce, from the Latin *divortium*, related to "divert," had become almost synonymous with "marriage," emotionally and semantically. Divorce was commonplace among the ancients, and only the Hebrews seem to have required a bill of divorcement, or any kind of written documentation.

With many tribes, divorce was a male decision, often a precipitate action. In most of the Arabic countries the male made his leave-taking official by saying "*Ittalck.*" ("Go to the devil.") three times in rapid succession. In other cultures the man merely walked off, although the Eskimo pointedly moved his belongings to another igloo. During Biblical times the Hebrew male was required to present a brief bill of divorcement to his wife, but she was bound to accept the document and its stipulations.

But post-biblical Jewish authorities made the proceedings more precise and more difficult. Divorce was valid only when obtained in a court of three judges, in company of two other witnesses, and the bill had to be drawn up by a scribe-expert, during a session of the court. The witnesses, alone, signed the document. The chief judge read it and in turn passed it to the husband. In the presence of the witnesses, he handed it to his wife, as he said: "Here is your bill of divorcement. Take it. From now onward be divorced from me and free to marry any man."

The wife returned the bill to the chief judge who tore the top off to preclude subsequent use in a fraudulent action. The language of the early decree, still adhered to in essence by orthodox Jews, goes: "On the_____day of the week, the_____ day of the month _____ in the year____ in the city of_____ situated on the river_____ I _____ the son of____with the surname of____who today am resident of____do hereby consent of my free will and without any restraint, set free, release and put away my wife ____ who at present resides at_____ .

"Up to this moment you have been my wife. But now you are released, set free and put away, so that you may be your own mistress, and may marry any man you desire. No one may hinder you from doing this, as from this day forth you are free to marry any man.

"Thus you received from me this bill of divorcement, a document of lease, a Bill of Freedom, according to the law of Moses and Israel."

The Anglo-Saxons were among the first to require specific grounds for divorce, but this wasn't difficult if the wife was "abusive," "passionate," "barren," "luxurious," "quarrelsome," "rude," or "habitually drunk."

Early in Roman history, dislike or disaffection by either partner was sufficient for divorce. This tenuous justification seems implicit in the story told by Plutarch (47-120 A.D.) in his *Life of Aemiliuus Paulus*: To the consternation of his friends, an unnamed Roman divorced his wife, who appeared exemplary to the man's friends. The man handed his friends one of his shoes, asking if they could tell him where it pinched, a sentiment repeated by Chaucer in *The Merchant's Tale*.

Later on one of the spouses had to declare his intention in a formal letter, carried by a messenger, or in a letter written, or delivered, in the presence of seven witnesses. In addition to expressing an intention to end wedlock, this private writ stated that the other person could retain ·all of her property. A judicial inquiry did not occur unless there was an issue about the care of children or an issue about the division of possessions.

"Caesar's wife should be above suspicion," the deathless injunction found in Plutarch's *Lives*, endures as an enigma to many students. In 67 B.C., Caesar married Pompeia, second of his three wives. In 63 B.C. he was elected to the powerful position of *pontifix maximus*, which had jurisdiction over the ceremonies of expatiation, marriage, regulation of the calendar, and administration of the laws of worship. The next year, when Caesar was made magistrate, *praetor*, and entitled to wear the purple-edged toga, the marital scandal broke at the observance of Bona Dea, the deity of all fertility. The rites of the "good goddess" were celebrated on May 1, to mark the dedication of her temple on Aventine Hill, and again in December in the home of one of the magistrates.

All males, including servants, were excluded, as always, when Julius Caesar's home was given the honor in 62 B.C. The women, dressed in black robes, had just begun their ritual when Publius Clodius, wealthy young nobleman and profligate, was discovered disguised as a woman. The outraged women beat Clodius and drove him into the street, but Caesar asked for a divorce.

No relationship between Pompeia and Clodius has ever been established, and Caesar brought no charges against the young man. But the desecration of his home by Clodius' presence brought shame to Caesar, and his marriage was dissolved shortly afterward.

Did Caesar exploit this issue? Was he seeking a way to get rid of Pompeia? Many cynics think so. Many subsequent dictators have exploited pretexts equally as flimsy, but no one will ever know just what it was that motivated mighty Caesar.

Since primitive man's first awareness of death, there has been a steady subconscious desire to defeat death, or to hold it in some sort of check. This seems to account for the Pyramids, as well as mummified bodies, and the Egyptian's *Book of the Dead*. Virtually all cultures have believed consecrated ground enhances resurrection, but the washing of corpses arose from superstition and not hygiene. Early man believed that evil spirits feared water.

The sarcophagus was made of stone which the Greeks thought consumed all flesh and bones, save teeth, within forty days. The original Greek for cemetery meant "dormitory" or "sleeping place." It is yet "house of eternity" for the Jews, and the Germans call it *Friedhof*, or "courtyard of peace."

The first "undertakers" were those who were asked to "undertake" funeral arrangements. The word "funeral" derives from the Latin *funnus*, or torch. Torches, or lights, were necessary to guide the soul to its eternal resting place. Catholics light votive candles on All Souls' Day, and orthodox Hebrews burn a lamp for twenty-four hours each year on the actual anniversary of the revered departed.*

While the spiritual and aesthetic implications of candles, perpetual lights, are well known, the original funeral candles probably emerged from fear and superstition. Candles frightened predatory spirits from the dead, and there was the belief, also, that the dead were afraid of lights. Perpetual lights kept the dead from harming the living, by the fear of the light and by providing the dead with the luxuries they had enjoyed in life. Light was a prime comfort, as well as a talisman. A corpse was less likely to abandon a well-lighted tomb to go searching for the luxuries of the quick.

"Coffin" comes from the Greek *kophinos*, or basket of plaited twigs. Many early coffins were made of trees (the oak was sacred) cut in half. The bottom, hollowed out, was the bed and the top of the tree was the lid.

Today's expensive "casket," the semantical replacement of "coffin" in American mores, has its counterpart in the ornate

---

*Shapur II, King of Persia from 310 to 370, the posthumous son of Hormurd II, was crowned before he was born. All of Hormurd's other sons were killed, or exiled, immediately upon the king's death, and the unborn child was proclaimed "Shapur II."

boxes, "chested burials," subscribed to by affluent people in history's early days. Simultaneously, the poor were taken to the burial ground in a coffin. The coffin was returned, for subsequent use, and the corpse was actually buried in a shroud.

Although the ultra expensive modern casket, perhaps the ultimate status-symbol, relates from that, coffins of a much cruder sort came in as popular receptacles for the dead to protect bodies from animals and from body-snatchers who sold cadavers to students and hospitals. And fear of the dead was salient, persistently. Often his feet were tied tightly, and some tribes even removed his head, putting it between his legs, obviously, to distort his sense of direction should he attempt to return to his former abode. To add to the deceased's consternation, he was carried from his home feet first, and frequently, in a special hole or passage made specifically for the funeral and then closed up. And the trek to the graveyard was done in the most circuitous way possible, the longest and most convoluted.

The first funeral wreaths, a magic circle to keep the body in its place, were initiated to placate the dead, to provide him a safe journey, and to keep him happy lest he return and haunt the living. The early Christian leaders tried hard to abort this custom, but endless momentum devolved from the Roman and Greek custom of crowning distinguished people with laurels, especially laurels of flowers with evergreen leaves.

And the original tombstones came from atavistic fear, also. The body was weighted with stones, and burial usually occurred where one had died. And in the days before formal cemeteries, the stones warned the living, made them wary. The initial inscriptions, reserved for people of high rank, exclusively, were written to attract attention, to invite pilgrims to pray for the soul of the deceased.

"Hearse," a French word, was a harrow, and as the name suggests, a triangular, iron frame, with spikes attached, used by Roman peasants, and adopted by the French. By the 13th century French peasants turned their field harrows over for use as huge candelabrum at wakes. The harrows grew larger, a framework developed, with black drapes, on which mourners pinned pieces of paper that contained memorial poems and greetings. A rail was placed around the harrow-hearse but it remained stationary until the 14th century when wheels were affixed and mourners pulled it, with the body on it, to the graveyard. ("Death wagon" and "dead wagon" had tremendous vibrance in America, especially in the south, until those terms, and "undertaker," were replaced by more disarming euphemisms in the 20th century.)

One of the most repulsive stories in all of history involves Inez de Castro, of Portugal, dubbed "the queen who reigned after her death." She became the morganatic wife of Dom Pedro, heir-apparent to the throne of Portugal in the 14th century. The Prince's father, fearing the powerful Castro family, opposed his son's marriage, and he denounced Inez's birth as illegitimate.

In 1355 Inez was assassinated, apparently by the king's agents, and Dom Pedro launched an insurrection which culminated in his being given "a large share of the government." The King died in 1357, being succeeded by Dom Pedro. According to tradition when Dom Pedro was coronated he had Inez exhumed and placed on a throne and crowned as queen. All the nobles of the realm had to pass and kiss her withered hand. Almost immediately Inez was reinterred, amid tremendous pomp, her body being placed in a sarcophagus of pure, white marble.

PART SEVEN
HOUSES, CLOTHING, AND PERSONAL HABITS

"Set not your House on fire to be revenged of the Moon."

Thomas Fuller, from *Gnomologia.*

"A man builds a fine house; and now he has a master, and a task for life: he is to furnish, watch, show it, and keep it in repair, the rest of his days."

Ralph W. Emerson, "Society and Solitude," from *Work and Days.*

"Fashion wears out more apparel than the man."

Shakespeare, from *Much Ado About Nothing.*

"Fashion is gentility running away from vulgarity, and afraid of being over-taken."

William Hazlitt, from *Conversations of James Northcote.*

"All orators are dumb when beauty pleadeth."

Shakespeare, from *The Rape of Lucrece.*

"The saying that beauty is but skin deep is a skin-deep saying."

Herbert Spencer, from *Personal Beauty.*

"I fill this cup to one made up of loveliness alone,
A woman of her gentle sex, the seeming paragon."

Edward Coote Pinkney, from " A Health."

HOUSES, CLOTHING, AND PERSONAL HABITS

When the House of Commons was dedicated, upon its reconstruction in 1944, Winston Churchill, the prime minister, said, "We shape our dwelling and afterwards our dwellings shape us."

The common names of many of the rooms in modern houses emerged from their original functions. "Parlor," from the Latin *parliatorium*, a conference room, through the French, *parler*, to speak, was the family's original "talking room." "Kitchen" is from the Latin, *cogyina*, through the Anglo-Saxon *cycene*, to cook, and in this century "kitchen" supplanted the old "cook-room." "Drawing-room" is a shortened version of "withdrawing-room." In the 16th century, British inns maintained special "withdrawing-rooms" which special guests used for conferences, to enable men of station and affluence to have privacy from crowds. By the 18th century the function had changed to mean a room to which women withdrew after a sumptuous meal, leaving men to talk freely, to revel with wine and tobacco. The attrition of time simply wore away "with."

"Hall" is from the Anglo-Saxon *heal, heall*, the public dwelling of a teutonic chieftan. His private residence, often a "palace," derives from Palatine Hill, one of Rome's famous seven hills. Originally, Palatine Hill was the chief section of ancient Rome, and according to tradition Romulus made his first furrow there, built a wall around the famous hill. Augustus, Rome's first emperor, was born on the hill, and he picked it as his official residence. Other emperors followed, but the insufferably vain Nero (Claudius Caesar Drusus Germanicus), emperor from 54 to 68 B.C., had all the buildings on Palatine razed. The new, splendid emperor's residence on Palatine became known as the "palace."

"Mansion," as "In my Father's house are many mansions," (John 14:2) usually induces visions of celestial opulence and grandeur. Historically, "mansion" is merely a dwelling-place, and John Milton wrote about the "mansions of hell." In time the residence of the lord of the manor became the "mansion." But even if "mansion" really means a room, something is lost in the "revised" version, "many dwelling places."

"Attic" comes from *Attica*, the hinterland of ancient Athens. When British architects of the 18th century ornamented the top floors of elegant homes with ornate Athenian pilasters, the modern word "attic" emerged. When the 18th century architectural fashion subsided, the narrow room beneath the roof lost its splendor but the word "attic" persisted.

Several experts tie the "lumber room" (frequently "plunder room" in America) to the Lombards, the banking family, some of whom migrated to London during the Middle Ages. The Lombards, in essence highly respectable pawnbrokers, kept pledges and other redeemable items in a special room in their establishment. This compartment, the "Lombard Room," was Anglicized into the "lumber room," and as such it endures as a storage room in the home.

(The three golden balls, as the sign of a pawnbroker, are said to derive from the Medici family of Florence. Prior to becoming pawnbrokers and bankers, the Medicis, as the name indicates, were doctors. Averardo de Medici, one of Charlemange's officers, killed a giant named Mugello. To perpetuate indicates, were doctors. Averardo de Medici, one of Charlemagne's officers, killed a giant named Mugello. To perpetuate his feat, Averado claimed the three gilded balls on Mugello's face. The three golden balls symbolized the Medici

family and the medical profession. The symbol was transferred to pawnbrokers later on when the Medicis entered
banking and pawnbroking.)

Infinite ingenuity and fatuity have been expended by men
in their specious attempts to circumvent, semantically, the
essential purposes of the bathroom or urinal. The
euphemisms, well-nigh endless, run from toilet, to water
closet, to "W.C.," to head, to john, to powder room, to privy,
to urinal, to comfort station, and on and on to the really
atrocious "little boys' " and "little girls' room." The medieval
monasteries contained a " necessaire," and the castle had its
"gardenrobe," semantically a forerunner of our cloak-room.

The outdoor privy, variously the "latrine," the "garden-
house," and "outdoor plumbing," had almost as many
synonyms. Some were "lavatories," although this is supposed
to suggest washing, and "latrine" is merely the contraction
of its original Latin root. "Privy" and *retirade*, prevalent in
Dutch countries, enunciated isolation. *Toilet*, from the French
"little cloth," was viable for much of the 20th century, and
some authorities even relate the word to the story of Saul and
young David: Saul had to "cover his feet," or "void his
bowels," and David, to show Saul how easily he could have
killed him, "cut off the skirt of Saul's robe privily."

Seat closets, made of brick, dating back to 2000 B.C.,
were found in excavations in the Indus Valley. In the 14th
century B.C., Cretans in their capital of Knossos built closets
over a conduit of running water. King Minos' lavish palace,
excavated by Sir Arthur Evans, contained astonishingly
modern closets whose pans were flushed by water, rainwater,
chiefly, from a cistern.

Sir John Harington's "privy perfection" of the 1590's is
often cited as the model for the modern water closet.
Harington, Queen Elizabeth's godson and a poet, put a

water-tower high atop his house. A hand-operated tap controlled the flow of water into the pan, and sewage was released into a cesspool by opening and closing a valve. Elizabeth had one of Harington's water closets installed in her palace at Richmond, but the public thought the invention was frivolous and unnecessary.

"Window" is from an Anglo-Saxon combination that meant "wind's eye," and before the advent of glass, windows were eyes to see through, from the inside to the outside. The modern window began as a small hole in the wall, covered by crude shutters or by a curtain. Albeit, the coming of glass added a dimension to art in the form of ornate, decorative windows, particularly in the use of stained glass. John Milton (1608-1674) put it this way in "Il Penseroso":

And storied windows righly dight,
Casting a dim religious light.

"Gothic" implies architecture of abundant splendor, but the Goths, a Teutonic tribe from the 3rd to the 5th century, never used it. The Goths, long in limbo, were allies with the Vandals in the destruction of much Roman and southern European culture. Labeled barbarians, the infamy of the Goth's misdeeds made the word synonymous with Philistinism.

Artists of the Renaissance, deriding the current architectural styles, revived the ancient classical style. The current crudities were tagged "Gothic." But the abusive term was misconstrued by laymen, and "Gothic" cathedrals became "far the most in harmony with the mysteries of religion." Indeed, it was the religious intensities of the 12th century which brought about the pointed arches and new designs that symbolized spiritual idealisms. Thus the new cathedrals, the "Gothic" cathedrals, ceased to be contradictions in terms.

"Pantry," of over-riding viability in insular America, comes from the Old English *pantrie*, from the Old French *panaterie*, or bread closet. "Piazza," "verandah (or veranda)", and "stoop" have some sporadic use in the American South even today. "Piazza" is from the Italian *piazzae* a public square in an Italian town, from the Italian *platea*, meaning broad street. "Verandah" is Hindu, or from the Portuguese, *verare*, to surround with poles, and "stoop" is from the Dutch *stoep* or front verandah.

The basement, home workshop, kitchen, and even the bathroom are quick with many "gadgets" and "doodads." In American English, "gadget" is a slang synonym for the novel and for almost any item whose name the speaker can't recall. "Gadget" originated in the American navy to mean small tools and mechanical devices of an infinite variety. When a sailor said, "Hand me that gadget" he could mean anything from a monkey wrench to a small nail. Two theories have been advanced to account for the origin of "gadget," but neither is supported by fast evidence: "Gadget" is derived, by some, from the French *gauchette*, diminutive of *gache*, a catch or a staple, and, again, it is derived from *gadge*, an obsolete Scotch word that meant gauge. In American English, "thingaumbob," "thingumabob," "thingamajig," and "doodad" are generally synonymous with "gadget."

Finally almost anything that is completely lifeless is still said to be "as dead as a doornail." For a long time the saying was explained in line with the ancient saw, "As the doornail is knocked on the head several times a day, it cannot be supposed to have much life left." The weakness is that there is no evidence that the original doornail was a nail, or piece of metal, on which the knocker struck. It is highly likely that the original application was to an ordinary nail in the door, and during the Middle Ages nails were used in doors as ornaments, and for utilitarian purposes. Such a commonplace object must have lent itself to copious comparisons. Shakespeare must have had this in mind in *King Henry IV* when Sir John Falstaff asks, "What! is the old king dead?" and Pistol replies, "As nail in door."

Despite the Old Testament contention that the sartorial art began when Adam and Eve sewed dresses of fig leaves, animal skins came first. And man's initial raiment has been described as a basic girdle, as an apron, and as something in between the two. The impulse to primitive tailoring must have been simple self-preservation, a protective force against nature. Obviously, modesty was a secondary factor, as was dress to show class distinctions. (There is the old saw that vanity induced tailoring because all naked people look alike, but many artist and realists will dispute the latter allegation.)

Always utilitarian, primitive man quickly found numerous translations for his early clothing. A cloak or robe became a blanket or bed, a saddle-blanket, or even a saddle itself, and merchants used robes to display their numerous wares. As the Writ tells us, when the Hebrews left Egypt, they wrapped their kneading troughs and their other scanty possessions into their garments. (Robes, most likely.)

Clothing not only came to distinguish the sexes, until hairstyles became similar in the 1970's, when the young of both sexes wore blue jeans, but it came, also, to symbolize one's personality.

"Trousers," probably from the Old English *trouse*, from the Old French *trebus*, from the Late Latin *tibraci* said to come from *tibia*, the shinbone, were necessitated by the horse. The first trousers—more often pants or britches in American English, until recently—were worn around a thousand years before Jesus by nomads in Central Asia. Apparently, the warriors of the Asian steppes found the habitual habit, a piece of animal skin wrapped around the body, uncomfortable when on a horse, incompatible with speed and dexterity. And the first trousers were gawdy, striped, checked, and sometimes embroidered, even to resemble some of the patches and splotches worn on trousers by young men today.

The barbarians from the steppes were excellent PR men for trousers because their "civilized" antagonists in flowing robes lost out in the ensuing cavalry clashes. The new fashion seems to have made its way into northern Europe after it was adopted by the Persians, Indians, and the Chinese. (When Julius Caesar invaded Britain, around 55 B.C., he was impressed particularly by the bright trousers worn there, and the Romans took the idea back to their empire.)

Trousers had an off-and-on saga in the Roman Empire. Noblemen branded trousers "worthy of slaves only," and at one point an imperial edict threatened trousers-wearing freemen with the loss of their property or banishment from Rome. However, the utilitarian advantages saved trousers. Then, almost apropos to nothing, trousers went out of fashion for several centuries.

The French Revolution is credited with giving trousers their greatest impetus in modern history. Knee breeches and silk stockings were construed as arrant privilege, and the guillotine. Trousers were a symbol of equality, and former noblemen quickly donned the workingman's blue pants to escape execution.

Again, England seems to have been slower to make the adjustment. There is the story that in 1814 the famous Duke of Wellington was turned from his club because he was wearing trousers. About this same time, 1812, Trinity College marked absent any student seen in pants, and an ordinance passed in Sheffield, and elsewhere, declared that "under no circumstances whatever shall any preacher be allowed to occupy the pulpit who wears trousers."

There is probably something to the theory that the turn to trousers in Great Britain was accelerated by the upper class belief that trousers were much better for their habitual gout than knee breeches.

Periodically, knee breeches, of a sort, would make several sporadic returns via an assortment of "knickerbockers" or "plus-fours." "Knickerbocker" comes, in modern semantics, from Cruickshank's drawings which illustrated Washington Irving's *Diedrich Knickerbocker's History of New York*. (1809) The elderly men depicted by Cruickshank wore wide pants, caught at the knees, soon known by the populace as "knickbockers" or as "knickers." (A *knicker* or *nicker* is a marble made of baked clay, and in colonial New York the man who made them was a *knickerbocker*.)

"Plus-fours," popularized by golfers, originated in the British army. These were called "plus-fours" simply because four inches were added to the inside seam of each leg of ordinary knickerbockers.

"Jeans," to attain epidemic proportions with youngsters of both sexes in the 1970's, or *jene fustian*, is from the Middle English *jene*, from Genoa, where they were first manufactured. "Levis," often a common synonym for "jeans," evolved from Levi Straus, of the famous family of late 19th century American merchants. Straus, conducting the family's mercantile business in the west in the 1870's, opening up a new territory for the family firm, devised fairly heavy, unusually durable jeans, with fore and hip pockets. These pants were heavily reinforced along the seams. The pants were great favorites with cowboys and miners, who called them "Levis."

"Bloomers," one of the most enduring misnomers in sartorial nomenclature, honors Mrs. Amelia Jenks Bloomer (1818-1894) who, in 1849, founded *Lily*, one of the prominent magazines to espouse women's rights and temperance. The issue of February, 1851 contained a description of a "sanitary attire" for women designed and worn by Mrs. Elizabeth Smith Miller, daughter of Gerrit Smith. The costume consisted of skirts that reached the knees and loose trousers gathered around the ankles, like Turkish pantaloons. Amelia Jenks Bloomer denied consistently that she created bloomers, but her name attached. Tremendous impetus fastened when women across the country said it was much easier to do household chores in "Mrs. Bloomer's creation." And many other women said it was easier to handle a baby in "bloomers." Curiously enough, Mrs. Bloomer abandoned the costume after eight years because she said her influence for women's reforms and for temperance was greater when she wore conventional clothing.

"Lindsey-woolsey," long common for coarse fabrics of cotton, or linen, woven with wool, is from the Middle English *lynsey wolyse,* apparently predicated on Lindsay, village of Suffolk where the fabric was made. "Cardigan," to mean a sweater or jacket that opens down the front, is from James Thomas Brudenell, Seventh Earl of Cardigan (1797-186), who devised the jacket or who had it made. "Raglan," the loose jacket with slanted shoulder seams extending in one piece of neckline, is named for Field Marshall Lord Raglan (1788-1855), British commander in the Crimea.

Shortly before his death Raglan is said to have read Alfred Lord Tennyson's "Charge of the Light Brigade," a somewhat fanciful description of the British defeat at Balaclava. Seeing a man who was about to return to England, Raglan is supposed to have said: "If you see Tennyson tell him to stop writing such rot." "Inverness," the loose overcoat, with detachable cape, was popularized first at Inverness.

"Havelock," cloth covering for a cap, with a flap to protect the back of the neck, was designed for wear in India by General, Sir Henesy, Havelock (d. 1857).

"Corduroy," is elusive. Frequently this thick, durable, coarse cotton fabric, with the surface ridged, corded, or ribbed like velvet, is derived from the French *corde du roi,* or "cord of the king." Most modern etymologists deem sheer fiction the repeated assertion that the word was applied to a fine cloth manufactured in France and worn by the king and his court when hunting. (This probably arose as a theory to account for the strange name of the cloth.) And there is the intermittent theory that the word started as *colourduroy,* or *couleur de roi,* "king's color," or the royal purple.

But the evidence convinces that "curduroy" is of English, not French origin. For, neither "corduroy nor *corde de roi* appears in French as the name of a fabric. (The *Oxford Dictionary* points out that a list of articles manufactured at Sens, France in 1807 included "king's cordes," that the term, foreign to the French, was borrowed from England.) One of the oldest extant uses appeared in the Hull *Advertiser* in 1795 when "old corduroy breeches" were available. In 1722 the London *Gazette* had mentioned "a grey duroy coat," and a writer in the same paper in 1746 wrote of "Serges, Duroys, Druggets" etc. And George Washington, after his marriage to Martha Custis in 1759, ordered via his London agent "a light summer suit of Duroy." Nonetheless, no direct relation between "duroy" and "corduroy" has ever been established.

Actually, "corduroy" is an Old English surname and it is not unlikely that the fabric acquired its name from an early manufacturer, and there is the equal possibility that *corde de roi* was adopted as a trade name for the fabric, without specific reference to any royalty. (Starting in the 18th century, "corduroy" was applied to many crude roads that were built by laying logs side-by-side transversely.)

"Cravat," necktie, is derived from *cravate*, the French name of the inhabitants of Crotia. (In English Croats, called "kro-ats.") The original "cravat," or "cravate," was a linen or muslin scarf which members of a regiment of Croat mercenaries wore around their necks, while in the service of Austria. About 1635 France organized a light cavalry regiment whose members were dressed in uniforms patterned after the Croats. Stylish Frenchmen immediately adopted this type of neckware, and the fashion spread around the world.

When it was first introduced to civilians, the cravat consisted of a simple scarf. Soon, though, Cravats edged with lace and tied in a bow, with long flowing ends, became marks of high fashion, In time, all "neckties" became known as "cravats."

The "vest," irrepressible yesterday, then in limbo, and now making a return, comes from the French *vests*, from the Latin *vestis*, or garment. Until late in the 19th century, this garment was known in British and American English as the "weskit," or the "waistcoat." Worn to be seen, the first waistcoats were expensive and elaborate. Most waistcoats were made of the finest materials, often quilted and now and then trimmed with silver or gold. Usually embellished with intricate handiwork, and made in brightest colors, it was intended to supplement the most flamboyant of personalities. Henry VIII's wardrobe held many lavish waistcoats, and when the Earl of Essex, once one of Elizabeth's favorites, was being led to his execution, he removed his doublet to reveal a brilliantly scarlet vest.

Despite the persistent old wives' tale that vests "protect the chest and stomach from wintry air and encourage a nice tendency to sweat during summer," the garment lost almost all of its practical and aesthetic appeal between the two World Wars. But early in the 20th century many Americans saw bright, elaborately-made vests as depicting a sort of personalized heraldry, and that may account for the garment's renewed popularity late in the 1970's.

"As public safety measures," during the 1890's, several American cities passed ordinances making it illegal for women to wear hatpins more than two inches long. (This preceded the popular advent of muggers.) Charles II (king, 1660-1685), to accelerate the wool trade, passed a law that required all English people to be buried in woolen. The law prompted John Dyer's facetious play of 1757, *The Fleece*, but when Dyer died a year later, he was buried in woolen!

Alexander Pope demurred, in *Moral Essays*, asking that his "cold limbs and face" be wrapped in "a charming chintz and

Brussels lace." His concluding line, "And—Betty—give this cheek a little red," revolutionary early in the 18th century, is standard with modern morticians."

According to the story generally credited, "cuffs," or "turn-ups," resulted from a small accident. Near the end of the 19th century a visiting Englishman was caught in a down-pour enroute to the wedding of Consuello Vanderbilt to a titled European. To salvage the hang in his trousers, and to keep them dry, he turned up the bottoms (a rainy day device still adhered to by many older men, even wearing cuffed trousers). Amid the excitement of his late arrival, he forgot to turn his trousers down. Many guests assumed "cuffs" were a new British fashion, and immediately after the wedding numerous American society leaders had tailors cuff all of their trousers. When the Englishman returned home, he found "turn-ups" all the rage there, never suspecting he was responsible for the fetish. During World War II trousers were cuffless, in the guise of saving materials. The change in fashion gave rise to the irrepressible joke, "I don't mind no cuff on trousers nearly so much as no trousers on the cuff."

The "derby hat," known also as the "bowler" and the "billycock," may have acquired its name from the fact that this style of headgear was worn by the Earl of Derby, who established the famous horse races at Epsom in 1780. (It could have been that the sporting gentry who attended the Derby wore "bowlers.")

There is the persistent story that this type of hat, the stiff felt with dome-shaped crown, was made originally by William Bowler, a Southwark hatter, and that it gained its first popularity via the patronage of William Coke, nephew of Sir Edward Coke (pronounced "Cook"). Young Coke proclaimed: "The bowler possesses all the good qualities that a man could desire in his headgear." (A London firm still advertises this as "Coke hats.")

Some authorities have assumed that "billycock,"first popular in the 18th century, is a corruption of "Billy Coke," but the *Oxford Dictionary* implies that this may have been a corruption of "bully-cocked."

The first American derbies were manufactured in South Norwalk, Connecticut, in 1850. For a long time the American derby symbolized ward politicians, drummers, and members of the sporting fraternity. But the most notable vibrance attached to drummers, to the loquacious traveling-salesmen who rode grimy day-coaches incessantly. Drummers wore almost as fraternal trimmings, derby hats impervious to soot and disfigurations, detachable celluloid collars and sleeves, spats, and vests that ran from bright to downright gawdy.

Many of the professional horse-and-mule-traders wore derbies and carried canes, to whomp mules on the rear rather than as ornamentation or aids to locomotion. As a very small boy the author attended a horse-and-mule trading session in Bill Blair's Mule Lot, just east of Kingsbury Street, in Oxford, N.C. I wanted a pony, desperately, even though this was totally unrealistic financially. A man who purported to be a mule-skinner showed me an unusually attractive pony, but I noticed that he wore a John D. Stetson felt hat. Since he wasn't wearing a derby, I assumed that the man was a fraud, that there must be something amiss with the pony, too.

With the wholesale turn to assorted pants by women in the 1970's a few die-hard male advocates of the mini-skirt predicted the flood of trousers would destroy the male's capacity for fantasy and rhapsody. Two or three irascible men amplified their revulsion for women-and-pants with a quote from Deuteronomy: "The woman shall not wear that which pertaineth unto a man, neither shall a man put on a woman's garment; for all that do so are an abomination unto the Lord."

Until the 19th century "pants" was unseemly, certainly

with people of station. "Pants" is an abbreviation of *pantaloons*, from Saint Pantaleone, a favorite of the Venetians. In the medieval Italian mask, or *commedia dell arte*, Pantaleone was the foil for the clown's jokes. Hence, "panteloon" used to be linked with the slang word "looney." Oliver Wendell Holmes, Sr. (1809-1894) said "pants" is a word made for "gents," not for "gentlemen."

The first "brassiere," from the Old French *brasiere*. or arm guard, is ascribed to Caresse (Mrs. Harry) Crosby, New York socialite who became luminous in Paris among the literary expatriates of the 1920's. According to the accepted story she was dressing for a dance in 1915, and she thought her gown fitted her poorly. Apparently, she did not need "gay deceivers," the bosom embellishment favored by many women of the era. On the spot with a little thread she fashioned a brassiere from two white handkerchiefs. She is generally credited with receiving $1500.00 from some facet of the garment industry for her invention. Hence, the weight of the evidence suggests that Caresse Crosby took out a patent on her invention.

"Buttons on sleeves," now decorative, came in when sleeves were unnaturally long. The early buttons were a simple expedient to keep elongated sleeves from hanging down and impeding locomotion. In the 17th century ornate, fragile cuffs were turned up and fastened by buttons. And if the weather was cold or windy, the wide sleeves were tightened and closed around the wrists.

(It may be apocryphal but buttons on military jackets are said to be the result of a king's displeasure when he saw some of his soldiers wiping their noses with their sleeves.)

But these buttons were retained after their utilitarian needs vanished. The first purely decorative buttons were hand-made, expensive, and fashioned in endless shapes and colors. With many men these ornate buttons, and cuff-links, had the same social significance as the school tie in Britain, or a form of modern heraldry.

Many (including this author) always leave the bottom button on their vest (waistcoat) unbuttoned. In the late 1930's, among neo-but-bucolic swingers, it was said that one could tell a sophisticate from hayseed by the open buttonhole. And this vain pomposity was augmented by the maxim, advanced by some tailors, that the whole male ensemble fit and blended much better with the bottom button loose.

But according to the generally-accepted story, a member of England's royal family dressed in a hurry for an elegant party. In his haste he neglected to button the bottom button of his waistcoat, and the other male guests, seeking to spare the prince's embarrassment, unbuttoned their bottom vest buttons.

The first "handkerchief" was a simple cloth used to protect the head and face from the searing eastern sun. It was brought to France by sailors where it was called *couvir chef*, or "a covering for the head." The cloth crossed the Channel to England, where it acquired its enduring name and its modern purposes. It came to England as a head covering, but, obviously, it failed to give protection against the harsh British weather.

But the British, not to be outdone commercially, improvised and found the head covering to be excellent for blowing the nose and wiping the forehead. Few trousers had pockets, and the English carried the new kerchief in their hands. Thus it became the "handkerchief."

Actually, the Romans anticipated the British when upper class men, patricians, carried utility napkins. When the Roman Empire fell, these napkins vanished, for a thousand years. The Anglo-Saxons came up with their "sweat-cloth," but this survives as a portion of the vestments of the Church of England. (During the Middle Ages many priests were reprimanded by their bishops for blowing noses on their sacred garments.) The word "handkerchief" came into fairly general use in England during the 16th century.

Wigs, found on mummified bodies in Egyptian tombs, have had many vogues and declines. The original wigs were the by-products of fear and superstition. Primitive man believed hair was the source of strength and longevity (the story of Samson), "the seat of the vital spirit of life." Wigs were fashioned when primitive man became aware of the loss of hair, and, parenthetically, strength and life.

And since the wig was a practical means of disguise, military and political spies began wearing it. The Greek theater liked brightly colored wigs, and the color of a wig represented the character of the actor. Tyrants wore black and comedians especially comic menials, were dressed in red wigs. Heroes were given blonde wigs, with lots of curls.

(During the days of Tacitus, 1st and 2nd centuries A.D., the most barbaric Germanic tribes exported tons of their blonde hair, to Rome, chiefly, for wigs.)

Nonetheless, wigs were off and on, denounced as evil by the early church. And it was not until the 17th century that they became fully accepted and worn in Europe. Louis XIII wore a wig to obscure his baldness, and courtiers at Versailles followed suit. The common people, anxious to ape nobility, started wearing the *perruque*. (From which English obtained "periwig" and "wig.")

It invaded England during the latter portion of the 17th century, to become an instantaneous symbol of rank. Ordinary Englishmen wore the full-bottomed, or "natural" wig, but grandees sported wigs that towered high above the forehead, in two enormous peaks, and fell far below the shoulders. By the middle of the 18th century, as many as forty varieties had been devised, among them "the staircase," "the wild boar's back," "the artichoke," "the comet," "the pigeon's wing," and "the turnip seed."

To help defray the excessive costs of the wars with the French, the British government imposed a severe tax on powder, an essential ingredient in the wig-maker's trade. The wig-makers petitioned George III for relief, complaining that men had "gone to dressing their own hair." When the taxation was relaxed, inflation made the cost of wigs high, and many men of station learned the trick of dressing their own hair so that they appeared to wear a wig. And in passing it is interesting to note that for a long time Hebrew law made the wearing of a wig mandatory for every married woman because her head hair was considered too titillating to be seen by anyone but her spouse. (Perhaps, James Howell had the Hebrew law in mind in 1621 when he wrote: "One hair of a woman can draw more than a hundred pair of oxen." In 1693 John Dryden had it: "She knows her man, and when you rant and swear,/Can draw you to her with a single hair." And Alexander Pope (1688-1744), in his famous "Rape of the Lock," put it: "Fair tresses man's imperial race ensnare,/And beauty draws us with a single hair.")

The fan, intermittently a comfort or an accessory with women and men, was a large palm leaf or a mass of birds' feathers swayed by slaves or servants. At their parties the Egyptians posted a servant with large fans of papyrus to stand behind each guest, to sweep away insects and to supply cooling air. The fan symbolized superiority and it was mandatory at state and religious affairs.

The original, naturally-grown fan was replaced, generally, by gadget-fans, usually constructed to fold into a small compass, and when unfolded and expanded to take the shape of a section of the ancient magic circle. Almost immediately the fan became vital in woman's sham-flight from man. Primitive women had learned that flight, and subsequent easy capture, accelerated desire and romance, and the more modern woman could sit behind her fan, in a superficial retreat of modesty, with her eyes operating as irresistible magnets just across the top of her fan.

The "umbrella," long an essential accoutrement, comes from the Latin *umbra*, or shade, and the "parasol," now a feminine embellishment, originated in France, in reference to the sun, obviously, just as their *parapluie* is a reference to rain. Umbrellas, likely the first status-symbol, were introduced in the East thousands of years ago, and they were cherished in China, Egypt, and Mesopotamia as early as the 12th century B.C. Too expensive and rarefied for commoners, most of the early umbrellas belonged to royalty. It is told that the inner chamber of an emperor of Siam contained "three umbrellas and nothing else." And the monarch Ava proudly billed himself as "The King of the White Elephants and Lord of 24 Umbrellas."

The early umbrellas, heavy and costly, were carried by servants to shield nobility from the sun. (There is the ancient myth about King Solomon's flying-carpet. Solomon carried his lavish entourage on his flying-carpet, and to protect his ladies from the sun, and possibly the rain, Solomon commanded a large flight of blackbirds to fly overhead. Shortly, the blackbirds solidified into a singing canopy.)

By the 17th century when cheaper materials were used, umbrellas became generally available. The traditional leather was supplanted by lighter cloths, such as silk, and whalebone was used for the ribs. Equally important as cost, the umbrella could be carried by the owner, without an umbrella-bearer. But many men, deriding the umbrella as effeminate, were adamant. Whether or not James Hanway (1712-1786) actually introduced the umbrella into England, he popularized it. Hanway took great pains to carry an umbrella each day, and he persisted, despite constant ridicule from males. And Hanway was bad-mouthed, predicatably, by the operators of sedan-chairs and hackney coaches, men who always did a brisk business during spells of inclemency.

But it protected against rain, and acted as a cane, and by the middle of the 19th century the old metallic-silk shade was virtually axiomatic in the British Isles. And there is this fascinating epilogue: The story, apparently not apocryphal, is that Hitler, seeing Neville Chamberlain's inevitable umbrella at Munich, sneered openly. If a nation's leader was so morbidly concerned with shielding himself from the rain his adherents had to be feckless.

Dozens of semi-ribald jokes about the man who lost his umbrella have permeated the conversations of American males. Sir Charles Bowen (1821-1889) seems to have had the last word in his stanza called "Umbrella":

The rain it raineth on the just
And also on the unjust fella;
But chiefly on the just, because
The unjust steals the just's umbrella.

Since the fifth century fishermen of the Aran Islands, on Ireland's west coast, have worn distinctive woolen sweaters, ones hand-knitted in a thick, oiled, cream-colored wool, wool called *Bainin* in Ireland. These warm, water-repellent sweaters are ideal to wear amid the ferocious gales of the Atlantic. They are elaborately patterned with closely knitted gables, bobbles, and embossed diamonds. In the past, and today to a limited degree, families evolved their own patterns, with a slight variation of the traditional stitches, so that drowned fishermen could be identified. Many of the designs convey symbolisms, often of a religious nature: Diamond means wealth. Double-zig-zag is considered symbolic of the vagaries, the ups and downs, of marital life. Cable: represents the fisherman's ropes of "lifelines." Trees of Life implies long life and strong sons to sustain the fisherman's career. The Ladder of Life symbolizes man's climb to celestial happiness. The Trelis depicts the small fields enclosed within stone walls that are found in the west of Ireland. Trinity Stitch —a witness to the "Three in One" and to the "One in Three." Honeycomb —symbolic of the theory that hard work brings a just reward, just as the busy bee produces golden honey. The

Lismore Cable represents the tie of a devout family to God. The Missal Stitch is in remembrance of the illuminated books that contain Masses for an entire year. The Spearhead and Chain was inspired by the harpoon with attached chain or twisted rope.

PART EIGHT
SOME ENDURING SURNAMES

"My name is Legion: for we are many."

Mark (5:9).

"Ah, what avails the classic bent,
And what the cultured word,
With the undoctored incident
That actually occurred?"

Rudyard Kipling, "Lines."

"What's in a name? that which we call a rose
By any other name would smell as sweet."

Shakespeare, from *Romeo and Juliet*.

Kipling's nativity may supply a partial answer to Shakespeare's deathless question. He was christened Joseph Rudyard Kipling, but one has difficulty associating Joseph, or Joe, Kipling with *Kim*, *The Jungle Book*, and *Barracks-Room Ballads*.

One could fill many pages with similar analogies, including Woodrow Wilson, who was christened Thomas Woodrow, who was even called "Tommie" by a few fellow-students when he was a freshman at Davidson College.

Lord Dunsany, the eighteenth baron of his line, was the author of many authentically eerie fairy tales and fantastic, plausible melodramas. The fine Irish author was christened Edward John Moreton Drax Plunkett, but one can not ascribe *The Gods of the Mountain* or *A Night and an Inn* to someone named Plunkett.

SOME ENDURING SURNAMES

Several surnames in American English are tied so completely to specific institutions and agencies that surname and agency constitute a perpetual hyphenation in popular semantics. *Robert's Rules of Order* was written by Brigadier General Henry Martyn Robert (1837-1923), born in Robertville, S.C. Robert graduated from West Point, and he fought throughout the Civil War on the federal side. The first, modest edition, 4000 copies, of *Rules of Order* came out in 1876. Robert said, "Where there is no law, but each man does what is right in his own eyes, there is the least of liberty." And he intended his *Rules* to provide a maximum of liberty within an essential framework of order. Subsequent, ever-expanding editions of the *Rules* were printed in 1893, 1915, and 1951. As a guideline, Robert appended a study outline. He suggested the simplest of his *Rules* be learned first, adding that it is better to know how to find a correct ruling than to worry about trying to memorize it.

Not just incidentally, Robert spent a stint teaching civil engineering at West Point. And in 1909 he designed a sea wall 17 feet high and 7½ miles to protect Galveston from Gulf floods. The same year Robert built a two-mile causeway to connect the island city of Galveston with the Texas mainland.

The "Mason-Dixon Line," almost axiomatic in Tin Pan Alley's flood of Dixie tunes, derives from Charles Mason and Jeremiah Dixon, two English astronomers, who surveyed the boundary between Pennsylvania and Maryland in 1763-67. An ambiguous description had produced protracted disputes about the boundary line between the Penn family, of Pennsylvania and the Calvert family of Maryland. The matter was taken to an English court of chancery, and the survey by Mason-Dixon was a legal compromise.

By 1767 Mason-Dixon had run a line 244 miles from the

Delaware River, every fifth milestone bearing the Penn and Calvert arms. In 1779 the line was extended to mark the southern boundary of Pennsylvania-Virginia (the section that became West Virginia in 1863). The phrase "Mason-Dixon Line" attained semantical and emotional viability in the era prior to the Civil War to mean the boundary line between Free States and Slave States.

"Boycott" derives from Captain Charles C. Boycott (1832-1897) who managed the estates of Lord Erne in Connemara, Ireland.* His abrasive personality and his harsh dealings made him anathema to the tenants from whom he extracted exorbitant rents for his absentee landlord. In 1880 Lord Erne's tenants formed an informal union to demand lower rents. Lord Erne and Boycott were adamant, and the tenants refused to work or let anyone else work the acreage, thus starting one of the original "sit ins," or "sit down strikes." Subsequently, the irate tenants tore down fences, disrupted the delivery of mail, and burned Boycott in effigy. Boycott appealed to the crown for protection. A gang of Orangemen, known as "Emergency Men," came from Ulster and harvested Erne's crops, under the protection of nine hundred soldiers.

But boycotts spread, being sanctioned by Charles Parnell's National Land League of Ireland. And the word, "boycott," became popular almost immediately to mean an organized economic or social taboo, especially a combination organized to ostracize an individual or agency in the hope of gaining concession to specific demands.

Somewhat less known is Joseph Roberts Poinsett's (1779-1851) association with the Christmas favorite, the poinsettia. President Monroe sent Poinsett to investigate some

*The home of the late Carl Sandburg at Flat Rock, N.C. is named "Connemara." Oddly enough, in light of the fact that Sandburg was one of Abraham Lincoln's principal biographers, Sandburg's home, Connemara, was so named by C.C. Memminger, Confederate Secretary of the Treasury, who occupied the residence as a summer home.

of the Latin American countries that were seeking independence, and Poinsett worked out some of the original trade agreements between the United States and several Latin and South American countries. He served as ambassador to Mexico from 1825 to 1829, and upon his return he introduced the lovely plant called the "poinsettia."

Poinsett, educated at the University of Edinburgh, served in Congress, and he was Secretary of War under Martin Van Buren. His really significant feature was his unswerving opposition to the doctrine of nullification, so popular in South Carolina during Poinsett's lifetime.

Few phrases have more persistent popularity than "Coxey's Army" in the sense of a crowd. In southern America, "Coxey's Army" often describes crowds at social functions that far exceed the original expectations. For instance, it is fairly commonplace to hear: "Mrs. Smith planned dinner for eight but ended up feeding 'Coxey's Army.' "

In 1893, the bankruptcy of the Philadelphia and Reading Railroad triggered the failure of many, many other businesses. Within a year more than two and one half million men, about 18.5% of the nation's labor force, were unemployed. A few agencies of local government made limited, almost fatuous, efforts to alleviate the situation, but there was the feeling that intervention by the federal and state governments would establish "dangerous precedents."

Jacob S. Coxey, affluent, self-made businessman of Massillon, Ohio, proposed that the unemployed be put to work building and improving public works, simultaneously two corrective measures. Coxey importuned a Congressman to introduce an appropriations bill. When Congress continued to delay action, Coxey declared that he would take a "petition with boots on it" to Washington. On Easter Sunday, 1894, "Coxey's Army" left Massillon for Washington. Coxey had expected 100,000 men, but only about one hundred unemployed men, and fifty newspapermen, began the trek.

In each of the towns the army passed through Coxey made speeches explaining the purpose of the march. Many townspeople fed the army, and Coxey encountered no hostility en route. A month after leaving Massillon Coxey marched down Pennsylvania Avenue. (The original one hundred and fifty had swelled to five hundred, although, many were newspapermen.)

Although Coxey had a legal permit to march, a law expressly prohibited any sort of demonstration on the capitol grounds. The path of the marchers was barred by a stout contingent of policemen. Coxey and two adherents (one was Carl Browne, whose espousal of the "Commonwealth of Christ" tagged the army with the nickname of "Commonwealthers") slipped through to parley. Police arrested the two men, but Coxey returned to his wife and child, also members of the army. Coxey handed a written statement to reporters, and when spectators cheered, the police lost their cool and started swinging nightsticks.

Around fifty of Coxey's men were hurt. The unprovoked attack stirred Congress to an investigation. On May 21 Coxey and the two men who passed the police line were given twenty days for carrying banners on the capitol grounds. Upon his release, Coxey was nominated for Congress as a Populist. And he was again the defeated Populist candidate for governor of Ohio in 1895. But in 1931 Coxey was elected mayor of Massillon, and he lived until 1951, attaining the age of 97.

The perennial multi-faceted, utility phrase, "Hobson's Choice," ascribes to Tobias (or Thomas) (1544-1631), who kept a livery stable in Cambridge. The phrase arose from Hobson's custom of assigning each customer the horse nearest the front door of the stable. In a 1712 issue of the famous *Spectator*, Richard Steele, or, perhaps, Joseph Addison, wrote: "Tobias

Hobson was the first man in England that let out hackney horses. When a man came for a horse he was led into the stable, where there was a great choice, but he obliged him to take the horse which stood next to the stable-door; so that every customer alike was well served according to his chance, from whence it became a proverb when what ought to be your election was forced upon you, to say 'Hobson's choice.' "

The saying was proverbial before Hobson's death. In l630, a year before Hobson's demise, Thomas Ward had this couplet in his poem "England's Reformation":

Where to elect there is but one,
'Tis Hobson's Choice; take that or none.

Apparently, Hobson usually kept forty horses in his Cambridge stable, and it is important to remember that his "choice" was amazingly antithetical to the spirit rampant during the era of James I and Charles I, in which gentlemen of station insisted on preferential treatment. And if Hobson was a plain, unpretentious man, few British monarchs have had longer, happier histories. An issue of the *Spectator* was dedicated to Tobias Hobson; Milton wrote a humorous poem about him; a prominent street in Cambridge perpetuates his memory; and his name is integral in an enduring proverb.

Hobson was extremely popular with the students and dons of Cambridge, and, according to an old account, "He raise'd himself to a considerable estate, and did much good in the town (Cambridge), relieving the poor and building a conduit in the public market."

(In American English there is some sporadic confusion over "Hobson's choice" with Richmond Pearson Hobson (1870-l937), an Annapolis graduate and officer during the

Spanish-American War. The "choice" attaches to Hobson's single-handed effort in blowing up the collier *Merrimac* to block the harbor at Santiago, Cuba. Hobson seemed to have the alternatives of escaping the explosion of the collier, or of having a dangerous swim back to his own ship, or of swimming to the harbor shore amid heavy fire from the Spanish. Apparently, he blew up the *Merrimac* and swam back to his own ship.

Hobson, from Alabama, served in the Congress from 1905-1915, where he was zealous for expansion of the American navy. He became ardent for Prohibition, giving lectures for temperance groups across the nation, before and after the enactment of the 18th amendment.

In popular jargon the "life of Riley," the epitome of luxuriance, attaches to the suddenly acquired opulence of several mythical Rileys, all of whom "bored with big augers." But Riley, as the quintessence of envy, seems to have come from the song "Is That You, Mr. Riley?" (1891) written, sung, popularized, and danced to by Pat Rooney, the famous vaudevillian.

In the song the destitute singer strolls down Broadway dreaming of what will happen when he strikes it rich. In the chorus, amazingly popular for two decades, his imagination is stirred by the excitement of the admiring crowds along Broadway. In his reveries he hears the cries of the admiring throng:

Is that Mr. Riley, can anyone tell?
Is that Mr. Riley that owns the hotel?
Well, if that's Mr.Riley they speak of so highly,
Upon me soul, Riley, you're doing quite well.

The chances are infinitesimal that Pat Rooney knew about Bolinbroke, the sinister, saturnine character in Shakespeare's *Henry IV*. While Bolinbroke pretended to be impervious to the adulation of the mob, secretly he construed this as a mark of greatness.

Insofar as anyone can say, "Uncle Sam" stems from Samuel Wilson, an army contractor, of Troy N.Y. The earliest printed reference to "Uncle Sam" as a synonym for the United States appeared in the Troy, N.Y. *Post* in September, 1813. Military historians say that "by 1815 the expression was known as a cant term in the army for the United States."

"Pandora," of the deathless box was the first woman to come into a world populated totally by men. A casket, containing all the evils of earth, belonged to her.

But her birth was predicated upon a diabolical ruse. Zeus, who despised earthlings, withheld the gift of fire, and when Prometheus (Forethought) stole fire from the gods and brought it to man, Zeus obviated the gift by ordering Hephaestus, god of the forge, to create a woman, one endowed with beauty and skills. Hence, Pandora (All-gifts) was despatched to Prometheus's brother, Epimetheus (Afterthought), as his bride. With her she took a box in which Prometheus had confined the woes that might plague the world.

Although Epimetheus had been admonished never to accept anything from Zeus, he married Pandora. However, he followed Prometheus' advice by ordering Pandora not to open the box. But one day in Epimetheus' absence, curiosity seized Pandora and she opened it. The imprisoned evils hopped out, to remain on earth ever since. A gauzy-winged creature named Hope was the last of the creatures to stream from the box. The assumption is that Prometheus, acting on his habitual foresight, had inserted Hope into Pandora's box so that there might be something to cling to, regardless of what occurred.

"Orion's hound," originally "Orion's hunting dog," became

a constellation when Orion was killed. Orion's image was placed in the sky, and the dog's image, *Canis Major,* was placed at Orion's heel. Sirius, the dog-star, the most brilliant, is at *Canis Major's* nose. *Sirius,* from the Greek for scorching, usually arises after the middle of July, and ancients were forearmed for a seize of debilitating heat and running sores that would not heal until the abatement of dog's days. In order to lessen the axiomatic epidemics of chills, fevers (malaria), and sores, the Romans sacrificed red dogs to placate Sirius.

Orion, in Greek mythology the son of Poseidon and Euryales, envisions Esau, the great hunter of the New Testament. Orion met Artemis, Apollo's sister, herself an indefatigable huntress. The two hunted, perhaps, sported, together. To protect his sister's virginity, Apollo sent a huge serpent after Orion. To elude the snake, Orion dived into the ocean,* but by dint of dark legerdemain, Apollo caused Artemis to fire an arrow. This killed Orion. When Artemis was unable to restore life to Orion, she placed his image in the sky, along with his hunting dog, as an act of eternal commemoration. The two are there today, and Orion is yet stalked by Scorpion.

"Dog Days," still proclaimed in the southern states as an important perennial fact, begins around July 16, with the rising of Sirius, the dog-star, the brightest fixed star and one comparatively close to our solar system. The Romans and Greeks believed the conjunction of the rising of Dog-Star and sun was responsible for the excessively hot, dry weather that usually came in mid-summer.

Today, in the American south "Dog Days" run from the middle of July until around August 11. And there is some current credence to the ancient myth that dogs are likely to go mad during this period of unrelieved torpor. (Health

---

*Perhaps, poetic justice is served since Poseidon, Orion's father was the god of the sea.

officials say dogs get rabies more often in early spring and late fall.) But there is some substance to the ancient belief that children acquire sores more readily during Dog Days. Creeks and rivers are likely to be low and brackish, and the chances of infection to swimmers are acute.

"Chauvinism," sometimes as "male chauvinist pig," became commonplace in the 1960's, and afterward, as an adjunct of the various Women's Lib movements. Nicholas Chauvin, who had fought under Napoleon Bonaparte, made such a fetish of his fulsome patriotism and his addiction to Napoleon, that he became the object of general derision. In 1831 *La Cacarde Tricolore* was built around Chauvin's character, and the word "chauvinism" slipped into popular speech. As has been noted, "jingo" and "jingoism" from a music-hall song of 1878, had a similar history.

"Mrs. O'Leary's cow" is credited with kicking over a lantern and starting the celebrated Chicago fire that may have been the most disastrous in the nation's history. More than three hundred people were killed, and ninety thousand were left homeless. The fire destroyed three and one-half acres of business buildings and homes, including much in the heart of Chicago.

The weather was dry and several fires had occurred early in October, 1871. Most of the streets were paved with pine blocks, and most of the sidewalks were made from seasoned wood. Pine and hemlock fences separated much property, and in several places fences blocked access to the river. As additional hazards, the industrial section contained seventeen grain elevators, many paint and varnish shops, and a large number of lumber yards and woodworking plants.

According to legend the immense fire of October 8, 1871, began in Mrs. O'Leary's stable, behind her residence at 137 De Koven Street on Chicago's West Side. If no one has ever really seemed to know how the conflagration started, the holocaust produced an anonymous ditty that was almost as popular as the lines about Lizzie Borden, and one of the same literary quality:

One dark night—when people were in bed,
Old Mrs. O'Leary lit a candle in her shed.
The cow kicked it over, winked its eye, and said,
'There'll be a hot time in the old town tonight.'*

Any reference to the Chicago fire reminds those who cherish the bizarre minutiae of history of the story about Robert Toombs (1810-1875), one of the most profanely eloquent of all of the unreconstructed rebels. Toombs lived in Washington, Georgia and when news of the disaster came to Washington, townspeople dispatched General Toombs to the local telegraph office to assess the bulletins that came over the wire. After a lengthy period, Toombs emerged, shaking his head:

"Gentlemen, sad to report, every known method of modern fire-fighting is being used in Chicago." Morosely, Toombs walked ahead a few paces, turned, and said brightly: "However, the wind is in OUR favor." Toombs, said to be the most imaginative and fluent orator in the pre-war South, served in the House of Representatives and as a Senator. Although he did not espouse secession until after Lincoln's election in 1860, he played a vital role in Georgia's Secession Convention and at the convention at Montgomery, Alabama that commenced the Confederate government.

Toombs, mentioned strongly as President of the

---

*No one seems to know when the ditty was written, but occasional attempts to make it current with the fire seem questionable. The last line appears to be a deliberate play on the enduringly popular song "A Hot Time in the Old Town." This jaunty song, taken by Teddy Roosevelt's Rough Riders during the Spanish-American War, and TR's campaign song from then on, was written by Joe Hayden and Theodore Metz, in 1895. The two men, musicians with McIntyre and Heath, a minstrel troupe, wrote the tune to stimulate ticket sales for an appearance of the minstrel show at the sleepy hamlet of Old Town, Louisiana. Even so, this was twenty-four years after the Chicago fire.

Confederacy, served briefly as the new nation's first Secretary of State. He entered the Confederate Army, armed with belligerence, principally. He became a brigadier-general but his inability to follow orders and to maintain discipline incurred the wrath of General James Longstreet, Toombs' commanding officer. Nonetheless, Toombs had a day of accidental glory in the summer of 1862 at Sharpsburg, Maryland (called Antietam in the north), said to be the bloodiest one-day battle in the history of warfare.

Toombs' small brigade was positioned on a hill just behind the stone bridge (still there) that spans the narrow Antietam Creek. Toombs' riflemen delayed the advance of General Ambrose Burnside's army corps most of the day. When Burnside finally over-powered Toombs' small force to cross the bridge, it was too late in the day for Burnside to be of active assistance to the large arm under General George B. McClellan. Ironically, the water was (is) sufficiently shallow for Burnside's corps to have forded the stream easily. Apparently, this fact was not known to the Federals.

Toombs expected to be promoted. When he was not promoted, he resigned, charging President Jefferson Davis with ingratitude and stupidity. He returned to Washington, Georgia from which he unleashed a constant barrage of vilification at Davis.

With the demise of the Confederacy, Toombs was a European expatriate* for two years. He returned to Washington, Georgia in 1867 to become a local patriarch. Although he practiced law, he refused to take the oath to the federal government. Late in his life someone asked Toombs why he didn't ask for an official pardon. "Pardon for what?" he thundered. "I haven't pardoned them yet." (Interestingly and curiously, some of the most intransigent, vociferous of the unreconstructed rebels had been strong union men prior

---

*The fascinating story of Confederate expatriation has never been published in depth. Sizeable colonies of former Confederate military and civilian leaders abounded in Mexico, Cuba, England, and Canada.

to Lincoln's election. The case of Lieutenant-General Jubal A. Early, post-war of Lynchburg, Virginia, has many parallels with Toombs' In Virginia's Secession Convention, Early voted against separation from the Union.

But after expatriation in Mexico, Early, too, refused resolutely to seek or to accept official pardon. A brilliant writer, Early refought the numerous battles of the Army of Northern Virginia in the endless pages of the *Southern Historical Society*. Longstreet was his post-war enemy, and Early's pen attacked Longstreet even more rapiciously than Early had attacked the Yankees during the war. Early won many literary battles from Longstreet. Then, the tide turned, and Longstreet won several signal victories. Early probably did not know that when Longstreet began to win, he had come up with two able ghost-writers, Joel Chandler Harris, creator of the Uncle Remus stories, and Henry W. Grady, Atlanta editor, and author of the once-famous essay, "The New South.")

In Robert Toombs' old age Washington, Georgia had a spirited town meeting to raise money for a municipal hotel, as an active facet of incipient industrialization and tourism. Toombs entered the hall belatedly, ascertained the proposition, and exploded: "This is arrant nonsense. We don't need a hotel. If a gentleman comes to town, he may stay the night with me, and if a son of a bitch comes, we don't want him to stay the night, anywhere."

Yesterday, country lawyers in the American south compared the prosecuting witness in all carnal knowledge cases to "Potiphar's wife." In other words, the hapless male defendant had been pursued blatantly by the predatory female.

When Joseph incurred the ire and jealousy of his brothers, he was sold into slavery in Egypt, where he became a servant in the house of Potiphar, a captain of Pharoah's guard. According to Genesis, Potiphar's wife (Zulikea, but unnamed, apparently, in the Writ) tried to get Joseph to seduce her. When her wiles failed, she tore Joseph's garment and gave it to Potiphar as evidence of an attack upon her.

Joseph stayed in jail until he interpreted Pharoah's dream about fat and lean cows and the fat and thin ears of wheat. He was released and he was given authority to try to arrest the imminent famine.

In the apocryphal account, a babe in its cradle sees Zuleika hand Joseph's garment to Potiphar. Whereupon, the baby says: "Look carefully, O, Potiphar. If it was torn from the front of Joseph's garment, he was pursuing her, but if from the back, she was pursuing him." When Potiphar looked he saw it was torn from the back.

The War of Jenkins' Ear, between England and Spain, began in October, 1739, supposedly by a mutilation of Robert Jenkins, commander of a British sloop. But while Jenkins' ear was an emotional factor, Spain's attempt to curtail England's foreign trade was the dominant cause of the war.

The Treaty of Utrecht, in 1713, gave England restricted trade with Spanish America. However, British privateers used the treaty as an excuse to seek broad access to South America. Many incidents of smuggling ensued. In 1731 Jenkins' sloop, *Rebecca*, bound from Jamaica to England, was halted by a Spanish coastal boat, and boarded. No contraband was found, but according to Jenkins, the Spaniards cut off one of his ears. Jenkins was told to carry his ear back to the King of England and say had the sovereign been Jenkins, why his ear would have been removed also.

Jenkins is supposed to have carried his ear, and the message, to George II, but the king was non-commital. However, in 1738 when affairs with Spain became anomolous, the Jenkins episode was recalled, and a committee in Parliament was formed to look into the matter. Jenkins' recitation was listened to carefully. When a member of the committee asked him what he had done, Jenkins replied: "I recommended my soul to God and my cause to my country."

Tobias Smollet, in his *Compleat History of England* (1811), wrote: "The maltreatment of so sturdy a patriot filled the whole House with indignation." A year later, 1739, England declared war on Spain.

Subsequent historians studied the Jenkins incident much less emotionally, and some were skeptical. Lord Mahon, in his *History of England* (1858) wrote: "Jenkins had lost an ear, or part of an ear, which he always carried about with him wrapped in cotton, to display to his audience; but I find it alleged by no mean authority that he lost it on another occasion, and perhaps, as seems to be insinuated, in the pillory."

Jacob, father of Joseph, brother of Esau, about whom one reads in Genesis, appears in several relevant phrases. "Jacob's ladder," often rope with rungs, was used for climbing on ships from the deck to the rigging. There is also the European herb, perennial, of the phlox family, with bright blue, or white flowers, and with a stalk whose twin leaves branch horizontally at regular intervals, like a ladder. In Genesis, Jacob dreamed of a ladder that stretched from earth to heaven. The ladder is quick with angels, coming and going. God sat at the top of the ladder, to bless Jacob and his descendants.

"Jacob's pillow" can designate almost any sort of commemorative stone. In Genesis, one learns that Jacob fled from Esau, after tricking Esau out of their father's blessing. Overcome by exhaustion and darkness, Jacob lay in a field, with his head on a stone. When he was awakened by a vision of divinity, Jacob used the stone to mark the holy spot, calling it Bethel, or "House of God."

"Jacob's stone," also the Stone of Scone, was the stone on which the kings of Scotland knelt to receive the crown, from the 9th to the 13th century. Tradition related this stone to the one which served as Jacob's pillow. But some historians say that Kenneth MacAlpine, crowned King of the Picts and Scots in 844, brought the stone from Dunstaffnage to his capital at Scone. The stone remained in Scone until 1296 when Edward I, of England, defeated the Scots and took the stone and placed it under the coronation throne in Westminister Abbey. Despite intermittent agitation, it has not been returned to the Scots.

"Jacob's well," is the public well in the town of Samaria, now Nablus. This is near the field that Jacob gave to Joseph. (Genesis) (Apparently, it was at this well that Jesus asked a drink of water, vainly, of a "woman of Samaria.")

Incidentally, "Jacob's coat," the bacillary layer of the retina, was described first in 1819 by Dr. Arthur Jacob, Irish ocular pathologist. "Jacob's staff," a navigational instrument for taking the elevation of the sun or a star, or to measure the angular distance between two stars, was invented, perhaps, perfected, in the 13th century by Jacob ben Mahir. Sailors aimed it as if it were an ancient crossbow to "shoot" the sun and the stars.

The obsolete pilgrim's staff was called "Jacob's staff," as is the cane that conceals a sword or a dagger. (Goldenrod and mullein are known as "Jacob's staff" and "Aaron's rod," alternately.)

"Aaron's beard," the perennial herb indigenous to rocky crevices, used to be endowed with medical properties. And at one time the herb's hairlike stamens were used to stanch bleeding, the same way cobwebs have been used in the southern states. "Aaron's breastplate" worn by Aaron, the first high priest of Israel, was made, allegedly, from instructions given by God to Moses. It was made of "gold, blue, and purple and scarlet stuff, and fine twined lines." It was set with twelve stones in four rows, one stone for each of the sons of Jacob, engraved with their names, and all held in place by a filigree of gold. The four rows of stones were sardius, topaz, and carbuncle; emerald, sapphire, and diamond; jacinth, agate, and amethyst; beryl, onyx, and jasper.

Few phrases have longer daily vibrance in the southern states than "Abraham's bosom,"* habitually preceded by "in" or "out of." In popular parlance the phrase is usually spoken to denote authenticity or continuity, but *sinus Abrahae*, "cave of Abraham," or *limbus Patrum*, "limbus of the fathers," was an area on the border of hell. In medieval theology, the saints of the Old Testment stayed there until Jesus delivered them.

St. Luke wrote: "The poor man (Lazurus) died and was carried by the angels to Abraham's bosom. The rich man also died and was buried; and in Hades, being in torment, he lifted up his eyes and saw Abraham far off and Lazarus in his bosom." St. Thomas Aquinas (1225-1275) may have made the original theological use of *limbus*, or border. Prior to St. Thomas Aquinas, the church had made two distinctions, only: heaven for those saved and baptized; and hell for the damned sinners.

Inevitably, an argument developed relative to the fate of those not good enough for eternal life but not bad enough for eternal damnation, and the concept of an intermediate zone, *limbus Patrum*, developed for those who led unblemished lives but were not baptized. Simultaneously, *limbus infantum*, or *limbus puerorum*, evolved for infants who died before they could be baptized, and for mental defectives for whom the rites could have no meaning.

In his *Divine Comedy*, Dante (1265-1321) has *limbus* as *limbo*, or "the first circle of hell." Dante and his tour-guide, Vergil, encounter in *limbo* the ghosts of such memorable men as Plato, Hippocrates, Homer, Hector, Caesar, and Socrates. As Vergil explains the strange situation:

In Abraham's Bosom is the title of Paul Green's (1894-) Pulitzer Prize winning play of 1927.

Ere thou pass
Farther, I would thou know, that these of sin
Were blameless; and if aught they merited,
It profits not, since baptism was not theirs,
The portal to thy faith. If they before
The Gospel lived, they served not God aright;
And among such am I. For these defects,
And for no other evil, we are lost;
Only so far afflicted, that we live
Desiring without hope. Sore grief assail'd
My heart at hearing this, for well I knew
Suspended in that Limbo many a soul
O mighty worth.

While the fatal flaw in "Achilles' heel" is widely understood, two different stories attempt to account for the omission that made Achilles vulnerable to death.

Achilles, the youngest of seven sons born to Thetis, the sea goddess and to Peleus, a human, was killed in the last days of the Trojan War, when struck in the heel by an arrow fired by Paris. Like his brothers, Achilles inherited his father's mortality. To obviate the common legacy of death, Thetis, "silver-footed Thetis," in Homer's words, placed each of her babies in a bed of flames. When their mortal portions were consumed by fire, the immortal elements would ascend to Olympus, to eternal life.

Thetis began the ritual when Achilles was in the cradle, putting the infant in the flames by night and annointing him with ambrosia by day.* But Peleus walked in, horrified at the ritual, and Thetis dropped Achilles, ran away and hid in the sea forever. Achilles was invulnerable, save for one ankle bone, singed by the flame but not burned entirely. Yet,

---

Ambrosia was the food, as nectar was the drink, of the Greeks and the Romans. Ambrosia is from the Greek *as,* not, and *brotos,* mortal. Ambrosia and nectar were a delight to the palate and both conferred immortality.

another version has Thetis carrying out the rites by water, not by fire, When she dipped the baby in the Styx she grasped one heel so tightly it was not touched by the magic waters. And as Achilles attained manhood he endured thousands of hazards, including the interminable Trojan War. There is the story that Apollo guided the arrow shot by Paris, and in another account Apollo assumed the visage of Paris.

"Custer's Last Stand" is the battle at the Little Big Horn, June, 1876, when Indians commanded by Sitting Bull liquidated Custer's force of 264 cavalrymen. Custer, breveted a major-general during the Civil War, was put on the inactive list afterward. He tried and failed to get a command under Juarez, in Mexico,* and in 1867 he was commissioned a lieutenant-colonel and attached to the famous 7th Cavalry. In 1867-68 he routed some Cheyennes at an inconspicuous village of Washita, in Oklahoma. Custer's next five years were relatively quiet ones spent doing western garrison duty.

A treaty of 1868 gave the Sioux a reservation in the Black Hills, western Dakotas, with the stipulation that the Sioux were not to molest surveyors and workers building a Union Pacific line through Nebraska and Wyoming. The provision was not violated, but in 1873 engineers for another railroad, the Northern Pacific, pushed across the Dakota plains, invading the reservation given to the Sioux. The Sioux retaliated with raiding parties, and in 1875 Custer and his troops were called to protect the railroad workers.

Almost coincidentally, eastern newspapers reported a large gold strike in the Black Hills, and some of the press urged that the federal government take over the Black Hills. Several congressmen urged caution, and early in 1876 tribal chiefs

---

*Benito Mussolini, the Fascist leader of Italy, executed by Italian partisans near the end of World War II, was named for Benito Juarez, the "Lincoln of Mexico," whom Alessandro Mussolini, Benito's father, admired greatly. Mussolini was called *Il Duce* (el doo-chay), simply, "the leader." *Duce* derives from the Latin *dux*, leader, which is also the source for "duke" and "doge."

were called to Washington to a no-decison conference. In the fall of 1876 the Sioux rejected two offers: payment of $400,000.00 for the mineral rights and an offer of $6,000,000.00 for outright sale of the Black Hills area.

During the winter of 1875-1876 the army, in a hasty decision, called the Indians back to the various agencies. The weather was bad, and travel was execrable, and many Indians did not make it back to the agencies. The entire Sioux nation was declared belligerents, and a large-scale military campaign was mounted against them. While Custer's 7th cavalry, as a portion of General Alfred Terry's force, was making its way through southern Montana, scouts brought back intelligence of a large Sioux encampment near the Little Big Horn River. Custer, badly underestimating the Indians' strength, attacked rashly and his entire force was destroyed.

Charles William Eliot (1834-1926) served as President of Harvard for forty years, but he became almost a household name in America as a result of his "Five Foot Shelf," the fifty volumes of outstanding poetry, philosophy, science, drama, and sundry literature compiled by Eliot, for Collier's. Eliot was assisted by William A. Neilson, of Harvard, and later president of Smith. On the left hand columns of huge sheets of paper Neilson put down various centuries, and the remaining columns were filled in with pertinent discoveries and events. When an age had been sketched in, Eliot and Neilson selected literature to explain and to interpret the age.

Prior to publication of the *Harvard Classics* Eliot had said that just fifteen minutes a day reading from the "five foot shelf" would culminate in a liberal education. Although pedants made jokes about the prescribed fifteen minutes a day, the set of books attained incredible popularity in the homes of America. Eliot, at Harvard, had written, "The best acquisition of a cultivated man is a liberal frame of mind," and his *Harvard Classics* did much to make that a delightful reality in the libraries and parlors of middle America.

"Ford's Peace Ship," the *Oscar II*, sailed from New York

on January 26, 1916, for a peace conference at Christiania, Norway, a conference that would make a reality of the popular slogan, "Get the boys out of the trenches by Christmas." Henry Ford's pacifism seems to have mounted in 1915, after conferences with Rosika Schwimmer, Hungarian journalist and suffragist, and with Mrs. Patrick Lawrence, British pacifist, who was touring America to propose an international peace movement and to protest war as a means of settling international disputes.

When the two men suggested a "Conference of Neutrals" in some non-belligerent country, Ford was more than anxious to finance the venture. Jane Addams, chairman of the recently formed Women's Peace Party, demurred insisting that the delegates pay their own expenses "or the voyage will attract many fanatic and impecunious reformers." Illness obviated Jane Addams' going, and Thomas Edison and John Burroughs, two of Ford's best friends, "politely declined."

Despite many physical and emotional obstacles the *Oscar II* docked at Christiania, for a formal peace conference scheduled for January 26, 1916. Five representatives were present from Sweden, Norway, Denmark, Holland, and Switzerland. Three people represented the United States. Henry Ford, smitten with a heavy cold, did not attend the peace conference. He returned home shortly after landing in Christiania, but he continued for a year to pay $10,000 a month to defray the expense of the conference.

Upon America's entry into World War I, Ford's pacifism was replaced by militant patriotism. In October, 1917, Ford exhorted his fellow Americans "To back our Uncle Samuel with a shotgun loaded to the muzzle with buckshot." And whereas Ford's peace ship venture had been derided and vilified, the essence of the peace conference emerged a few years later in Woodrow Wilson's Fourteen Points.

The "Styx," mythical river of Hades, from the Greek *stygrin*, to loathe, is the river over which travelers hoped

Charon would ferry them to the Elysium Fields, Hence, the "Stygian crossing" has come to mean transport into the next world. If the mythical "Styx" is one of the best known rivers in any language, we have neglected the three other rivers of Hades: "Acheron," or flowing with grief; "Cocytus," or weeping; and "Phlegthon," or to burn. (Heat may produce a clammy humor. Thus, the Greek *phlegma*, from which we get the English "phlegm.")

"Frankenstein," almost revered, along with Dracula, by intense cults of youngsters in the 1970's, actually identifies Victor Frankenstein, young Swiss medical student, who attends a German university, in Mary W. Shelley's novel of 1818, *Frankenstein Or the Modern Prometheus.*

From materials found in cemeteries and in dissecting rooms, Victor Frankenstein constructs a monster and he endows the creature with life via galvanism (roughly, neo-electrodes). The soulless monster, spurned by every living creature, becomes psychotic because it has all of the human desires and no way to express these desires. Frantic by dint of its unrequitements, the monster commits a series of atrocious crimes. Finally, it kills Victor Frankenstein, thus inflicting terrible retribution upon the mortal who usurped the prerogative of the Creator.

Mary W. Shelley, Percy B. Shelley's second wife, did not give the monster a name in her novel. This natural omission continues to lead millions of people into the error of referring to the monster as "Frankenstein."

For his famous play, *Pygmalion*, George Bernard Shaw expanded the Greek legend of Pygmalion, in mythology, the king of Cyprus. Pygmalion makes an exquisite statue of a woman, Galatea, and he falls in love with the stone. He prays to Aphrodite for a wife similar to the statue. The goddess hears Pygmalion, and the statue becomes a woman, and he marries her.

But intermittently, some student revives the old theory

that Bernard Shaw was thinking, also, of Frankenstein, of the transformation of cemetery materials into the monster.

"Belshazzar's Feast" occurs in literature several times, often as a chapter heading, to indicate that the action will involve upon a succulent, lavish, or lascivious dinner, bash, or soiree. The original was given by Belshazzar son of Nebuchadnezzar. After the ceremonial wine was served in golden and silver goblets taken from the temple in Jerusalem, a hand appeared, mysteriously, to write upon the wall, "Mene, mene, tekel, upharsin."

This has been construed, literally as "He counted, counted, weighed, and they divided." (The fifth chapter of Daniel.) The writing, presumably in Aramaic, has been translated also, as "numbered, numbered, weighed, and divisions." And Bergen Evans suggested that these may be the names of weights. Thus "a mina, a mina, a shekel, and half-shekels." But Daniel translated them to mean, "God hath numbered thy kingdom and finished it. Thou are weighed in the balances, and art found wanting. Thy kingdom is divided, and is given to the Medes and Persians."

At the feast Daniel was called by Belshazzar and he was promised lavish gifts if he could translate the words. Despite the ominous nature of Daniel's translations, the gifts were forthcoming. According to the story, Belshazzar was killed that very night, and his kingdom was taken over by Darius, the Mede.

Nebuchadnezzar had brought the sacred goblets from the temple in Jerusalem, and the ancient implication was that retribution was exacted of Belshazzar for defiling the holy vessels.

Bluebeard's name still appears in some news and feature stories as a generic word, or as a catchall, and his legend has several versions. The story told generally is that seven beautiful women were killed by Bluebeard for entering a forbidden room. Fatima was rescued by her brothers, but just barely. The best known of the Bluebeard stories was published around 1697 in Charles Perrault's (1628-1703) collection of tales: *Histories ou contes du temps passe avec des moralites,* or *Stories or Tales of the Past with Moral Lessons.*

As many as eleven beautiful women died, in a Middle-European version, and the famous Grimms (Jacob Grimm, 1785-1863) have two sisters imprisoned and being released by a third sister. Several attempts have been made to give verity to the French tale, which, originated, apparently, in the coastal province of Brittany. Andrew Lang (1844-1912), who edited Perrault's tales in 1888, wrote in his introduction that Bluebeard *(Barbe-Bleu)* had been identified as a 6th-century Breton prince, one Cormorus or Cormorre, and again, as the Baron Giles de Rais, or de Retz, a marshall of 15th century France. But Lang makes it clear that the fundamental elements of the tale are found in countries in which Cormorre and de Retz are unknown.

"Robin Hood's barn," means the vast outdoors, from the legend that the famous British outlaw, hero of ballads, stabled his horses under the canopy of the sky. (In common parlance, "To go around Robin Hood's barn" has ancient, continued use to mean the attainment of the desired result by devious or circuitous methods. When a student arrived at the right answer, or conclusion, after desultory wanderings, his teacher often said the student had been "around Robin Hood's barn."

"Robin Hood In Barnsdale stood" is the only extant line, or phrase, from a song once said to be immensely popular. British jurists, and a few American judges, used to admonish attorneys who spoke irrelevantly, "Robin Hood in Barnsdale stood," and the phrase has limited pertinence in common American parlance to denote vacuity.

For whatever it is worth, a small cave near Ravenshead Oak, at Newstead Abbey (Lord Byron's birthplace), is known as "Robin Hood's barn," from the legend that the outlaw,

Friar Tuck, Little John et al stabled their horses here.

"Praise from Sir Hubert" has declined in recent years to mean the accolade, but it still has some use, especially among older writers and conversationalists, to bestow encomiums. This expression seems to have been suggested by a quotation from Thomas Morton's (1764-1838) play *A Cure for the Heartache*, produced in London in 1797. Sir Hubert Stanley is a gentle, impoverished baronet whose family pride forces him to live beyond his means. At the end of the final act, Sir Hubert says to Young Rapid, son of Old Rapid, the tailor: "Mr. Rapid, by asserting your character as a man of honor, in rewarding the affection of this amiable woman, command my praise; for bestowing happiness on my dear Charles, receive an old man's blessing."

Young Rapid replied: "Aprobation from Sir Hubert Stanley is praise indeed." Many Americans have spoken it, "Praise from Sir Hubert is praise indeed."

"According to Hoyle," almost synonymous with "cricket" in American English, relates to Edmond Hoyle (1672-1769), Englishman, who wrote about games. Apparently, Hoyle made a living teaching various card games, whist, particularly.

In 1742, as an aid to his students, Hoyle published *A Short Treatise on the Game of Whist*, containing the first systematic code of rules for the game. Later Hoyle published a general book on games. Playing a game "according to Hoyle" means playing by the rules, although the applications of the phrase are so numerous it often has the same relevance as "kosher."

T.B., in Maryland, one of the oldest, shortest names on the American map, has no relevance to tuberculosis, as many people have always assumed. (Many have supposed that the village housed a sanitorium.) The letters are the initials of Thomas Brooke, whose father, Robert Brooke, acquired enormous acreage in the vicinity in 1648. The stones placed by early surveyors on the limits of the plantation bore the initials of Thomas Brooke. According to local tradition, one of the "T.B." stones was found within the village's limits, when a settlement arose. The inhabitants fell into the habit of referring to their village as "T.B."

"Halley's comet," first seen in 1682 by Edmund Halley (1636-1742), British astronomer, has attained tremendous vibrance in American mores because it reappeared the years Mark Twain was born and died — 1835 and 1910. Halley made concerted calculations by which he established, for the first time in science, that comets return to the solar system.

The word "comet" is from the Greek *kometes* or "long-haired," and Halley, a mathematical prodigy, had begun his study in 1680. He noted certain discrepancies between the theoretically plotted orbits of Jupiter and Saturn and the orbits they were seen traveling. Consequently, Halley spent eighteen months on the island of St. Helena, below the equator, to verify his data, from a different latitude.

Upon his return to London, Halley met Isaac Newton, who had confirmed the elliptical patterns of comets. And Newton suggested that comets probably move in ellipses, so protracted that a complete circuit would require longer than a human's lifetime. Hence, Halley began computing the orbit of a comet that had appeared in 1683. For twenty years he pursued this, collecting enough material to figure out the orbits of twenty-four comets, dating back to 1337.

Halley's analysis showed that the comets of 1531, 1607, and 1682 traveled in paths almost identical. Thus, he reasoned that the three seen were the same comet. Halley concluded that the comet had an orbital period of approximately 75½ years, and he predicted another appearance in 1758 or in 1759, one that was fulfilled when the comet was seen on March 13, 1759. And since Halley's time, and based on his computations, around thirty appearances of his comet have been tabulated, ranging from 467 B.C. to 1910.

And Halley's comet became a "black cat." Its episodic appearances seemed to coincide with disasters. The ancients tied several catastrophes to it, and in more modern times it coincided with the war of 66 A.D., the one that saw the fall of Jerusalem; the devastation of Italy by the Huns in 373; and the Battle of Hastings in 1066. (Halley's Comet is woven into the Bayeux Tapestry that depicts the death of Harold by the hands of William the Conqueror.)

And the weeks prior to May 18, 1910, the projected appearance, saw the nation aglow with excitement and fear. Many people predicted the seas to boil and soil to be scorched when the earth passed through the comet's tail.

A group of reputable French astronomers believed the gases in the comet's tail would poison the earth's atmosphere. And in America as the date drew closer, newspapers everywhere reported suicides and attempted suicides. "Anticomet pills" (sugar concoctions) were tremendous sellers at a dollar a box. But aside from some minor, sporadic electrical disturbances, nothing untoward happened in 1910.

Halley's "bearded star" is expected again in 1986.

Henry Hudson's (d. 1611) name conjures the fabulous ship, *Half-Moon*, and the immense bay, 472,000 square miles, that lies just below the Arctic Circle in Canada. Hudson, famous English navigator, explored the region in 1610, while attempting to find a northwest shortcut to the East Indies.

Hudson subscribed to the prevalent belief that after a mariner passed the first belt of arctic frigidity, he would encounter warm weather and open sea lanes. Muscovy, joint-stock trading company, acting on this impulse, hired Henry Hudson in 1607 to find a route eastward via the northern polar region. In April, 1607 Hudson, with his son, John, and ten seamen, put to sea. He got as far as Spitzbergen, but ice barriers sent him back. The next year, 1608, Hudson sailed again, and although he probed the Barents Sea for a northwest passage, the venture failed. (It was on his voyage that two of Hudson's sailors saw a mermaid and recorded their meticulous impressions in the logbook.)

In 1609 Hudson sailed on the *Half-Moon*, outfitted by the Dutch East India Company. He got as far as Novaya Zemlya when his crew balked, refusing to proceed farther in the enormous cold. Hudson wisely figured that if he returned to Amsterdam his sponsors would call his action insubordination.

Hudson had a map Captain John Smith had given him which indicated a passage westward at 40 latitude, the approximate present location of Philadelphia. But the only opening Hudson found was a mouth of the river now known as the Hudson. After he had gone upstream about 150 miles, to the present location of Albany, he realized this route would not take him to China.

On his return to the Netherlands, Hudson put in at Dartmouth, England, and his ship was seized and the English sailors taken off. Hudson's fourth, and last, voyage, an English company entirely, proceeded directly to Davis' "overfall" (now Hudson Strait). He reached this location the middle of June, 1610, two months out of London. Moving westward he entered the enormous bay. (Mariners believed that proximity of the magnetic pole caused ships' compasses to become erratic.) Confident he had found the passage to China, Hudson spent several months combing the east shore. The last day of October he dropped anchor in James Bay. In ten days the ship was frozen in tightly.

One seaman died during the ensuing harrowing winter. Discontentment bordered on mutiny continuously. In spring Hudson and Henry Greene had a tempestuous quarrel over the division of the dead seaman's clothing. Greene incited a mutiny, and Hudson, his son, and seven men (sick men it appears) were put adrift in a small boat. Hudson was never seen again. Some of the mutineers got back to England, to be thrown into prison.

The enduring "Ixion," of "Ixion's wheel," seems to be the first murderer in Greek mythology. His bizarre, convoluted saga began with a blatant perfidy, Ixion, son of Phlegyas, King of the Lapiths in Thessaly, courted Dia, and he promised Eionius, her father, lavish gifts for his permission to marry Dia. But Ixion had second thoughts, and when Eionius came to Ixion's palace to claim his presents, he tumbled into a deep pit of live coals which Ixion had camouflaged. For his infamy, Ixion became an outcast. No one would speak to him, much less purify him. But, ultimately, Zeus looked down from Olympus, took pity, and called the pariah to his table.

Almost immediately, Ixion tried to seduce Hera, Zeus' lovely wife. Zeus could read Ixion's mind, and he caused a cloud, Nephele, to assume Hera's shape. Ixion made love to Nephele, who bore him a son, Centaurus, progenitor of the centaurs. As eternal punishment, Zeus had Hermes to bind Ixion to a fiery wheel which rolled through the heavens (or the underworld) perpetually. Bound to the wheel hand and foot, Ixion remained in revolving agony.

Interestingly enough, Ixion was punished for sinning against Zeus, not against Eionius, a mortal. The latter sin was expiable. And the obligation to seek absolution is embodied in Ixion's name: *Ixion* means suppliant, or comer, from the verb *ikein*, to come.

While "Pete" persists as a nickname, as a utility noun, and occasionally an unnatural adjective, the sonorous "Peter" has declined as a Christian name in the latter portion of the 20th century. Some etymologists ascribe "parrott," along with *Pierrot*, French for sparrow, and the stormy "petrel" to St. Peter, the first because of its garrulity and the second because mariners saw it walking on water.

"Peter," itself, is Latin and Greek, and there is the intermittent speculation that Jesus made a pun when he put his hand on Peter to proclaim (Matthew 16:18), "Thou art Peter, and upon this rock I will build my church." The same word appears in "petrify," to become stone, and in "petroleum," from *petre*, stone, and *oleum*, or oil. "To peter out" originated in the mining camps of the American west to mean that a vein of ore had solidified into stone. The domestic "pet" may be a shortening of the French *petit*. "To be in a pet," and the earlier "to take the pet," meant to sulk, usually because one was not a "pet," was not "petted." And the "petty" person is likely to be "pettish." Albeit, "in petto," the breast, whence the English "pectoral," has no relevance to what used to be called "petting party."

Millions of school children know about the resounding kiss planted on Leigh Hunt by the recondite "Jenny":

Jenny kissed me when we met,
Jumping from the chair she sat in;
Time, you thief, who like to get
Sweets into your list, put that in.
Say I'm weary, say I'm sad,
Say that health and wealth have missed me:
Say I'm growing old, but add, Jenny kissed me.

Jenny was Jane, Mrs. Thomas Carlyle, apparently every bit as irascible as her husband (1795-1880). Leigh Hunt (1784-1859), a friend of the taciturn Carlyles, came calling. As he entered the room, Jane bounced from her chair to kiss the poet. He was so astounded, and pleased, he wrote the celebrated poem. (Hunt's father, lived for a time in Philadelphia, where he married Benjamin West's sister-in-law.) Leigh Hunt, poet, essayist, and critic, and his brother, John, started a weekly newspaper, the *Examiner*, organ of incessant attacks upon British royalty.

In 1813 the two brothers were sentenced to two years imprisonment for referring, in print, to George IV as a "corpulent Adonis of forty." Leigh Hunt is probably known best for his somewhat maudlin poem "Abou ben Adhem," standard memory-work yesterday and a poem declaimed on virtually every schoolhouse stage in America.

A few syndicated columnists, such as Sydney Harris, run sustaining quizzes about bizarre minutiae, types of hodgepodge quizzes. "Quiz," itself, is a modern coinage, and it seems to have been added to the dictionary solely because of a bet. In 1780, one Daly, manager of a Dublin theater, and some intimates had regular discussions about the innate gullibilities of their friends. And Daly bet that he could make the Dublin public accept a meaningless assortment of letters as a new word.

Daly and some friends went about the streets of Dublin late one night with buckets of red paint splashing four red letters, on pavement, on fences, and vacant buildings. Shortly, almost everyone in Dublin asked what the word meant. The word spread to other counties almost directly, and there was even an attempt by a few pedants to construe "quiz" as an abbreviation for "inquisition."

"Hodgepodge" and the British "hodgepotch" are variants of the older noun "hodgepot," in British law the gathering together of the various properties for equal distribution to the children of a parent who died interstate, probably from "hodge" and from the vulgar Latin, *pottus*. In addition to the word's numerous current implications, during the 19th century "hodgepodge" was synonomous with "double-talk," and "don't hodgepodge me" was spoken almost precisely as today's "don't jive me" is spoken.

PART NINE
BETWEEN-THE-ACTS
INCLUDING THE REAL OR IMAGINARY VAGARIES
OF A FEW AMERICAN TOWNS

"Whence are we, and why are we? Of what scent
The actors or spectators?"

Percy B. Shelley, from "Adonais."

"Oh, it offends me to the soul to hear a robustious
periwigpated fellow tear a passion to tatters, to very rags, to
split the ears of the groundlings, who for the most part are
capable of nothing but inexplicable dumb-show and noise. I
would have such a fellow whipped for o'erdoing Termagant; it
out-herods Herod."

Shakespeare, from *Hamlet.*

In this famous scene, Prince Hamlet is lecturing his fellow
players. In the old mystery plays King Herod was always
represented as a ranting, bullyragging ruffian, and ham actors
playing Herod could vent all of their bellicose fulminations,
all the way from A to B, as Dorothy Parker put it. Termagant
is the name the Crusaders gave to a pagan deity whom they
believed the Mohammedans worshipped. He, too, ranted and
stormed in the old mystery plays, and the flowing robes that
formed his stage costume caused him to be confused with a
woman. Today, "termagant" is applied to women, exclusively.

"They have the time, the time of their life,
I saw a man who danced with his wife,
In Chicago, Chicago, that toddling town."

Fred Fisher, from the song "Chicago."

One does not hear "toddling" today. The word appeared as "in-jargon" during the 1920's in the same sense that "cool," "neat," "groovy" et al did almost half a century later.

BETWEEN-THE-ACTS
INCLUDING THE REAL OR IMAGINARY VAGARIES OF
A FEW AMERICAN TOWNS

"The Seven Seas," heard almost daily, is a figure of speech to mean all of creation's oceans and seas. However, when pressed for an answer, many people reply that these seven seas are the Arctic, the Antarctic, the North and South Pacific, the North and South Atlantic, and the Indian Ocean. This imaginary explanation was integral in the vernacular of several languages before the names of some of the oceans were known to many of the inhabitants of Europe and Asia.

"The Seven Seas" appears in the literature of the ancient Chinese, Hindus, Persians, and Romans, and, perhaps, others, and in each instance the phrase refers to different bodies of water. (Some of the allusions are to mythical seas.) In Persian literature the seven seas were the streams forming the Oxus River, and the Hindus applied the words to the bodies of water in the Punjab. With the ancient Romans the seven seas, their *septem maria* meant a group of salt water lagoons, near Venice.

In modern literature, Rudyard Kipling popularized *The Seven Seas* as the title of a book of his poems published in 1896. Kipling said the term could be regarded as an allusion to the seven oceans, but that it was an extremely old figurative name "for all of the waters of the world."

The famous, magical "Seven League Boots" were worn by Hop-o-My-Thumb, fabled character in the old nursery story. (A league varies from 2.4 to 4.6 miles, from country to country, but in English-speaking countries a league is three miles. "League," of course, was popularized in Tennyson's "Charge of the Light Brigade": "Half a league, half a league, onward etc.") Hop-o-My-Thumb is the tiny hero in Charles Perrault's fairy tale. In the fable, Hop-o-My-Thumb saves himself and his little brothers from an ogre by means of his boots, which cover seven leagues at each bounce. And Hop-o-My-Thumb is used often as a generic name for pygmies and dwarfs. "Seven League Boots" has come to mean anything which enhances speed or achievement.

(As previously stated, the figure 7 was considered holy and magical by ancients.)

It is in *As You Like It* that Shakespeare introduces the "Seven Ages of Man," with poetic descriptions of each condition: the infant; the school-boy; the lover; the soldier; the justice; the lean and slipper'd pantaloon; and second childishness, "sans teeth; sans eyes, sans taste, sans everything."

The "seven-hill'd city" (Rome) appears in Lord Byron's "Childe Harold":

The Goth, the Christian, Time, War, Flood, and Fire,
Have dwelled upon the seven-hill'd city's pride;
She saw her glories star by star expire,
And upon the steep barbarian monarchies ride,
Where the car climbed the capitol.

In *Major Barbara*, Bernard Shaw defined "the seven deadly sins" as food, clothing, firing, rent, taxes, respectability, and children." Shaw added, "Nothing can lift those seven millstones from man's neck but money; and the spirit cannot soar unless the millstone is lifted."

Conversely, the 1866 *A Catechism of Christian Doctrine for General Use* lists the "seven capital sins" as pride, covetousness, lust, anger, gluttony, envy, and sloth.

Matthew (18:22) admonishes forgiveness, "Until seventy times seven." And in Isaiah (4:1) the prophet warns of the carnage of war: "And in that day seven women shall take hold of one man."

"Hocus-pocus" was picked up by the American populace from tank-town magicians who used the words as an incantation to attend their slight-of-hand executions, as well as to divert attention when performing some trick of questionable merit. The phrase now runs a wide gamut, from double-talk to the secretive dexterity of a T-quarterback in football.

Many of the vaudeville and tent-show magicians embellished their patter with Latin words, frequently bogus phrases, and some authorities think hocus-pocus is an inadvertent corruption of *hoc est corpus filli*, of the Catholic sacrament by which bread is transformed into the body of Jesus. The original verbal debasement appears to have been perpetrated innocently. The bush-league magician simply did not know the translation of the Latin words he mouthed so glibly.

Intermittently, someone points out that whenever "hocus" is spoken rapidly it seems to come out as "hoax."

"Vaudeville" and "tank-town," aforementioned, have prompted frequent discussion, much of it erroneous. According to *Variety*, the official trade-paper of the American entertainment world, "vaudeville" was spoken shortly after the Civil War. If a single person can be credited with the introduction of vaudeville, the person has to be Tony Pastor, born in New York City in 1837.

To attract women to his Tony Pastor Opera House, 201 Broadway, he gave dress patterns, pots, pans, sacks of coal, bags of flour and sewing materials as door prizes. Later on his Tony Pastor Music Hall in Union Square became the Mecca for vaudeville. It was Pastor who introduced Lillian Russell, and it was he who changed her name from Helen Louise Leonard. The Four Cohans, including George M., Pat Rooney, Eddie Foy, Emma Carus, Nat Goodwin, May Irvin, Weber and Fields, and Harrigan and Hart appeared in Tony Pastor's vaudeville productions. And Pastor was the first American to send vaudeville shows on the road.

As an eight year-old, Pastor sang at Temperance meetings. Before he was thirteen, he had organized a neighborhood circus, operated an adult peep-show, appeared as a black-face minstrel on the New York-Staten Island run, starred as a song-and-dance act, "the talented child," with Barnum and

Bailey, and he had staged variety, or vaudeville, shows in schoolhouses and courthouses.

But if Tony Pastor was the first to stage vaudeville, the word seems to have been used, officially, first in 1871 when H.J. Sargent, in Louisville, Kentucky, billed his traveling troupe as "Sargent's Great Vaudeville Company."

"Tank-town" was popularized by vaudevillians to satirize any place that had a municipal water tank, and a tank displayed conspicuously. "Jerk-water town," generally synonymous, arose from the days when trains made unauthorized stops for water at streams adjacent to the track. Water was carried in leather buckets from the creek to the locomotive, and this process was known as "jerking water." In time "jerk-water" was applied to towns at which trains stopped principally to replenish the engine's water supply.

In the 20th century "tank fight" emerged to mean a boxing match that was fixed, and "to go into the tank" still means to take a dive, to pretend to be knocked out.

"Abracadabra," also intoned by small-time and amateur magicians, is an ancient antidote against illness. It is mentioned first by a Roman physician in the 2nd century A.D., in the reign of Caracall. It was particularly efficacious against toothache, rheumatism, swellings, ague, and fever. Different scholars have called the magic formula Aramaic and Hebrew, and it is suggested that it is formed of the initials of the Hebrew words for Father, Son, and Holy Ghost. Again, it is construed as a corruption of *bracha* and *dabar*, the Hebrew words for "blessing" and "word." Finally, others contend "Abracadabra" was the name of an ancient demon, one whose identity faded centuries ago. This probably attaches to the old theory that if a person learned the specific name of a supernatural power, the power passed to the person, himself. By applying the name to himself, he was capable of similar good or evil. Hence, the saying of Abracadabra's name brought the power to heal toothache or rheumatism.

Nonetheless, there was a hitch: The whole word had to be written on a top line. On each successive line, the word was repeated, minus one letter, until one letter remained. The finished script formed a magic triangle:

```
A B R A C  A D A B R A
 A B R A C A D A B R
  A B R A C A D A B
   A B R A C A D A
    A B R A C A D
     A B R A C A
      A B R A C
       A B R A
        A B R
         A B
          A
```

In 1976 incessant stories in newspapers, on radio, and on television about the Alaskan pipeline focused considerable attention on the far north, and several letters-to-editors asked the origin of "mush" and "mushing," meaning the sledge dogs. The early French Canadian *voyageurs* yelled "*Marchon*," literally, "let us march," to their sledge dogs. English-speaking dog drivers in the Northwest corrupted *Marchons* into "mush on." In time, "mush on" was shortened to "mush."

Entirely coincidentally in 1976, frequent news stories about slow, erratic, and expensive postal service occasioned much spoken and written derision of "Neither snow, or rain, nor heat, nor gloom of night stays these couriers from the swift completion of their appointed rounds." These exultant words, carved over the central post office building in New York City, are a paraphrase of a reference to the ancient postriders of Persia.

Herodotus, aforementioned, writing around 430 B.C., tells how King Xerxes of Persia, in 480 B.C., attacked Greece and sacked Athens. Nonetheless, allies of the Greeks destroyed the Persian fleet near Salamis, forcing Xerxes to withdraw his large army into Asia. "The King sent off messengers to carry intelligence of his misfortunes to Persia. Nothing mortal travels so fast as these Persian messengers. The entire plan is a Persian invention, and this is the method of it. Along the whole line of road there are men, they say, stationed with horses, in number equal to the number of days which the journey takes, allowing a man and a horse to each day; and these men will not be hindered from accomplishing their best speed the distance which they have to go, *either by snow, or rain, or heat, or by the darkness of night.* (This author's italics.) The first rider delivers his dispatch to the second, and the second passes it to the third; and so it is borne from hand to hand along the whole line, like the light in the torch-race, which the Greeks celebrate to Vulcan. The Persians give the riding-post in this manner the name of *Angarum."*

While the Alaskan sledge-drivers are hollering "mush," many other Americans, ones in the south notably cry "Sick'm'" the colloquial form of "seek him" or "seek 'em." During the Elizabethan period the prevalent word for this was "tarre." In *Troilus and Cressida*, Shakespeare has Old Nestor to say:

Two curs shall tame each other; pride alone
Must tarre the mastiffs on, as 'twere their bone.

Several of Shakespeare's passages imply that the sound represented by "lo," "low," "alo," and "alow" fastened to incite hunting dogs. Indeed, the English word "harass" probably derives from the Old French *harer*, meaning to set or to sick a dog on.

"The Fourth Estate," meaning newspapers, or their official representatives, is attributed to Lord Macaulay, to Edmund Burke, and to Thomas Carlyle. And "Fourth Estate"was applied to various strata of society before it became hyphenated with newspapers. In France and in England, the three estates of the realm consisted of the church, the nobles, and the commoners.

In the 17th century "Fourth Estate" had limited use to mean the British army, and in 1752 Henry Fielding (1707-1754), author of *Tom Jones*, used "Fourth Estate" in a newspaper article to mean the British mob. Thomas Carlyle, in *Heroes and Hero Worship*, published in 1840, wrote: "Burke says there were Three Estates in Parliament; but, in the Reporters' Gallery yonder, there sat a Fourth Estate more important far than they all. It is not a figure of speech or a witty saying; it is a literal fact, —very momentous to us in these times."

Carlyle's (1795-1881) convoluted passage prevents one's knowing whether he intended the passage to be Burke's (1729-1797) precise words. Scholars have not found the phrase among Burke's writings, and no one knows where Carlyle obtained his information. In 1837 Carlyle had published his *The French Revolution*, and a chapter, headed "A Fourth Estate," has this sentence: "A Fourth Estate, of Able Editors, springs up."

Some students believe that Carlyle coined the phrase, himself, and ascribed it to Burke. And to compound this enigma, in 1828, Lord Macaulay (1800-1859) in an article in the Edinburgh *Review,* wrote, "The gallery in which the reporters sit has become a fourth estate of the realm."

During the tenures of Presidents Nixon and Ford, the extraordinary peregrinations and diplomatic missions of Henry Kissinger prompted at least one writer to say the Secretary of State "has solved all problems save those of the Holy Roman Empire." That is the strange name given to a nebulous empire that existed in Central Europe from 992 to 1806. The Roman Empire established by Augustus Caesar in 27 B.C. was split into the Western Roman Empire and the Eastern Roman

Empire when Theodosius died in 395. The Western Empire ended in 476, and in 800 Charlemagne was proclaimed Emperor of the West at Rome, and westerners construed Charlemagne's empire as a direct legatee of the old Roman Empire. Then, in 962, when Otto the Great was crowned in Rome, the political entity known as "The Holy Roman Empire" came into existence. This was conceived by Germans, who prefixed "Holy" around 1160, after the death of Frederick I. It consisted of numerous small German states in Germany, Austria, and Northern Italy. The Diet was the administrative component, and provincial governors were called Electors simply because they elected the emperor from among their number.

Each emperor proclaimed himself the logical successor to Caesar's mantle, with all the authority implicit therein, but in actual practice the various states and principalities that composed the loose-jointed Holy Roman Empire considered themselves to be autonomous. Apparently, it was Voltaire (Francois Marie Arouet, 1694-1778) who first denounced Holy Roman Empire as a misnomer because it was not holy, it was not Roman, and it was not an empire.)

Francis II of Hapsburg, was the last titular head of the strange empire. In the latter portion of its political history, the empire was barely more than a phrase, a name. And in 1806 Napoleon and his legions brought about its total dissolution, in every conceivable phase.

Several queens and saints lend their names to an interesting assortment of entities. "Queen Mary's thistle," *Onopordon acanthius*, the national flower of Scotland, in the language of flowers, developed by the Greeks, stands for austerity. And many consider austerity representative of Scottish personality and terrain. Apparently, the royal prefix was attached near the close of the 16th century when some handmaidens presented Mary with a handful of the purple-topped thistle, the wildflower that is covered with small, thread-like white hairs.

At the time of the presentation of the wildflowers, Mary, Queen of Scots (1542-1587) was being held captive at Fotheringay Castle, by her cousin, Queen Elizabeth. And, for whatever it is worth, Mary is credited with introducing the straw hat to the English-speaking world. This occurred when she returned to Scotland from her exile in Lorraine, in the 16th century, and brought with her a number of expert straw-plaiters.*

"Queen Anne's bounty" relates to a fund established for the poorer members of the clergy by the sovereign (1665-1714). For several centuries Roman Catholic clergymen turned over to Mother Church the profits from the first year of a new parish appointment. From then on, one-tenth of the annual parish profits, called "first fruits," then *annates*, and, finally, *decimae*, went to Rome. In 1534 when Henry VIII broke with Rome, these stipends along with "Peter's pence," went to the crown.

In 1704 Queen Anne, resolutely anti-Catholic, but excessively pious, granted a charter which, in essence, utilized contributions from the richer parishes to supplement those parishes that were bringing in 50 pounds annually, or less. This lasted until 1926 when the charter was retired by Parliament.

("Peter's pence" refers to the penny a year paid by each English household to the Vatican. The custom extended from the 7th century, or perhaps, from the 8th century, until Henry VIII obviated the practice in 1534.)

(The tax was paid on August 1, and the English penny replaced the Latin *denarius*, which survived as the sign *d*, and was written *pending*. The statute provided that every family having land worth 30 pence annual rent was subject to the

---

*The ancient Romans wore straw hats, but as a general vogue, straw hats seem to have disappeared for several centuries. Straw hats were not general in America until the 1890's. "Wool hat boys," originally meaning those too poor to buy straw hats in summer, quickly became synonymous with "redneck" as a political opprobrium.

tax, and August 1 was celebrated as the feast of Saint Peter. Two lines from an anonymous poem of the 13th century say:

From Rome he broughte an heste that me here nome
Petres peni of ech hous that smoke out of come.

After 1860 "Peter's pence" was used only in the sense of voluntary contributions to the papal treasury.

"Queen Anne's free gift" was an endowment sponsored by the British queen for ships' surgeons. During Queen Anne's time (daughter of James II and queen from 1702-1714) ships' surgeons were paid twopence monthly for each man aboard ship. Queen Anne's fund supplemented this pittance.

The wild carrot, *Daucus carota*, with flat blossoms and a circular cluster of tiny florets, with intermittent purple dots, is called "Queen Anne's lace." It is set in a delicate, lace-like pattern reminiscent of the court flounces fashionable during Queen Anne's tenure. Botanists count as many as 2500 general species, edible and poisonous: carrots, parsnips, dill, anise, caraway, parsley, and celery. It is highly possible that the poison used to carry out Socrates' death sentence came from the deadly alkaloids of the water hemlock, or fool's parsley.

"Saint Crispin's day," October 25, was brought over to the New World by some of the English colonists, and the feast day had limited celebration in colonial America. The brothers, Crispin and Crispinian, martyred in Gaul around 286 A.D., are the patron saints of cobblers and leather workers. The brothers fled Rome and the executions of Diocletian around 284. They made their way to the present area of Soissons, France where they preached Christianity and where they supported their physical needs by cobbling shoes. Maximianus, ruler over Gaul under Diocletian, had the missionary brothers' heads cut off. Shortly, their festival was observed across Europe, and in Soissons, particularly. The religious ceremonies of the feast day, October 25, were followed by merry-making in which the shoemakers' guilds were prominent. And in England, from the 15th century on, the day was celebrated in conjunction with the British victory at Agincourt, in 1415.

The French outnumbered the English several times over, but a hard rain turned the narrow battlefield into a quagmire. The heavily-armored French troops could not maneuver, and the lightly-clad English archers and infantrymen inflicted horrible casualities. This was one of the more memorable battles of the Hundred Years War (1337-1453). The triumphant British army was commanded by King Henry V, and Shakespeare, in *King Henry V*, gives the monarch-military chief, this speech:

This day is called the feast of Crispin
And gentlemen in England, now a-bed,
Shall think they were accurs'd they were not her
And hold their manhoods cheap, whiles any speaks
That fought with us upon St. Crispin's Day.

"Saint Martin's summer" is the European equivalent of America's Indian Summer, although "Saint Martin's summer" usually comes in November and Indian Summer in October.

St. Martin, Bishop of Tours, 4th century A.D., is credited with many miracles. Impressed into the Roman army at fifteen, he left it to become " a soldier of Christ."

While serving in the Roman army, he was beseeched by a beggar, and St. Martin slashed his cloak in two with his sword, and gave half of the garment to the beggar. The same night Jesus, wearing the same piece of half-cloak, appeared in a dream to give St. Martin His special blessings. When the Saint died, in 401, the barge bearing his body is supposed to have floated up stream on the Loire to Tours without wind or sails. And along the way the trees burst into radiant blossom, and "unearthly music" was heard until the ship glided effortlessly to its destination at Tours.

"Saint Swithin's Day," July 15, feast day of the Bishop of Winchester Cathedral* carries the superstition that if rain falls on the day, rain will continue for forty days, and if the day is dry, fair weather will persist. "Swithin," perhaps, "Swithun," Bishop of Winchester from 852 until his death in July, 862, is said to have built many bridges and churches.

He had asked to be buried outside the Cathedral, so that his grave would be accessible to commoners. This was not done, and a monsoon of forty days delayed the saint's burial. This was taken as a divine sign that Swithin's wishes must be followed. A chapel was built over his grave. (According to the ancient saying, when rain falls on July 15, St. Swithin is "christening his apples.")

Around 310 A.D., the Roman Emperor Maxentius is said to have bound Catherine of Alexandria on a large wheel filled with unusually sharp knives, the instrument of horror that comes down as "Saint Catherine's wheel." In the legend, Catherine, a beautiful woman and an intense Christian, upbraided Maxentius for his paganism. He ordered Catherine to appear before him and fifty men of learning to defend her faith. When the fifty savants conceded the argument to Catherine, Maxentius ordered them executed.

Maxentius tried to seduce Catherine, and he implemented his overture by offering to cast aside Faustina, his legal wife. Catherine refused the tryst, and Maxentius had her imprisoned and flogged. Faustina took a party of two hundred to the jail to commiserate with Catherine, and the Saint converted the entire retinue to Christianity. Maxentius put the whole group to the stake, and the lethal wheel was prepared for Catherine, but when Catherine was bound and the wheel started turning, the knives flew among the spectators, killing and maiming

---

*In the late 1960's Rudy Vallee came out of semi-retirement to popularize the engaging "hip song," "Winchester Cathedral," a jaunty lyric that has absolutely no relevance to "Swithin" or to his cathedral.

them at large.

The executioner cut off Catherine's head with his sword, but several angels descended and carried the Saint's body to Mount Sinai.

Actually, a devout, educated Catherine of Alexandria did live, and she seems to have been exiled for seeking converts. But the symbolism of the awful wheel has made her the patron of wheelwrights and millers, and her piety placed ministers and nuns beneath her protection. St. Catherine's voice is supposed to have been one of the heavenly sounds that directed Joan of Arc to save France. (These are voices Joan of Arc professed to hear while she was in the forests of Domremy.) Although St. Catherine has been the patroness of coeds for a long time, the women's libbers must not be abundantly conversant with the legends that attach to her.

"Salome's dance," better known in America as "The Dance of the Seven Veils," is the exhibition performed before Herod, the governor, or tetrarch (literally, ruler of one-fourth of a province). Herod rewarded Salome's dancing with the gift of John the Baptist's head. According to the story, based in Mark, chiefly, John the Baptist incurred Herod's wrath when John denounced Herod for forming a sexual alliance with Herodias, wife of his brother Philip. (Herod was married to an Arabian princess.) Albeit, Herodias, not Herod, was John's nemesis. Mark says that Herod acknowledged John as a good man, promised to "keep him safe."

Salome, Herodias' daughter, danced on the state occasion of Herod's birthday, and Herod was so enraptured he agreed to fulfill any request Salome made of him. Herodias influenced Salome to ask for John's head. Herod was unwilling, but he was tied to the oath he made in front of his banquet guests. Thus, a guard decapitated John. The head was brought to Salome, who gave it to Herodias.

In Mark's account Salome is referred to as "the girl," and she is supposed to have married her uncle, Philip the Tetrarch. Obviously, Salome derives from the Hebrew *shalom*, or peace, the word that produced innumerable Salems in

many of America's most perfervid Protestant sections. Oscar
Wilde's (1865-1900) play, *Salome*, produced in 1893, adds a
twist to Mark. In the play Herod is in love with Salome, his
step-daughter, and she is enticed to dance against the wishes
of Herodias, her jealous mother. Simultaneously, Salome loves
John the Baptist, who has spurned her advances harshly.
Hence, his head on a platter is Salome's revenge. (William
Congreve's famous couplet, "Heav'n has no rage like love to
hatred turn'd/Nor hell a fury like a woman scorn'd," is from
his play *The Mourning Bride* (1697). Subconsciously, perhaps,
Congreve echoed something Coley Cibber had written in 1696,
in his *Love's Last Shift*: "We shall find no fiend in hell can
match the fury of a disappointed woman—scorned, slighted,
dismissed without a parting pang." If Congreve was familiar,
after a fashion, with Cibber's passage, he condensed it and
gave it wings.)

"Seward's Folly" was an allusion to the purchase of
Russian America, as the vast area was called at the time of
the transaction in 1867. The American state department had
known for ten years that Russia was anxious to sell Alaska,
and William H. Seward (1801-1872)*, Lincoln's Secretary of
State, and an avowed proponent of Pacific expansion, offered
$5 million. The Russians wanted $10 million, and the deal was
consummated at $7 million.

Seward and President Andrew Johnson were roasted, and
the enormous purchase was ridiculed not only as "Seward's
Folly," but also "Seward's icebox," "Icebergia," "Walrussia,"
"Seward's iceberg" and other epithets. Seward's diplomatic
purchase acquired 600,000 square miles of frozen terrain, and,
apparently, it was Seward who called the new territory

*At the time John Wilkes Booth was assassinating Abraham Lincoln, Lewis Paine,
ex-Confederate soldier and Booth's accomplice, entered the home of the ailing
Secretary Seward. Paine inflicted serious knife wounds on Secretary Seward and on
his son. Fortunately both recovered.

"Alaska," from the Aleutian *alasshah*, or *alayeksa*, meaning "a great country."

What is known historically as "Sutter's gold" refers to the immense strike made near the present site of Sacramento, California in 1848, by John A. Sutter (1803-1880). Sutter's find, in his mill race launched the episodic gold rush of 1849.* Sutter seems to have immigrated to America from southwest Germany in 1834. He lost his possessions in an accident on the Missouri River, and he worked a while as a fur trader.

He is supposed to have boarded ship for a five-months voyage to the Sandwich Islands and to Sitka, Alaska. He came to San Francisco in 1839 (Yerba Yuba then, and under Mexican dominion) where he bought launches for himself and for some Kanakas whom he brought from Alaska. Sutter and his party explored the Sacramento River, building a settlement at the junction of the Sacramento and Rio de los Americanos.

The Mexican government granted Sutter 49,000 acres, and he called his settlement New Helvetia. A Mexican citizen and government official, Sutter expanded his original adobe into Sutter's Fort. Among the establishments were a tannery, a carpenter's shop, a forge, and a sawmill. The revolt of Californians in 1846 ended Mexican authority.

In 1848 Sutter and one of his partners built a second sawmill at Coloma, about forty miles from the fort. The partner, seeking to deepen the mill race, found yellow grains gleaming in the exposed rocks. This find occurred January 24, 1848. The partner raced to the fort to show the yellow grains to Sutter, who tried hard to keep the news a secret. However,

*Edgar Allan Poe's (1809-1849) poem, "Eldorado," and Stephen Foster's (1812-1864) song, "Oh, Susannah," are enduring artistic residuals of the gold rush of 1849. Not just incidentally, Foster was born, near Pittsburgh, on July 4, 1826, the same day that ex-Presidents John Adams and Thomas Jefferson died, and fifty years from the date each had signed the Declaration of Independence.

the news leaked out and Sutter was ruined. His acres were devastated by squatters, and in the ensuing litigation the U.S. Supreme Court determined the title to most of his domain was faulty. For the final thirty years of his life he seems to have subsisted on an annual pension of $250.00, granted him by Congress. His efforts to have Congress validate his claim were denied repeatedly.

Historians figure that from 1849 to 1852 in excess of 100,000 people abandoned their homes in the eastern portion of the country to seek Poe's Eldorado. Many of these came by way of Panama, and some around by Cape Horn.

"Mary had a little lamb" must be America's primary contribution to the art of the nursery rhyme. It is probably our best known poem, and "Mary's lamb" must be the best known animal in our husbandry. But tempestuous dispute about authorship has erupted. Sarah Josepha Hale, of Boston, editor of *Ladies Magazine* (to be merged with *Godey's Lady's Book*), said she wrote the poem in 1829.

Lowell Mason (1792-1872), composer, had asked Ms. Hale for a poem he could set to music. (Mason, alternately a banker and a choir director, was a professional, or certainly a semi-professional musician, although he did his utmost to make this clandestine. He is remembered today, if at all, for three hymns extracted from longer works: "Nearer My God to Thee," "My Faith Looks Up to Thee," and "From Greenland's Icy Mountains." Mason is responsible for teaching music in the public schools, and for the music conventions that culminated in numerous summer festivals and the summer schools for the training of music teachers.)

Ms. Hale says she supplied Mason with "Mary Had A Little Lamb," and in 1830 the jingle was contained in a 24-page pamphlet, *Poems For Our Children*, long an American favorite. So far, so good, but in 1880 a fund-raising rally was held to preserve Boston's famous Old South Church. A popular device was the gift of some item to be auctioned for

the benefit of the church, and as Mrs. Tyler unraveled a pair
of stockings knitted, she declared, "from the first fleece shorn
from Mary's lamb."

Mrs. Tyler cut the wool into short strands, and these were
tied into bundles and wrapped on cards. They were sold at
ten cents a card. The Boston papers picked up Mrs. Tyler's
explanation: In 1817, when she was eleven (née Mary Sawyer)
she had a pet lamb. One day it followed her to the
schoolhouse at Redstone hill, and a young man, John
Roulstone, saw the lamb following Mary to school, and
Roulstone dashed off the familiar jingle.

But, Ms. Hale never wavered, and scholars attribute the
poem to her. All the same when Henry Ford bought the
Redstone schoolhouse in 1926 as a landmark, Ford's
commemorative plaque credits Roulstone with the first twelve
lines and Sarah Hale with adding twelve lines more.

Almost parallel in popular imagery is "Tall oaks grow
from little acorns." The original version appears in David
Everett's poem of 1791, "Lines Written for a School
Declamation":

You'd scarce expect one of my age
To speak in public on the stage;
And if I chance to fall below
Demosthenes or Cicero,
Don't view me with a critic's eye,
But pass my imperfections by.
Large streams from little fountains flow,
Tall oaks from little acorns grow.

During America's bicentennial, many references to "Paul
Revere's ride" were printed and spoken, and at least once the
alleged journey was re-enacted. In Henry W. Longfellow's
(1807-1882) poem ("Listen my children, and you shall hear/
Of the midnight ride of Paul Revere."), written many years

after the Revolution, Revere rides all the way from Boston to Concord, spreading the alarm. But the ride seems to have been consummated to Concord only in the poem.

Revere (née Appolinaire, 1735-1818) is still famous as a silversmith, but no 19th-century dictionary seems to mention the exploit Longfellow ascribed to him. Revere had carried dispatches along the seaboard as an official courier for Boston's Committee of Correspondence, and by all accounts, including Revere's, he knew the British were coming by sea. Thus, the lanterns in the Old North Church were superfluous. (The lights seem to have been placed in the belfry for the benefit of patriots waiting on the Charleston (Massachusetts) shore.)

He was instructed by Joseph Warren, President of the Massachusetts Provincial Congress, to ride to Lexington to warn John Adams and John Hancock of the imminent approach of the British. He borrowed a famous horse, Brown Beauty, from Dean John Larkin. His goal was the Lexington home of the Reverend William Clark, where Adams and Hancock were staying. Around midnight Revere was challenged by William Monroe, posted as a sentinel in Clark's yard. Clark told him the people inside had retired, to be quiet, not to make any noise.

"Noise. You'll have noise enough before long. The regulars are coming," Revere shouted. Shortly afterward, Revere was taken in custody by British scouts. After several hours of questioning, he was released, to return to Boston astride Brown Beauty.

"When Greek meets Greek," or "That's Greek against Greek," still popular in daily conversations, began as "When Greeks joined Greeks then was the tug of war." The speech appears in the fourth act of Nathaniel Lee's (1653-1692) tragedy, *The Rival Queens, or the Death of Alexander the Great,* written in 1677. The line is a reference to the tenacious resistance put up by Greek cities to the invading Macedonian armies led by Philip and then by his son, Alexander the Great. For several centuries the phrase has been spoken to imply the intensity of the conflict that is likely to result when two men, or teams, or groups, of equal strength and resolve, clash.

In American English "The Greeks had a word for it" means almost anything the speaker has in mind, and, often, meaning is predicated on intonation. The late Zoe Akins brought national attention to the phrase, especially to the word "it," in *The Greeks Had A Word For It* her successful play, first produced on Broadway in 1929. "It" is *hetaera*, a companion or female paramour; or what might be termed a top-drawer call-girl today.

The upperclass male in ancient Greece insisted on educated, refined mistresses. The idea was that such a woman was much more a satisfactory and amiable companion than the cloistered wives of the classical era.

No synonym for incomprehensibility has ever surpassed "It's Greek to me." Although Shakespeare sent this winging down from *Julius Caesar*, it was an established proverb before Elizabeth I's time. In *Julius Caesar* this exchange occurs between Cassius and Casca:

Cassius: "Did Cicero say anything?"
Casca: "Ay, he spoke Greek."
Cassius: "To what effect?"
Casco: "Nay, and I tell you that I'll ne'er look you in face again; but those that understood him smiled at one another and shook their heads; but for mine own part it was Greek to me."

"Robbing Peter to pay Paul," invoked many times each day in conversations, is not a Biblical allusion as many Americans seem to believe. The exact phrase, "He robbeth Peter to pay Paul," appears in John Florio's *Firste Fruites*, published in 1579. But Florio was merely repeating a bromide that had been current for a century. Fuller, in *Church History of Britain*, said the proverb derived from the refusal of Dean Williams to appropriate lands belonging to St. Peter's, at Westminister Abbey, to implement the maintenance of St. Paul's Cathedral.

However, counterparts exist in other European languages, such as the French proverb, "To strip Peter to clothe Paul," and despite the validity of Fuller's contention, alliteration may have been the dominant factor.

In 1975-1976 sporadic arguments popped up about that modern atrocity, "fore-head," for the older, much better "for-ed." When "fore-head's" usurpation began in the middle of the 19th century, Henry W. Longfellow (1807-1882) wrote a poem to show, among other things, how "forehead" should be pronounced:

There was a little girl
Who had a little curl
Right in the middle of her forehead.
And when she was good
She was very, very good,
And when she was bad she was horrid.

The "little girl," "Edith, with golden hair," appears in Longfellow's "The Children's Hour," with her sisters, "grave Alice" and "laughing Allegra." And Longfellow thought Edith, and her sisters, were precious, and never horrid. Unfortunately, Longfellow, a consummate scholar and professor, was unable to induce his fellow countrymen to preserve the older, better pronunciation of "for-ed."

"Liliputian," which has come to mean infinitesimal, almost anything tiny, comes, obviously, from Jonathan Swift's (1667-1745) *Gulliver's Travels*, published in 1726. While Swift wrote the novel as a savage satire on current conditions in

Great Britain, this extraordinary novel is read today as an adventure story, as engrossing fantasy. In the novel Lemuel Gulliver visits four bizarre countries.

In Liliput the tallest person is not more than six inches high. Gulliver exhausts a six months' food supply with a single meal, and wades out into the water and captures the entire navy of an invading enemy. In Brobdingnag the smallest dwarf is taller than the church steeples Gulliver has known in England. Next he visits the floating island of Laputa, inhabited by scientists "up in the air." The fourth voyage is to the land of the Honuyhnhnms, or noble, highly intelligent horses, that are waited upon by the utterly servile Yahoos.

The sojourn in Liliput is much the best known of the mythical countries, so much so that the several movies called *Gulliver's Travels* present Liliput, only. In addition to the enduring word for anything small, "yahoo" is synonymous politically and intellectually with "redneck." Although, "yahoo" used to be a rough-handed, jocular term of fatherly endearment. In this sense, "yahoo" was interchangeable with "rascal" and "rapscallion."

"Pariah" and "nincompoop" have a strange way of surfacing during political campaigns. "Pariah," now a fugurative outcast, comes from the Tamil (Indian) *paraiyan*, or drummer. The "pariah," a lower caste servant, beat a drum when upper caste whites had their festivals. And, interestingly enough, in medieval Europe, the leper, perhaps, the most pitiable "pariah," had to beat two sticks together when he walked the roads to warn others of his approach.

Periodically, someone suggests that "nincompoop" was, successively, a shortening and a corruption of *non compos mentis*. An earlier form of "nincompoop" was "nickumpoop," suggesting that the first portion attaches to Nicodemus, in the Bible, who doesn't impress with his intelligence.The second portion is related to the Dutch *poop*, or fool, from which English obtained "poop," or lummox. And "poop" may have been compounded previously with another shortening of Nicodemus in the early English "poopnoddy," or fool.

Such a delightfully entrancing story accounts for the origin of "Printer's Devil" one may go over-board to give the legend credence. According to the story, Aldus Manutius, famous Venetian printer of the late 15th and early 16th centuries, employed a black boy as a shop helper. The Venetians of that era were unfamiliar with Negroes, and many believed in witchcraft; thus, they suspected that Manutius' black helper was an evil genius or devil. Demand for an investigation permeated Venice, and Manutius is supposed to have issued this statement: "I, Aldus Manutius, printer to the Doge, and the Holy Church, have this day made public exposure of the printer's devil. All who think he is not flesh and blood are invited to come and pinch him."

The black boy is alleged to have endured semantically as "Manutius' printer's devil." But the phrase probably arose from the obvious fact that helpers were blackened with ink during the period of hand presses. Joseph Moxom, in his *Mechanical Exercise* (1683), wrote: "The Press-Man sometimes has a Week-Boy to Take Sheets, as they are Printed off the Tympan. These boys do in a Printing-House, commonly black and Daub themselves; whence the workmen do jocosely call them Devils; and sometimes Spirits, and sometimes Flies."

(Manutius and his black devil printed many question marks, a form of punctuation with a fascinating, bizarre history. The Latin to indicate a query is *questio*. This word was placed at the end of a sentence, but it took up valuable room. Then an early proponent of shorthand abbreviated *questio* as QO, but since there were no breaks between words, QO was mistaken for the ending of a word. Printers and writers began to place the Q above the O, Q/O, and it didn't take long for the Q to deteriorate into a squiggle, for the O to contract into a dot. Thus, the evolution of the question-mark, "?.")

Manutius printed Greek classics on his Venetian presses. He was born in 1450, about the time Johann Gutenberg began experimenting with moveable type. Several scholars have tagged Manutius the "father of punctuation." If punctuation involved a process of gradual evolution, the tie to Manutius is not specious. Until his time it was the policy to write letters together in lines without breaks for words or sentences. For a while there was a haphazard system of dividing words into sentence fragments by use of dots and points, borrowed from the Greek grammarians of Alexandria. The Greek grammarians in Alexandria had used dots and points, and Aristophanes, who died about 180 B.C., is supposed to have "devised a complete system of punctuation with dots." But this system vanished, and by the 9th century punctuation was so completely abandoned that Charlemagne ordered his scholars to revive the system.

Printing necessitated some conventional system of punctuation, and Manutius is likely the first to use some form of punctuation regularly. His marks, with numerous variations and developments, are still in use.

French dancing masters may be responsible for the enduring juxtapositions of "p's and q's" as in "Mind your p's and q's." In French this means feet (*pieds*) and wigs (*queues*). The more pragmatic British, uncertain about the proper accents, shorted *pieds* and *queues* to "p's and q's."

Capital letters give no clues, but children learning to print the alphabet may experience some difficulty with "p's and q's," and the bromide was reinforced by the constant injunctions of schoolmasters. Again, the proprietors of many of England's pubs kept blackboards on which they recorded the pints and quarts of ale served to a specific customer. Pints and quarts were entered under "P's" and "Q's," and the man apprehensive about being over-charged asked the publican to "mind his p's and q's." And if a customer showed signs of becoming intoxicated, his friends pointed to the black board, told him "to watch his p's and q's" and so on.

Undoubtedly, some of the profanity that attended the drinking of the p's and q's was called "billingsgate." For several centuries the fishmongers of Billingsgate, London, especially the women, were so notoriously profane that "billingsgate" and "fish-wife" became active synonyms for verbal scurrility. It is told that Jonathan Swift used to visit the fish-market at Billingsgate to sharpen his wits with verbal exchanges with the women.

Once when a fish-wife had showered the Dean with a flood of vile epithets, Swift, in desperation, yelled, "Oh, shut up, you old isosceles triangle." Whereupon, the poor woman broke down and cried saying that Swift's vulgarity had exceeded all the limits of human decency.

This fish market is on the left bank of the Thames, below London Bridge, on the site of an ancient watergate that protected the city from the river side. Geoffrey of Monmouth, historian of the 12th century, told that Billingsgate acquired its name from *Belin*, the name of King of the Britons about 400 B.C., who built a wharf and watergate near the present site. Apparently, a specific wharf of the Thames was called Billingsgate as early as 949 A.D. A market was in operation there at the time of the Norman Conquest. Even today the Billingsgate Market is one of London's most impressive sights.

Foul-mouthed language was established as "billingsgate" by the 17th century, and much of the early "rhetoric" is printed in Edmund Gayton's *Festivous Notes on Don Quixote,* published in 1654.*

---

*Intermittent attempts to equate "billingsgate" with the American "bunk" and "buncombe" are not valid. At the close of the famous debate on the Missouri Compromise, 1820, Rep. Felix Walker, "Old Oil Jug," from the North Carolina mountains, made a long irrelevant speech. When implored to speak on the subject, Walker explained, "I am talking to Buncombe (county)." This became "bunk" and "bunkam."

Few pubs and American bars keep raw or steamed oysters on hand during the season today. Yesterday many of the saloons on the Atlantic Seaboard states, particularly those that catered to specific clientele, had "oyster bilings" behind the grog shop to commemorate special occasions, and raw and steamed oysters were served as the deluxe portion of the institution's famous lunch.

Almost since antiquity, the oyster has been touted as an aphrodisiac. Pistol, speaking from the Garter Inn, in *The Merry Wives of Windsor*, says, "The world's mine oyster/Which I with sword will open." Thomas Fuller (1608-1661), in *Worthies of England*, writes a cliche that is credited to James I and others: "He was a very valiant man who first adventured on eating oysters." Before the advent of refrigeration there was some validity to the "R month" admonition. This may have been published originally in 1599 in Henry Buttes' *Dyet's Dry Dinner*: "Please take heed that it is unseasonable and unwholesome in all months that have not a R. in their name to eat an oyster."

Richard Sheridan (1751-1816), the great dramatist, may have been in print first with the oyster's bisexuality, In *The Critic* Sheridan wrote: "An oyster may be crossed in love." In *Don Juan*, Lord Byron says "Oysters are amatory food," and he goes on to embellish Sheridan's contention:

An oyster may be crossed in love, and why?
Because he mopeth idly in his shell,
And heaves a lonely subterraqueous sigh,
Much as a monk may do within his cell.

Actually, the sexes are separate in some species of oysters and mixed in some other species. The later conjunction must produce some classic bewilderment and consternation, difficulties so formidable that man with his one-sex system should remain silent. If one may endow oysters with the speech so common to animals in the fables of Aesop, Perrault, La Fontaine, and Joel Chandler Harris, it is almost rudimentary to hear the two-sexed females saying to her mate: "No, not tonight. The woman in me has been ironing all day."

Britishers "queue up" at pubs and movies rather more often than Americans, even if "queue" and "queueing" attained an innning of viability during and after World War II in American English. Actually, a psychologist might say that "queueing up" at a liquor store during and right after World War II, and at other places wherein rationing necessitated long lines, seemed to leaven some of displeasure of waiting.

In its predominant sense of a pigtail, "cue" derives from the Latin *coda*, via the Old French *coe, keue, cue*, which became the French *queue*, and spelled the same in English to mean a pigtail.

(Occasionally, some linguist suggests that "cue," the stage-word, comes because the hint, the "cue," is at the end, the "tail" of an actor's speech, although the word is not used this way in French.)

In billiards, the shooting stick was the first called the "billiard," and the tapering, tail end was the "cue." Cue, of course, came to be the entire stick.

The "queue," pigtail, is associated with the Chinese, historically. Until 1644 Chinese males wore their hair long and tied in a bun or knot at the top of their head. But when the Manchus conquered China in 1644 they required the men (only) to shave the top and fore parts of their heads and to wear the remaining hair at the back of the neck. This was a mark of subjugation, of loyalty to the new masters. (Historians say the Manchus borrowed the idea for the tonsure and braided "queue" from neighboring Tartar tribes.)

At first the Chinese resented bitterly the pigtail, but after a few generations had worn it, the Chinese were so proud of their tonsures and pigtails they spent hours each week in braiding and brushing. (Americans called these "queues" ponytails and monkeytails, and at one juncture tons of combings from "queues" were shipped to the United States to be made into hair nets.)

At the apogee of the influx of Chinese to California, San Francisco passed an ordinance which required Chinese within the city's jurisdiction to cut off their pigtails. But in Ho An Kow *v.* Nunan, Associate Justice Stephen Field, expressing the Supreme Court's unanimous decision, ruled for plaintiff, amplifying his opinion with the statement that the court found the ordinance to be "special legislation imposing a degrading and cruel punishment upon a class of persons who are entitled to equal protection of the law."

Curiously enough, when a Chinaman died, his head was dressed in the cue that dates back to 1644. If the perpetual "queue" symbolized domination by the Manchus during life, death was eternal liberation from the ancient oppressor. Indeed, millions of Chinese cut off their pigtails in 1911 when the Manchus were overthrown and when a republic was established. Proponents of the revolution insisted on an end to the "queue," and within a few years of 1911 most of the pigtails were gone.

It was long-haired American boys in the 1960's, not Chinese, who made limited reintroduction of the venerable "queue," although none seems to have been activated by the old, old Chinese myth that one was jerked to heaven by his pigtail.

"Laconic" is, or has been, a popular, if garbled, term which Americans have applied to Chinese. This word, meaning brief, pithy, or concise, is an adjective formed from Laconia, the name of an ancient Greek country of which Lacedaemon, or Sparta, was the capital. The Laconians and Spartans were celebrated for their pointed, brisk, and sententious speech. There is the tradition that Philip of Macedonia sent the following message to the citizens of Sparta: "If I enter Laconia, I will level Lacedaemon to the ground."

The city fathers held a conference and after considerable deliberation and cogitation, sent Philip this message: "If."

Perhaps, the classic among all laconic messages is Julius Caesar's *Veni, vidi, vici,* or "I came, I saw, I conquered." This intelligence was in a letter Caesar wrote to announce his victory over Pharnaces at Zela, in Pontius, in 47 B.C.

Many teachers of writing and of rhetoric have insisted that all writers and incipient writers are "in Caesar's debt" for classic conciseness, completeness, and succinctness of his deathless message. Others have contended that it hasn't been often in history that the vanity of the author and the vanity of the conqueror have to compete for supremacy. Suetonius adds this foot-note: "In his Pontic triumph he (Caesar) displayed among the show pieces of the procession an inscription of three words, 'I came, I saw, I conquered,' not indicating the events of the war, as others did, but the speed with which it was finished." Caesar said "the die is cast," or *Iacta alea est,* when he decided to cross the Rubicon. This is quoted by Plutarch (46-120 A.D.) in his *Life of Caesar.* Plutarch explained that the phrase was a "proverb frequently in their mouths who enter upon dangerous and bold attempts."

The Rubicon, a small stream, formed the boundary between ancient Italy and Cisalpine Gaul. In 49 B.C. Caesar was given command of the Gallic legions, but he had no authority in Italy, and when he crossed the Rubicon he knew this action would start a civil war. Plutarch writes that when Caesar came to the Rubicon he meditated, alone, for a long time, "computing how many calamities his passing over the river would bring to mankind."

Then, "with a sort of passion, uttering the phrase with which men usually prelude their plunge into desperate and daring fortunes, 'Let the die be cast,' he hastened to cross the river." Suetonius adds this foot-note: As Caesar stood meditating, a "wondrous apparition" appeared, "sounding the war-note." In a word, Caesar's crossing the Rubicon was adherence to the "signs the gods had pointed out."

(There is lingering confusion about the word "die." Some high school literature teachers, assuming that Caesar cast "dye," from the Anglo-Saxon *deag* or *diah*, as a marker to determine water currents etc. in the Rubicon, tell their students that "die" should be spelled "dye." While that is a reasonable conjecture, Caesar seems to have been thinking about "dice." A "die" was (is) from the Old French *de*, through the Latin *datus*, meaning given or thrown. Among "die's" several meanings is one of the small cubes ("dice" in popular parlance) used in gaming, in the game called "craps." Caesar, obviously, used the word in the sense of fate's attending the casting or throwing of a die.)

Anent the reference to writers being in Caesar's "debt" for the clarity and pithiness of *Veni Vidi Vici*: For generations students have been bugged and dismayed by the redundant "b" in "debt," and many have assumed that this is the survival of an obsolete pronunciation. However, the unnecessary "b" is the result of pretentious meddling and tampering. "Debt" is from the Old French *dette* and early in the English language the word was spelled "det" and "dette." It is spelled "dette" in *The Vision of Piers Plowman* and in the *Canterbury Tales*. Then from the 14th through the 16th centuries, pedants, assuming that the word was derived directly from the Latin *debita*, or owed, spelled it "debt" to conform to what they erroneously assumed was its Latin progenitor. (Almost as many students are miffed and perplexed by the cumbersome abbreviation of "Jhn" as "Jn.," in the tenuous guise of saving time via a single letter. "Jno." came about during the period when "John" was in the process of formation. The English form is derived from *Johannes*, first contracted to "Johan."

In time the "a" was dropped, or an "o" was substituted

for it, and the name was spelled "John" or "Johon." But occasionally it was written "Jhn." because of the omission of the first rather than the second "o" in "John," or because "h" and "o" were transposed in "John." In the early years of its use, the word was probably pronounced in two syllables, and centuries ago when there was a common practice to use "n" for "h," "John" was abbreviated "Jh." or "Jn."

(John is derived indirectly from the Hebrew "Yohanan," which means "Jehovah has been gracious." Its evolution is *Yohanan* in Hebrew, *Joannes*, in Greek, *Johannes*, in Latin, *Jean*, in French, and "John" in English.)

"Rigmarole," almost inevitably pronounced "rig-ga-ma-role" in the American south, produces two theories. Many scholars believe it is a corruption of "ragman-role," although not in the current sense of "ragman." A "ragman" was an official who got up the feudal tax lists, but "ragman" was also an ancient name for the devil. (As in *The Vision of Piers Plowman*.) In this connotation it became synonymous with coward. Insofar as one can tell, these two theories crossed, and "rigmarole" came out of the crossing as a hybrid meaning garrulous nonsense, or the devil's wagging his tongue interminably.

It's within the realm of peradventure that the ragman spouted "rigmarole" as he assembled his tax lists, and, perhaps, his fulminations and blandishments were as disenthralling to his feudal clients as the gobbledygook of the IRS is to beleagured Americans of 1976. (The late Maury Maverick, Congressman from Texas, is credited with coining "gobbledygook" in 1944, to condemn long, vague, pompous talk or writing. In the New York *Times* magazine supplement, May 21, 1952, Maverick wrote: "When concrete nouns are replaced by abstractions, simple terms by pseudo-technical jargon, the result is gobbledygook.")

Joseph Dun, a petty official during the reign of Edward VII (king from 1485-1509), the man who gave us "dun," to mean due bill, seems to have functioned as a part-time ragman. Several stories have been published about Dun's prowess as a demon bill and tax collector. In 1708 the *British Apollo* carried this explanation: "The word 'Dun' owes its birth to one Joe Dun, famous Baliff of the Town of Lincoln. It became a Proverb... 'when a man refused to pay his debts, why don't you Dun him?' That is, why don't you send Dun to arrest him? It (dun) is now as old as since the days of King Henry the Seventh."

Samuel Johnson defined "dun" from the Saxon word *donon*, meaning to clamor. Maitland, in his *American Slang Dictionary*, derived "dun" from "din," in the context of noise, and, intermittently, some pedant ties it to the French word "donne," signifying to clamor. But the earliest known published reference appears to occur in *Microcosmographie or a Peece of the World Discovered in Essayes and Characters*, published in 1628 by Johon Earle (1601-1665), ultimately Bishop of Salisbury: "An Universitie Dunne... He is an inferior Creditor of some ten shillings or downwards. He is a sore beleaguer of Chambers."

Today's skillful, persistent collector of due bills is charged often with "reading the riot act" to some hapless creditor. And the "or else" lecture, bristling with invective or with baleful admonitions, is spoken by irascible wives to husbands who have lost the grocery money gambling or carousing with the boys.

By extension the "riot act" means to give warning of severe rebuke, but it originated in the Riot Act passed by Parliament in 1714. (The first year of the reign of George I.*)

*Walter Savage Landor (1775-1864), Britsh poet and friend of the Brownings, left this commentary on the Georges:

George the First was reckoned
Vile, but viler George the Second;
And what mortal ever heard
Any good of George the Third?
When from earth the Fourth descended,
God be praised, the Georges ended.

This legislation expressly forbade "tumultuous and riotous meetings," and it provided that if twelve or more persons assembled unlawfully and disturbed the peace, a sheriff, mayor, or justice of the peace should read this proclamation to the foregathering: "Our Sovereign Lord the King chargeth and commandeth all persons being assembled immediately to disperse themselves, upon the pains contained in the act made in the first year of King George for preventing tumultuous and riotous assemblies. God save the King." And several of the American states enacted similar legislation.

If the four Georges have never inspired poets and historians, and if they cause no visible jealousy on Parnassus, they probably needed as badly as any monarchs the active services of some good public relations men. One and two were pariahs, foreigners, and the vanquished Stuarts had all of the emotionalism that frequently attaches to lost causes. (It isn't excessively far-fetched to compare this to the replacement of Jefferson Davis, after Appomattox, with Grant, in the old Confederacy.)

Number One couldn't speak English, and his anomoly calls up the time Battling Levinsky fought Mike McTeague on Dublin, and on St. Patrick's Day. Number Two said he hated all "boets and bainters," and the Third, derisively tagged "Farmer George," thought Shakespeare pretty sad. George IV praised Jane Austen and he befriended Sir Walter Scott, but he imprisoned Leigh Hunt, the popular poet, for fairly bland cracks Hunt and his brother made about the monarch.

They were constant grist for the mills of wags and caustic humorists, just as Herbert Hoover was during the Great Depression, and just as President Ford's small accidents and listless statements made him during the 1970's.

"Board," as in board and lodging, is derived often from the "festive board," the buffet that was served almost perpetually during winter on a sideboard, from the Anglo-Saxon *bord*, or piece of sawed wood. But in Elizabethan England, and previously, stapled, polished boards were placed atop an ordinary, stout table. Meals were taken on the loose board, and afterwards the board was washed and turned over to be used on the other side.

Apparently this is the origin of "board," as in boarding house, as it is for "turning the tables." In many Elizabethan homes food was served in a wooden bowl called a "trencher," and, this gave rise to "trencherman" to mean one possessed of a prodigious appetite. No eating utensils were used save for a hefty knife, often the same blade that had killed the game that was being eaten. And such rarefied people as Queen Elizabeth, Shakespeare, Marlowe, and "Rare Ben" Jonson ate much of their food with their fingers.* In lieu of napkins many elegant Elizabethans wiped their greasy fingers on shaggy dogs, four-legged finger-bowls, kept for this purpose, principally, and dubbed "house dogs."

Coffee and tea were unknown during this period, and, as is true today, Europeans drink little water, compared to Americans. Many Britishers drank beer and ale from gallon-sized flagons, made of leather or wood. This was taken with meals, and carried to the field for plowing and farming chores. If a man could straight-arm a gallon of beer, hoist it with one arm, unaided, and drink without spilling he was applauded as having "lots of elbow grease."

The Elizabethans never saw a banana, which comes to us through the Spanish (and allegedly via Guinea) and originally Arabic, meaning finger, but some of the actors, i.e., comedians, probably cavorted with air or water-filled bladders, yellow-colored, similar to the phallic symbols carried on the

---

*Haggis, the celebrated, traditional Scottish dish, eaten with the fingers long ago, is remarkably similar to "ponhaw," a Tuscarora word for hog liver (haslet) or sheep liver, cooked in a bladder with grits or other fine grain products.

ancient Greek stage.

Today's inevitable "gone bananas," with the fairly obvious tie to the convolutions of monkeys, arose from the days when vaudevillians tilted with inflated yellow bladders, and the preeminent comic on a vaudeville bill was proclaimed the "top banana." Throughout much of the 20th century "banana-head" had limited use to mean a stupid person, but "banana oil" was spoken widely to denote arrant nonsense. To have one's "banana peeled" had ribald connotations, but it was cherished also by high school students from the 1920's through the 1940's to mean that the smart-aleck was exposed and chastised. Kids who improvised backyard games played with homemade bats, called these bats "banana sticks." Actually, "banana stick" was prevalent from around 1915 until around 1945 to mean many oddments fashioned from inferior wood, especially from abandoned pieces of wood.

As difficult as it is today to imagine the American supermarket and the home without bananas, few Americans ever saw a real banana until the Philadelphia Centennial of 1876. At this paean to "Culture, Science, and Progress," bananas were such an intriguing novelty some were wrapped in foil and sold for a dime a piece, a hefty sum, comparably, when a loaf of bread cost a nickel.

If the boosters of 1876 said little about it, and if some historians are slow to pick up on it, many of the male pilgrims who went to the Philadelphia exposition came home titillated by the hypnotic gyrations of "Little Egypt," whose wibbly-wobbly undulations forecast those of the hootchie-kootchie dancer, the stripper, the bubble-dancer, the fan-dancer, and many others to come.* The highly sensual dancing at Philadelphia by Little Egypt had been done before,

---

*H.L. Mencken coined the word "ecdysiast," from *ecydyais*, from the Greek *ekdusis*, a stripping-off, as a snake sheds its skin, as the professional designation for a stripteaser of the 1930's who wanted a more dignified word for her occupation.

in the "back rooms" of county fairs and carnivals, but no single, generic name for the stripper seems to have appeared until Little Egypt stunned and excited her bug-eyed auditors at the centennial.

Little Egypt, and her innumerable progeny, her daughters and granddaughters, were the main attractions on the mid-way of thousands of fairs and carnivals. Indeed, Little Egypt was hale and extraordinarily dexterous until Sallie Rand came along with her fan at the Chicago World's Fair of 1933.

"Hootchie-kootchie," the old carnival term, apparently from "hooch," or "hootch," meaning white lightning, and "kootch," a woman's hips and hindquarters, caught the nation's attention at the St. Louis World's Fair of 1904, in the Andrew Sterling-Kerry Mills song, "Meet Me In St. Louis, Louis."

The chorus, sung by half of current America, goes:

Meet me in St. Louis, Louis,
Meet me at the fair,
Don't tell me the lights are shining
Any place but there;
We will dance the Hoochee Koochee,
I will be your tootsie wootsie
If you will meet me in St. Louis, Louis
Meet me at the fair.

Although the promoters of the fair exploited the song in a manner in which a place-tune had never been used, the lyrics were prompted by a Broadway bar-tender named Louis. The beer he drew was called "a Louis," as in "Draw me another Louis, Louis." The words fascinated Andrew Sterling, then a successful lyricist. After two or three sets of trial lyrics about Louis and Louis, Sterling thought of the St. Louis Fair, scheduled to open within a few weeks.

The nation sang "Meet Me In St. Louis" as it had not sung

any popular song previously, and throughout the months of the fair, the St. Louis newspaper reported that the Sterling-Mills song "shared daily honors with 'The Star Spangled Banner.' "

Epicurus, Greek philosopher erroneously credited with teaching a doctrine of refined voluptuousness, is cast often, in common parlance, as "sitting in the laps of the Gods." In this context, "gods" may be an inadvertent substitute for "luxury." Homer wrote the phrase, and it is a conversational twist to "The issue lies in the laps of the gods," found in the *Iliad*. The ultimate fate of patients who were enduring the "crisis" in pneumonia was said to rest in the lap of the gods. This ascription applied to momentous verdicts being pondered by juries, and "the lap of gods" had considerable currency as a synonym for "touch and go," to mean a close issue that hinged on intangibles. In some portions of the southern states, "third lieutenant" connoted the same sort of suspense.

The "third lieutenant" actually came in to designate the officer-candidate who had completed the required training but had not been commissioned formally, and each of these phrases contained a potent degree of incipiency.

When things didn't work out satisfactorily, when one's services or one's social situation were terminated summarily, he left "bag and baggage." But this appears in *As You Like It* as, "Come, let us make an honorable retreat, though not with bag and baggage." "Bag and baggage" was a military term, an army's collective property. The phrase was applied usually when a besieged garrison surrendered but was allowed to march out with all of its equipment.

Each rifleman who marched out carried his weapon and a bullet in his mouth. This pap to individual and collective dignity meant that although the army had surrendered it was prepared to resent and to resist any affronts to its honor. Thus, the historical sense of "bag and baggage" implied an aggressive defiance that no longer attaches to the phrase.

With the election of Jimmy Carter and the new emphasis on southern mores, considerable copy devolved upon "tacky" and "tawdry." "Tacky," New Orleans dialectical word, meant unseemly intoxication originally, and it came to mean almost anything not quite respectable. But, curiously enough, "tawdry," showy or cheap, had a religious nativity. St. Etheldrede (630?-679) started a monastery at Bly for men and women over which she was Abbess for seven years, 670-679 (?). In 674, St. Etheldrede, or St. Audrey, as she came to be called, gave the land on which the world-famous Abbey at Hexam, England is built.

For many years an annual fair at Hexam perpetuated Etheldrede-Audrey or St. Awdrey, as Shakespeare spelled it. A local lace, elegantly made, and known as "tawdry," after "St. Awdrey," was the piece de resistance at the fair. The lace-work supplied the language with "tawdry," a far cry from the denigration the word came to impart.

In 1976 headlines on drama pages of some newspapers proclaimed: "*Mardi Gras* A Smash in Gotham and London." This allusion was to a musical predicated on Storyville, the old redlight district of New Orleans. Mardi Gras, literally "fat Tuesday," is the French name for Shrove Tuesday, the day before Ash Wednesday, the advent of Lent. "Shrove" is the past tense of "shrive," or confess, making shrift, and confession is made on Shrove Tuesday, prepatory to the forty days of fasting during Lent.

In America, Mardi Gras galvanizes the New Orleans festival, but the celebration originated in Europe. In Italy, France, and other Catholic countries the day before the beginning of Lent is a holiday-carnival. This is Pancake Tuesday in England. Britishers, anxious to use up all of their lards and greases before Lent, made pancakes. (Lavache, the clown in *All's Well That Ends Well*, says his answer fits all questions "As fit as a pancake on Shrove Tuesday.") In Catholic countries Fat Tuesday refers to the old custom in which a fat ox, symbolizing the passing of meat, was paraded through the streets of Paris, and in other Catholic cities. Because Lent was forty days of fasting, Mardi Gras merged as a day of lavish carnival, a term derived through Italian from the Latin *carnem levare*, or "to put away flesh (food)."

Mardi Gras was brought to America by French colonists, and celebrations occurred between 1702 and 1710 at Fort Louis de la Louisiana, the original site of Mobile, Alabama. A society to sponsor Mardi Gras balls and festivals was formulated in Mobile in 1830. Mardi Gras was celebrated, unofficially, by young men in New Orleans as early as 1827, and, apparently, these celebrations were revived and intensified between 1837-1839 by "gentlemen of New Orleans" who had just returned from visits to Paris.

It was not until 1859, however, that a full-blown Mardi Gras festival was instituted in New Orleans, by former residents of Mobile. On Mardi Gras, New Orleans is under the rule, ostensibly, of a King of the Carnival. Mobile and Galveston, Texas observe Mardi Gras with elaborate merry-making, and the day is a legal holiday in Louisiana, Alabama, and Florida.

Mardi Gras and New Orleans conjure "Dixie" and "Dixieland," as a type of music and as a "country within a country." As a synonym for the southern states, "Dixie" has teased etymologists for a long time. Although the Mason and Dixon Line is bound to be a factor, so is the old ten dollar bill, emblazoned with the French word *dix* on one side. This was widely circulated in and around New Orleans before the Civil War, and in the region it was called a "dixie."

There is also the legend that some slaves, owned by one Dix, of Harlem, N.Y., were sold to the deep south. According to the story, New York's cold weather obviated regular, harsh toil, but once in the deep south they were required to work endless hours in the biting sun. Their work-chants were redolent with poignant laments for the days of relative ease back in "Dix's land."

Daniel Emmett (1815-1904), professional song-writer and minstrel-show man, wrote "Dixie's Land" as a walk-around for Bryant's Minstrels. That is, it was sung and danced to by a few soloists in the foreground while the remainder of the company — about eight men — stayed in the background on the stage. "Dixie" or "Dixie's Land" was played and sung first in April, 1859 at Broadway's Mechanic's Hall.

When Jefferson Davis was inaugurated at Montgomery, Alabama, on February 18, 1861, "Dixie" became the Confederate national anthem. The original tempo, *allegro*, was changed to a military quick-step by a Confederate bandmaster.

If the lyrics sung by the north are forgotten today, several anti-southern sets of lyrics were put to "Dixie" and sung in the north:

Away down south in the land of traitors,
Rattlesnakes and alligators,
Right away come away, right away come away,
Where cotton's king and men are chattels,
Union brothers will win the battles,
Right away come away.

Emmett, leading minstrel-show man of his time, died in Mount Vernon, Ohio. He was reduced to doing manual labor, and in his last years he was supported by the Actor's Fund, of New York City.

"Gotham," or New York City, in the headline about the musical *Mardi Gras*, was popularized in Washington Irving's *Salmagundi Papers*, of 1807. Irving's good-natured joshing of his fellow-citizen's alleged conceit took off from Gotham, the village of Nottinghamshire, whose inhabitants were proverbial for conceit and feigned stupidity.

It is said that King John, ruler of England 1199-1226,

announced that his royal procession would pass through Gotham on a mission to find a location for a new palace. To be spared the burden of additional taxation to support the palace, the Gothamites hit upon the expedient of appearing hopelessly stupid. When King John's advance agents reached Gotham, everyone in the village was engaged in some foolish pursuit.

Some were trying to drown an eel in a pond; others were lifting horses into haymows and pulling the horses around; some were joining hands around a bush to fashion a cage for a cuckoo; and still others were putting carts on barns to shade the shingles from the sun.

The King was told that Gotham was the home of fools, whereupon, the Gothamites observed: "We ween there are more fools pass through Gotham than remain in it."

Several American towns are endowed, somewhat similarly, with various whimsicalities. Harold Ross, publisher of the *New Yorker,* said his magazine was not "for the old lady in Dubuque." In Fred Fisher's hit tune of the 1920's, Chicago became "that toddling town," and "the place that Billy Sunday could not shut down."

The city fathers of New Rochelle, N.Y. brought a suit, or an injunction, against George M. Cohan (1878-1942) when his infectious song, "Forty-Five Minutes From Broadway," lampooned the town as the haven for bumpkins. Albeit, the city fathers decided that the enormous derisive publicity was capital advertisement for their town, and Cohan, the tunesmith who made New Rochelle lyrically synonymous with hopeless gaucherie, became an honorary citizen.

It was John Collins Bossidy (1860-1928), in "On the Aristocracy of Harvard," who stitched up Boston and privilege:

And this is good old Boston,
The home of the bean and the cod,

Where the Lowell's talk to the Cabots,
And the Cabots talk only to God.

When one of the Cabots tried to use an injunction to prevent a man named Kabotschnik from changing his name to Cabot, Franklin P. Adams ("FPA" 1881-1960) wrote:

Then here's to the city of Boston,
The town of the cries and the groans,
Where the Cabots can't see the Kabotschniks,
And the Lowells won't speak to the Cohns.

Another version, an anomynous offering goes:

Here's to good old Boston,
The home of the bean and the cod.
Where the Lowells can't speak to the Cabots,
For the Kabots speak Yiddish, by God.

There is a reasonable, if unsupportable, belief that "as smart as a Philadelphia lawyer" was actually applied to Andrew Hamilton, attorney of Philadelphia, in reference to his successful 1735 defense of John Peter Zenger, the editor, in the first freedom of the press case tried in colonial America.

Albeit, the legendary shrewdness of the Philadelphia lawyer was an American proverb prior to 1788. Whenever anyone got into serious legal, emotional, political, or economic trouble the response was likely to be, "Well, it would take a Philadelphia lawyer to get you out of that mess."

There is a strong possibility that the magnetic phrase arose simply because Philadelphia was our largest colonial city, our only real city, at a time when most Americans lived on farms. "Philadelphia" was likely synonymous with the subsequent "big city" this or that. Too, the colonial and early American lawyer, an educated man, comparably, at a time when many of his contemporaries were barely literate, enticed a strong portion of suspicious awe. Even his clothing, semi-formal raiment in a era of home-made apparel, and his Latinized parlance, set him apart, made him the object of a queasy type of admiration.

Some of his admiration-mingled-with-fear survives in the late Carl Sandburg's whimsical "The Lawyers Know Too Much":

Why does a hearse horse snicker
Hauling a lawyer away?

American English has been redolent with mythical institutions, such as "Up in Mabel's room," and mythical thoroughfares, such as "The Old Ox-Road," as contained in the popular song-ballad of the 1930's. But despite· the fact that "Pick's Pike" seems to. be a pigeon Latin play on Pike's Peak, the once-famous thoroughfare was the chief military supply line from Lashio, Burma into southwest China during World War II.

In view of the Japanese control of Burma, maintaining a supply line into China was one of the most formidable chores presented by the direst exigencies of World War II. The old military road from Kunming to Lashio, built in 1937-1939, was abandoned when the Japanese staked out Burma in the early spring of 1942 and captured Lashio. In December, 1942, American army engineers began an alternate military road down from the north, beginning at Ledo, in eastern Assam, in India. This route curved south and east to join the Burma Road just across the Chinese border.

General Stillwell, in overall command, as an assistant to Chiang Kai-shek, kept a Chinese division ahead of the bulldozers and the men, but heavy rains and malaria slowed construction. In ten months the road had been carried only to

Naga Hills, around forty-five miles from Ledo. In October, 1943, supervision of the military road passed to Brigadier-General Lewis A. Pick of Auburn, Alabama. Pick, a resourceful, ingenious engineering officer, completed the remainder of the road, some 420 miles, in fifteen months. It was the commanding general's close association with endless facets of the work that prompted laborers and American soldiers to call the road "Pick's Pike." And this stuck, even if it was designated Stillwell Road, at Chiang's suggestion.

"The riddle of the sphinx" means the monster, with a woman's head and a lion's body, that wound round a cliff on the road to Thebes. The riddle asked of all who passed, was: What is it that walks on four legs in the morning, on two at noon, and on three in the evening? The answer was man, crawling as a child, walking erectly as a man, and leaning on a staff in old age.

When Oedipus answered the riddle correctly, the sphinx threw itself off the cliff. Oedipus was rewarded, to his immense chagrin, by being made King of Thebes, with Jocasta, for his queen-wife.

Some confusion about Thebes arose early in 1977 when the fantastic artifacts from the tomb of King Tut-Ankh-Amen were exhibited at the Smithsonian, when there were stories of the young king's affection for Thebes. Luxor and Karnak now stand on parts of the site of the ancient Egyptian Thebes. In evidence are some of the world's most splendid ruins, ruins of incredible temples, tombs, obelisks, and statues. Thebes developed from scattered villages, and the city emerged when a Theban family established XI Dyansty, around 2160 B.C.

Thebes became the royal residence (for Tut-Ankh-Amen, too), and the seat of worship of the god Amon. The city became famous for the necropolis where Egyptian kings were entombed on the west bank of the Nile. The city went into decline when political and economic focus shifted to the Nile delta. For a time in the 11th century B.C. Thebes was a separate political entity. The city was sacked by Assyrians in 661 B.C. and by the Romans in 29 B.C.

Traditionally, Cadmus founded the other Thebes, the chief city of Boeotia. By the end of the 6th century B.C Thebes began its active opposition of Athens, and it supported Sparta against Athens in the Peloponnesian War. But Thebes joined Athens against Philip of Macedonia, and after a revolt in the city, Alexander the Great subdued it in 336 B.C. Cassander rebuilt the city, in 335 B.C., after Alexander the Great had devastated it, but Thebes never attained its former greatness.

"Balaam's ass," Anglo-Saxon *assa*, any of several quadrupeds, is likely to be appended to the dolt, the boor, the oaf, the willful clown. (Here the overt machinations of the adult ass often conjure the uproarious gyrations of the blindfolded child who is trying to pin the tail on the donkey at a birthday party.) In *Othello*, Shakespeare has it, "Egregiously an ass," and in *Pudd'nhead Wilson's Calendar* Mark Twain leaves this conundrum: "Instead of feeling complimented when we are called an ass, we are left in doubt."

The famous, often garbled, story of "Balaam's ass" is found in Numbers, a part of the Hexateuch, or the Five Books of Moses and the Book of Joshua. After their sojourn of forty years in the wilderness, the Israelites are encamped on the plains of Moab. The Israelites have whipped two Palestinian armies, and Balaak, King of Moab, thinks he will be the third. So, Balaak orders Balaam, kind Gentile prophet, to go and put a curse on the Israelites so that they will be defeated in the imminent battle.

After demurring, Balaam saddles his ass and takes off, although he knows he will not be able to speak any words save those put into his mouth by God. En route, an angel, invisible to Balaam and to a party of Balaak's soldiers attending him, stand in the middle of the road. The ass sees the angel and turns from the road. Whereupon Balaam whips the ass with a stick. But the ass lies down, and it doesn't move, despite the continued fury of Balaam's blows.

The animal asks what it has done to merit such harsh treatment, and Balaam answers that it has made sport of him. He adds, "If my stick had been a sword I would have slain thee."

Finally, Balaam sees the angel, and when he climbs the hill he blesses the Israelites instead of damning them with a curse. He makes a prophecy of a great victory for the Israelites.

With the exception of the snake in the Garden of Eden Balaam's Ass seems to be the only talking animal in the Bible, although folklore is permeated with the talking animals.

The books of the Hexateuch are a combination of two accounts, one written around the 10th century B.C. and the other later. The earlier version uses *Jahweh*, to name God, and this is called the J version. The later account, which uses *Elohim* to name the Deity, is called the E version.

Many Americans were baffled by the statement that President Ford "leaves office without taking any 'Parthian shots.' " Figuratively a "Parthian shot" is applied to any thrust made in parting, whether verbal or physical. However, the image derived from methods of combat ascribed to the ancient Parthians.

The Parthians, innately warlike, specialized in firing arrows from horseback, and some of their deadliest volleys were shot as they feigned retreat. A favorite military tactic was to ride rapidly towards the enemy, firing darts ahead, suddenly to whirl, fake withdrawal, only to send endless arrows at their pursuers.

Parthia, which lay southeast of the Caspian Sea, became a separate kingdom about 250 B.C., under Arsaces. Although Parthia was attacked by the Romans persistently, the kingdom maintained its independence until it was conquered by the Persians in 226 B.C. Shakespeare used the image of the parthian shot in *Anthony and Cleopatra*, and, again, in

Cymbeline, wherein Iachimo says, "Arm me, audacity, from head to foot! Or like the Parthian, I shall flying fight."

"Herculean labors" is attributed to endless facets of extraordinary physical attainment, even if few Americans are tagged Herculean for spiritual or creative successes. And once the "Herculean feat" is accomplished, the person who did it may be hailed "One of the seven wonders of the world," or a "seventh wonder afoot." Hercules (Greek *Heracles*) was commanded by Eurystheus, King of Mycenae, to perform twelve, ten, originally, seemingly impossible tasks. Hercules, offspring of Zeus and Alcmene, a mortal, was foreordained by Zeus to become "the greatest of all heroes" and the "ruler of all the sons of Peleus" (the Mycenaeans).

On the day Alcmene was to give birth to Hercules, Zeus decreed that the first male child born that day would become a ruler and a hero. Zeus' wife, Hera, angered by Zeus' infidelity with Alcmene, used her black magic to delay Hercules' birth and to hasten the delivery of a child expected by the wife of King Sthenelus of Mycenae. Although Zeus was trapped, he obtained a compromise and Hera agreed that Hercules might become immortal, if, when he grew to manhood, he performed ten labors stipulated by Eurystheus:

1. To kill the Nemean lion. This animal was impervious to injury by stone, bronze, or iron. So, Hercules strangled it, skinned it, tanned the hide and wore the pelt for a cloak and the head for a helmet.

2. To destroy the hundred-headed Hydra, indigenous to the Lernean Swamp, which brutalized the countryside with its fiery breath. As fast as Hercules cut off one of the Hydra's heads, two heads sprang up. However, Hercules enlisted the aid of his nephew, Iolaus, who placed a pitch torch to each stump as soon as Hercules cut off a head.

3. The capture of the wild boar that ravaged the Mount of Erymonthus. Hercules drove the beast northward and when it

was inundated in a snowdrift he put a net around it, swung the net to his shoulder, and he carried the boar to Eurystheus, but the King was so terrified he hid in a large bronze jar buried in his courtyard. Eurystheus raised the lid intermittently, timorously, to peep at the approaching Hercules, the scene caricatured by Grecian vase-makers many, many times.

4. The capture of the golden-horned hind, sacred to Artemus, that had, perforce, to be captured alive. Hercules chased the hind for a year, and when it stopped to drink from a stream he pierced its forefeet with a single arrow.

5. To drive away the iron-feathered, man-eating birds, sacred to Ares, the birds that lived in the Stymphalian marsh. Athena gave Hercules a bronze rattle. He flushed the man-eating birds with the rattle, killed many in flight, and the remainder fled.

6. Augeas, King in Elis, had a stable of three thousand cattle, all immune to sickness and death. His stables had not been cleaned in thirty years. Stipulating that he would get one-tenth of the cattle, Hercules cleaned out the stables in a single day by diverting two rivers, Alpheus and Peneus, from their beds.

7. To bring back from Crete the white bull, cherished by Pasiphaw. Working unaided Hercules subdued the bull, and rode on its back as it swam from Crete back to Greece.

8. To capture the flesh-eating mares of Diomedes of Thrace. Hercules killed Diomedes, fed him to his own mares. Immediately the wild mares were tame enough to be hitched to a chariot. Hercules drove them back to Eurystheus, consecrated them to Hera, and set them free on Mount Olympus.

9. To get from Hyppolyte, Queen of the Amazons, a girdle given her by her father, Ares, god of war. Hyppolyte, agreeably susceptible to Hercules, offered him the girdle. Unfortunately, Hera started a rumor that Hercules meant to

betray (in the manner of the dastard of an 1890's story-song) Hyppolyte, and the Amazons prepared to attack him. Hercules, thinking he had been double-crossed by Hyppolyte, killed her, and carried the girdle to Mycenae.

10. He was ordered to steal the red cattle of Geryon, the horrible winged man-monster with three heads (sometimes three bodies). These cattle, on the island of Erythea, west of the Mediterranean, were guarded by Eurytion, enormous herdsman, and by Orthus, savage two-headed dog, and brother to Cerberus, guardian of the gateway to Hades. Hercules killed Eurytion, Orthus, and Geryon, in turn, and he drove the cattle from the western mouth of the Mediterranean — where he had paused to set up the pillars of Hercules — overland and by sea to Mycenae.

(This should have ended the labors, but Eurystheus contended that two did not count because Hercules was aided by Iolaus, in one and because he received pay, one-tenth of the cattle, for cleaning out the Augean stables. Thus, two more labors were required.)

11. He had to fetch a branch from the tree of golden apples which grew in the garden of Atlas, and was guarded by Atlas' three daughters, the Hesperides, and by Ladon, hundred-headed dragon. En route Hercules freed Prometheus, who told Hercules not to pick the fruit, personally. When Hercules reached the garden, he killed the dragon, and he agreed to hold up the sky while Atlas broke a bough from the tree of golden apples. But Atlas decided to carry the apples back himself. Hercules pretended to acquiesce, and he asked Atlas to hold the sky a minute so Hercules might adjust his cloak. Atlas fell for the ruse, and Hercules sped off with the golden apples, leaving Atlas to hold up the heavens forever.

12. To bring Cerberus back from Hades. Cerberus had three heads, a serpent's tail, and a mane of serpents' heads. Hercules obtained permission to possess the dog if he could do it without weapons. Despite the stings of the snakes, Hercules

choked Cerberus into submission. After he had exhibited the dog to Eurystheus, Hercules carried it back to the underworld.

"The Seven Wonders of the World" is the common name given to a group of ancient works of engineering and art, and it is supposed that the first list of "seven wonders" was prepared by Antipator of Sidon in the second century B.C.

The second, slightly different, set is contained in a treatise called *The Seven Wonders of the World*, included in the works of Philo of Byzantium who lived around the second century B.C., albeit it is now believed that the treatise was written as late as the sixth century A.D.

The list generally accepted contains: the pyramids of Egypt; the hanging gardens of Semiramis at Babylon; the temple of Diana at Ephesus; Phidias: statue of Zeus at Olympus; Mausolus' tomb at Halicarnassus, erected by Mausolus' wife, Artemisia; the Pharos, or lighthouse and watchtower, at Alexandria; and the Colossus at Rhodes.

Other lists have been forthcoming, such as "The Seven Wonders of the Middle Ages," of the "Modern World," "The Seven Wonders of the Natural World" et al. But little value attaches because these lists change constantly, via physical, natural, and scientific discoveries. The "wonders" of the ancient world were fixed at "seven" because of magical and sacred connotations of the figure 7.

In *As You Like It*, Shakespeare, in the passage that begins, "All the world's a stage," enumerates the "Seven Ages of Man," from the "mewing and puking infant," to "second childishness, sans teeth, sans eyes, sans taste, sans everything." And it was once widely held that the seventh son (child) of a seventh son was endowed with supernatural talents. Throughout the Middle Ages it was generally believed that such a person was impervious to normal diseases, and by laying on his hands could cure sickness and foretell the future. (Even in the 19th century it was accepted that such persons were born to be doctors.)

Benjamin Franklin says in his *Autobiography* that he was the youngest son of the youngest son for five generations in his paternal line. Franklin was the fifteenth of his father's seventeen children, by two marriages, and the eighth of his mother's ten children. He was named Benjamin, for Benjamin, youngest of Jacob's twelve Biblical sons, because his parents intended him to be the last offspring. They seem to have missed the mark, by two younger daughters.

There is, also, the ancient contention of gourmets that the turtle's body contains seven kinds of delicious meats. This is another way of saying that the meat is as tender as any other furred, scaled, or feathered animal. And the Chinese used to believe that one could acquire the turtle's longevity by eating its flesh, especially the turtle's green fat.

The ancient argument, "Which weighs more, a pound of feathers or a pound of lead?" was revived many times in 1976, probably as a by product of the talk about the imminent switch to the metric system. Technically, a pound of feathers is heavier than a pound of gold or lead because feathers are weighed by avoirdupois weight, 7,000 grains in a pound. Gold and other valuable metals are weighed by Troy weight, 5,760 grains in a pound. (Obviously, by the same system of measures feathers and gold weigh the same.)

Avoirdupois,, originally *avoir du pois*, is the old French word meaning "goods of weight." (In common parlance in America "avoirdupois" is used in terms of human flesh.) *Avoirdupois* is used in all English-speaking countries to weigh all commodities save precious metals, stones, and drugs. The latter are measured by Troy weight, from Troyes, France. In the *avoirdupois*, system a pound contains 16 ounces of 437 grains, each, while a troy pound has 12 ounces of 480 grains, each.

There is an old saying in the American south that a pound of feathers is lighter than a pound of lead even when weighed by the same measurement. If the two are weighed in a vacuum and then weighed in air, feathers "seem" lighter because they are less dense than the metal and weight-for-weight displace more air. Often bodies that appear to have the same masses in air have different masses in a vacuum.

PART TEN
THE BIRDS AND THE BEES

*"I think I could turn and live with animals, they are
     so placid and self-contain'd;
I stand and look at them long and long.
They do not sweat and whine about their condition;
They do not lie awake in the dark and weep for their
     sins;
They do not make me sick discussing their duty to God."*

Walt Whitman, "Song of Myself," from *Leaves of Grass.*

*"I never saw a wild thing
Sorry for itself."*

D.H. Lawrence, from "Self-Pity."

*"Animals are nothing but the forms of our virtues and
vices, wandering before our eyes, the visible phantoms of our
souls."*

Victor Hugo, from *Les Miserables.*

"I heard a little bird say so."

Jonathan Swift, from "Letter to Stella," May 23, 1711.

"One brid in the hand is worth two in the bush."

14th-century proverb and probably older.

"Brid" was the old form. Chaucer's *The Manciple's Tale* begins: "Tak any brid, and put it in a cage." The "r" shifted positions, as it did in the common pronunciation "hundred."

THE BIRDS AND THE BEES

"To show the white feather," still fairly common, came from the cockpit long, long before "cockpit" was associated with an airplane. The phrase came from the ancient belief that a white feather in the tail of a gamecock meant that the bird was a mongrel, and, hence, lacking in courage and aggressiveness. Even today cockfighters (an illegal, barbarous sport) say that when a purebred bird fights a mongrel the latter "cannot stand the gaff" and shows the "white feather," reveals its inferiority. (A gaff is a metal spur placed on the leg of gamecocks when they are put into the pit.) Obviously, selective breeding should result in birds more suitable for the sadism of the pit, but it is difficult to understand just why the old phrase "to show the white feather" refers to birds of inferior breeding.

In medieval England hard plumage was desired for gamebirds but little importance was attached to color and markings. Indeed, the ancient phrase may have arisen from the observation that a pure-blooded gamecock with white feathers in his wings would "show the white feathers" when he drooped his wings to acknowledge defeat.

If gamecocks and cormorants aren't birds of a feather, precisely, several references to the large sea birds common to Japan, China, and other parts of the Orient, surfaced in the summer of 1976, after a long hiatus. While the word almost disappeared from print and speech, the late Inglis Fletcher called one of her novels in her colonial Carolina series *Cormorant's Brood*, using the word in the sense of predators.

Cormorants have been trained to fish for Orientals since the dawn of history. Astonishingly agile under water, they devour fish so greedily their name has become synonymous with gluttony and voracity, just as the title of Inglis Fletcher's novel indicates. The young cormorants are trained to fish and to return their catches to their master's boat. A leather collar is placed about a cormorant's neck to keep it from swallowing a fish.

The sight boggles Occidental minds, but in the Orient it is commonplace to see a fisherman on a raft controlling a large flock of cormorants by means of cords attached to their collars, and some cormorants will fish for their masters without such controls. And if a fish is too large for one cormorant to handle, it is not unusual for another bird to assist the first bird. A single, well-trained cormorant may bring as many as one hundred fish to the boat within an hour.

Oddly enough, cormorant fishing was introduced into western Europe in the 17th century, and in several courts the Master of Cormorants became an official in the royal household. (If few American farmers are cognizant of the fact, the white-breasted cormorant is responsible for the production of the enormous quano deposits on the islands off the coast of Peru. Of course, some of this fertilizer ends up in American corn, peanuts, cotton, and tobacco fields.)

One of the most poignant of the American Indian legends, and one tragically forgotten today, accounts for the tribal reverence of the turkey. At the start of a particularly bitter winter, all of the fire in creation went out save for a few coals in the hollow of a tree. A brave, vigilant turkey, alert to the imminent disaster, fanned the coals until a crackling fire erupted. The noble bird was badly singed and burned, and that is why the turkey is pock-marked and bald to this good hour.

Because the migratory habits of birds were unknown to primitive men they believed, including Aristotle, that the autumnal disappearance was ascribable to hibernation in caves, treehollows, and marshes. Storks frequented marshes, and primitive people thought the souls of unborn children waited in these watery places, for birth. Simple juxtaposition gave rise to the myth that the stork found these embryos and delivered them to mothers-in-waiting.

And today it is exhilarating to see a stork, tall and graceful, its white plumage set off by its black wing quills, with its red beak and legs, as it glides so effortlessly about marshlands, or as it stands on one leg atop a chimney. Such winged poetry makes one forget the crack attributed to Charles F. Potter, in the early 1900's: "The bird of war is not the eagle but the stork."

"Halcyon days," still invoked fairly often to conjure the safe innocence of youth, comes down from Greek mythology: Ceyx was drowned enroute to consultation with an oracle. His wife, Halcyone, or Alcyone, daughter of the wind god, Acolus, discovered his body when the sea washed it ashore. Halcyone, overcome with grief, threw herself into the serf, and the compassionate gods turned them into the birds known as "halcyons," usually identified as species of kingfisher.

The halcyon was said to spend the seven coldest days of the winter building upon the waves a floating nest of fishbones upon which to lay its eggs. An extra week was required for brooding, and since a nest could not survive the wind and high waves for seven days, the gods invoked unutterable calm during the period of fourteen days. Hence, the week before, and the week after, the winter solstice (shortest day of the year) became the "halcyon days."

Later on in history, it was assumed, that the halcyon, or kingfisher, itself, was endowed with the power to subdue the wind and the ocean. This myth has some continuing pertinence in the custom along the Atlantic Seaboard of hanging a dried kingfisher up by its head so that the bill can point the direction of the wind, the same as a weathervane. This belief was old when colonists settled along the Atlantic

Seaboard. In *King Lear*, Shakespeare has Kent to say: "Such smiling rogues," meaning Goneril's steward, Oswald, "Renege, affirm, and turn their halcyon beaks with every gale and vary of their masters."

"As the crow flies," almost axiomatic to denote the shortest distance between two points, is a misnomer. The bromide must be the result of careless observation for, crows zigzag perceptibly. Indeed, the shortest distance between two points might be labeled a "beeline," much more properly. When seeking their hives, bees fly in a line that is almost straight. The Bee Line Highway, which connects Kansas City, Missouri, and Canon City, Colorado, is built along the shortest ground route between the two towns.

Anyone who listens closely to the humming sounds made by wind on powerlines may hear anything from a minuet on a cello to the noise of bees swarming. Indeed, forest rangers in Padres National Forest, California, have reported telephone poles damaged by black bears that mistook the humming music for bees. The bears, on several occasions, have climbed the poles seeking honey. Similar accounts have come from brown bears and telegraph poles in Russian Siberia.

Experts say wires strung from pole to pole are set into oscillation by the wind almost as the strings of a violin are set into vibration by a bow, and the natural frequencies of vibration are akin to piano strings. Frequently, several of these frequencies are produced simultaneously to make harmonies. The intensity depends upon the direction and velocity of the wind, and the tightness of the wires between poles. And the wooden poles are pretty fair conductors of sound.

Considerable publicity has attached to efforts to obviate the extinction of the American eagle. In the ancient myths eagles dropped turtles, tortoises, on stones to break the shell, to make the meat accessible. Aeschylus (525-456 B.C.), Athenian poet and "the father of Greek drama," is said to have been struck on the head and killed by a tortoise dropped by an eagle.

In manner reminiscent of the fate of Achilles and Balder, the gods had warned Aeschylus that he would be killed by a falling object. Sedulously avoiding all congestion, Aeschylus stayed in the safety of open fields, but an eagle mistook the poet's bald head for a rock. This yarn appears in several pieces of literature. Sir Thomas Browne (1591-1663) ridicules it in his *Vulgar Errors*, and it appears in the *Life of Aeschylus*, 11th century, appended to the Medicean manuscripts of Florence.

Aeschylus died in Crete, and he is buried in Gela, a place-name that used to be fairly popular in the American south.

Each fall residents of the southern states are electrified by the almost perfect V-shaped formations of those ebullient transients, the "wild geese." Many admiring observers assume that the foremost bird's duties are similar to those of the "point" on a battalion of skirmishing infantry. The front bird is assumed to break the wind for the entire formation.

This is not true, certainly not essentially true; for, a certain amount of wind is most helpful in sustained flight. The wedge formation allows the other geese to see the lead-bird more clearly, especially when flying at an angle. When the wind blows on the side of the V Formation, one prong of the V is usually considerably longer than the other prong. When this occurs the geese assume positions that coincide with the spaces between the birds on the windward side. Thus, each flyer is exposed to the full wind current.

Oliver Wendell Holmes, Sr. (1809-1894) said "A goose flies by a chart which the Royal Geographic Society could not improve." And Thoreau (1817-1862) leaves this inimitable entry of March 21, 1840 in his *Journal*: "The wild goose is a more cosmopolite than we; he breaks his fast in Canada, takes a luncheon in the Susquehanna, and plumes himself for the night in a Louisiana bayou."

Throughout history, the horse has profited immeasurably by press agents and the mule has suffered. Long before Benjamin Franklin published *Poor Richard's Almanack* "horse-sense" was an inevitable encomium, and "mullishness" endured as wanton adamance or perversity. Experts say the antithesis is true, that the mule's innate intelligence far transcends that of the horse. This is attested to by obvious, daily contrasts. Left alone, a horse eats and drinks until his system is endangered. The mule eats and drinks what its body requires.

If the restive horse catches a foot in a wire fence, he will injure himself painfully and seriously in frantic efforts to jerk the hoof free. Conversely, the mule will stand docilely until a man comes to extricate his foot. Given a load too heavy to pull, the horse breaks into a foaming lather amid exasperated lurches amid wild, futile efforts to move the wagon. The mule, sensing the load is too much for his strength, stands until some of the weight is taken off. Many contrasts in basic equipoise occurred in World War I, prior to the general motorization of armies. Under shell-fire, many horses' uncontrollable nervousness made their presences hazardous. Conversely, the mule maintained his cool.

But few sagas are more tragically poignant than the mule's. An Ishmael, a pariah, he is born without the inspiration of parents and he lives without the hope of progeny. And if the meek inherit the earth, no one has ever seemed to serve as guardian *ad litem* for the mule. Considering his ostracisms, his physical and verbal flagellations, and his classical want of human affection, the mule endures as a mute, four-legged Philip Nolan, eternally without country or friends, but put into social and physical limbo by an ancient caprice of nature.

Simultaneously, the horse's intelligence, fidelity, and prowess are embalmed in countless stories, poems, books, songs, and drawings. The mule, lampooned mercilessly in

comic strip cartoons, is derided in an old, bucolic satire that
no author ever wanted to sign:

Johnson had an old gray mule,
He hitched him to a cart;
John loved the mule,
The mule loved John,
With all his mullish heart.

The rooster crowed and Johnson knowed
That day was about to break;
So he curried mule with a three-legged stool
And brushed him down with a rake.

Yet "Brer Mule's" strong back has meant bread upon the
table and a few books upon the shelves for endless families.
He labored six days a week, gruelling year in and out, for his
rudimentary measure of fodder. His annual tribute was
reduced to the assertion of old farmers, a tribute to the
animal's sense of health, "Whoever saw a dead mule?" At
times, this has been leavened with the left-handed
compliment: "White mules don't die. They become Baptist
preachers." Yet, here and there the simple, pathetic destinies
of a few lone men and their long-suffering mules were
inseparable. Among some of the more anomolous dirt-farmers,
those with personal sagas as cheerless and hopeless as "Brer
Mule's," each was the other's desperate alter-ego. This
attained classic chronology in 1963 when an enfeebled,
impoverished dirt-farmer in Samson County, S.C. left this
suicide note penciled on a piece of wrapping paper: "My old
mule is dead and I mought as well be dead to."
    In a more insular society, the fortunes and destinies of
some poor men and their mules were so inexorably
interwoven it almost seems a breach of faith and decency that
the two are not buried in the same grave.

"Darwin's finches," birds seen by Charles Darwin along the Galapagos Islands —in the Pacific and approximately 650 miles west of Ecuador — had direct bearing on the great scientist's concept of "natural selection." Charles Darwin (1809-1882) made exploratory voyages on the famous *Beagle* between 1831 and 1836. He counted at least fourteen species of finches on the Galapagos Islands, with varying sizes and shapes of bills and with variegated markings.

Finches are known across the globe as the bullfinch, canary, goosebeak, chaffinch et al. Some are distinguished by spectacular yellow plumage and others by dull gray or brown plumage. Darwin was fascinated by the fact that the birds on the Galapagos had characteristics he had never seen before. While Darwin was tabulating the beak structures—ranging from thick, conical, long and slender, and short—he put down the diet the birds ate: Some of the finches subsisted on insects; some ate nuts, of varying sizes and thickness; others lived on cactus. But no two species ate the same food.

Darwin had no theory at this juncture, but in October, 1838, after returning to England, he studied Thomas Malthus' (1766-1835) *Principle of Population*, in which Malthus said that people in a given area are bound to exhaust their food supply from over-population. The excess population is reduced by war, disease, or famine to numbers that can be sustained by agriculture.

Darwin decided that his Galapagos finches had solved this problem. They multiplied rapidly on their isolated islands and the seed-producing capabilities of the islands having been over-reached, the birds that survived would be the one that made use of other foods. A finch with a stouter beak would crack a harder seed or even a nut; one with a slender beak could ream out wood-burrowing insects, previously un-obtainable. The finches that switched to other foods would survive, and the remainder would die. Albeit, Darwin ascribed the variations in plumage to diet, solely, a supposition corroborated by the fact that the feathers of the European bullfinch turn black if the bird eats nothing but hempseed.

The voyages on the *Beagle* implanted in Darwin's mind the idea of "natural selection," the revolutionary study he implemented during the next twenty years. By 1859 he was ready to announce to the world his theory of the evolution of the species. His classic, *Origin of Species*, swung scientific thought from Isaac Newton (1642-1727) to himself.

However, Darwin's book was vilified by Samuel Wilberforce, an acknowledged mathematician, at an important meeting of the British Association for the Advancement of Science (an ultra-conservative society of scientists.) Wilberforce shared the platform with Thomas H. Huxley (1825-1895) who became known as "Darwin's Bulldog." Huxley thundered: "If the question is put whether I would rather have a miserable ape for a grandfather, or man highly endowed by nature and the possessor of great means of influence yet who employs these faculties and that influence for the mere purpose in introducing ridicule into a grave scientific discussion, I unhesitatingly affirm my preference for the apes."

Fundamentalists, such as Gladstone, in England, and William Jennings Bryan, in America, were Darwin's most un-relenting adversaries. Curiously enough, Gladstone (1809-1898) declared that Darwin's scientific investigations confirmed the story of Creation as told in Genesis. Bryan (1862-1925) died at the conclusion of the famous, or infamous, Scopes trial, the "monkey trial," in Dayton, Tennessee upholding Genesis against "heretics" such as Darwin and Clarence Darrow. The "monkey laws" enacted by the Tennesses legislature made it a felony for the teaching in any state supported school of any doctrine about the Creation not contained in Genesis.

The "dove," likely the most familiar bird in the Bible, received its first mention when Noah sent it out from the Ark, when it returned with an olive branch it its beak as a sign that it had found dry land. (Genesis 8:11) Of the many varieties of dove in the Holy Land, the Rock, or Pigeon, Dove, and the Turtle Dove are the most common. Doves, characteristically gentle, are the symbol of beauty and peace, as in the "Song of Solomon.": "For lo, the winter is past, the rain is over and gone;/The flowers appear on the earth; the singing of the birds is come, and the voice of the turtle (dove) is heard in our land."

Psalms (55:6) implements the image with, "Oh that I had the wings of a dove!" And Alfred Lord Tennyson, in *The Princess*, rhapsodizes, "The moan of doves in immemorial elms,/And murmuring of innumerable bees." Matthew, Mark, Luke, and John all speak of Jesus' baptism in terms of the "Spirit of God descending like a dove." Ever since, the dove has become synonymous with the Holy Ghost, or the Holy Spirit, the third member of the Trinity.

The "cuckoo" was spelled "cookow" in the Bible until the late translations appeared. (Early translators probably had in mind the European bird). Because it eats snakes and lizards occasionally it has the image of "unclean." (Deut. 14-15 and Leviticus 11:16) The cuckoo has an amazing talent to imitate the calls of other birds, and its habitual singularity is enhanced by the fact that some cuckoos lay buff eggs with black spots and others lay blue eggs.

Frequently it lays its eggs in a nest that contains eggs of similar coloration, leaving its own eggs to be hatched by a surrogate parent. As a taunting imitator, a parodist of man's follies, the cuckoo ranks with the American mocking bird. In *Love's Labors Lost* Shakespeare has this as

The cuckoo then on every tree
Mocks married men; for thus sings he:
'Cuckoo!
Cuckoo, cuckoo.' O word of fear,
Unpleasing to a married ear.

(In the American south married men, out late at night roistering, swear their resident mockingbird mocks them at dawning with "Sixes and sevens, sixes and sevens" and with "O, my aching head, O my head.")

Many poets, including William Wordsworth (1770-1850) have heard the cuckoo as an unseen voice:

Thrice welcome, darling of the Spring!
Even yet thou art to me
No bird, but an invisible thing,
A voice, a mystery.

The "raven" is the first bird alluded to in the Bible, in Genesis 8:7: "At the end of forty days Noah sent forth a raven," to ascertain if the flood had subsided. Although male and female unite for life in testament to fidelity, the raven's reputation as an ominous, avaricious bird is merited. It feeds on carion, and it will attack smaller, weaker creatures, often plucking out the eyes of tiny birds.

Despite its general unsavoriness, the raven is highly intelligent and it can be taught to talk, if in parrot fashion, as in Edgar Allan Poe's (1809-1949) well-known but somewhat artificial poem, "The Raven." The poem must have been suggested by "Grip," the raven in Dickens' novel, *Branaby Rudge*. Poe, who reviewed *Barnaby Rudge*, said Dickens had passed over an opportunity: "Its croakings might have been *prophetically* heard in the course of the drama. Its character might have performed, in regard to that of the idiot (Rudge), much the same part as does, in music, the accompaniment in respect to the air."

Proverbs (30:17) speaks of "ravens of the valley" picking out "the eye that mocketh at his father..." "and the young eagles shall eat it." In *Othello* the Bard crystalizes the predatory image of the raven in:

O, comes o'er my memory,
As doth the raven o'er the infected house,
Boding to all.

Jesus picked the "sparrow" to represent the most humble of men:, "Are not two sparrows sold for a farthing? And one of them shall not fall to the ground without your Father (knowing)" (Matthew 10:29).

Here and there in the scriptures "sparrow" must be interchangeable with almost any small bird, but many varieties of sparrows were as familiar to ancient Hebrews as to modern Americans. Perhaps, David, or whoever wrote Psalm 107:7, had this in mind when he said: "I am as a sparrow alone upon a house top."

It is difficult to think of American mores without the irrepressible English sparrow. Ornithological historians say there were none in America until 1850. Nicholas Pike, one of the directors of the Brooklyn Institute, had eight pairs brought over. Then in 1852, when Pike was enroute to assume the consul generalship of Portugal, he arranged for another shipment, and some of these were released as the ship entered New York harbor. In all the total number of English sparrows brought over between 1850 and 1852 was fewer than one hundred, of both sexes.

The declared objective was to use the sparrows to protect shade trees from foliage-eating caterpillars. From the outset there were a few demurrers. An infinitesimal minority wrote letters-to-editors to brand the English sparrow as pest, a bird that ate seeds and buds rather than pernicious insects, both contentions substantiated by the continued presence of the English sparrow.

Subsequent to 1852, additional sparrows were released in St. Louis, Cincinnati, San Francisco, and, perhaps, elsewhere. Multiplying almost as rapidly as rabbits, the sparrows drove off many of the more desirable native birds.

But during the era when the horse, next to the railroad, was the principal means of transportation and for the hauling of goods, many terse observers hailed the English sparrow as an indefatigable, unpaid sanitation worker. (The horse and the sparrow produced many unseemly jokes: The habitual format usually went: "Two can't live as cheaply as one unless it is a horse and a sparrow.") After the automobile took over, the sparrow's chief economic value was its habit of destroying weeds by eating enormous amounts of the seeds that produce weeds.

When a hunter in southern America says he is "going bird hunting" he means, almost beyond peradventure, that he is out for partridges (quail). Nonetheless, the Bible distinguishes between "partridge" and "quail." The "Sand Partridge," with bluff and brown plumage, is almost inconspicuous in the wilderness of Judea. A fast runner, it tires quickly, and is caught often in the pursuer's bare hands. David may have been thinking of this when he said to Saul (Samuel 26:20), "As when one doth hunt a partridge in the mountains."

The "quail" mentioned in Numbers, the Psalms, and Exodus, is not much larger than a robin, according to ornithologists. The small bird, with brown and black feathers, with white belly, was hunted for food long before the Hebrews immigrated to the Holy Land. Numbers must exaggerate the size when a veritable flood of quail is described: "...two cubits" (from *cubitum*, or elbow, in English 18 inches). It is not a good or strong flyer, and while migrating it covers a short distance, often settling on the ground for the night. Hence, it, too, is caught with the bare hands, although nets may be used in mass hunting.

The "phoenix," used occasionally as a symbol for the resurrection of Jesus, is a mythical bird, one endowed with pristine beauty. Unusually large, it lived a normal span of five hundred years. Some Biblical scholars think Job was referring to the phoenix (Job 29:18) in the word translated as "sand." It is not among the birds enumerated in the Bible.

Howard Nemerov (1920-) has this stanza in his poem, "The Phoenix":

By incest, murder, suicide,
Survives the sacred purple bird
Himself his father, son, and bride
And his own word.

Three centuries earlier, Sir Fulke Greville (1554-1628) used "The Phoenix King" to mean a facet of love:

Love is of the phoenix kind,
And burns itself with self-made fire,
To breed still new birds in the mind,
From ashes of the old desire.

"Bees," linked almost inevitably with "birds" in the cliche relative to sex education for the very young, were imported to New England from Europe sometime between 1638-1640. (One marvels at the mind of the man who boarded a crude, small, bouncing wooden ship in 1638 with a parcel of bees.) The Indians, who branded the bee, "the white man's fly," always associated the honeybee with colonists from Europe. The buzzing, stinging tormentor was no portion of their own environment. Swarms escaping soon in American history to take up residence in hollow trees in the far-flung wilderness, led to the belief that honey, or hive, bees are indigenous to America. By 1800 honeybees had crossed the Mississippi. Stephen Austin, on his initial exploration to Texas, in 1821, wrote in his diary that he found a bee tree and obtained from it a gallon and a half of excellent honey.

"Bee," from the Anglo-Saxon *beo*, was common Teutonic. Jonathan Swift's *Battle of the Books*, published in 1704, contains the comment that its bee is responsible for honey and wax, "thus furnishing mankind with the two noblest of things, which are sweetness and light." In *Culture and Anarchy*, published in 1869, Swift develops this as the contribution of the artist.

"Honey" was not an early word, the Old English *hunig* and the German *Honig* having replaced the Gothic *mility*. And "mealy-mouthed," an opprobrium today, began as the antithesis. "Mealy-mouthed," earlier "meal-mouthed," meant "honey-mouthed." (The "meal" from which cornbread is made comes from the Anglo-Saxon *mael*, meaning pleasure or point of time, in the sense that one acts at an appointed time.)

Today, "honey-dew" means a melon, but Coleridge (1772-1834) ends his fascinating "Kubla Khan":

For he on honey-dew had fed,
And drunk the milk of paradise.

Euphemistically, anyway, the "scapegoat" may outlive all of the other animals. Even so, Leviticus 16:9-10, is one of the most enigmatic passages in the Writ : "The goat shall go for a scapegoat into the wilderness." On the formal, ritualistic Day of Atonement, the High Priest was charged with bringing two goats into the tabernacle. By lot, one was dedicated to Jehovah (or Jahweh) and the other for Azazel, whom scholars of recondite minutiae believe to have been a demon of the wilderness. Upon the second goat (presumably an "es—cape" goat) the High Priest transferred all of the transgressions of his people. Then the second goat was allowed to escape and go to Azazel.

It was William Tyndale, in his translation of 1523 who came up with "scapegoat": "To let him go for a scapegoat into the wilderness." Thus, it is reasonable to assume that the word "scapegoat" evolved from Tyndale's pronunciation of "escape."

"To get one's goat" may be a contraction of "goatee," the chin tuft that resembles a goat's beard. If this assertion is sound, "to get one's goat" means, literally, to humiliate him by pulling his beard.

Nevertheless, horse trainers have a theory that merits serious consideration. Frequently, goats are placed in the stalls of restive thoroughbred horses, for company and therapy. Indeed, many nervous thoroughbreds form close attachments to these stall mates. Gamblers, according to the story, sometimes stole the goat the night before a race on which they had large bets. Because unscrupulous men "got his goat," the horse ran poorly the next day.

PART ELEVEN
GAMES AND GAMBLING

*"If he, being young and inexperienced, play for great shekals
of silver and gold,*
*Take his money, my son, praising Allah, the kid was ordained
to be sold."*

Quoted by Rudyard Kipling, as a Hindu maxim.

*"The gambling known as business looks with austere disfavor
upon the business known as gambling."*

Ambrose Bierce, from *The Devil's Dictionary.*

"No man can lose what he never had."

Izaak Walton, from *The Compleat Angler.*

*"The winners tell jokes, and the losers yell, 'Deal, damn it,
deal!' "*

Ancient Granville County, N.C. aphorism.

GAMES AND GAMBLING

Charles Caleb Colton's (1780-1832) *Lacon* is even less resilient with modern readers than Emerson's (1803-1882) somewhat ponderous essays, but Colton pontificated, "Gambling is the child of avarice, but the parent of prodigality." In an appallingly large number of cases Colton's bromide is applicable, but on the tenuous plus side, gambling has enlivened the languages of the universe with vital plasma.

Other mortals may be saints and sinners by turn, and their hours may gravitate between ardor and lethargy. They may dwell among roses one month and among ragweed the next month. But the inverterate gambler breathes to wager. This anecdote may be apocryphal, and it seems to have counterparts in several communities, but the following version came to the author first-hand:

An acquaintance had spent the entirety of an intensely cold and icy Christmas season playing "red-dog" in the unheated, back room of a tobacco warehouse. He took his meals, cold sandwiches and coffee brought in, at the "red-dog" table. The game went on from nine each morning until long after midnight when physical exhaustion brought a temporary hiatus. Not once during two straight weeks of hard play did the gambler remove his overcoat, muffler, or hat.

Betimes, his lovely wife and his two small children made Christmas preparations amid the warmth of the man's attractive home. One morning he stumbled home from the game at four a.m. He had slept three hours when his wife shook him, to say she needed his help in acquiring gifts for Santa Claus to bring their children. "Get up, get up." He opened one eye to mumble, "I'm up. Deal, goddam it, deal."

Other mortals may tie their personal almanacs to notable events, to the precise unfolding of history, but the gambler, like the old-time vaudevillian, reduces presidential elections or assassinations and enormous events such as floods and moon-landings to runs of good or bad luck he had at the time. If someone mentioned the Johnstown flood or the San Francisco earthquake and fire to the tank-town vaudevillian, he would reply: "Yep, I had a split-week, three shows a day, in Altoona, Pa. I was between a dog act and a lady ventriloquist but I killed the audience."

The gambler remembers the 20 to 1 long-shot that won the race when John Kennedy was murdered; and when the astronauts went to the moon, his first four cards at high-low were the two, three, four, and five of diamonds, but his last three cards were "big black bastards." One of the numerous legends about "Steamboat Bill," the flashily-dressed Mississippi River gambler, is, for all of its preposterous license, an eternal testament to the insatiable gambler's real, undeviating nature:

The *Delta Queeen's* boilers exploded, and planks, furniture, crew, and passengers were catapulted upward. As "Steamboat Bill" ascended he drew abreast of a drummer from Cairo whom he offered to bet he would sail higher. When the zooming drummer declined the wager, Bill offered him two to one that he would come down quicker than the man from Cairo, Illinois.

"Money makes the mare go" as quoted by the experts, Peter and Iona Opie in their *The Oxford Dictionary of Nursery Rhymes*, goes:

Wilt thou lend thou mare to ride but a mile?
No, she's lame, going over a stile.
But if thou will lend her to me spare,
Thou shalt have more money for thou mare.
Ho, ho say you so!
Money shall make my mare go!

The famous Opies say the rhyme is an addition to *The Second Part of Musicks Melodie* (1609), found in the British Museum.

The ditty became a nursery rhyme, and the concluding line, rendered verbally as "Money makes the mare go (or trot)," became a standard cliche. While the original application seems to have been to the racing-course, the proverb has attached to endless endeavors, usually in the sense that if one really needs a job done, or a favor, he should be prepared to pay for it.

"He knows the ropes" sprang from the race-track, the ropes being the reins or the harness, and the winners were jockeys or drivers who knew how to handle their ropes. But, as many students know, Richard Henry Dana popularized the phrase in *Two Years Before the Mast*, published in 1840: "The captain who 'knew the ropes' took the steering gear." Hence, many readers assume the phrase is of nautical origin. But Dana's putting the words within quotation marks seems to prove that he was using it out of context.

"It is difference of opinion that makes horse races" appeared in Mark Twain's '*Pudd'nhead Wilson's Calendar*, although Twain's words have a variety of regional examples.

The "compulsive gambler" (a colloquialism, perhaps, from "gambit") finds enduring residence in Twain's "The Celebrated Jumping Frog of Calaveras County: "If there were two birds sitting on a fence he (Jim Smilley) would bet (probably from the Middle English *abet*, "abetting") you which one would fly first." Jacques Saurin's (1677-1730) "Nothing is sacred to a gambler" is rivaled in gaming parlance only by the idiomatic, "As homeless as a poker chip."

Bergen Evans, and other authorities illustrated Saurin's maxim with an incident at Will's, London's famous gambling house, in the 18th century. A pedestrian fell on the sidewalk in front of Will's and one member took odds from another member that the man was dead. When other members sought to go to the aid of the fallen man, the first gambler objected strenuously, denouncing any assistance as unethical. The question was referred to a committee of Will's, and by the time the committee ruled in favor of assistance, it had already been determined that the poor man was dead.

The poker chip, used to facilitate the game and used also as a palpable ruse ("We're not playing for money") is a little "chop," and both words are imitative, beginning as references to wood. Around 1650 "chip" meant a chessman, and the round disk came to the gaming tables around 1850. "Let the chips fall where they may" came from wood-chopping, obviously, although moderns probably think of metal or celluloid disks. ("Hue (or hew) and cry," echoic, comes from wood-chopping, from early forestry, also. "Hew not too high,/ Lest the chip fall in thine eye" was proverbial by the 14th century.)

"The candy " is the large pot or wager, and "rolling the candy" in French pool refers to the ten, eleven, twelve, thirteen, fourteen, and fifteen balls. "The candy kid," a ladies man ("lounge lizard" yesterday) is a gaudily-dressed "high-roller." "The candy man," in gambling, sits quietly, often amid feigned vacuity, while someone else raises the bet, but when he "calls," he wins. It is said of him, "The big possum walks just before day."

"The candy kid" invariably uses fanciful synonyms for many of the individual cards. Two's are "snakes" or "puppy feet"; three sixes are "chill tonic," after "666"; sevens are "walking sticks"; and three sevens are "young man leaving home" (21); eights are " bug-eyes"; jacks are "mules" and other male animals; queens run a wide gamut from "stenographers" to "whores"; kings are the "klan"; and three kings are "ku klux klan"; aces have endless synonyms to indicate male virility; a heart or diamond flush is "an Indian massacre;" and a club or spade flush is a "black funeral."

"Playing cards," ascribed to the devil's diabolical invention, came from China, around 975 A.D. The first ones, circular, were made of wood or plant fibre, painted in rich, bold colors. Cards reached Europe, via the Arabs, and some of the oldest ones extant, from Venice, were painted brightly but lacked numerals and suit-designations. In lieu of numerals and suits there was an extensive galaxy of figures and emblems: the sun, the moon and stars, the "Wheel of Fortune," justice, the emperor and empress, "the klovers," the mountebank, the fool, the devil, and "the Hanging Man."

Soon afterward, cards were divided into suits, such as, cups, for faith, swords, for justice, money, for charity, and clubs, for fortitude. The state (Italy) had a monopoly, and a lucrative source of special taxation. By the end of the 15th century, playing cards were so evident in France, a major industry arose to manufacture them. Around 1505 a British royal decree forbade playing cards to servants and apprentices, save during Christmas holidays. James I, Mary Stuart's son, king from 1603-1625, was such a compulsive card player he kept two courtiers at hand constantly, one to hold his cards and one to suggest which card to play, "to throw."

Around 1400, French card makers came up with the four suits known today, allegedly to represent the four chief classes of French society: Hearts, to depict ecclesiastical authority, represented the clergy. Spears, which became spades in England, symbolized the military. Clubs, originally pictures of a clover leaf, suggested farmers and peasants; and the simple shape of a diamond represented the French middle class. Many of the middle class were merchants, and diamond-shaped tiles were used to pave their exchanges.

If the ace, "two (or three, or four) balls of fire," is the big dog in the meat-house, its etymology is uncertain. One of the oldest traditions has the "ace" invented by the Celts which they called *as* because in their language "*as*" meant the first of all things. A theory more plausible ties the "ace" to the Romans who referred to it as the *unit*, the "one," the *unus.* The Greeks, supposedly, corrupted this into *onos* and the Germans corrupted it into "as," ultimately "ace."

The most likely suggestion is that "ace" came from the Roman coin, *as*, which served as a unit of weight, also, (Many gamblers swear that the "ace," in cards, and "ace," or single spot on dice, comes from "ass" because it makes players make asses of themselves.)

Thousands who play poker for large stakes and for friendly, penny-ante stakes, always call a pair of aces and a pair of eights "the dead man's hand." James Butler "Wild Bill" Hickok is said to have had aces and eights, in a draw poker game, when he was killed by one Jack McCall at Deadwood, South Dakota in August, 1876. Many southern card players call two aces and two eights the "spook hand" because in several versions of wild-card games it wins over any other combination, including royal straight flushes and five of a kind.

"Passing the buck," popularized by Harry Truman's desk sign, "The Buck Stops Here," emerged from the card table. In many poker games a marker, to keep track of the deal, was passed from player to player. If a player preferred not to deal, or if he "strapped the pot" in draw poker, matched the original ante, and got the last "open," he was said "to pass the buck."

("Buck," long synonymous with a dollar, arose in the days of American barter when the skin of a male, or buck, deer was more valuable than the hide of a doe.)

In many games of poker, and pool, a "kitty" is accumulated, for some aforestated purpose, with two or more players contributing portions of the pots or pool games they win. Since "kit," meaning several kinds of container, dates back to around 1400, "kitty" may have arisen to mean a "small kit of money." And some authorities suggest there may be a tie between "kitty" and *kiste*, or *kist*, the old Scottish and North of England word that meant a money box or a money chest. And in some parts of rural Southern America people used to speak of a "kit of eggs," to mean a basket of eggs. Of course, "kit bag," as in "Pack Up Your Troubles In Your Old Kit Bag," the popular tune of World War I, had considerable vibrance in British and in American English.

"Faro," dormant as a gambling game, was revitalized in western movies. Basically, "faro" is roulette played with cards, although in sagebrush saloons there are references to "crooked faro wheels." (A cowboy is asked: "Why do you play that faro wheel? Don't you know it's crooked?" "Hell yes, but it's the only wheel in town.") "Faro," a corruption of pharoah, ties to the legend that the king of hearts represented the Egyptian Pharoahs.*

The origin of the word "bridge" has tantalized etymologists much of this century. A modified version of Russian whist, "bridge" was prevalent in the social clubs of Constantinople and Alexandria as early as 1865. The game worked its way to the Riviera and into Paris, and it was played in London around 1894. The British called the new game "bridge whist" until the system of bidding was superseded by auction bridge.

"To bridge" is an old verb meaning to bend a card so that a confederate may cut the pack where the bent card is positioned. (*Webster's International Dictionary* has the same definition for "bender.") In euchre, "bridge" is used when one side has scored four points and the other side has scored only one point. And it is asserted frequently the "bridge" is derived from the Russian word *britch*. However, chronology runs counter because it is fairly evident that the Russians appropriated *britch* from the British "bridge."

*For whatever it's worth, Cleopatra, the "dark Queen of Egypt," married two of her own brothers, and she was descended from four generations of brother-sister marriages.

Bridge whist was so called because the dealer could name trumps, or he could "bridge" this choice over to his partner. Too, there is the outlandish theory that "bridge" stemmed from a Leicestershire village, around 1898. Two married couples played bridge whist in each other's homes on alternate nights, and a treacherous foot-bridge stretched between the two homes. The couples fell into the habit of saying, "Thank God, it's your bridge tomorrow night."

Several experts think auction bridge, predecessor to contract bridge, originated among British army officers who were stationed in India, late in the 1890's. The January 3, 1903 issue of the London *Times* alluded to it as "the new game of auction bridge for three players." It seems to have become a four-handed game at the Bath (England) Club in 1907.

The violent demise of Joseph B. Elwell, unchallenged expert on auction bridge, author of the standard text, introduced a new format in American detective fiction, along with an extraordinarily different fictional sleuth, and a new author. Elwell, barely five feet high, a profligate, and a most fastidious man, owned forty wigs and a dozen sets of false teeth. But he was found by his maid bereft of hair and teeth, seated in a chair, a bullet hole in his forehead.

The cartridge had ranged upward, and this led New York City detectives to reason that Elwell may have been done in by a small, spurned woman, who fired from a coat pocket. Elwell must have known the killer and the killer's mission. Otherwise, such an inordinately vain, dandified man would not have been exposed sans false teeth and hair-piece. However, no suspects emerged, and for a while detectives wondered if some aggrieved husband hadn't arranged for a midget hit man.

The murder of Elwell is unsolved, except on paper. Willard Huntington Wright, author of copious, poorly-paid critical pieces, solved the Elwell case in fiction. He called it *The*

Benson Murder Case, the first in a long series of murder mysteries written under the name S.S. Van Dine. And *The Benson Murder Case* introduced Philo Vance as the cultured, meticulous sleuth who must be America's closest, if yet distant, approximation of Sherlock Holmes and G.K. Chesterton's Father Brown.

"Fantan," which came from China, is a game in which gamblers bet on the number of beans, or coins, or other counters, that remain when a hidden pile is divided by four. In a second version of "fantan" sevens, and their equivalents (five-two, four-three et al) are played in sequence, and the winner is the first player to discard all of his cards. "Fantan" derives from the Cantonese *fan t' an*, from *fan*, meaning division, and *t'an*, or distribution.

"Euchre," played with the 32 highest cards from a 52-card deck, is the game in which Ah Sin, the picaresque hero of Brete Harte's poem, "Plain Language From Truthful James," excels. In euchre each player is dealt five cards, and the winner must take at least three tricks. Despite the decline of the gambling game, the art of "euchring someone" has fairly wide connotations, usually in conjunction with "out" or "out of" something.

In Brete Harte's infectious narrative, written in 1870, the two white gamblers intend to fleece Ah Sin, the "heathen Chinee," who professes total ignorance of euchre. The climax comes when Ah Sin lays down a "right bower," the hand the narrator's confederate had stacked to deal to the narrator.

"Roulette," faro played with a wheel and a basin for the black and white balls, is French, from the Old French, *roulle*, from the Late Latin, *rotells*, diminutive of the Latin, *rota*, a wheel.

"Pinochle," sometimes "penuckle," is played with from two to four people, with a special deck of 48 cards, with the ultimate catch being a combination of the queen of spades and the jack of diamonds. The word is an extended use of the French *binocle*, pinze-nez, from whence "binovular," from the New Latin *Vinoculus*, or the two eyes.

With the possible exception of the cross-word puzzle, no avocation of the 1920's was so compulsively magnetic as the new game, new to America, called "mah-jong," from the Cantonese *ma chiang*, or house sparrow, the figure emblazoned on the leading pieces of one of the "mah-jong" suits. This game, with four players, employs domino-like tiles, of various designs. Tiles are drawn and discarded until one player wins with a combination of three tiles, each, and a pair of matching tiles. (There is a rough parallel here to a full-house in draw poker.)

"Chess," played so often by so many people of diverse stations that any explanation of the game's nuances is redundant, comes from the Middle English *ches*, short for the Old French *esches*, the plural of *eschec*, or check in the game of "chess."

"Checkers," or "chequers," still called "draughts" by many senior Americans, must be older than recorded history. This excerpt appears in Blucher's translation of the *Odyssey*:

"When the goddess Athene descended from the heights of Olympus and reached the gate of Odysseus she found the lordly woers taking their pleasure at draughts in front of the doors."

If checkers suffers from intellectual comparison with chess, Edgar Allan Poe (1809-1849), in an excess of fervor, tried to even the score: "The higher powers of the reflective intellect are more decidedly and more usefully taxed by the unostentatious game of draughts than by all the elaborate frivolity of chess."

"Skin," the ubiquitous southern colloquialism, has long attachment to an infinite variety of gambling games. Several theories attempt to account for the origin of "skin": In hot weather small-time small-town gamblers stripped to their

BVD's in back rooms and along creek banks; although these dice and card games were played for loose change, the play was so intense vigorous players were said to be "after skin." And in games in which a player was dealt all his cards face down (the opposite of stud poker), he held his five cards so tightly, fanning his entire hand in a tiny space, the gambler "skinned his cards."

Even if "skin" means a manner of playing, rather than any specific game, "Brown berry" means a type of set-back, or seven-up – "high, low, jack, and game "–in which the bidder who goes set pays each of his opponents the same amount every player puts in the pot at the start of the game. Seven-up, or pitch, is played with six cards to a man, without a draw or a widow. In the habitual seven-up, or pitch, each player puts up a dollar, for instance. If he is set, he puts in another dollar. If he is caught at the post, doesn't make a point, and his score remains at seven, or above, he puts in an additional dollar. The winner, the player who goes from seven to zero first, wins the whole pot. "Brown berry" varies in that the bidder who is set pays everyone else a dollar instantly.

"Brown berry," heard daily in almost limitless contexts, is a complete mystery to etymologists. In the "Prologue" to *The Canterbury Tales*, Chaucer has it:

His palfrey (horse) was as brown as is a berye.

Yet, no botanist knows what a "brown berry," is, although there is intermittent speculation that "brown berry" meant a coffee berry. But coffee, in any form, was completely unknown in Chaucer's time. The vigorous persistence of "brown berry" ties, undoubtedly, to simple alliteration. The phrase has endless uses, often as a simile, in October, and during summer sun-tanned bodies are linked with "brown berries." In certain games called "skin," the "brown berry" is the ultimate, the financial accolade, the whole kit and caboodle.

It has been claimed that "dice" were invented during the seige of Troy, as therapy for soldiers who played the game in their tents during lulls in the fighting. Nonetheless, Herodotus (5th century B.C.) "the father of historians," credits the Lydians with the invention of dice. Herodotus says that hungry people were supplied with dice during a famine. They were given food one day and dice the next day. Albeit, many gamesters find scant thereuptic value in dice, today.

Archaeologists have unearthed vases that depict soldiers in the Trojan War watching dice being thrown, and Homer tells how young Patroculus killed a friend in a dice game argument. Several of Rome's imperial palaces contained dicing rooms, and paintings on some Roman tombs show dice games, the implication being that the game was one of the bonuses of eternal life.

The Germans obtained dice from their more civilized Roman neighbors. According to Tacitus (lst and 2nd centuries A.D.) the Germans were so obsessed with throwing dice they sacrificed anything, even their freedom, to continue a game. (Apparently, Tacitus predicates this on the fact that many Germans sold themselves into Roman slavery.)

Some of the early dice, stamped with small circles, or with demi-gods, were used in fortune-telling, but the Greeks, especially the women, played with five knucklebones, thrown into the air, much as jackrocks, and caught with the back of one hand. If a die was dropped the contestant had to pick it up without dislodging the ones already caught. In the next evolution the four sides of knucklebones were stamped with four faces —convex, concave, flat, and a profile. Bones (Dice shooters still chant, "Roll those bones.") were made from stone, wood, lead, bronze, and ivory, and stamped with dots to represent the various numbers.

"Crap," or "craps" throughout southern America, is

Louisiana French, from "crabs," the lowest throw at hazard, a dice game with several similarities to "craps." Much of the crap-shooter's parlance is the result of alliteration: "Little Joe (a four) from Kokomo;" "eighta from Decatur;" "nine on the Frisco line" etc. "Boxcars," a twelve formed from two sixes, has the general outline of a boxcar, and "snake eyes," two aces, have that appearance.

A dice shooter "craps out" if he throws a seven before he pulls his point, or if his initial roll is a two or three. And he must surrender the dice to the next shooter. "Crap out" has well nigh limitless uses in the sense of cowardice, exhaustion, evasion of duty, or failing to contribute to a social, political, or intellectual foregathering.

There is some confusion, as well as controversy, relative to the chronology of "crap," a taboo meaning excrement, and "crap" in the sense of "crapping out." This argument may remain insoluble, but it seems reasonable to assume that the taboo came from dicing parlance. By the 1920's "crap" had come to mean insincerity and mendacity, and as an interjection for incredulity and astonishment, it became synonymous with "bull." Such eminent writers as the late John O'Hara, James T. Farrell, and Arthur Miller used "crap" to run a wide gamut from worthless, to insincere, to unpleasant, to ugly. After World War II "crap" as in "Stop all that crap," meant fulsome noise, pandemonium. (Milton coined "pandemonium in *Paradise Lost* for the name of the capital of Hell. By natural transfer, "pandemonium" came to mean diabolical noise and arrant confusion. Undoubtedly, this portion of *Paradise Lost*—Book I, line 756—is responsible for the southern colloquialism, "As surely as hell is a city." "Bedlam," synonymous with "pandemonium," comes from the French *bella dame*, beautiful lady, and it was used in early England to mean grandmother. But it came to mean an old, ugly woman, and a hag, ultimately. However, in the sense of meaningless sound and volatility it stems from Bedlam, the old London insane asylum.)

After 1950 "bazooka" meant any of several kinds of wild-card games, and in this context "bazooka" appears to have no more semantical relevance to wild-card games than "red dog," "Chicago" and the remainder. Beyond peradventure, "bazooka" was coined to mean a wild-card game, or a seven card stud game in which the best and poorest hands split the pot, simply because the prowess of a specific gambler suggested the power of a "bazooka," or a loser compared his ineptitude to being attacked by a "bazooka."

The "bazooka," the musical instrument, was invented by the late Bob Burns, famous as a radio comic in the 1930's. Burns made a "bazooka" in 1905, in his native Arkansas, when he found two pieces of gas pipe that fit, one over the other. Burns turned the pipes into a crude trombone.

"Bazooka" is made from adding an ending to the hobo word "bazoo," slang for brash talk. ("He blows his own 'bazoo' too loudly.") (Toy noise-makers of the 1890's and early 1900's were "kazoos," "zuzus" etc.) It is highly possible that Bob Burns thought of the similar-shaped "bassoon" when he called his cacophonious music-maker a "bazooka."

The "bazooka," meaning a rocket-projectile gun, made of straight tubing, open at both ends, was so-named in 1943 by Major Zebulon Hastings, ordnance expert of the U.S. Army, from Bob Burns' home-made instrument. Burns said, "Both are pretty devastating."

"Billiards," from the Old French billart, or staff, any one of many games played on an oblong table, with ivory balls propelled with a cue stick, is interchangeable with "pool" in American English. Indeed, even wherein a neon sign proclaims "Billiard's Parlor," patrons are likely to refer to the institution as "the pool room."

"Pool room," or "hall," stems from the days when many neighborhood billiards' parlors and short-order cafes that had a billiards' table in the rear held weekly lotteries. The drawing usually occurred on Saturday night, and the "pool" was given to the lucky number. In some communities the weekly "pool" was in the form of cash money, but here and there the "pool" consisted of coal or flour or meat. The drawings for the neighborhood lottery occurred in the billiards' parlor because that institution was open on Saturday night. Very shortly this was spoken of as the "pool room."

At the apogee of the neighborhood "pool," "geetus," "geetis," and "geedus," became synonymous with money, and the scene of the lottery became the "geetus hole," later "geetus box" in underworld lingo to mean a bank vault. "Geets," pronounced with the same sound as the "gee" in McGee, became money, more especially the purchasing power, and the influence, of money.

About this same time, circa 1890, "Kelly pool," the game in which each player gets two pills from a shaker, emerged. In Kelly, the rotation in which a player shoots is determined by the pill he puts back on the table, as he retains, surreptitiously, the number of the pill that corresponds with the number of the ball he must sink to win the "Kelly pool."

This game is known, generally, as "Straight Kelly," to differentiate it from "Crazy Kelly," the game in which one wins if his ball is made accidentally by a competitor. And there is this enduring mystery: Throughout the southern states that border on the Atlantic, "Kelly" is pronounced, almost universally, as "Keeley." "Keeley" is so firmly intrenched the man who says "Kelly" runs the risk of sharp criticism for effete affectation.

It is assumed that "Keeley," in this context, came from the Keeley Institutes, the drying-out places famous for their speedy "Keeley Cures" for inebriation. The logical assumption is that a man who had phenomenal success at "Kelly pool" was said to have given his opponents "the Keeley Cure." Or, a chronic loser may have sworn off Kelly, stipulating that he had received "the Keeley Cure."

No historian has been able to determine when billiards began, but Shakespeare refers to the game in *Anthony and Cleopatra*, written around 1607. It is assumed that the Knights Templar brought a form of billiards to England from the Crusades in the 11th century. Insofar as any record indicates, the game identifies with Louis XI, King of France from 1461-1485. Louis played the game regularly, and it is established that Charles IX ordered a table built for his court in 1571.

In Charles' time, and afterward, the table had a wooden bed and sides, and the balls were propelled with a mace. By 1735 the mace was replaced with a wooden stick, and in 1798 Captain Minguad, a French political prisoner, used his confinement to improve the stick, particularly by putting a tip on the end. Jack Carr, Britisher of the early 19th century, introduced chalk for the cue, and it was Carr who put "English" on the cue-ball. By 1825 a slate bed replaced the wooden bed. The table was built a little higher, for comfort and skill, and sides of India rubber replaced their wooden predecessors around 1835, and around 1855 the standard tables were improved by the addition of rubber cushions.

The game multiplied our stock of spoken words. Many of the words, phrases, and expressions that emanated from billiards and pool attained additional idiomatic meanings and are spoken and understood almost universally, and often by non-players: "Ball on," "bank shot" (now inevitable in basketball), "break,"* "bridge," "called ball," "caron shot," "draw shot," "English," "frozen," "kiss," "kiss shot," "miscue" (now has almost limitless connotations), "safety,"

---

*"Break" runs a wide, diverse gamut, from the sense of good or bad luck to social faux paus, and it was used in both senses by the late Sinclair Lewis in his novel of 1914, *Our Mr. Wrenn*. Baskets of tobacco, placed upon an auction warehouse floor for sale are yet designated as good and bad "breaks of tobacco." This comes from the era in which tobacco was packed into 1000 pound hogsheads, and the tops were broken into by buyers to determine the quality.

"scratch," and "set-up"* are a few of the words and phrases that sashayed from pool rooms to invade homes and offices.

Historically, the game of "American football" dates from a match played between Rutgers and Princeton on November 6, 1869, won by Rutgers, six goals to four. In the ensuing century-plus, American football, via constant modifications, barely resembles the tug-of-war that occurred in November, 1869.

Curiously enough, Shakespeare refers to "football" in *King Lear*, written around 1607: "You base football player." The reference must be to some version of soccer, and a quarter-century earlier, Philip Stubbes, in his *Anatomie of Abuses* (1583), gives some crude form of football the back of his hand fully: "Rather a bloody and murdering practice than a felowly sporte or pastime. For dooth not everyone lye in waight for his Adversary seeking to over-throw him, though it be uppon hard stones? So that by this meanes, sometimes their necks are broken, sometimes their backs, sometimes their legs, sometimes their armes; sometimes one part thrust out of joynt, sometimes another; sometimes their noses gush out with blood, sometime their eyes start, sometimes hurt in one place, sometimes in another...And therof groweth envie, malice, rancour, and what els; murther, homicide, and great effusion of blood, as experience dayly teacheth."

Beyond question this is about some form of what came to be called "Rugby." Interestingly enough, several tribes of American Indians had developed a stick-ball-game from which the white man evolved his game of lacrosse. Although the evidence is not palpably clear, there is reason to believe that some tribes, the Algonquins, notably, had developed the long-handled stick with basket attached, the device in which the

---

*"Set-up," meaning a treat, or meaning ginger ale or water brought by a waiter for a chaser, has been prevalent since the 1870's. It appeared first, in both senses, in American saloons. The free lunch was a "set-up." "Set-up" in the sense of an artful ruse, subterfuge, or trick came from the billiard parlor.

hard ball is caught or carried in the modern game of lacrosse. And there is reason to assume the Indians played a version of the school boy game called "Fox-In-Wall," the game in which live tackling appears sometime.

Canada introduced rugby to America in 1874, when McGill University played a match with Harvard. Undoubtedly, this rugby match was responsible for the football game played between Rutgers and Princeton five years later. Then around 1950 Canada picked up a slightly modified game of football from America. In Canadian football the field is 110 yards long and 65 yards wide, adding to forward passing. The game is scored the same as American football, save for the "rough point," one score when a player is tackled in the end-zone (like a safety in the American game) and one point when the ball is kicked over the end zone (a touchback in America).

The Canadian game is played with twelve men to a side, and the extra man is designated as the "flying wing." There are only three downs in Canada, and although the names of the backfield men are the same as in the American game, in Canada the center is called "snap," the guards are "inside," the tackles are "middle," and the ends are "outside."

"Baseball," "America's national pastime," evolved from the British games of cricket and rounders, and there is much tempestuous contradiction to the assertion that Abner Doubleday originated the sport at Cooperstown, New York in 1839. (All the same "baseball" had its official centennial in 1939.) Some form of "baseball" was played in the northeast states prior to the Civil War, and it was extremely popular with Union soldiers during the four years of fighting. It is highly likely that the first baseball played in the south took place at Hilton Head Island, S.C. by federal occupation troops. And Sherman's troops appear to have played the game in and around Raleigh, N.C., following the surrender of the Confederate forces commanded by Joseph E. Johnston.

Alexander Carthwright and Henry Chadwick, about whom very little else is known, are credited with the development of baseball in the pre-Civil War era. It is highly probable that the form of "baseball" played in the northeast states before the war was what is known as "One-eyed Cat" and by other "cat" euphemisms. This game, an improvisation, was a by-product of sparsely settled communities. It could be played with two to a side. The habitual format, home base and one other base, suggests cricket, and in the various "cat" games a runner was out if a fielder hit him with a thrown ball, between the two bases.

And, the "cats" and "baseball" may have taken off from the colonial and early republic game called "ante-over," as well as from the English sports, cricket and rounders. In ante-over, one side threw a homemade ball over a barn. The throwing side yelled "ante," and if the receiving team, on the opposite side of the barn, caught the ball on the fly, its members yelled "over."

Then the "overs" threw the ball at the "antes," "until all their chillun are dead." The game combined many of the elements of "hiding," "chase," "hare and hounds" et al. The fleers could hide in ditches or climb trees, and there are reports of games that covered several rural miles and occupied the best portion of a day.

The efforts of the aforementioned Carthwright and Chadwick culminated in 1857 in a national baseball association, even if the association was loosely effected. The National League was formed in 1876, and in 1900 the Western League, a minor league, became the American League. By 1903 the American League was the second big league, officially. Both the big leagues began night baseball in 1935.

James Naismith (1861-1939) started basketball in Springfield, Mass. in 1891, as an adjunct to a physical education program for business men in the Springfield Y.M.C.A. According to the accepted story, Naismith put up his peach baskets because his adult pupils didn't respond to volley ball.

"Soccer," or Association Football, a kicking game, derived its name from an abbreviation of "association." Played on a field 120 by 75 yards, soccer seems the most popular of international sports, and in the 1970's the game obtained a strong toe-hold in many American high schools. For many centuries, "soccer" was not distinguished from "football." Differentiation occurred in 1823 with the advent of Rugby Football, a game that combined passing with kicking.

"Tennis," a French game, is from *tenez*, meaning "take it" or "play." As early as 1742 the French, playfully, adopted *l'oeuf*, their word for egg, to represent zero, or "no score," in tennis. When "tennis" worked its way across the Channel, British ears heard *l'oeuf* as "love." "Racket," through the Arabic *ruhah*, comes from the French *raquette*, the palm of the hand.

"Golf," from the Dutch *kolf*, or club, defies the attempts of historians to begin its chronology. The first written reference seems to have appeared in 1457 when James II's Scottish Parliament enacted a decree that stipulated the "fute-ball and golfe be utterly cryed down." This decree was passed to enhance the national defense. Scotsmen were neglecting their archery practice to play "golfe."

This official decree was repeated in 1471 and in 1491, although many of the Scottish sovereigns were devotees of the game. Mary, Queen of Scots, early exponent of distaff golf, played at St. Andrews. Golf may have stemmed from the Roman field game called *paganus*, literally, "countrymen," played with a club and a ball stuffed with feathers. Several historians think the Roman legions brought their *paganics*, or golf equipment, to the British Isles and to parts of Europe.*

The Netherlands' *hetkolven* was played along roadways,

---

*There is this ironic commentary. Golf was so compulsive in 15th-century Scotland it menaced the national defense. Then in America, up through the first three decades of the 20th century, golf was equated with money and privilege. Sarah Cleghorn's brief "The Golf Links" is one of the supreme strokes of irony of the 1920's:

The golf links lie so near the mill
That almost every day
The laboring children can look out
And see the men at play.

and, there is the persistent, sensible, but un-supported theory that roadway, or "overland," golf, evolved from the boys' marble game called "span and shoot." This form of marbles was played by many rural and small-town boys until well within the 20th century, because it provided entertainment all the way to the schoolhouse and back. The parallel with golf becomes more acute when one remembers that the dirt road and the byways along the schoolhouse route contained holes, dug intermittently.

Dutch immigrants brought *hetkolven* to New York state, and by 1659 Fort Orange, N.Y. passed an ordinance prohibiting games of *hetkolven* in the public streets. Other villages forbade the game on the Sabbath. And some of the first Dutch settlers played golf on ice during winter, with a puck. Although newspapers of the 18th century contain several loose allusions to "golf societies" and to "golf clubs," Foxburg (N.Y.) appears to be the oldest in continuous use, having been established officially in 1886. Albeit, public notices circulated in Charleston, S.C. in 1786 tell of plans to organize a "golf society, for ladies and gentlemen." In the absence of concrete evidence, one assumes that a golf club, in the sense of links and social foregathering, did occur in or around Charleston, S.C. at this time. No written records survive, and one assumes that congenial men and women hit a ball along the beaches and across open, rolling meadowland. The club used was a stout stick, with a knob, and although the ball may have been made of gutta percha, it was more likely to have been a piece of leather stuffed with feathers. That early golf was played along the seaside is attested to by the irrepressible use of the word "links" to mean a golf course. "Links," from the Anglo–Saxon *hline*, ridge or hill, meant sandy stretches along the seashore that "linked" with arable lands along the interior.

"Croquet" perhaps, from the French *crochet* or hook, the French *croc*, a shepherd's staff, was enormously popular in

Ireland early in the 18th century. The "wicket" from the French *guichet*, appears in the game called cricket. Originally, wicket was a small gate or door, usually placed near, or forming a part of a larger gate or door. In "croquet" the wooden balls must pass through the wickets. In cricket, the wicket is one of the two frameworks at which the ball is bowled. The cricket wicket consists of three vertical stumps stuck in the ground less than a ball's length apart, and spaced by two balls placed in grooves atop them.

The "domino" theory in international politics comes, of course from the ancient game played with 28 small pieces, one with a blank face and one with pips or dots. The original "domino," via the Latin *dominus*, master, was a hood worn by the canon of a cathedral. The most common version of "dominoes" is the draw-game played by two or four who pick a specified number of face-down dominoes. The underlying principle is to match the number on one domino half with that of the half already played on the table.

"Domino," the priest's hooded cloak, came to mean a mask over the top portion of the face, which the hood might hide. (Hence the popular phrase "to hoodwink" someone.) The French *Faire domino*, to put on the hood or cap, was spoken when the last domino was put down, and the game was won, evolved into the name of the game, itself.

One of the first references to "wrestling" appears in Greek mythology, with the appearance of Antaeous, the gigantic wrestler, whose strength was invincible so long as he touched the earth. But, undoubtedly, some form of rough-hewn catch-as-catch-can pre-dates recorded history. Genesis (32:22), speaking of Jacob's sojourn in Jabbok, tells how Jacob wrestled a "man." (In the Sunday school lessons of yesterday Jacob always "wrestled an angel," and the assumption, of course, is that the angel took the shape of a man for the bout with Jacob.) Jacob won the match, and, as a bonus, his adversary gave him a blessing which entailed the change from

Jacob to Israel.

Hand, or Indian, wrestling, which reappeared as a popular barroom and tavern contest during the 1960's and the 1970's, was as popular in colonial America as it was likely to be bestial. Local champions were pitted against each other, for comparably large side-bets, in taverns and ordinaries. Often, the loser's arm came down on a lighted candle stub, red coals, or a mass of broken glass.

"Wrist," vital in all "wrestling," is from the Anglo-Saxon *wrest*, to turn. In addition to the *hand-wrist*, there was a *foot-wrist*, until it was replaced by "ankle," from the Anglo-Saxon *ancleow*. The English word, "wrest," is the Anglo-Saxon *wrest*. However, our English word, "wrestling," has a direct counterpart in the Anglo-Saxon *wraestlian*, meaning a hand-to-hand contest between two unarmed men.

Next to running for speed and endurance, "wrestling" may be the oldest sport, and in view of today's preposterous frauds as shown regularly on television, the ancient Greeks brought ineffable grace to "wrestling," the object being to launch every attack with the poetry of movement. Even so, "wrestling" was arduous and debilitating. Plutarch says it was the hardest from of known athletics.

"Boxing," from the Middle English *box*, to slap or to strike, extremely popular among the Greeks and Romans, was done with the fists armed with strips of rawhide, the *cestu* often knotted and loaded with lead or iron.

Rules to govern "boxing" were developed in Europe early in the 18th century, and "boxing" became a "science," if a lethal science. In 1719 the prowess of a giant named Figg was so celebrated he was painted by the great realist, Hogarth, and Figg's "science" was perpetuated by Broughton, long-time champion of the British Isles. By the middle of the 18th century, matches, "prize fights," were staged regularly, and a championship belt became a portion of the prize. (These belts go back to the time of the Seige of Troy. Homer, in describing the games at the funeral of Patroclus, mentions such a belt.)

Thin, hand-gloves came in around 1860, and with the turn from bare fists, the new rules formulated by the Marquis of Queensbury were adopted internationally. Obviously, the modern roped "ring" is square. The term comes from the days when matches, often arranged spontaneously, took place outdoors. A ring was drawn in the dirt with a stick, and the spectators circled around the ring.

"Backgammon," known as "tables" in the British Isles, was popular among the early Greeks and Romans, and the game pervaded Europe after the 10th century A.D. This game, a combination of skill and chance, is played by two opponents on a specially marked board, divided into two tables, each of which has twelve alternately colored points or spaces. The moves are dictated by throws of the dice, and the object, of course, is to remove one's disks.

"Backgammon" boards, with dice and the pieces, have been found in Babylonian excavations, and "parcheesi," trademark for a board game, probably began in India, from "backgammon," with four players instead of two players. "Parcheesi," an outgrowth of the Indian game *parchisi*, is closely related to "backgammon." "Gammon," from the Old French *gambon*, through the French *gambe* meaning leg, is an old word for a filtch of salted and smoked, or dried, bacon, and until fairly recently "gammon" had considerable use in the American south to mean the lower end of a side of bacon. (The southern housewife would say, "I cooked the greens with a gammon.") "Gammon" in the sense of fastening a bowsprit to the stem of a boat, or ship, by lashings of rope or chain, is a fairly persistent nautical term. And as a colloquial word, "gammon is synonymous with chicanery or humbuggery, in the context of talk intended to confuse or to deceive. "To talk gammon" and "to influence with gammon" were heard in street conversations until fairly recently. And the person who made a habit of such talk was a "gammoner."

The gambling game, "blackjack," evolving from "black" and "knave" (jack), is known also as "21," the object of the game being to come closer to 21 than the dealer. To have "blackjack," itself, is to draw with one's first two cards any combination of an ace (11) and any face-card (10).

"Rook," almost axiomatic as a parlor game prior to auction bridge and still played by many children, takes its name from the crowlike, Old World bird, *corvus frugilegus*. In this points-game, the four suits are green, red, black, and yellow, with cards numbered 1 through 14 for each color. Many decks are stripped from 1—4, a 5 is five points, a ten, ten points; a 14, fifteen points; and the rook, a wild card, is 20 points.

"Rook," interchangeable with swindle, from the Middle English *rok, ruke*, through the Old English *hroc*, is the chess piece that may be moved in a straight line over any empty squares in a rank or file. This is called "castle," also, apparently, from the Arabic *rukh*. A man-made habitat for almost any birds is called a "rookery," and the crowded tenement is a "rookers" in British and in American English.

The "rookie," in military and in baseball parlance, was produced by the alliteration of "recruit," influenced by "rook."

"Author," from the Middle English *autoru*, through the Old French *autor*, from the Latin *auctor*, or creator, is responsible for "authors," ("Give me all your Longfellows") played in insular America by thousands of children, for pleasure and as an adjunct of learning.

Since no precise history of the chronology of "authors" appears to be available, there is the interesting speculation that this parlor game was an outgrowth of the picture-cards that came with many brands of cigarettes, from the early 1900's until World War I, and into the 1920's, among certain specific brands.

The first cigarette packages, prior to the advent of cellophane, were flimsy, highly susceptible to perspiration moisture, and to handling. The opened package became shapeless, quickly, and the cigarettes ("coffin tacks") were likely to be misshapen or crushed. The late James B. Duke, head of the giant American Tobacco Company, is credited with suggesting that his brands be bolstered with a card, inside the package.

Then Duke decided he had an excellent opportunity for relatively free advertising by putting colored pictures on the pieces of paste-board. Soon the cigarette packages of America were stuffed with colored photographs of famous authors, athletes, scenic wonders, wild life, and other indigenous subjects. Boys, semi-professional collectors of a specific series of the cigarette cards, hung around drug stores and tobacco stores to cadge the bright pictures from smokers.

Accelerated swapping occurred when a collector needed specific items to complete a collection. Thus, a boy would say to his friend, "I'll swap you two Ty Cobbs for one James Fenimore Cooper." Some of these collections were extensive, and many boys sought reference books to bone up on the subjects in their special collections.*

The "rail-bird," the "coffee houser," must have been around since the era of knuckle-bones. For the past half-century, the old word "kibitzer" has encompassed most of the meddlesome busy-bodies who give unasked for advice to card players, to people playing various games. "Kibitzer"

*I remember one such collection was exhibited in the classroom when this author was in the fifth grade. Photographs of authors were arranged on a large piece of thick paper that was fastened to boards. In what may have been the first example of "Show and Tell" in the public schools of North Carolina, the small lecturer pointed to the likenesses of Emerson, Carlyle, Mark Twain et al, giving the dates of each author depicted, plus a brief bibliography.

derives through Yiddish, the street gamin of all spoken languages, from the colloquial German *kiebitz,* the name of the Old World bird that is known in English, variously, as "green plover," "lapwing," and "peewit."

European farmers say this bird not only stands around fields to watch them work, but actually gives other birds a shrill warning upon the approach of hunters. In the 16th century German card-players applied this derision to spectators who annoyed them with incessant chatter. It is alleged that *kiebitz* was imitative in its origin, suggested by the bird's monotonous, characteristic cry.

In the American south, and in North Carolina, especially, no synonym for card or pool sharp has more intransigent pertinence than "lamp-chimney salesman." Throughout the 20th century "lamp-chimney salesman" has attached millions of times to the stranger who feigns total ignorance of pool, poker, or whatever, and wins the money. The "lamp-chimney salesman" attained celebrity, grudging admiration intermingled with opprobrium, in the exalted era of county fairs, when every small county seat town, or market town, was quick with human traffic.

The "lamp-chimney salesman" pretended to be a farmer, and often he effected overalls. If the weather was hot, he was certain to wear a wool hat, and if the weather was cool, he was sure to wear a "plow-boy's straw hat," the kind that used to sell for fifty cents at "time" stores. He rolled his cigarettes, and he carried his change in an old Bull Durham sack. He had memorized local news from the weekly paper, and as he discoursed about recent births and deaths, he chewed on a long broomstraw.

It is generally conceded that at some point in history such a semi-professional, itinerant gambler really did sell lamp-chimneys. But the sobriquet fastened in southern mores, and even today the man at the country club who has an amazing run of luck in the high-low game is tagged a "lamp-chimney salesman," and usually by a friendly gambler who never saw a lamp-chimney in his life.

The southern poker player who effects the mannerisms which he thinks may devolve upon big-time gamblers in Las Vegas is often "Sam Savvy." "Savvy" was acquired by south-westerners from the Mexicans. "Do you savvy?" is equivalent to the Spanish *sabe usted*, or "do you know?" The American ranchers who first encountered *sabe* spelled and pronounced it "savvy" because in Spanish the "b" and the "v" are pronounced almost alike, and in many words are inter-changeable. When employed as a noun "savvy" means puissant mental grasp, intimate knowledge of the subject or the game at hand.

Hardly any gaming phrase for "Don't make me have bad luck" has such consistent vitality as "Don't hawk me." Many card players exude signs and portents through their very pores, and anything from a hat on a bed to a crooked picture on the wall is seen as the direct cause of a run of inferior cards. Such a victim of bizarre superstition will throw in his cards, and depart the game, adding, "There's no point in my playing with the 'hawk on me.' "*

"Black cat," "mo-jo," and "mouse" are interchangeable with "hawk," but in poker, dice, and blackjack parlance the swift bird of prey has almost devoured the other three. One supposes this axiomatic word arose from the predatory nature of the hawk. The Anglo-Saxon for "hawk," *hafoc*, was cried by Saxons hunting the bird.

"Cry havoc and let slip the dogs of war," which appears in Shakespeare's *Julius Caesar*, implies to moderns that there is fearful carnage ahead. But this meant "plunder" to

---

*Here and there in the southern states, some gambler, relatively shorn of superstition, is said to have a hawk stuffed to be displayed when he is host for the poker game, and the author has actually seen a woodcarving of a hawk, perched much as the raven in Poe's poem.

Shakespeare and to his auditors. In Shakespeare's time the phrase meant that the battle was won and that the victors were about to be rewarded with spoils, with the "plunder." "Havoc" is from the Old French *havot*, plunder, of Teutonic origin.

Gamblers ascribe "luck," from the Middle Dutch *gheluc*, to everything from finding a pin to the phases of the moon, and the causes of bad luck are as numerous. However, in general, when a gambler says, or feels, his luck is changing, he has in mind the essence of the late Ogden Nash's observation:

You can take it as understood
That your luck changes only if it's good.

The author knows a diabetic poker player, a man who has taken large injections of insulin daily for many years, who drank, inadvertently, a cup of lavishly sugared coffee just prior to a five-card stud game in which he had an extraordinary run of luck. During the progess of the lengthy game, he drank cup after cup of heavily sweetened coffee, and he stuck with this potation until his luck changed. He ascribed the poor run of cards to his wife's throwing away the pair of dirty socks he had worn in every game while he was on his winning streak.

When a southern gambler has an uncanny streak of good luck, his associates chant, "Let's blackball him," "Let's icehouse him," or "Let's sabotage his charms." These jocular threats are implemented when the dealer pretends "to deal around" the "hot player," when the mess attendant is instructed to "put salt petre in his drink." The ancient Greeks had an urn to represent each candidate, and the voter tossed a white pebble into the urn to approve. The voter registered disapproval by tossing in a black pebble. In modern society the rule is followed in secret organizations to the extent that a single antagonistic vote constitutes rejection, the "black ball."

"Ice-house him" is an obvious reference to the family ice-house maintained here and there prior to electrical refrigeration. In this connection many youngsters ask why ponds used to freeze over but do not always freeze over solidly today, even amid such low temperatures as were commonplace in the harrowing winter of 1976-1977. The people who had family ice-houses maintained special ice-ponds, small bodies of shallow, relatively still water, saturated with grass and vegetation. Such bodies of water were designed to freeze.

The ice was cut with long saws, to be carried by wagon or sled to the ice-house. The ice-house was built under-ground, much in the manner of the infamous World War I dug-out. One glass-door, a bleary-eyed Cyclops, was above ground. The ice was packed with dirt and sawdust until summertime.

Most gamblers who enjoy hot streaks are vigilant to eat, dress, walk, talk, and act precisely as they did when the streak commenced. Their greatest horror is to deviate, even by a tiny fraction, from their established order. Thus, to hide the lucky man's tie, or to hand him his soft drink before he is handed his sandwich, is to "sabotage his charms." A "sabot" is a wooden shoe made of a single piece of wood and hollowed out to fit the foot. Many French and Flemish peasants used to wear sabots because they were inexpensive and because they protected the feet in wet weather. "Sabotage," "sab-o-tazh," acquired its destructive meaning in the early days of French industrial machinery. Frenchmen who wanted a respite from toil, and those with a grudge against management, would kick their wooden shoes into the machinery, foul it, and pretend this was an industrial accident.

"Sabotage" was first defined in 1887. It was recognized as a weapon or organized labor when the General Confederation of Labor, in France, took official cognizance of the term. Shortly afterward, 'the Industrial Workers of the World, the famous "Wobblies," recognized "sabotage as an instrument of industrial warfare as effective as the strike."

"Sabotage" attained universal popularity during World War II to describe the actions of resistance groups who blew up bridges, derailed trains, and destroyed ammunition dumps, and the like. Earlier in France, the people who wore wooden shoes were called *sabotiers* but during World War II the resistance agents who engaged in sundry demolition were called *saboteurs*, "sab-o-ters."

The unsuccessful or inept athlete, coach, or manager is fired, and he usually vanishes into limbo. Conversely, in the gambling fraternity, the habitual loser, the unlucky, compulsive gambler, has all sorts of local and national legendry fastened to him. Indeed, in the long haul the flamboyant tales of his prodigious ineptitude and hard luck attain wider, longer celebrations than the stories of the ultra successful gamblers who "bore with a big auger." There was the farmer who owned two valuable plantations. He lost one plantation trying to catch an inside straight, and he lost the other plantation when he caught an inside straight. Most of these tales are too ribald for printed recitation, but one of the more self-effacing of the so-called smutty stories involves the gambler who spent his hours away from the tables, the ball game, and the race track at the bar of the same saloon.

His bad luck and poor judgment were such factors in the daily mores of the saloon that everytime he said "I'll bet" a dozen takers crowded the bar to ask, "How much?" Only rarely did he state the nature of his projected bet. If he said, "I'll bet ten bills," he was covered before he stated the condition.

In desperation he sought medical help, thinking an explanation might lie within his body or personality. After a lengthy examination the doctor said, "You are perfectly healthy and sane, save for one small physical irregularity. You have three testicles."

Aglow with the prospect of instant wealth, he returned to the saloon, skipping and whistling. With supreme confidence he snapped, "I'll bet a grand," and the thousand dollar bet was covered immediately. One fellow asked, yawning, "What's the bet?"

Still beaming, he said, "I'll bet that between us the bartender and I have five balls."

The bar-tender almost jerked him over the bar as he rasped in the man's ear, "Well, by God, you better have four."

"St. Louis," "Louie," and "Brownie" are generic names for chronic losers in many small towns, wherein each gambler knows his associates fairly intimately. This derisive designation stems from the days when the St. Louis Browns were in the big league, when their hapless play on the diamond fetched the perennial jingle:

First in shoes,
First in booze,
And last in the American League.

The player who calls with chronically weak cards is tagged "Sanka," for abundantly clear reasons; and if few inveterate gamblers have the time or inclination to read poetry, "namby-pamby," and "namby" and "pamby" attach to puerile players and to "klutz" cards. However, those who say the words most often wouldn't stop playing long enough to hear the brief explanation of the phrase.

"Namby-pamby," a jingle of Henry Carey's, published in 1729, goes:

Let the verse the subject fit,
Little subject, little wit,
Namby-pamby is your guide.

Carey's caustic ditty arose from the fact that Ambrose Phillips, the great Alexander Pope, and Carey were all writing pastoral poetry simultaneously. Ironically, but, perhaps, typically, the public preferred Phillips' sacchrine mouthings, and Carey dubbed him "Namby-Pamby." Pope picked up on this and he used Phillip's moniker in *The Duncaid*, published in 1733.

It is fortuante for Pope's estimable reputation the *The Duncaid* is buried with the woodbine, but "Namby-Pamby" ingratiated with the public and it endures in all sorts of daily speech long, long after those pastorals Carey and Phillips wrote are ashes.

Carey has achieved considerable semi-anonymous tenacity. He wrote "Sally In Our Alley," still heard and sung intermittently today, and several historians believe Carey wrote "God Save the King." And he is inevitable via his marvelous coinage, "Namby-Pamby."

For many generations thousands of card players have declared, especially after a night of big winnings, "Well, I'll be buried in the Potter's Field, surely." Apparently, the original "Potter's Field" was bought with the thirty pieces of silver that Judas threw away before he hanged himself (Matthew 27:7). The name arises from the fact, or legend, that ancient potters obtained their clay in these burying grounds.

This type of free cemetery became "God's Acre" later on.

Such burying grounds were supposed to provide graves for those who died far from home, and, more especially, itinerant mendicants.*

If no single irrefutable definition for "poker" is extant, several reputable scholars ascribe it to the Middle English *poke* from the Old French *poque*, a sack. It has meant a "beggar's wallet," particularly in Scotland, and in archaic Scottish dialect, a *poke* was a pocket. A reasonable assumption is that "poker," perhaps, by some hobson-jobson process, came to mean the card game from *poke*, in the sense of a beggar's wallet, plus *poke* in the sense of jabbing, searching, and investigating.

The non-poker connotations of "fourflusher" exceed, vastly, the gambling uses of the old word. Today, "fourflusher," to mean a cheat or a braggart, is widely used by thousands of people who don't play poker. (At cards today, the old-time "fourflusher" would have a "busted flush," if called, and if not called, he would have "run a sandy," won the pot without a winning hand.)

The word originated in draw-poker with the man, trying to get five cards of the same suit, who ended up with four cards of the same suit and one card of a different suit. That used to be called a "bobtailed flush." Although betting on a bobtailed flush is entirely legitimate, his bluff, his "four card flush" is exposed if he is called.

The man who succeeds with the four-card flush, or with any other sort of bluff, acts good-naturedly on that distortion of the Golden Rule which E.N. Westcott put in his once-celebrated novel *David Harum*: "Do unto the feller the way

---

*In the old west such impoverished itinerants were buried on various Boot Hills (from the feeling that one who died with his boots on must lead a fuller more virile life).

he'd like to do unto you an' do it fust." (In the same novel, Westcott (1846-1898) says, "They say a reasonable number of fleas is good fer a dog—keeps his mind from broodin' over bein' a dog.")

It is palpably obvious that many insatiable gamblers talk against their luck,* talk down their chances of making a specific hand. They do this on the theory that "talking the luck down" actually enhances the chances of good luck. In this reverse psychology, they emulate, subconsciously, the Jews who are meticulously careful to placate the Evil-Eye. (The old-time small-town Jewish dry goods merchant, an undeviating devotee of reverse psychology, said of himself that if he sold shrouds, people would stop dying; if he sold umbrellas, drought would be interminable; if he were a druggist, no one would ever get sick. And he spoke these baleful lamentations most profusely and tearfully when the cash register was dingling with merry regularity.)

Birds sing for other mortals, but for the losing gambler they exist solely to bombard his head with "bird do's" (excrement). And if he wins a hefty pot, his apologetic explanation usually goes this way: "Well, even a blind hog finds an acorn once on a blue moon."

Canny gamblers say that one can tell a smart poker player from a poor one because the smart man isn't reluctant to cash in when his luck is bad. Conversely, the inferior player, sure his luck will change, stays in the game and loses much more. And the same seventh or eighth sense is said to apply to knowing when to stop when he is improving every hand. Indeed, in more than three hundred years few observers have improved upon the dictum written by George Herbert

---

*On the theory that whoever or whatever controls events is essentially malignant and will do the opposite of what one asks.

(1593-1633), in a poem called, peculiarly enough, "The Church-Porch":

If yet thou love a game at so dear a rate,
Learn this, that hath old gamesters dearly cost:
Dost lost? rise up: dost win? rise in that state.
Who strive to sit out losing hands are lost.

In those poker games that have gone on, without interruption since Lord Cornwallis, or Nathaniel Greene, or Daniel Morgan rode through town almost two centuries ago, it is as banal to say that whiskey was present as to say the cow gave milk and not Pepsi-Cola. George Ade (1866-1944), author of those hilarious and incisive parables, must have been writing from the literal, bitter experience of hangover from bad cards and bottle in his "Remorse," published in 1903 but equally as pertinent in 1976:

A dark brown taste, a burning thirst,
A head that's ready to split and burst...
No time for mirth, no time for laughter—
The cold gray dawn of the morning after.

The word "fan" encompasses the devotees of dozens of games, although it is associated with the militantly loyal adherent of a specific team or sport. If the "fan," in normal context, is a vociferous spectator, an alumnus or an aficionada, the word has hourly applications to card players and to others who gave unstinted time and patronage to a game.

In the sense of an enthusiast, and this carries over to avocations and entertainments, "fan" is put down frequently as a contraction of "fanatic." But the theory, often advanced, that "fan" derives from the verb "to fan," to blow upon or to stimulate to action, seems irrelevant to most philologists.

"Fan" came into general use sometime after 1880. Chris Van der Ahe, owner of the St. Louis Browns, stated that one Charles Haas "is the greatest baseball fanatic I have ever seen."

Sports writers began calling baseball enthusiasts "fanatics," and around 1890 this was shortened to "fan" by headline writers. (At the outset, headline writers spelled the word "fann.") Curiously enough, several centuries ago "fan" was often used as a contraction for "fanatic," in the literal meaning of the term.

There seems to be no substance to the theory, advanced sporadically, that "fan" comes from "fan" in the sense of striking out at the plate. However, one minor theory is worthy of enumeration: This entry appears in Francis Grose's *Dictionary of the Vulgar Tongue as Revised and Corrected by Pierce Egan*, published in 1823: " 'The Fancy': one of the fancy is a sporting character that is either attached to pigeons, dog-fighting, boxing etc." For a long time in the British Isles, and for a considerable period in the United States, "fancy" was applied to prize-fighting enthusiasts. However, no known etymologist appears to give credence to the theory that "fancy" was borrowed by baseball, and shortened to "fance" and to "fan."

On occasion, the most fervent fan may be taken in as a "patsy," a "pigeon," a "mark," or as a "sucker."* ("Cedar-bird," widely heard a generation ago to mean a dupe, has almost disappeared, as has "Sally" or "Sally Ann." The latter two, vibrant with hoboes as early as the First World War, emerged from "Sal," verbal abbreviation of Salvation (Army). In hobo parlance "Sally Ann" meant any refuge where food, shelter, or clothing was obtained free of charge. Perhaps, because the hobo was a helpless mendicant, the gullible card or horse-player was tagged as "Sally Ann," too.)

"Sucker" ties to what the French call an April fish, *un*

---

*Some students question P.T. Barnum's saying "There's a sucker born every minute." "Sucker," meaning a dupe, wasn't resilient until after Barnum's (1810-1891) death.

poisson d'Avril, young, inexperienced and easily caught in French rivers in early spring. This fish, a "sucker," in American English, is one of the endless examples of the April Fool. (The Scots call an April Fool a "cuckoo," and "cuckoo" has had limited use around American gaming tables.)

"Patsy," popularized as the fall guy in the late John O'Hara's *Pal Joey*, 1949, was popular on the street before 1949, often in the sense of a feckless or cowardly person. "Patzer," a notoriously inept chess player, is ascribed to Yiddish. But since there seems to be no Yiddish, German, or Hebrew word or combination to suggest "patzer," it must have been a by-product of "patsy." "Mark," an easy victim, began as a carnival word, and it was appropriated by the underworld in the same sense and to mean, also, the amount of money stolen in a robbery. ("Marker," an I.O.U. accepted as a wager, may have originated in literature originally in the stories of the late Damon Runyon.) "Pigeon" seems to have started in New Orleans, around 1885, to mean a professional gambler. By 1950 "pigeon" was an easy mark, and there may be some association with "stool-pigeon," an older term that came from the mechanical decoy used by hunters. (Curiously enough, "pigeon-eyed" meant intoxicated as early as 1740, and "Pidgeon Ey'd," in this context appeared, in the *Pennsylvania Gazette*, of Philadelphia, in an issue of 1737.)

Surprisingly enough, "the black ox is on me" is still spoken by many older card, chess, and checker players, and by assorted, venerable gamblers, to mean bad luck, bad health, misfortune, and the adversities of age. John Heywood has "The black ox has not trod on his foot" as one of his proverbs (*Proverbs*) of 1546. John Lyly's *Sapho and Phao*, written in 1591, has this sentence: "Now crow's foot is on her eye, and the black ox hath trod on her foot."

This doleful phrase is an allusion to the black cattle sacrificed by pagans to deities such as Pluto, lord of the nether world and its supreme judge. (White cattle were sacrificed to Jupiter.) The altar in Rome on which black cattle were sacrificed was twenty feet below ground, and it was never exposed, save when cattle were being sacrificed.

Gertrude Atherton's best-selling novel of 1923, *Black Oxen*, took its title from a line in William Butler Yeats' "Countess Cathleen": "The years like great black oxen tread the world." But among the Arabs, the "black camel," unknown to American gamblers, apparently, is the symbol for violent death and bad luck.

When a poker player tosses in a second-best hand, in face of a powerful hand, he may say, "That's strong medicine," from the Latin *medicina*, from *medicus*, healer, and the man who has good cards consistently is referred to as "strong medicine," probably from the accumulated effects of sage-brush and Indian literature. And a strong hand is a "pill," hard to swallow, and the fellow who seems always to catch out in the clutch is a "pill," and "a damned bitter pill."

(The first patented pills, "Lee's Windham Pills" and "Lee's New London Bilious Pills," were marketed in 1796 by Samuel Lee, Jr., of Connecticut. Lee obtained a patent on April 30, 1796 for a "compound of bilious pills." However, the first compressed pills to be manufactured were made by Jacob Dunton, wholesale druggist of Philadelphia, during 1863-1864. Dunton's pills were simple chemicals, such as potassium chlorate and ammonium chloride. Dunton seems to have sold all of his wares to druggists, some of whom packaged the chemicals.)

The big winner who leaves a game long before the session ends probably says he has to attend a funeral or sit up with a sick friend, and the losers probably respond, "See you in the funny papers." The first newspaper comic strip, called "Hogan's Alley," depicted a humorous set of characters. This was drawn by Richard F. Outcault for the New York *World*, in 1893. On November 18, 1894 the first of Outcault's six-box cartoon series, "The Origin of a New Species," appeared in the *World*. A little later this six-box series was called "The Yellow Kid," the first successful newspaper colored section.

"Put it in shorthand," snarled by dyspeptic losers, is synonymous with the ubiquitous, "The winners tell jokes and the losers yell, 'Deal, damn you, deal.' " Although many people assume shorthand is a product of modern business accelerations, types of abbreviated writings go back to antiquity. Early shorthand is related closely to paleography, and many antiquarians have tried to tie shorthand to hieroglyphics, to assert that it was used by the Egyptians, Hebrews, and Persians a thousand years before the birth of Jesus.

And lectures were taken down in abbreviated writings, as were the poems chanted at the Phythean, Nemeon, and Olympic Games. Specimens of *notae*, Greek shorthand, are to be found in the Vatican Library, in the British Museum, and at the Bibliotheque Nationale, in Patis. Tiro, the brilliant freedman, Cicero's amanuensis, was heralded for his speed in abbreviated writing, and *Notae Tironianae* became the official designation for shorthand. Plutarch, in his *Life of Cato, the Younger* tells how Cicero distributed *notari* throughout the Senate Building to record the speeches of Caesar and Cato, on the memorable occasion of the vote on Cataline.

Some scholars assume that St. Paul dictated some of his *Epistles*, notably to the Colossians, with Tychicus acting as shorthand expert and with Onesimis as transcriber.

The first "modern" shorthand book, published in England in 1588, was dedicated to Queen Elizabeth by the author, Dr. Timothy Bright. Young Charles Dickens, soon to captivate his fellow countrymen with *Sketches by Boz,* and with the *Pickwick Papers*, also by "Boz," began as an expert shorthand reporter in Parliament.

PART TWELVE
MINOR PROGRAM NOTES ON
INDIGENOUS AMERICAN MUSIC

"Untwisted all the chains that tie
The hidden soul of harmany."

John Milton, from "L'Allegro."

"Hell is full of musical amateurs."

Bernard Shaw, from *Man and Superman.*

"If music be the food of love, play on;
Give me excess of it, that surfeiting,
The appetite may sicken, and so die."

Shakespeare, from *Twelfth Night.*

"Some to the church repair,
Not for the doctrine, but the music there."

Alexander Pope, from *An Essay on Criticism.*

"Wagner's music is better than it sounds."

Attributed to Mark Twain and to Bill Nye.

"The Most High has a decided taste for vocal music, provided it be lugubrious and gloomy enough."

Voltaire (Francois Marie Arouet) from *Philosophical Dictionary*.

"Music is love in search of a word."

Sidney Lanier, spoken to an interviewer and put into a letter of 1878.

MINOR PROGRAM NOTES ON INDIGENOUS
AMERICAN MUSIC

Joseph Addison, in "Song For St. Cecilia's Day," leaves an enviable nosegay: "Music, the greatest good that mortals know,/And all of heaven we have below." Albeit, Vachel Lindsay must have been closer to the mark with this cursory summary in two of his gallivanting lines from "General Booth Enters Heaven": "The banjos rattled, and the tambourines/ Jing-jing-jingled in the hands of Queens."

The progressive turn in the 1970's to nostalgia (New Latin translation of the German *Heinweh*, homesickness, the Greek *nostos*, a return) has revitalized extensive interest in several prominent forms of indigenous American music (Latin *musica*, from the Greek *mousike,* or the art of the muses.) This infectious revival, a source of effervescence to older people, and an exciting, new experience for younger people who cut their teeth on rock and blue grass, focuses on "ragtime," the "blues," and "jazz," principally.

"Ragtime," tagged "the new music" at its incubation, originated in New Orleans, and although what we call "ragtime" was really "jazz," this designation followed "ragtime" by several years. There are palpably obvious, fundamental reasons to explain the advent of the new music in New Orleans: There was intimate contact with the African bamboula, and Sunday dancing, prohibited almost everywhere else by blue laws, was vibrant at New Orlean's Place Congo, and elsewhere.

Prostitution, always licensed, was concentrated after 1897 in Storyville, New Orlean's rambunctious, free-swinging red-light district, the apex of minor vice and the new, febrile music. Liberated blacks, seeking paying employment and new homes, found semi-social acceptance in New Orleans that was wanting in other major American cities of that era. (In New Orleans venerable grandees and young chevaliers consorted openly with their quadroon paramours.)

The music of brass bands, indelible in the city's day-to-day mores, was axiomatic at funerals, weddings, carnivals (such as Mardi Gras), political and lodge parades, on riverboats, and at all holiday celebrations. And, perhaps, more important than all else, New Orleans was a center for the manufacture of wind instruments, the first that most of the recently-freed blacks had ever seen, and these clarinets and saxaphones were readily available at fairly inexpensive prices.

Wind instruments brought much wider gratification to blacks than they had acquired previously from spontaneous work-songs or from banjos and bones. Fortunately for American artistry, few learned to read music. Expertise was obtained by constant experimentation which culminated in new performance techniques and in extraordianry sounds and timbres. Not contaminated by exercise-books or by formal instruction, and dependent upon the ear and not the eye, they endowed standard melodies with the imaginative verve of their native intelligence.

Thus, the new music was redolent with color combinations, dissonances, and disjointed counterparts previously unheard, The new music exuded deviating pitch, strong syncopations, febrile emotions, and marked accentuations, all of the "low-down" throaty sounds which had stamped Negro spirituals and work-chants. Undoubtedly, this super-hyperthyroid, explosively energetic music would have been anathema in other localities, but it was the sort of robust, animalistic magic to which the denizens of Storyville's sporting-houses responded naturally and enthusiastically. And bistros such as Pete Lala's Cafe, the 101 Ranch, Lulu White's Mahogany Hall, the Tuxedo Dance Hall et al, provided part-time work for black musicians.* The musician received the stimulation

---

* But the ablest of these musicians averaged only about two dollars a night, and many doubled as barbers, shoe-shine boys, and waiters during the day.

essential to creativity, and in Storyville he was a real personage, a bona fide celebrity.

"Ragtime" and the "blues" were the basic components of New Orleans "jazz." "Ragtime," probably from "ragging," the name given the clog-dancing of the blacks, is marked by strong syncopations in the treble –playing a strong beat weakly (or the other way around), as the bass maintains a rigidly even rhythm.

Syncopation had been apparent in pre-war minstrel-show tunes such as "Old Dan Tucker" and "Zip Coon." Yet, the application of syncopation against a steady bass rhythm did not emerge until the mid-l890's. Historically, Kerry Mills' "At a Georgia Camp-Meeting," 1897, is the first published "rag."* Then in 1899 Scott Joplin's "Maple Leaf Rag" crystalized, for all time to come, the "ragtime" style. Joplin, a Negro, developed his original style while playing piano in the honky-tonks in and around St. Louis. He seems to have been discovered by a St. Louis music publisher in 1899 when he was playing piano in the Maple Leaf Club in Sedalia, a suburb of St. Louis. Joplin's first published composition, "Original Rag," came out in 1899, to be followed later the same year by "Maple Leaf Rag."

In addition to "The Entertainer," "Spaghetti Rag," and other exhilarating "rags," Joplin, often erroneously designated today as an illiterate,** wrote an instruction book, *School of Ragtime*, and in 1903, a ragtime opera, *A Guest of Honor.*

---

*Mills always said he wrote "At A Georgia Camp-Meeting" "to put an end to all damned 'coon songs.' " If so, endless, localized lyrics have been applied to the contagious music, for an assortment of pep-rallies, political bonfires and the like. With lyrics by Andrew Sterling, Mills published "Meet Me In St. Louis, Louis," in 1904, for the St. Louis' World's Fair, and "Lonesome" (1909), with lyrics by Edgar Leslie, sold a million copies of sheet music.

**The same specious charge is made, intermittently, about James A. Bland, composer of "Carry Me Back to Old Virginny," "In the Evening By the Moonlight," "Oh, Dem Golden Slippers," "Hand Me Down My Walking Cane" et al. Bland (1854-1911) graduated from Howard University. His father, also a college graduate, was the first Negro in history to serve as examiner in the U.S. Patent Office.

Almost simultaneously, Ben Harney, "ragtime professor" of New York, wrote "Mister Johnson, Turn Me Loose," "You've Been A Good Old Wagon" and other "salty dogs," and Charles Trevathan composed "May Irvin's 'Bully' Song," in "ragtime," for the great star's appearance in *Courted Into Court.*

By 1899 "ragtime" was so irrepressible, the *Musical Courier* attacked the new music in editorials, branding it "vulgar, filthy, and suggestive," calling it "the pablum of theater." However, Rupert Hughes, to attain fame and derision as George Washington's biographer, defended the new music in the *Musical Record*, in 1899: "If ragtime were called *tempo di raga* it might win honors more speedily... Ragtime will find its way gradually into the works of some genius and will thereafter be canonized."*

It was Irving Berlin (née Israel Baline, born in Russia in 1888) who endowed "ragtime" with his personal touch and enormous vitality in 1911 with "Alexander's Ragtime Band." (Berlin duplicated "Alexander's unparalleled success three years later with "Everybody's Doin' it," from the context of ragtime, probably an even better composition.)

Before 1911 was out, "Alexander" had sold a million copies of sheet music, and "ragtime" had routed the vaudeville novelty-song, the sentimental ballad, and the perennial freshet of dialect tunes. At "Alexander's" phenomenal apogee, a Chicago newspaper man, cruelly lost to posterity, wrote: "If we were John D. Rockefeller or the Bank of

---

*Hughes, uncle of Howard Hughes, was correct, essentially, in his high-blown prophecy. The "genius," George Gershwin (1898-1937) was "canonized" for "Rhapsody In Blue," performed at New York's Aeolian Hall on February 4, 1924. This first jazz concert was conducted by Paul Whiteman, and it was George Gershwin's brother, lyricist Ira, who called the revolutionary composition "Rhapsody in Blue."

England we should engage the (Chicago) Coliseum and get together a sextet including Caruso. After the sextet sang 'Alexander's Ragtime Band' about ten times we should, as a finale, have Sousa's Band march about the building tearing the melody to pieces with all sorts of variations."

Berlin returned to the composition of sentimental ballads, but "Alexander" changed American mores enormously and inexorably. Prior to 1911 American couples were quickly fatigued by such strenuous dances as the schottische, polka, and waltz. Only the young danced regularly, and they required rest between sets. However, the 2/4 and 4/4 rhythms of ragtime simplified dancing. Almost anyone who could walk could learn to dance to ragtime. And for the first time in American history, dancing was introduced in restaurants and hotels, especially during meal hours. Tea-dances, during the day or late in the afternoon, swept the nation, and the demand for after-theater dancing was so persistent the principal cities opened their first night-clubs. Several factories had dancing during the noon break, and the papers told how Mrs. John D. Rockefeller was taking lessons privately. Almost everybody was "doin' it," "it" being the one-step, two-step and the almost limitless animal dances — the fox-trot, the turkey-trot, the bunny-hug, the camel, the grizzly bear — inspired by ragtime.

The "blues," created formally and officially by W.C. Handy (1873-1958), began as a profound lament in which the wails of a lonely or disadvantaged black sang the cruel life of an entire race. The "blues" yet uncoined, followed the Civil War, as itinerant blacks sang laments, with improvised lyrics, on street corners and in saloons. The subject, almost inevitably, was oppression or sadism by white bosses, a two-timing sweetheart, and financial disaster.

The lyric usually was improvised; and by Handy it was constructed from three-line stanzas, with the second line repeating the first to enunciate and to dramatize the plight of the singer; and many were in the classical iambic pentameter pattern. The melody spread itself over twelve bars, composed of three four-bar phrases. Handy added the flatting of the third and seventh steps of the diatonic major scale, subsequently called the "blue-note." It was the astringent dissonances that came in when the accompaniment provided a harmony shorn of blue notes, "breaks" in the melody, which allowed the singer to exclaim "Oh Lordy," and the like, which permitted the New Orleans musician to embellish the melody with fascinating figurations.

Handy, a minister's son of Florence, Alabama, became a teen-age virtuoso with a trumpet which he bought from a traveling circus musician, for a dollar. He joined a circus band, almost starved in St. Louis, until, in 1896, he became chief cornetist for Mahara's Minstrels. After 1903 he organized a jazz band which toured the small towns of Mississippi.

His first "blues" tune was a campaign song for Edward Crump, long a legend in Tennessee politics. In 1909, Crump, known as the "Red Snapper," and more a power in Memphis and in Shelby County than Richard Daley was in Chicago and in Cook County, ran for mayor of Memphis, on a reform platform, ironically enough. One of Crump's most formidable planks was to rid Memphis of panderers, known locally as "easy-riders."

Handy's blues tune, "Mr. Crump," proclaimed, "Mr. Crump don't 'low no easy-riders here." In 1912 Handy published "Mr. Crump" as "The Memphis Blues." With Crump ensconced as mayor, Handy refurbished the lyrics somewhat: "I don't care what Mr. Crump don't low/Go get me an easy-rider anyhow." A shrewd New York publisher bought the song for fifty dollars and it was reissued in 1913 with new lyrics.

Since Handy received nothing from the prodigious sale of the sheet music, he rented a room on Beale Street. In his autobiography *Father of the Blues*, he tells of his attempt to duplicate the national success of "The Memphis Blues": "A flood of memories filled my mind. First there was a picture I had of myself, broke, unshaven, wanting even a decent meal, and standing before the lighted saloon in St. Louis without a shirt under my frayed coat. There was also from that period (when Handy was standed with the circus band) a curious and dramatic little fragment that up till now seemed to have little or no importance. While occupied with my own miseries during the sojourn, I had seen a woman whose pain seemed even greater. She had tried to take the edge off her grief by heavy drinking, but it hadn't worked. Stumbling along the poorly lighted street, she muttered as she walked, 'My man's got a heart like a rock cast in the sea.' By the time I had finished all this heavy thinking and remembering, I had figured it was time to get something down on paper, so I wrote 'I hate to see de evenin' sun go down.' If you ever had to sleep on the cobbles down by the river in St. Louis you'll understand the complaint.' "

Thus was born the words and music of "The St. Louis Blues," by far the best known of all "blues" tunes. But it was turned down by numerous publishers. Handy, in association with another man, formed his own company and published the classic in 1914. It would sell more phonograph records than any other piece of serious or popular music. Forty years after publication the song was earning for Handy an annual royalty of $25,000.00.

The contagion abroad has almost matched the unbounded fervor the song has induced in America. Cherished by Queen Elizabeth, her uncle, King Edward VIII, had the pipers of Scotland play it for him, and it was played at the wedding feast of Prince George of England and Princess Marina of Greece. And when the Italians under Mussolini* invaded

*"Mussolini" is derived from the same source as "muslin." Marco Polo

Ethiopia in 1936, "The St. Louis Blues" was the battle song of the beleaguered Ethiopians.

After 1914 Handy added to his distinguished repertoire with "The Beale Street Blues," "The John Henry Blues," "The Harlem Blues," and "The Joe Turner Blues." But "The St. Louis Blues" is his masterpiece and a continuing legacy for Americans. A public park in Memphis honors Handy's name.

"Blues" singers such as Ma Rainey and Bessie Smith carried on Handy's tradition, with both women becoming cults among their fans. It was the late Carl Van Vechten who saw Bessie Smith as "a woman cutting her heart open with a knife until it was exposed for us all to see, so that we suffered as she suffered."

Obviously, the "blues" was a basic style with the premier "jazz" men of New Orleans, with their genius for improvisation. One musician would come up with an idea, and another musician would embellish it. Then the two joined forces, each going his own way, but also with the other in mind. Then a third man would come in with an extravagant cadenza, as the whole band joined.

With the New Orleans jazzmen, improvisation was not merely high art for the soloist but for the combinations of instruments in which different rhythms were combined, conflicting tonalities assembled, and dissonant sounds blended. And this might go on for several hours at a single stretch.

There were "hot" musicians and "hot" bands in New Orleans as early as 1880, but "jazz" came of age in the 1890's with Buddy Bolden, cornetist, barber, editor of a scandal-sheet, a "devil with the ladies," and in the words of the late Louis Armstrong, "A one-man genius that was way ahead of 'em all." Contemporaries swore that the sound of Bolden's

---

wrote: "All those cloths of gold and silk which we call muslins are of the manufacture of Mosul, and all the great merchants termed Mussolini, who convey spices and drugs, in large quantities from one country to another, are from this province.

cornet could be heard "several miles away on a clear day," that the hypnotic filigrees pouring from his cornet constituted an "overtly sensual experience for many listeners."

While white musicians were in a limited minority, Jack "Papa" Laine is often referred to as the "father of white jazz." Laine, Bolden's protege, organized two extraordinary groups, the Reliance Brass Band and Jack Laine's Ragtime Band. In New Orleans competition between bands was splenetic and personal; and when two bands crossed on a street, a musical donnybrook always ensued. Kid Ory wrote: "They (the bands) used to have 'cutting contests' every time you'd get on the street."

The format was to tie the wagons holding two bands together to make them continue their playing, continue their musical free-for-all. Once when a competitor stole Buddy Bolden's crowd, the cornetist took a stand near by to play his favorites blues and rags. When the crowd flocked back, enraptured by Bolden's ingenious improvisations, he exclaimed, "All my chilluns come home."

Late in 1916, Storyville, the Xanadu of "jazz," was closed by orders from the war and navy departments in Washington. With the fabulous Storyville empire one with Nineveh and Tyre, an exodus of black musicians to Chicago occurred. And when, in 1924, Louis Armstrong formed his band to play at the Dreamland Cafe, Chicago had become the "jazz" capital of the world.

And it was in Chicago that the nation became cognizant of the word "jazz," which some etymologists assume to have come from the French word *jaser*, to prattle. Still others derive it from the minstrel-show word "jasbo," and it has been ascribed to a nebulous New Orleans musician, Charles, and that the contraction to "Chas," or "Jas" gave the name "jazz" to his magnetic music. Other pundits trace "jazz" to "jass," prevalent in bawdy-houses during the Elizabethan period.

But beyond peradventure, "jazz" was a street, or gutter, word, one with a specific sexual connotation, long before it meant a type of popular music.

In addition to making the word "jazz" official, Chicago may take credit for "jam-session," the cutting contests in which musicians foregathered solely in after-work hours to improvise for each other's sheer delight. Bix Beiderbecke,* whose phrasings made him an acknowledged aristocrat among jazz musicians, gave him a "mystic halo," in the late Paul Whiteman's words, was king of the jam-sessions.

In addition to witnessing the advent of many stellar jazz luminaries, Chicago is responsible for some of the new jazz styles. "Boogie-woogie" was born on Chicago's South Side in the 1920's, even though it did not attain national celebrity until a decade later. The music, with emphasis on rhythm and not on melody, was played at monthly parties given to raise the rent and called "pitchin' boogie." (Like "jazz," "boogie" had a sexual synonym not taught at Sunday School.) The highly imaginative piano improvisations heard at the rent-raising parties came into general speech as "boogie-music" or as "boogie-woogie." It was associated first with the piano pieces of Pine Top Smith, composer of the scintillating "The Pine-Top-Boogie-Woogie." In these pieces a blues melody was set against an accompanying brief rhythmic figure, often eight beats to the bar, repeated without variations throughout the selection, thus creating a powerful rhythmic momentum.

---

*Beiderbecke has produced one of the most astonishingly viable modern cults, if one limited to pristine devotees of jazz. He moved from Chicago to New York where his unhappiness and wretched health were due in large part to excessive drinking. Dorothy Baker's *Young Man With a Horn*, a superior novel in every way, is about Bix Beiderbecke; and in 1950 the novel was made into a movie, in which Kirk Douglas played the part of Beiderbecke.

Several authorities say "swing," as such emanated from Chicago's Congress Hotel, on November 6, 1935. If this is not completely accurate, historically, the nation became "swing" conscious immediately after this date, and from Benny Goodman's engagement at the Congress Hotel. Goodman, Chicago native, was weaned on recordings of New Orleans and Chicago jazz, and he had played in many jam-sessions with such aristocrats as Jimmy McPartland, Bud Freeman, and Frank Teschmacher.

As a word and as a format, "swing" was not new. Jazzmen had used "swing" to mean improvised melodic rhythm, and as early as 1932 Duke Ellington had written "It Don't Mean A Thing If It Ain't Got That Swing," with the words by Irving Mills. The style was a variation of New Orleans improvisation, with this departure. Group notated improvisations preempted the prominent functions once the province of solo improvisations. Too, the melodic line retained a clearly enunciated beat as the harmony was sprinkled with spiced-up dissonances.

Anyone who has listened closely to the old recordings made in the 1920's by Fletcher Henderson's fine orchestra is aware of a definite "swing" in Henderson's orchestra, and although it was Benny Goodman who gave the world "swing," Goodman attained his early prominence playing Henderson's old arrangements. By 1937 Goodman was "The King of Swing," and on the first day of an engagement at New York's Paramount Theater the house was jammed with "20,000 swing-happy youngsters." The fervor engendered was so enormous extra policemen and firemen had to restrain the young audience once the concert began.

In January, 1938, Goodman gave a swing concert before a packed house at Carnegie Hall. When Goodman walked out the audience cheered loudly, wildly for fifteen minutes. In May, 1938, a "Carnival of swing" occurred at Randall's Island, in New York's East River, at which 23,400 young jitterbugs danced for six uninterrupted hours to the music of various "swing orchestras."

Even so testy demurrers erupted from pulpit and press, if scarcely heard for the sound of "swing" and the gyrations of jitterbugs.* The Dean of the New York School of Music wrote a bill, aborted, which would declare "swing" illegal. Protestant ministers here and there vilified "swing" as "obscene," "degenerate," and "debasing." William Allen White, famous editor of the Emporia, Kansas *Gazette*, said " 'swing' squeaked and shrieked and roared and bellowed in syncopated savagery."

As boogie-woogie and swing were ebullient off-shoots of jazz, "Be-bop," sometimes called "Re-bop," came from "swing." "Be-bop," cyclone music that eschewed an articulated melody, let the accentuation fall on the upbeat. Usually, the harmony changed several times in each bar. It produced tremendous nervous excitement, and this nervous excitement came much more from manner than from matter.

The high priest of "Be-bop" was Dizzie Gillespie, trumpeter and leader of a small orchestra that played a night club on New York's 52nd Street. When "Be-bop" flashed out, in 1945, kids began wearing berets of the sort favored by Dizzie Gillespie, his heavy eyeglasses, whether or not they needed glasses, and his goatee, if they could grow one.

---

*"Jitterbug," meaning someone, though usually not a musician, who understood swing, catapulted in 1938, and soon it meant a type of personality and a manner of dancing, as well. The zoot-suit, with the reet-pleets, worn by Jerry Leney, in the old cartoon strip Joe Palooka, was typical of the apparel worn by American's jitterbugs. The jitterbug, with his "hip jive," became a national type, and, as such, he appeared in formal literature in 1956 in J.D. Salinger's novel *Catcher in the Rye*, and in Stephen Longstreet's definitive *The Real Jazz Old and New*.

The extension and intensification of black studies, enhanced by the current penchant for nostalgia, revive interest in Negro spirituals. Although a few soloists have sung spirituals on television and radio, these songs were written by groups of blacks and they are meant to be sung by groups.

We forget that the first slave came ashore at Jamestown, Virginia a year before the *Mayflower* docked. Early in the 18th century there were around 75,000 black slaves in the colonies, and early in the 19th century the number had grown to around one million. Their innate instinct to express their feelings in song and dance was evident from the outset. Jefferson, perhaps, the first white man to be thoroughly cognizant with this inherent instinct, wrote, in *Notes on Virginia*: "With accurate ears for tune and time, they have been found capable of imagining a small catch."

Syncopated beats, shifting accents, variety of rhythm, and facets of the voodoo chant were abundantly evident in what came to be called spirituals. From the first, the slaves sang at their work, and this natural impulse was encouraged by their masters who thought singing was an antidote to obviate the desire for rebellion. And on the plantation the slave was introduced, if obliquely, to European harmony and melody, both of which were quickly interpolated into his own work-chants and religious songs.

But it was the New World impact of Christianity that gave enduring force and distinction to the slave's music. Almost immediately he identified closely with the suffering and death of Jesus, with stories of bondage in the Old Testament. And his music, an indigenous American art form, is vastly different from all other forms of American folk-music.

This music is stamped by mobile changes from major to minor themes without formal modulation. It is characterized by the wild freedom of its rhythm and intonation, by its reverberating moods, and by the injection of notes, like the flatted third or seventh, foreign to the standard scale. "Roll, Jordan, Roll," the first spiritual to be printed as sheet-music, was published in 1862. In 1867 several other spirituals were collected in *Slave Songs of the United States*, edited by Allen, Ware, and Garrison. Basically, spirituals fall into these categories: The call-and-answer technique carries over from African tribal songs. The leader throws out a line, and the group answers repetitiously. Here, the tempo is fast and the mood spirited and passionate. Enduring examples are "Joshua Fit the Battle of Jericho," "Shout for Joy," and "The Great Camp Meeting."

The second type is statelier, with slower tempo, and is much more majestical. A long, sustained phrase is the essence of the melody, as in "Deep River," "Sometimes I Feel Like a Motherless Child," "Nobody Knows De Trouble I've Seen," and "Swing Low, Sweet Chariot." The third set, perhaps, the best known group, consists of a highly syncopated melody, a melody made up of snatches of rhythmic patterns. Examples are the classics, "Little David, Play On Your Harp" and "All Gods Chillun Got Wings."

The Crucifixion was a daily alter-ego. The slave was being crucified by his master, and the most intense rapport was established with the suffering and death of Jesus. Indeed, it is doubtful that music, nay more, the language, has a more nobly moving petition to the Curcifixion than "Were You There When They Crucified My Lord?" and "Never Said A Mumbalin' Word." (Curiously enough, "mumbalin', misconstrued as "mumblin'," was taken out of context by whites to be used as a euphemism for a more graphic participle.)

The Old Testament offered allegories which became musical counterparts in the slave's life. By invoking the Israelites, he could lament his own subjugation. And if it was dangerous to speak openly of his desire for freedom, he could accomplish this with the haunting refrain of "Let my people go," from the memorable "When Israel Was In Egypt Land." "I Am Bound for the Promised Land" meant Philadelphia or Boston as much as heaven. Frederick Douglass (1817-1895), first great black militant, wrote, "A keen observer might have detected in our repeated singing of 'O Canaan, Sweet Canaan, I'm bound for the land of Canaan,' something more than a hope of reaching heaven. We meant to reach the North, and the North was our Canaan."

If many of the Negro spirituals are majestic in their simple grandeur, the primitive fervor of some carried over to the ragtime composed in the 1890's by Scott Joplin and others. This is abundantly obvious in "I Know the Lord Has Laid His Hands On Me" and "The Old Time Religion." Even so, the public at large did not hear spirituals until 1871 when the "Jubilee Singers" of Nashville, Tennessee's newly-created Fisk University went on national tour.

The "Jubilee Singers," twelve Fisk students originally, came in existence when the school's treasurer heard students singing spirituals to and from classes. At the Gilmore Music Festival in Boston in 1872, at which Johann Straus conducted waltzes, an audience of ten thousand arose to exclaim, "Jubilee forever." At the end of a year, the twelve singers had cleared $150,000.00 for Fisk University, had gained for the college invaluable publicity, and had introduced spirituals to the nation.

"Jubilee songs," as the nation first called spirituals, fascinated the Bohemian composer, Anton Dvorak, who had come to New York City in 1882 as a guest director. Dvorak assembled this catalogue to describe Jubilee songs: "pathetic, gay, tender, passionate, melancholy, solemn, religious, and bold." Dvorak helped himself to authentic Negro music, notably in *Symphony From the New World*, composed during his American visit. The symphony's first movement contains a passing quotation from "Swing Low, Sweet Chariot," and the second movement has the character of a bona fide spiritual, although it is original with Dvorak.

Henry T. Burleigh, the black composer, who came under Dvorak's influence, arranged "Deep River," in a version that was played in concert by Fritz Kreisler and sung by Frances Alda, of the Met.

The work songs format of the colonial era endures in field and factory, on levee and loading platform, in the 20th century. A classic example is "Casey Jones," surely, the best-known and the best song in the history of railroading. In 1906 a crack Illinois Central train, engineered by John Luther "Cayce" (from his home town, Cayce, Illinois) crashed into a line of boxcars near Vaughan, Mississippi. "Casey," as he became in the lyrics, yelled to his fireman, Sim Webb, who leaped to safety. Casey's body was found in the wreckage, one hand on the throttle and the other on an air-brake lever. A few days later, Wallis Saunders, an engine-wiper, who found Casey's body, made up some lyrics using as a model a black ballad called "Jimmie Jones." Quickly, the song, with numerous sets of lyrics, was taken over by railroad workers, and other laborers, across the nation.

In 1909, Lawrence Seibert and Edward Newton, vaudevillians, heard black workers in New Orleans singing their own set of Casey Jones lyrics. Almost immediately, Seibert wrote four stanzas and choruses, and Newton "ragged" the melody he heard in New Orleans. The fact that the song was introduced in Venice, California accounts for an otherwise baffling portion of the lyrics: "Go to bed children and hush your cryin',/You gotta another Papa on the Frisco Line." Not just incidentally, "Casey Jones," one of the century's most consummate hits, was rejected by the first New York City publishers to whom Seibert and Newton submitted the manuscript.

Perhaps, because of bicentennial interest, much discussion in 1976 focused on "Dixie," the song, and as a synonym for the old Confederate States, upon "John Brown's Body," and on "Yankee Doodle," and on the word "Yankee."

The facts and suppositions about "Dixie" and Dixie have been related in the text previously. The lyric of "The Battle Hymn of the Republic," alone, is a product of the Civil War. In December, 1861, Julia Ward Howe, pioneer suffragist and poet, heard "John Brown's Body" sung by passing soldiers. Bitterly disappointed at the low quality of the lyrics, she decided to write a new version.*

Her poem, published in the *Atlantic Monthly* in February, 1862, brought her $10.00 and lasting reknown. Shortly, the poem was reprinted widely and issued as sheet music by at least three publishers. After the chaplain of an Ohio regiment of volunteers taught his men the music and words, "The Battle Hymn of the Republic" became a favorite war-time anthem with the Union forces.

The music, by William Steffe, had appeared in the mid-1850's as a camp-meeting rousement, "Say Brothers, Will You Meet Us?" And as was almost axiomatic during the era, frequent parodies appeared, topical and ribald alike. The most popular, "John Brown's Body," was sung regularly by units of the 21st Massachusetts Regiment, stationed at Fort Warren.

But the "John Brown" of the song is not the anti-slavery zealot who was hanged for his 1859 attack on Harper's Ferry. The "John Brown" of the original lyrics was a slovenly, naive soldier in the 21st Massachusetts whose unending gaucherie and ineptitude made him the constant butt of jests and

---

*A minister seems to have suggested to Julia Ward.Howe that she should write a new set of lyrics. The same night, according to Mrs. Howe, the opening line, "Mine eyes have seen the glory of the coming of the Lord," came to her as she slept in Washington's Willard Hotel. Arising, she completed the lyrics that night.

derision. Then during the period of the Civil War the personality of "John Brown" became that of the Kansas python.

The words and music of "Yankee Doodle," a fife song, were popular several years prior to the Revolutionary War. The melody, obviously English, has never been identified with a specific author, but one of the best known applications of the tune was in an English nursery song, "Lucy Lockett." The melody seems to have appeared in the American colonies in 1755, just as General Braddock was assembling his rag-tag American forces to fight the French and the Indians at Niagara.

Dr. Richard Shuckburgh, one of Braddock's surgeons, taunted the disheveled Americans, telling them that "Yankee Doodle" was a current British song hit. And the colonials seem to have taken seriously the nonsense lyrics that Dr. Shuckburgh improvised for the old melody. British soldiers used the new lyrics to mock the colonists everytime they marched through a New England village.

As frequently occurs, the derided became the deriders, and colonials taunted their British enemies with the same song. The Continentals played and sang "Yankee Doodle" en route to Lexington, Massachusetts in 1775; and it was sung and played at Concord. It was played when Cornwallis surrendered at Yorktown, and the prisoners of war who were marched through New England heard "Yankee Doodle" almost every mile of their forced march.

"Yankee," is from the Dutch *Jan*, diminutive of *Janke*. In the New World this became "Yankee," or the word that the Dutch colonists applied to the English colonists. (As a personification of England, "John Bull" originated in John Arbuthnot's pamphlet, *The History of John Bull*, published anonymously in 1712. Arbuthnot depicts John Bull as a fat, obstinate, hearty, but good-natured country squire type.)

In the same satire, "Lewis Baboon" represents the

French, and Nicholas Frog typifies the Dutch. In Flanders, however, the Dutch nickname was *Jan Kees*, or Johnny Cheese. *Gringo*, the Mexican appellation for Americans, may possibly have ensued from the Spanish word *griego*, or Greek, as in, "It's Greek to me." Nonetheless, there is the more popular theory, and a most reasonable one, that *gringo* emerged from the beginning words of song-poem by Robert Burns which the Mexicans heard American soldiers sing during the Mexican War:

Green grow the rashes O
The happiest hours that ere I spent
Were spent among the lasses O.

(It is as logical to assume that Mexicans heard "Green grow" as *gringo* as it is that white colonists in North Carolina construed the Indian word *tau*, or "river of health," as tar. While it is true that the historic Tar River flows through much of the terrain once prominent in the old tar, pitch, and turpentine industry, the chances are that "Tar" is due to faulty ears.)

PART THIRTEEN
NAMES OF STATES AND TOWNS

"In the youth of a state, arms do flourish; in the middle age of a state, learning, and both of them together for a time. In the declining age of a state, mechanical arts and merchandise."

Francis Bacon, from *Of Vicissitude of Things.*

"I come from a state that raises corn and cotton and cockleburs and Democrats, and frothy eloquence neither convinces nor satisfies me. I am from Missouri. You have got to show me."

William D. Vandiver, in a speech at a naval dinner in Philadelphia in 1899.

"Nothing could be finer, than to be in Carolina, In the morning."

From "Carolina In the Morning," music by Walter Donaldson, lyrics by Gus Kahn.

"Cain was the first builder of towns."

Rabelais, from his "Works."

"God made the country and man made the town."

William Cowper, from *The Task.*

NAMES OF STATES AND TOWNS

In "American Names," his galloping poem of 1927, the late Stephen Vincent Benét exults in the indigenous magic and music of several flavorsome American place-names.

I have fallen in love with American names,
The sharp names that never get fat,
The snake-skin titles of mining-claims,
The plumed war-bonnet of Medicine Hat,
Tucson and Deadwood and Lost Mule Flat.

In the third stanza Benét exclaims:

I well remember Carquinez Straits,
Little French Lick and Lundy's Lane,
The Yankee ships and the Yankee dates
And the bullet towns of Calamity Jane.

The seventh and concluding stanza puts Benet's rippling names-saga into enduring dramatic focus:

I shall not rest in Montparnesse.
I shall not lie easy at Winchelsea.
You may bury my body in Sussux grass,
You may bury my tongue at Champmedy.
I shall not be there. I shall rise and pass.
Bury my heart at Wounded Knee.*

---

*Of all the sacrileges of accelerated urbanization and modernity, one of the most unforgivable and distressing to this author is the mania of city planners to ax distinctive and indigenous names as living sacrifices to the so-called progressive image. This dreadful compulsion attained unholy consummation in the 1960's when Raleigh, North Carolina's capital city, changed Ramcat Road to Lake Wheeler Drive. Raleigh's parent county, Wake, formed in 1771, was named for Margaret Wake (1733-1819), wife of North Carolina's royal governor, William Tyron. Margaret Wake Tryon was from Ramsgate, England, rendered "Ramcat," locally, and Ramcat Road was one of the original throughfares in the county, in this section of North Carolina.

The names of the fifty American states reflect much distinctive etymology, legendry and lore. The Latin *statio*, from the Greek *statos*, supplies English with words such as "status," "stature," from the Latin, *statuere, statutum*, to establish, to stand up. The English "statist," or politician, by way of the 18th-century German, gave us the noun "statistics," whose first meaning was the supplies and paraphernalia of a state. (Thus, "states," or "United we stand"):

"Alabama," is an Indian tribe of the famous Creek Confederacy, and *Alabame* is Choctaw, meaning "I clear the thicket." "Alaska," is an Eskimo word meaning "the great country or land"; "Arizona" · probably evolved from the Spanish *Arida zona*, or dry belt, or, perhaps, from the Indian *ari zonac*, a small spring of water; "Arkansas" was the Algonquin name for the Quapaw tribe of Indians.

"California" probably traces from the Spanish term for an earthly paradise, as is found in *Las Serges de Esplandian*, title of an early 16th-century chivalric romance. Albeit, folk etymologists insist, militantly, that "California" comes from the descriptive prowess of Catalan missionaries who visited the region in 1769 and pronounced the land *calor de forni* or "as hot as a furnace"; "Colorado" is from the Spanish meaning "the colored country"; "Connecticut seems to have come directly from the Indian word *Quonecktacut*, "River of pines."

"Delaware" acquired its name from Lord De La Ware, governor of Virginia, who visited Delaware Bay in 1610; "Florida" is from the Spanish meaning flowery, and there is the legend it was named by Ponce de Leon in 1513 on the "Feast of Flowers," or Easter; "Georgia" honors King George II of England, but the British tie was severed under George III; "Hawaii," is from the native word, *Owhyhe*, the place Captain Cook was killed in 1779.

"Idaho" is a corruption of the Indian word, *Eda hoe*,

which means "light on the mountain"; "Illinois" corroborates the opinion that etymology is many parts guess-work, but the general assumption is that it came from an Indian word that meant "River of men." "Indiana," obviously, was the "State of the Indians"; "Iowa" perpetuates the Alaouez, the name of a Sioux tribe, or "the sleepy ones." But the tribe's own name for themselves was *Pahoja,* "gray snow."

"Kansas" is "folk of the south wind," popular designation of the Kansas tribe of the Sioux nation; "Kentucky," although rendered often as an Indian phrase meaning "Dark and bloody land," seems to come directly from the Iroquois, *k en-tah-ten,* "the land of tomorrow"; "Louisiana" was named for King Louis XVI, by Robert de la Salle, in 1682.

"Maine" is the name of a province owned by Queen Henrietta Maria, wife of England's Charles I; "Maryland" was also named for Henrietta Maria; "Massachusetts" is from the Algonquin *Masadchu-es-et,* which means "Small place at big hills"; "Michigan" is from the Indian word and place, *michi gama,* "Great water"; "Minnesota," the Sioux word translated as "sky-blue water; "Mississippi," Indian Choctaw likely, *maesi sipu,* "fish river." "Missouri" was one of the Sioux tribes; "Montana" means mountainous, from the Spanish.

"Nebraska" was an Omaho Indian word, "wide river"; "Nevada," the Spanish for "snow clad"; "New Hampshire," obviously, from the English county of Hampshire; "New Jersey" is from the Channel Island, Jersey. In 1664, the same year the King of England sold the Carolinas to eight Lords Proprietors, the Duke of York gave a patent to Lord John Berkley and to Sir John Cartaret, for what became New Jersey. Cartaret had been chief administrator of the Channel Island of Jersey; "New Mexico" is from the Aztec word *mexilti,* the title given to the Aztec's war-god; "North Carolina" honored England's Charles I (from the Latin, *Carolus)* when Charles II granted a new patent; "North

Dakota," the "Badlands," in popular legendry, is a Sioux word, meaning "alliance."

"Ohio," in Iroquois, meant "great." "Oregon's" most likely sources are *origanum*, "the wild sage," *oregones*, the Spanish word meaning "big-eared"; *oyerun-gen*, Shoshone for "Place of plenty," *aura agua*, in Spanish "golden water," and *Wauregan*, Algonquin, meaning "beautiful water." "Oklahoma" comes from the old Choctaw word for "red folk."

"Pennsylvania," almost unique among American states with a Latin base, *Pennsilvania*, "Penn's Woods," honored Admiral William Penn. His son, William, the famous Quaker, was given a charter to the land in 1681 by King Charles II. (The territories, the "Philippines" and "Puerto Rico," obtained their names from the Spanish, *islas Filipinas*, "islands of Philip," colonized from Mexico and named for Spain's Philip II, and from the Spanish meaning "rich port.")

"Rhode Island," originally Providence Plantation, was named for the Isles of Rhodes by the state's General Court in 1644. (For "South Carolina" and "South Dakota," see North Carolina and North Dakota.)

"Tennessee" was known as the State of Franklin, or as Frankland, from 1784-1788. *Tennese* was the old Cherokee Indian word for the tribe's principal village and river; "Texas" is from the Indian word, *Tejas*, meaning allies.

"Utah" emerged from the Utes, a tribe of Indians; "Vermont" in French is "green mountain." "Virginia" was named by Sir Walter Raleigh in 1584 for Queen Elizabeth, "the virgin queen." "Washington" began as Columbia. In order to avoid confusion with the District of Columbia the state's name honored George Washington. "West Virginia," (see Virginia). "Wisconsin" is Indian, meaning "the meeting of rivers." Earlier spellings were the Indian words *Ouiscousin, Misconsing*, and *Ouiisconching*. The present spelling was determined by Congress. "Wyoming" is Indian for "hills and valleys," apparently, from Pennsylvania's "Wyoming Valley," popularized through Campbell's poem, "Gertrude of Wyoming."

There is this engaging novelty: There is only one spot in the fifty states where one can build a house with each of its four corners in a different state. The spot is the common meeting point of Utah, Colorado, Arizona, and New Mexico. In this mythical house the occupant would sleep in New Mexico, have his bath in Arizona, eat in Colorado, and sit on his porch in Utah.

This four states' boundary is at the intersection of the 37th parallel of north latitude and the 109th meridian of west longitude. The position was determined in 1868 by E.N. Darling, a surveyor, who buried a sandstone three feet underground on which he chiseled the notation. There are no human inhabitants for a large area around this boundary point. It is inaccessible to the ordinary traveler and it is used in winter, only, as grazing land for cattle and sheep.

In official jargon, the American Union consists of forty-six states and four "commonwealths": Virginia, Massachusetts, Pennsylvania, and Kentucky. However, these four are "states" in the purview of the Constitution. Although "commonwealth" implied greater self-government than "state," originally, the two words have the same meaning today, in principle, and in the political and economic operations of the various "states" and "commonwealths."

Louisiana is singular in that its political subdivisions, called counties elsewhere, are "parishes." (In colonial days some of the old thirteen colonies, South Carolina, for instance, used "parish" in lieu of "county.") Shortly after the United States purchased the vast Louisiana Territory from France in 1803, the legislative council of Louisiana's Governor William Claiborne divided the territory that now comprises Louisiana into twelve settlements, designated as "parishes."

When these poorly-defined districts proved to be politically unwieldy, the 1807 legislature of the Territory of Orleans divided the territory into nineteen districts. These were called "parishes" because the old French and Spanish ecclesiastical parishes were the basis for the new political divisions. This unusual designation persisted when Louisiana was admitted into the Union.

It was from the political sense of "state" that the word came to mean a place reserved for ceremonial occasions. Around 1650, as Samuel Pepy's (1633-1703) readers know, the captain's room aboard a ship became the "stateroom," and "stateroom" was a place set aside for assemblies of official governmental representatives.

Nonetheless, there is this extraordinary addendum: Around 1844 Captain Henry W. Shreve, for whom Shreveport, Louisiana is named, built sleeping cabins on his Mississippi River steamboat, and he named these cabins for the states that bordered on the Mississippi and Ohio rivers.

For a while these sleeping rooms were known along the river as "states," and as "staterooms," ultimately. In 1845, the year Texas came into the Union, the pilothouse was built on the hurricane, or third deck of riverboats. The pilothouse was called "the Texas" (see Mark Twain's *Life on the Mississippi*) because it, too, "was annexed to the states."

It is possible that Captain Shreve was unaware of the long existence of "stateroom" in British English, although it is possible that his device for utilizing the names of the states that bordered on the Mississippi and the Ohio was prompted by awareness of "stateroom." Whether or not, it was Shreve, in 1815, who made the first steamboat voyage up the Mississippi and Ohio, as far as Louisiana.

Many American towns have had their names changed at some point in their history. Among this almost interminable list, several of the colonial Kingstons, named for one of the British Georges, usually, became "Kinston," as in Kinston, North Carolina, after the Revolution. New York was New Amsterdam, of course, and Atlanta was Marthasville and

Terminus.* Lynchburg, Virginia was Big Lick, and Richmond, Virginia was Byrd's Landing. "Asheville (N.C.), in the Land of the Sky," seems to enhance the figure much more readily than Morristown, the city's original name.

Portland, Oregon was decided by the flip of a coin. In 1843 William Overton and Amos Lovejoy, going up the Columbia River in a canoe, selected the future site of Portland as a good place for the location of a town. Overton sold his interest in the tract to a man named Pettigrove, and in 1844 the site was surveyed, streets laid off, and the first log house erected.

Pettigrove, who had lived in Portland, wanted to call the embryonic town "Portland," but Lovejoy, a native of Massachusetts, wanted to call it "Boston." The two agreed to flip a coin, a penny, with heads representing Portland and tails representing Boston. The penny came up heads. The new town became Portland.

Nations, states, commonwealths, and municipalities have "controllers," usually spelled "comptroller." The latter spelling, a source of consternation to multitudes, stemmed from an erroneous derivation from *compte*, an obsolete form of "count," suggested by the French word *compte*. (Count was derived indirectly from the Late Latin *computum*, from *computare*, to calculate.) In the 14th century, according to the *Shorter Oxford Dictionary*, "count" was "refashioned after Latin, as *compte*." Because a controller's business is to examine and to verify, it was supposed by the public the word to describe his profession should be spelled "comptroller." Indeed, many official scribes leaned heavily on this spelling.

However, this erroneous spelling endures only in certain

---

*Atlanta's famous Peach Tree Street was a botanical misnomer at first. The peach trees that now grow along this lengthy, teaming thoroughfare were planted after the street was named. According to tradition, Indians were trying to say "pitch tree," but white ears caught this as "peach tree."

official usages, such as Comptroller General of the United States, or Comptroller of the United States Post Office Department, etc. "Controller" is the correct spelling for normal purposes, and in each case the word is pronounced the same, "kon-trole-er." "Control" comes from the Latin *contre*, counter, and *rotulus*, roll. And the present French form of "controller" is *controleur*, and not *comptroleur*, as many seem to suppose.

"Cop," now likely to be derogatory, or certainly mildly derisive, may ascribe to the Old English verb, "to cop," meaning to take hold or to catch or to apprehend. However, several authorities tie "cop," as a synonym for policeman (the Greek *polis, polit*, order in a place, which gave us "politics," also) to the large, luminous copper buttons worn by the Irish and London constabularies organized by Sir Robert Peele in 1829. (In London policemen are still "bobbies" or "peelers.")

A subsidiary theory ties "cop" to the Italian-American "coppo," first a denigration that implied the speaker's adamance on superiority of law and order. And, finally, "cop" is related to John "Copperstock" Haines, Mayor of Chicago, who, in 1858, dressed his policemen in short, blue frock-coats called "copper-stock coats" by the citizens of Chicago. Beyond peradventure, this derivation is applicable to 19th century Chicago, but the ancient verb "to cop" and the copper buttons worn by Sir Robert Peele's policemen take chronological and etymological precedence.

"Cop," as in to "cop a plea," is a corruption of the Yiddish word *chop*, meaning to steal or to deprive. "Cop out," almost axiomatic in the 1960's and in the early 1970's to mean a retreat from something, some sort of overt apostasy often attended by fecklessness, originated as a colloquialism to mean being arrested, or to be caught in the act. One of the more vibrant of the early uses of "to cop out" meant to plead guilty, and in this sense the phrase appeared in issues of the *New Yorker* in the early 1950's.

"Cop a heel," in abeyance today, used to be fairly viable to mean an escape, especially from prison or from a policeman's clutch. ("Cop a mope" had the same general meaning, and "cop a feel," used by such eminent writers as Max Shulman in *Barefoot Boy With Cheek*, remains a vulgarism.) And, obviously, the word "cop" is responsible for an infinite variety of coinages such as "copectic," "kopesetic" et al, all of which meant fine, excellent, or all right, and some of which appear in the works of the late Carl Van Vechten, published in the early and the mid 1930's.

("Dick," whose original origins were salacious, and "bull" have been interchangeable with "cop" intermittently the past half century. Albeit, each is usually modified, as "store dick" or "railroad bull." And much of the literature, movies, radio, and television pseudo-dramatic writing of the past half century has bristled with "private-eye," "private dick," "gumshoe," "shamus" and others.)

"Gumshoe," from the rubber soles worn by certain private investigators and by second story men, alike, had fairly wide currency in metropolitan America as early as the beginning of the 20th century, although the word did not attain general recognition until the avalanche of detective fiction and assorted "whodunits" in movies and in television.

"Shamus," popularized in the stories of Raymond Chandler, Peter Cheyney and others, probably comes from the Hebrew *shaman*, a caretaker or custodian of a synagogue. In various literature the word is spelled "shamus," "shammus," "shomas," and "shommus," with the first being the most prevalent spelling. Although the most common pronunciation rhymes with "Thomas," New York City's Irish call it "shay-mus."*

"Sheriff," yet preceded with "High" among many older southern Americans, is from the roots of *shire* and *reeve*. Originally, the British sheriff was the reeve, the king's repre-

Shaman is medicine man in American Indian.

sentative, in a shire or county.* "Shier, " synonymous with county today, rhymes with "wire" "shirr" or "sherr." The division of England into shires came from the partitioning of the nation among local chieftans.

One theory derives "shire" from the root of "shear," to cut off, and thus, Berkshire is a corruption of Baroc's share, a leading chieftan. A second theory derives "shire" from the Anglo-Saxon *scir*, to distribute or to appoint. In either case, partitioning is implicit. Under Norman law the Anglo-French *counte* (from the Latin *comitatus*, a count's domain) was introduced as a substitute for shire.

Some Americans habitually make the mistake of saying, "the county of Berkshire." "Berkshire," or "the county of Berk," is the proper, coherent way of speaking.

"Mayor," the chief magistrate of a town or a borough, is from the Latin *major,* greater, via the Old French *maire.*

"Governor," from the French *gouverner*, from the Latin *gubernare*, to steer, from the Greek *kybernan*, to steer, is a comparison of the control of a nation to the steering of a ship.

"President," obviously, one who presides, comes from the Latin *praesidens, entis*, present participle of *praesidere.*

The American sheriff, especially the 18th and early 19th century southern sheriff, is responsible for "kick the bucket," which has come to mean virtually any kind of death. In pioneer and in frontier times "justice" was likely to be swiftly summary. In some of the old capital offenses,**such as horse-stealing, the high sheriff often impaneled a jury as soon as the alleged culprit was apprehended. A guilty verdict was almost

*The Arabic *sherif*, or *shereef*, ("shrf" in vowel-less Arabic) means, literally, "noble" or "the great one." While the word is not related etymologically to the English word "sheriff," the high station indicated almost had parallels in old-time England.

**For those who cry that execution is a deterrent, there is 'this oblique commentary: Off and on in the 19th century, and up until the 1850's, North axiomatic from the quasi-jury, and the sheriff threw a rope over a stout limb, affixed a noose around the prisoner's neck, placed the condemned man on an upended water bucket, kicked the bucket with his foot, and dispatched the felon to "kingdom come."

"Lynch," actually short for "Lynch law," should be adjudged to endure as a word that is purely historical. Among the tenuous claimants for this stained distinction are Captain William Lynch and Charles Lynch, both Virginians of the late 18th century. Each is credited, or charged, with summary executions, in 1776 and in 1780. Usually in the retelling, William's victims were horse thieves and Charles' were marauding British soldiers.

And South and North Carolina back into this dishonor by dint of Lynch's Creek, along whose banks the anti-British Regulators of 1770 meted out instantaneous justice, or injustice. And here and there in each state a hill or lane belonging to man named Lynch was the scene of a spectacular hanging, usually of more than one person. (In one of the accounts, Lynch, who owned the "boulevard," or lane, was murdered for his money, and the two men who killed him were "lynched" the same night.

"Kangaroo court," a sham trial or one in which the defendant is always guilty, is of unknown origin. There is the reasonable theory that this is a relic of trials on pirate ships in the days of the Spanish Main, but the kangaroo may have been associated with mock trials when Australia was a penal colony. There seems to be little dispute that Australian prisons, as elsewhere, convened permanent kangaroo courts for the punishment of minor offenses, such as petty thefts and unsanitary cells, among the prisoners, themselves. The fine, usually a few cents, was put into a central fund for the benefit of the prison population.

Carolina had as many as twenty-seven crimes which carried the death penalty, and all sorts of intensely personal violence was rampant.

Although "kangaroo court" has many innocuous implications, such as sham trials by agencies like the boy scouts, in their harsh extremities they are equated with "drumhead trials." This began as a type of military "lynch law" to try men on the battle field or on the march, without the amenities of a regular court martial. But in time "kangaroo" and "drumhead" came, in the larger sense, to mean precipitate, condign action by mobs acting as vigilantes.*

Towns, states, and nations are run on money, from the Middle English *moneye*,** from the French *moneie*, from the Latin *moneta*, and *Moneta*, epithet of Juno, whose temple in Rome housed the mint.

Strangely enough, "penny" is not the official or legal name of any American coin, even if this colloquialism has attached to the American cent since the advent of the country's coinage system. Actually, the British penny circulated widely in America even after the Revolution. Several states had

---

*"Condign," derived from the Latin *cum,* with, and *dignus*, worthy is used to mean harsh or severe punishment today. The original meaning is deserved or appropriate, not harsh. Punishment could be severe or mild so long as it was merited. And "condign" has had several meanings in its long history. In *Love's Labor Lost*, Moth asks, "Speak you this in my praise, master?" And Armado replies, "In thy condign praise." But in modern English, condign has come to be coupled with punishment, and severity is the over-riding adjunct.

**Munaye" has had sporadic verbal currency, as in G.W. Hunt's British musical-hall song, 1877-1878, to which "jingoistic" attached:

We don't want to fight, but by jingo, if we do,
We've got the ships, we've got the men,
We've got the munaye, too.

issued one-cent pieces, but "cent," as the official designation of a coin appeared in a Congressional action of August 8, 1786: "Cents: The highest copper piece, of which 100 shall be equal to the dollar."

In October of the same year Congress forbade the circulation of all "foreign copper coins." Thus, the English penny was obviated, but in popular parlance "penny" was superimposed on the "cent," and it has endured tenaciously ever since. "Penny" has a better literary ring than the truncated "cent."

Although "penny" comes from the British word, the American plural is always "pennies" and never "pence." To make allowance for the constant fluctuations in modern currency, an English penny, basically, is worth around two American "cents," and the British halfpenny is the equivalent of our "cent." But even if "penny" has no legal status in the United States, our language is quick with endless phrases, such as, "penny-whistle," "penny-wise," "penny-ante," "penny-in-the-slot" and many others.

The five cent piece, the "nickel," traces its etymology to the time when pixies, elves, and goblins were blamed for small mishaps and thanked for small, unexpected favors. According to the story, some copper miners found a shiny metal but investigation revealed it was destitute of copper. The mining superintendent, a wag with a knowledge of mythology, was importuned for an explanation.

He told the chagrined, puzzled miners, "Nicholas, the officious elf, stole the copper, as a joke." Whether or not, the five cent's piece chief composition, at one time, was nickel, and a "nickel" it became. This is an abbreviation of the German, *Kupfernicklel,* or copper nickel. "Nickel," from "Nicklaus," appears in happier guise as St. Nicholas, or Santa Claus.

The American five-cent piece is responsible for jitney, a small bus or private car that carried passengers, beginning around 1915, and ultimately, a synonym for any car, but in subsequent use usually a battered automobile. In 1915 the street cars and trolleys of Los Angeles were immobilized by a strike. A man with an open touring car began picking up passengers at the old trolley stops, at five cents a head. At that time, "nickel" and "jit" were synonymous, nationally, and the accidental public carrier became a "jitney."

In *This Side of Paradise*, the late Scott Fitzgerald used "the old jitney waiter" to mean an inferior waiter. During the 1920's the editors of America's numerous small, activist magazines were tagged "Jitney St. Georges," and until recently "jitney bag" had lively, if restricted, use to mean a coin purse or a small handbag.

And, of course, the "nickel" is responsible for "two-fer," irrepressible the first fifty years of the 20th century.

"Dime," from the Latin *decima*, (pars), the Latin *decem*, ten, and *decimus*, a tenth, was a *disme*, originally. Gouverneur Morris, a member of Continental Congress committee for a new coinage system recommended a coin to be called a *disme*, the old French spelling. However, the Mint Act of 1792 changed this to "dime."

In England during the 13th and 14th centuries, a dime was a tithe, the tenth portion of everyone's income that was paid to the church. In the King James version, Genesis (14:20) reads, "He gave him tithes of all." John Wycliffe translated this: "He gave him dymes of alle things."

"Yankee dime," meaning a kiss, was ubiquitous in the American south throughout much of the 19th century and well into the insular era of the 20th century. Originally, "Yankee dime" meant payment of a debt with a kiss. Dixie Lochinvars did innumerable chores for their lady-loves to claim payment with a "Yankee dime." The phrase attained its greatest viability after the Civil War when all hard money was scarce. Here and there, a "Quaker nickel" was a kiss, and a "Yankee dime" was a kiss and a hug. If some Lochinvars had their hearts and loins set on a "Yankee quarter," this "unseemly phrase" was never spoken in polite company.

The pliable Spanish dollar, widely circulated in the American colonies, and on which the American dollar came to be based, is responsible for the incessant "bits," as in "two bits." The Spanish silver dollar, or "piece of eight," was cut into wedge-shaped pieces for use as small coins, for change. In the 17th and 18th centuries English colonists called a one-real piece, a "bit," a two-real piece "two bits" etc.

"Shinplaster," which usually manages to reemerge at times of extreme inflation, surfaced during and after the American Revolution when the colonies, and states, were swamped with nearly worthless paper money. The original "shinplaster," brown paper smeared with tar and vinegar, was placed on sore shins, and Americans said their paper money "is fit only to plaster the shin."

There is a reasonable theory that "shinplaster" is a corruption of the French word, *cinque plastres*, a five-dollar bill of dubious worth, circulated in the West Indies about the same time this nation was flooded with semi-worthless paper specie. Despite any validity of this claim, the Americans who said "shinplaster" were thinking of tar and vinegar on brown paper. Indeed, "shinplaster" returned to deride small notes issued by private banks during the financial panic of 1837, and again in 1862 when a metal shortage, and the wide-spread hoarding of hard money, forced the federal government to issue its first fractional paper currency. (The fifth and final issue of fractional currency was printed between February 1874 and February 1876.

"Dollar" comes from the period around 1520 when coins were minted from silver of *Joachimsthal*, or Joachim's Valley. These were called *Joachimsthaler*, by tabulations of *schicks*, and were referred to sometimes as *Schlickenthaler*. (The

German *thale* gave us the English word "dale.") Both the names of the coins were shortened to one word, "Thaler," from whence we obtained the English word "dollar."

Although most cash-drawers contain an assortment of coins, as well as paper money and checks, the word "cash" in American English usually conjures paper, or folding, money. While "cash" derives from the Old French *casse*, meaning a money box, one of its most active colloquial synonyms, "mazuma," comes from the Yiddish *nezyneb* meaning ready (cash).

For several years after the mid 1960's "bread," as money, attained tremendous currency in hip and cool parlance.* However, "bread" in this context appeared in limited fashion as early as 1935 in the "jive" of "cool cats and far-out chicks." "Bread" meant the boss, one who paid over the money, and in its earliest use "bread" was brought into shop and office conversations as an admonition to one's associates that the boss was watching or listening.

"Breadbasket" has been a synonym for the stomach since around 1755, and "dough" has meant money since around 1855. Although "dough" came to mean money, per se, and was used forty years ago by so eminent a crtic as the late Henry S. Camby, in such an eminent magazine as *Harper's*, "dough" meant money obtained unethically, from 1855 through the 1890's, especially in the sense of political graft or any sort of bribe money.

Beginning in the middle of the 19th century the nation chewed on a diet of innumerable "dough"

---

*"Hep," conversant with the intricacies of current mores, has been used off and on most of the 20th century, and "cool," in context of 1960's meaning, was applied to Christy Mathewson by several sports when Mathewson pitched three shut-outs during the World Series of 1905.

idioms: "Dough-ball" was applied by town to gown as long ago as 1850 to mean any college student, and in most small college towns it meant a boring pedantic person, apparently, from the fact much fishing bait was made from stale bread and cinnamon. "Doughboy," popularized during World War I, dates back to 1847 to mean an American infantry soldier. Because of the frequent questions about "doughboy," and a number of preposterous explanations, all of the theories known to this author are enumerated: It is suggested that "doughboy" emerged from the Mexican War, in 1847, (1) from the adobe, often pronounced "doe-by," huts occupied by some American infantrymen, and (2) from the baked mixture of flour and rice cooked by infantrymen in campfire ashes; it was revived during Albert Sidney Johnston's 1850's expeditions against the Mormons, when artillerymen said a certain bugle call seemed to say, "Dirty, dirty doughboys"; during the fighting against the Indians in the west American soldiers cleaned their white trimmings with pipe clay, and if the infantryman became wet his whiting turned to a type of dough; again, infantrymen in the Indian warfare were called "dobe crushers" and "mud crushers;" and, finally, "doughboy," a dumpling, known by this name in England as early as 1685, was applied facetiously to federal soldiers during the Civil War because their globular buttons were said to resemble the doughboy dumplings.

None of these has positive confirmation. However, General William Sibert, commander of the first American division to reach France in 1917, asked for suggestions for a nickname to correspond to the British Tommy Atkins. Servicemen voted for "Sammy," "Yank," and "Johnny Yank," but "doughboy" was preferred by the majority.

"Dough-head" meant a stupid person, and "doughnut" still has limited use to mean an automobile tire; "doughnut foundary" or "house" used to be a cheap rooming-place or cafe, and a "dough-roller" cooked in a logging camp; and occasionally, for a railroad section gang "To dough up" meant to whip someone, and "to dough up brown" meant to whip someone thoroughly.

"Sheets," originally enough money for a bed in a flop-house, used by James T. Farrell in his *Studs Longian* trilogy, came to have restricted use for any kind of money; "lettuce," "kale," and other green vegetables became idiomatic for money, via the numerous correlations with "the long green." "Shekel," from the Hebrew word, was a silver dollar, as early as 1870. In this sense the word faded when silver dollars went out of use, or virtually so. Indeed, some authorities trace "shekel" to "Mene, mene, tekel, upharsin" (Daniel 5:25) and to the translation, "A mina, a mina, a shekel, and half-shekels."

PART FOURTEEN
SHIPS AT SEA

" 'The time has come,' the Walrus said,
'To talk of many things;
Of shoes-and-ships-and sealing wax-
Of cabbages and kings-
And why the sea is boiling hot-
And whether pigs have wings.' "

> Lewis Carroll (Charles Lutwidge Dodgson), from "The Walrus
> And the Carpenter."

"I must go down to the seas again, to the lonely sea and sky,
And all I ask is a tall ship and a star to steer her by."

> John Masefield, from "Sea Fever."

"The dragon-green, the luminous, the dark, the serpent-
haunted sea."

> James Elroy Flecker, "West Gate," from The Gates of
> Damascus.

"I remember the black wharves and the ships,
And the sea-tides tossing free;
And Spanish sailors with bearded lips,
And the beauty and mystery of the ships,
And the magic of the sea."

> Henry W. Longfellow, from "My Lost Youth."

SHIPS AT SEA

Josephus Daniels (1862-1948), long-time editor and publisher of the Raleigh, North Carolina *News and Observer*, Ambassador to Mexico under Franklin Roosevelt, served as Secretary of the Navy throughout Woodrow Wilson's two administrations, the only cabinet official to do so. For a while, anyway, Daniels was anathema to the Navy League, to Washington's deeply-intrenched, ultra social naval establishment, for his persistent reforms.

Too often it is forgotten that it was Daniels who started several technical training schools for enlisted naval personnel, thereby upgrading the competency of the navy immeasurably and giving badly needed education to professional sailors. It was Daniels who made appointments to Annapolis available to qualified enlisted men, and it was he who brought into the Naval Academy the first civilian instructors.*

But Daniels was the object of current derision when he abolished the Wine Mess aboard ships. And he was subjected to supercilious laughter when he attempted to replace such recondite terms as "larboard" and "starboard" with "left" and "right." Sardonic wags said Daniels tried to abolish "larboard, starboard, and cupboard with one fell-swoop."

As someone must have suggested, linguists are likely to go overboard on "larboard." The Middle English *lere* means empty, and the helmsman always stood on the steer-side, the "starboard." The early form, "leereboard" still exists, but years ago no one seems to have known how to spell it. Too, the Dutch term, *laanger*, or lower, is used also to mean left. It is suggested, periodically, that "lar" may be short for *laager*.

"Board," common Teutonic for plank, is the side of a ship, hence, "starboard" and "larboard." "Galley," from the Old French *galie, galee*, was a large, low usually one-decked ship

---

*Alphonzo Smith, scholarly English teacher of Greensboro, N.C. and O.Henry's biographer, was the first.

propelled by oars as well as by sails, and used in the Mediterranean in the Middle Ages, chiefly. It is also the cooking quarters on a ship. But Mark Twain compounded a mystery in the 37th chapter of *Huckleberry Finn*, published in 1884, with his line, "She grabbed up the basket and slammed it across the house and knocked the cat galleywest."

Although Twain had written "galleywest" in a letter, this seems to be the first printed reference. While it is patently evident that it means to smithereens, it has no relationship to a ship's cooking quarters or to a point on the compass. Scholars believe that Mark Twain picked it on the Mississippi somewhere, that it had come there, and elsewhere, from the English dialectal "collywestern."

At one time there seems to have been a place in England called Collywestern, and when things went bad, unaccountly but irretrievably, many Englishmen blamed such adversity on "Colly Weston," adding, "It's all because of Colly Weston." But no one really has any intelligent idea what or who Colly Weston was.

"Mark Twain," venerable call of a leadsman, means two fathoms, or twelve feet, of water, in the parlance of riverboat pilots. Samuel Langhorne Clemens (1835-1910) used "Mark Twain" for the first time in 1863, as a reporter for the Virginia City, Nevada *Territorial Enterprise*. Under the date of February 2, 1863, Clemens signed "Mark Twain" to a letter sent from Carson City, then the territorial capital, to the *Enterprise*. (Today this letter would be classified as "editorial correspondence.") "Mark Twain" was employed first by Captain Isaiah Sellers, for a series of bombastic items he wrote for the New Orleans *Picayune*. Sellers' features usually began, "This is my opinion for the benefit of the citizens of New Orleans."

Clemens, as a young cub pilot, wrote a lampoon of Sellers' series, for another New Orleans paper, which he signed

"Sergeant Fathom." Apparently, Clemens had been trying to think up an apt pen-name when he got the news, in Carson City, that Sellers was dead, that he would not use "Mark Twain" again.

"Schooner," name of a ship, derives from *scoon*, old Scottish dialectical word meaning to skip or to skim across a surface. According to the story, generally credited, the first vessel of this type was built in 1713 at Gloucester, Massachusetts, by Captain Andrew Robinson, a Scotsman. When Robinson's ship was launched, a spectator exclaimed, "Watch her scoon! O, see how she scoons." Robinson smiled: "Then a schooner let her be."

The story gains credence from the fact that during the 18th century the word was often spelled "scooner" and "skooner." And the covered wagon, used by immigrants going west, the wagon of similar design, became the "prairie schooner."*

"Scylla and · Charybdis," horrible monster and a fatal whirlwind, appear in the *Odyssey* (translation by T.E. Lawrence, "Lawrence of Arabia" (1888-1935), who changed his name to T.E. Shaw): "On this side Scylla, while on that Charybdis in her whirlwind was sucking down the sea."

The two words have come to stand for the dreadful, inexorable alternates in ultimate choices. Odysseus was warned by Circe that not even Poseidon, god of the sea, could save him from Charybdis. Hence, he decided to suffer from Scylla, who lived in an inaccessible cave, concealed in a rock.

"Mother Carey's Chickens," stormy petrels, is a corruption of *Mater Cara*. This is the sailor's nickname for the web-footed petrel, the albatross' cousin, and the term is applied also to snow that falls at sea. The phrase seems to have originated with sailors from the Levant (Turkey, Syria,

---

*There is even the suggestion that Studebaker, or one of the builders of prairie schooners, applied the phrase "mobile home" to the wagon.

Lebanon, and Israel). Ancient sailors rejoiced when these birds wheeled and dipped near their ships. For dear Mother Mary had sent her chickens as a sign that a safe harbor was near by.

Many people, older ones as well as school children, are bugged by the name "Hampton Roads," to mean a body of water. "Hampton" comes from the adjacent city, and "road," in singular or plural usage, is a nautical word meaning a roadstead for a ship, a sheltered place just beyond a harbor where a ship may "ride at anchor." Actually, "Hampton Roads" is the channel through which the waters of the James, Nansemond, and Elizabeth Rivers flow into the Chesapeake Bay.

It was along Hampton Roads that the age of the steamship emerged, in shot and smoke, on March 9, 1862 when the *Monitor* and the *Merrimac* (renamed the *Virginia* by the Confederates) slugged it out, with the whole world watching, in essence. The first clash may be called a draw, and although the *Merrimac* damaged the *Monitor* in a subsequent fight, and sank some wooden Federal ships, the *Merrimac's* own damage caused her to withdraw. The famous iron-clad was scuttled when the Confederates abandoned Norfolk, in face of the offensive launched down the Virginia peninsula by the Union army commanded by General George B. McClellan.

("Blimps," non-rigid, lighter-than-air airships, fly above Hampton Roads periodically, and they used to be a familiar sight there. And the word continues to tease etymologists. The late Frank Vizetelly thought the word probably evolved from the "b" in balloon and the word "limp," and *Webster's International Dictionary* says that "blimp," in this context, was probably suggested by "limp.")

And there is the story that the first model of lighter-than-air craft, one that proved unsatisfactory, experimented by the British in World War I, was designated as "A-limp." A satisfactory model was designated "B-limp." And some students believe that "blimp" came from the British colloquialism "blimp," meaning a blister.

"Slush fund," now used generally to mean money collected during a political campaign to influence public opinion, originated at sea, in the British navy. In the 18th and 19th century it was traditional to sell all of the slush, the surplus grease and lard from the galley, to perpetuate a permanent fund for the benefit of enlisted men. Any of the surplus slush, or grease, that was not needed to slush the spars and masts was collected in tins. ("To slush" is an old verb meaning to lubricate or grease.)

In more recent decades the "slush fund" was raised from the public sale of worn-out equipment, and from personal effects abandoned aboard ship; and military garrisons hit upon the same expedient to raise money for the entertainment of enlisted men, to provide for the disabled, and to aid the widows of former servicemen. Although the United States Navy has ended the "slush fund," enlisted military personnel on some posts collect a cash "slush fund" to buy athletic equipment for their games.

The "Horse latitudes" was applied by seamen to a treacherous part of the North Atlantic between 30 and 35 degrees, a region beset, alternately and inexplicably, by complete calms and tempestuous winds. Although "Horse latitudes" began as a nautical term and endures as one, some gamblers who experience hot and cold luck, in close proximity, say they have fallen over-board onto the "Horse latitudes."

Seamen of the 18th and 19th centuries described malignant lightning storms, followed by the most intense calms, the fairest, most gentle weather one hour and the most maniacal weather the next hour, as the salient feature of the ocean region.

Three theories seek to account for the origin of the words. The least likely is the one that ties the origin to the colonial era when ships carrying horses from Europe and New England to the West Indies threw them over-board, frequently, when ships were becalmed and fodder ran out. More realistic, if wanting in authenticity, is the story that many horses were killed by storms, and by violent seas and seasickness, in the region. Without verification is the even more realistic theory that the phrase emerged because the wild and eerie wind conjured the affrighted neighing and frantic pawing of a terrified horse.

Washington Irving (1783-1859) in his *Life of Christopher Columbus.* is enthralled by these incredible calms. Irving uses "calm latitudes" to describe the North Atlantic region in which Columbus was becalmed on his third voyage, in 1498. Irving ascribes the unmitigated calm to the trade winds meeting and neutralizing each other. Irving says: "The whole sea is a mirror, and vessels remain almost motionless, the crews panting under the heat of a vertical sun."

"Doldrums," figuratively any spell of listlessness, boredom, or apathy, and also said to be characteristic of bad luck at cards, is the region near the equator that abounds, also, in squalls and calms.

There is the old story that sailing ships, such as the ones Herman Melville (1819-1891) shipped on, traveled faster than the wind. All evidence is that no sailing ship ever traveled faster than the wind that blows directly astern.

But light racing ships and iceboats have been credited with attaining speeds twice faster than the wind that drives them. This depends upon the wind-angle of the boat. Normally, the sails of an iceboat are trimmed so that the direction of the boat and the wind do not coincide. An iceboat attains its greatest speed when the wind blows at an angle of 120 degrees. The U.S. Hydrographic Office states: "An ice boat can sail faster than the wind when it sails at some angle to it. The momentum is increased by every puff of wind striking the sails obliquely until it is finally equalled by the increase of friction engendered. Thus the continued bursts of wind against the sails cause a greater accumulation of speed in the boat than is possessed by the wind itself."

Summary: Under normal circumstances the speed record for iceboats is around 75 miles per hour, but amid 70-mile gales, iceboats have traveled 140 miles an hour.

(That's a pretty fair sample of "gobbledygook," the word that was originated in 1944 by the late Maury Maverick, Congressman from Texas, to characterize the maddening habit of governmental agencies to make the simple complex and convoluted.)

Venice became the "Bride of the Sea" from a medieval custom, the "marriage of the Adriatic," in which the Doge of Venice cast a wedding band into the sea, and proclaimed, "We wed thee, O sea, with this ring, in token of our true and perpetual sovereignty." In a word, the church was saying that as woman belonged to her husband, so the sea belonged to Venice.

Each year on Ascension Day, the Doge and his attendants led a procession of gondolas. This was at the time Venice was called the "Mistress of ths Adriatic" because her ships visited virtually all the known ports of the civilized world. The "marriage" ceremony originated around 1000 B.C., under the Dogeship of Pietro Orseolo. Apparently, the first ring thrown into the sea perpetuated the victory of the Venetian fleet, at Istria, over the anti-papal forces of the Holy Roman Emperor. The first gold ring cast into the sea is supposed to have come from the Pope's own finger. The ceremony passed after Napoleon subdued the thousand-year-old republican government of Venice, in 1798.

Children hold "seashells" to their ears to hear a noise that seems to simulate the distant rumble of waves. They ask their parents what causes these roars, and the parents usually say the sound in the seashell is the echo of the ocean. Unromantically, the roar is produced by the combined echoes of the ordinary sounds on the beach, around the shell. The smoothness of the shell's interior, and its singular shape, enables the slightest vibration to produce an echo. This effect is intensified by the fact that the shell, itself, magnifies the pulses in the child's head, as well as heightening the sounds produced in the immediate vicinity.

Many people especially rural dwellers, maintain stoutly that lightning never strikes water. Whether or not lightning ever strikes the open ocean may be a moot point, but the U.S. Weather Bureau thinks lightning does strike the open water, sporadically. And the common belief that lightning kills fish is augmented by the report, given credence by wire services, that in August, 1932, fishermen picked up more than one hundred stunned fish, after lightning struck Upper Saranac, N.Y., near Doctors Island.

The "South Seas," mentioned by Maugham, Melville, Masefield and other writers, was the British English term for the Pacific Ocean. From the beginning of their awareness of the ocean, the British spoke of it in the plural.

The Pacific became the "South Seas" because Nunez de Balboa was looking southward when he first saw it in 1513. Balboa,* looking from an eminence on the Isthmus of Panama, called it the Golden Sea, originally, because he was seeking gold. The next day when he waded into the water, to proclaim it and all the land it touched, for Spain, he christened it *Mer del Sur*, or "Sea of the South."

Many of the British writers have written "South Seas" to mean that portion of the Pacific Ocean that lies below the equator. However, in general, "South Seas" is applied to the

---

*As all school children used to know, John Keats (1795-1821) confused Cortez with Balboa in his ebullient sonnet, "On First Looking Into Chapman's Homer: "Then felt I like some watcher of the skies/When a new planet swims into his ken:/Or like stout Cortez, when with eagle eyes/ He stared at the Pacific."

more distant, less developed islands below the equator.

"Savanna," or "savannah," from the Spanish *zavana*, now *sabana*, a treeless plain or a tropical or subtropical grassland, perpetuated in American English by the charming, aptly-named city, Savannah, Georgia, ties to one of the birds that sings from the ground. Almost all of the other birds sing from the wing, or while perched on some elevation, but the *savanna sparrow*, native American, that breeds in Eastern America, sings from the ground. (The oven bird and the wood thrush follow this practice, also.)

For whatever it's worth, we are obliged to Matthew (10:29) for, "Are not two sparrows sold for a farthing? and one of them shall not fall on the ground with your Father." This, obviously, preceded "His Eye Is On the Sparrow," as a literary title and an image.

Chaucer, in his Prologue to the *Canterbury Tales*, has it "As lecherous as a sparrow." And if one may be unbecomingly immodest, this author ends a poem, "Dial For Theology":

...I am reminded, high and low,
That God's eye is on the sparrow, eternally.
But from what I have observed, from my insular post,
Such celestial surveillance never helped any sparrows.
I think it would be more the sparrow's point
If He kept his eye on men with shotguns and rifles,
And particularly on small bastards bearing B-B guns.

The phrase may have been an accepted proverb at the time, but William Camden (1551-1625) in *Remains*, appears to have been in print first with "The early bird catches the worm." (Again, little is said from the pathetic vantage of the early worm that is devoured every time the phrase is spoken.)

In a letter of 1711, the immortal Jonathan Swift said "I heard a little bird say so." The eternal, "A little bird told me" may spring from a passage in Ecclesiastes (10:20): "For a bird of the air shall carry the voice, and that which hath wings shall tell the matter."

William Blake's (1757-1827) "Auguries of Innocence" employs the bird in a cage in this manner:

A robin redbreast in a cage
Puts all heaven in a rage.

Whether or not Arthur J. Lamb (1870-1928) was a devotee of Blake, his story-song of 1900, "A Bird In A Gilded Cage," employs the same idea, after a fashion:

Her beauty was sold for an old man's gold,
She's a bird in a gilded cage.*

"Sargasso" and "Sargasso Sea," written more often than spoken, are invoked to convey several senses of immobility or inundation. "Sargasso," or gulf weed, is from the Portugese *sargace*, perhaps, down from the Latin *salix*, willow or sallow.

The Sargasso Sea is that portion of the North Atlantic Ocean that extends between the West Indies and the Azores, from about latitude 20 degrees north to latitude 35 degrees north. The sea, relatively still, is the center of a great swirl of ocean currents. The area is a rich field of study for marine biologists, and it is known far and wide among seafaring men for the abundance of gulf weed (*sargasso*) on the surface of the water. It is the abundance of the gulf weed and the relatively still sea that first induced the idea of immobility, and civilians picked up "Sargasso Sea," in this context, from sailors.

---

*In one of his essays, Montaigne says: "Marriage may be compared to a cage; the birds outside despair to get in and those within to get out."

(The word "ocean" is Old French, through the Latin *oceanus* from the Greek *okeanos*. Homer used the word as the mighty river that encompasses the earth. In its corporate sense, "ocean" means the body of salt water that covers three-fourths of the earth's surface. "Sea," one of the bodies of salt water smaller than the ocean, is from the Anglo-Saxon *sae*.)

The late John Masefield, poet laureate, playwright, and novelist, compiled a list of nautical terms used by him in *The Bird of Dawning*, novel of 1933. The novel's time, around 1870, involves the last, exciting days of majestic sailing ships in the annual race to bring tea from China to England. The awesome era of steam began at Hampton Roads in 1862, but the old tea races supply Masefield with an appropriate epilogue to the long history of sails. Masefield's list follows:

"A.B.," an "Able-bodied" seaman: Formerly one who had served five or seven years at sea; "Amerline": A light line or cord. "Bagwrinkle": After-supports to masts. "Beam Sea": A sea breaking at right angles to a ship's course. "Binnacle": The case which held the compass. "Bonnets": Extra sails laced to the feet of courses. "Booms": The space filled with the ship's spare spars, and the spare spars themselves. "Braces": Running rigging by which the yards are trimmed to one side of the other. "Break" of the "Poop": The forward end of a ship's afterstructure. "Breaker": A wooden cask or small barrel. "Broaching-to": Suddenly shifting course so that the ship's head points into the direction from which the wind is coming. "Backstays": After-supports to masts. "Brought aback": In such a position that the sails are pressed by the wind against the masts. "Bulkhead": A ship's partition or wall. "Bulwarks": The ship's sides, especially those parts of them which fence the upper deck. "Bunts": The central positions of square sails. "Caught by the Ice": Taken unawares by a dangerous and sudden shift of wind, as in a revolving storm. "Checked": Secured against rolling about.

"Clinker-built"': Having overlapping planks. "Clipper": A name given to a ship of speed and beauty. "Clove": A simple fastening. "Clue": The lower corner of a square sail. "Coaming": A raised rim around an opening in a deck. 'Cockbilled": Pulled askew. "Coir": Coconut fibre. "Companion": A hatchway, or opening to a cabin. "Cringle": A round, flanged ring of metal sewn into sails at particular points. "Crojick" or "Cross-jack": The lowest yard upon the mizen mast of a full-rigged ship; also the sail set upon this yard. "Crutch": A movable rowboat; "Davits": Curved iron appliances to which ships' boats may be hoisted. "Day's work" or "dead reckoning": A means of computing a ship's position from her course and the distance traveled. "Dodger": A screen. "Dog-watch": A short evening watch, from four to six, or from six to eight. "Drogue":A floating sea-anchor, to which a ship or boat may ride in foul weather. "Dungaree": A thin stuff like coarse cotton. "Fall": A stretch of running rigging, especially that part handled in hauling. "Fetch-bag": A canvas bag, with a wooden bottom, used for sailmakers' tools. "Fid": A wooden marlin-spike. "First watch": From eight p.m. to midnight. "Fo'c's'le" or "forecastle": A deckhouse on other living space allotted to seamen. The men living in such space. "Fife Rail": A teak ledge stuck about with belaying pins for the securing of rigging. "Forenoon watch": From eight a.m. to noon. "Frapped": Wrapped and tied round. "Gear": Things proper to the work at hand; such as running rigging. "Grummett": A ring or garland of rope. "Gudgeon": A metal socket. "Gunwale": The upper edge of a ship's planking. "Halliards": Ropes by which sails are hoisted. "Handy-billy": A portable tackle or pulley for obtaining greater power. "Hank": A twist or roll of light wire or twine. "Harness cask": A tub containing salt meat. "Jibboom": A spar secured to the extremity of the bowsprit. "Jiggers": Small arrangements or pulleys. "Jury rudder": A makeshift rudder improvised in case of an accident. "Killick": Small grapnel anchors for boats, usually with four prongs. "Kites": Light topmost sails. "Lazarette": A strong-room in which provisions are stored. "Leeches": The edges of sails. "Liverpool Pennants": Rope yarns used instead of buttons. "Log Ship": A quadrant of hard wood used in estimating a ship's speed. "Luff": To turn the ship towards the direction of the wind.

"Main bites": A strong wooden frame, surrounding the main mast, to which much gear is secured. "Mainyards shack": An arrangement by which the wind presses the sails of the main mast against the mast and stops the ship. "Marler" or "Marline-spike": A steel spike, about fifteen inches long, used in splicing ropes. "Middle watch": From midnight until four a.m. "Midshipman's nuts": The hard central portion of a ship's biscuits.* "Mizen mast": The aforemast of a ship's three masts. "Morning watch": From four to eight a.m. "Nettles" or "Knittles": Light cords such as are used to spread and support hammocks. "O.S.": An ordinary seaman, not yet able to qualify as "A.B." "Paddy's milestone": Ailsa Craig. "Painter": A line by which a boat may be secured to anything. "Pannikin": A tiny cup containing nearly half a pint. "Pantile": A ship's biscuit, usually a round, hard object weighing four ounces. "Picul": The load a seaman can carry at one time; about 120 pounds. "Pin" or "Belaying pin": An iron or wooden bar to which ropes may be secured. "Poop": A ship's after-superstructure. "Puff-balls" or "save-alls": Extra sails laced to the feet of square sails. "Quarter": A little to one side of the after-end of a ship. "Ratching" or "Reaching": Beating against the wind. "Rickers": Short lengths of wood, poles or light spars.

---

*The word "midshipman" originated in the British navy because young men being trained to become officers were assigned quarters amidships on the lower deck. In time cadets became "midshipmen," and the cadets at Annapolis are still so designated.

"Round-house": A part of a deckhouse set aside for the berthing place of a ship's warrant officers.* "Royals": Light sails set above the topgallant sails in a square-rigged ship. "Scupper": A channel at the ship's side for the carrying of water. "Scuttle-but": A tub containing drinking water.** "Sheer": The line, curved or straight, of a ship's rail. "Shrouds": Lateral supports to masts. "Sight": Observation of sun, moon, or star to determine ship's position. "Skids": Supports on which a ship's lifeboat stand. "Skysail": A little sail set above the royals in lofty square-rigged ships. "Slops": Clothes, kit, tobacco, knives etc. issued to sailors during a voyage, and charged against their wages. "Slush": Melted fat. "Spanker gaff": A spar by which the head of the spanker, a fore and aft sail set upon the aforemost mast of a ship, may be extended. "Spunyarn": A light tarry line spun from rope yarns. "Splice the main brace": Drink and be merry. "Stary": Powerful forward supports to masts. "Steerage way": Motion sufficient to enable the ship to be steered. "Stern sheets": A clear space at the after-end of a boat. "Strait": A streak or line of planking. "Studding sail": A sail set at the extremity of a yard to increase the area of a ship's canvas. "Tack block": A purchase pulley used at the corners of certain sails. "Thimbles": Small metal rounds or eyes spliced into ropes or sewn into sails, for various purposes. "Thole-pin": A wooden pin fitted into a boat's gunwale as a fulcrum for an oar. "Topgallant masts": Upper spars "Transom Stern": Shaped like the straight back-board of a ship. "Triced": Hoisted.

*Rail-roading terminology obtained "round-house" from nautical language. In baseball there is the "round-house curve," and some politicians and gamblers "Are so crooked he couldn't lie down in a round-house."

**"Scuttle-but" came to mean gossip because sailors gathered around the scuttle-butt on ships to chew the fat.

"Truss": An iron crutch or hinge supporting a yard upon a mast. "Trust-to-Gods" or "Hope-in-Heaven": Little topmost sails. "Watch": A division (usually one-half of a ship's company). The space of duty kept by each division at one time. "Weft": A flag knotted in the middle as a signal of distress. "Whack": An allowance.

PART FIFTEEN
CHRISTMAS AND SAINT NICHOLAS

" 'I have often thought,' says Sir Roger, 'It happens very well that Christmas should' fall out in the middle of winter.' "

Joseph Addison, in *The Spectator.*

"Thou has conquered, O Galilean."

Death-bed utterance attributed to the Roman Emperor Julian.

"He had a broad face and a little round belly,
That shook, when he laughed, like a bowlful of jelly."

Clement C. Moore, from "A Visit From St. Nicholas."

"Yes, Virginia, there is a Santa Claus. Not believe in Santa Claus? You might as well not believe in fairies."

Frank Church, from an editorial of September 21, 1897, in the New York *Sun*, in answer to a question from Virginia O'Hanlon.

"At Christmas play, and make good cheer,
For Christmas comes but once a year."

Thomas Tusser, from *Five Hundred Points of Good Husbandry* (1557).

"I heard the bells on Christmas Day
Their old, familiar carols play,
And wild and sweet
The words repeat
Of peace on earth, good will to men."

Henry W. Longfellow, from "Christmas Bells."

CHRISTMAS AND SAINT NICHOLAS

At times, Christmas, so fearfully traduced by blatant gimmicks and sordid, commercial machinations, has all of the dignity of a pool room towel. Pandering store and street-corner Santa Clauses have become so astronomically prevalent many beleaguered folks equate "yo, ho, ho" with a wrong number in the middle of the night. Even so, the jolly old elf retains much of his ancient magic for young innocents for whom the rapt expectancy of Christmas Eve's sugar-shivers is all bound round with the centuries' old wine of anticipation.

Eugene Field died in 1895, but the small, picaresque hero of "Jess Afore Christmas" has managed to circumvent light years of maudlin developments:

Now, all the whole year round,
There ain't no flies on me,
But jess afore Christmas,
I'm ez good ez I kin be.

And, a stanza in the late Robert Frost's "From Plane to Plane" speaks for millions of parents, even before Saint Nicholas became Santa Claus, even before gifts-giving was transferred to the English Christmas:

That's where I reckon Santa Claus comes in—
To be our parents' pseudonymity
In Christmas giving, so they can escape
The thanks and let him catch it as scapegoat.

Fact, fiction, and legend are almost comparable to a platter of scrambled eggs amid all the excitement and transition from Saint Nicholas to Santa Claus, from Gifts Day, on December 6, to the visit down the chimney on Christmas Eve. But Saint Nicholas (4th century A.D.), often called the "Boy Bishop," is an historical fact. Saint Nicholas lived in and around Myra, in Asia-Minor. He became the patron saint of boys, young men, and sailors, and, as a saint, he had enduring popularity and importance in the Eastern Church. The most famous painting of Saint Nicholas, by Bicci de Lorenzo, is in the Metropolitan Museum.

He was buried at Myra, and his remains were interred there until the 11th century. Overly-zealous merchants of Bari, on the Adriatic, exuding pious, and perhaps, fraudulent, indignation at what they branded as neglect of the Saint in Myra, carried his bones to Italy, to Bari's Church of Saint Stephen. Today, Saint Nicholas' tomb at Bari is the object of regular pilgrimages.

Several legends seem to have arisen during the saint's lifetime. Once when he was making a pilgrimage to the Holy Land, a fearful storm came up, and Saint Nicholas raised his hand to placate the fury of the weather. Thus, many seaport churches commemorate him, as the mariners' patron. And another legend, one that probably accounts for the custom of hanging up stockings at Christmastime, was circulated while he lived, or very shortly after his death.

Two sisters, about to be forced into prostitution because of extreme, unrelieved poverty, hung their wet stockings by the fire to dry. (This was before the advent of chimneys, when smoke-holes were commonplace.) Saint Nicholas knew of the young sister's awesome decision, and as he rode above their poor home on his gray ass, he dropped some gold coins down the smoke-hole. The coins fell into the stockings while the sisters slept, and they arose the next morning to discover that they had been delivered miraculously from the awful fate of prostitution. When they sought an explanation for their deliverance, local elders explained that they had been visited by elves while they slept.

In this legend, as in some of the other tales about Saint Nicholas' benefactions, the largesse is always accomplished in secret. Saint Nicholas comes and goes as swiftly, as mysteriously, and as majestically as Santa Claus does today. But, now and then, the saint's charity is discovered accidentally, by one other person, almost always a nobleman, who grabs at the flying saint and just manages to catch hold to his flowing robe.

The nobleman takes a vow of eternal secrecy. No one must ever know about Saint Nicholas' good deeds. The fact that the saint's confidante is always a nobleman suggests that commoners of the era were not considered safe repositories for such prodigious secrets. And in these tales of disarming detection, the nobleman's always grabbing the saint's robe seems to have parallels in religious literature, perhaps, with some of the symbolism of those who touched Jesus' terminal robe.

Although nothing approximating the precise date is extant, within a century or two of Saint Nicholas' demise, his feast day, December 6, became a children's holiday in the Netherlands, a day of gifts to the young. The saint flew about Dutch homes, on December 6, traveling on a gray horse, or a white ass, or via his robe, to leave gifts for good children.

Expectant children fixed hay, oats, some sort of fodder, for the horse or the ass, and in their wooden shoes they placed sweet cakes, or cakes and honey, for Saint Nicholas. He fed the fodder to his steed, and when he ate the cakes, he placed his own gifts in the children's wooden shoes. But if the children in a specific home were bad, the fodder was untouched, and rods (ashes and switches in America's insular era) were found in the wooden shoes.

One of the most significant developments was the election in some countries of a "Boy Bishop," an *Episcopus Puerorum*, to serve from December 6 to "Christmas Day" (December 28, old calendar). The "Boy Bishop" exercised burlesque episcopal jurisdiction throughout the period, and with his juvenile "dean" and prefendaries parodied various ecclesiastical functions. This tradition, essentially disarming was prevalent throughout the English cathedral and grammar schools. This pageantry was celebrated at Sarum, in Salisbury, England, most particularly.

New York's transplanted Dutchmen brought Saint Nicholas to the New World in the guise of Santa Claus, and, as in England, gifts to children and the general exchange of presents, attached to Christmas. From descriptions written by Washington Irving (1783-1859)(*Knickerbocker's History of New York*) and others, Santa Claus is dressed in brown and he smokes a long clay pipe. In the limited festival parades of the 18th century, Santa Claus rides in a horse-drawn vehicle that seems to approximate the 19th-century phaeton.

Santa Claus, as he is recognized today, stepped from Clement Moore's poem of 1823, "A Visit From St. Nicholas," better known to moderns via the popular adaptation, " 'Twas the Night Before Christmas":

" 'Twas the night before Christmas and all through the house
Not a creature was stirring, not even a mouse."

Moore (1779-1863), born in New York City, wrote the poem in 1822 for the amusement and edification of his own children, and the poem was published, without Moore's awareness, in the Troy, N.Y. *Sentinel* on December 23, 1823. It is unlikely that in the entire history of literature a single publication ever established so widely and firmly an image or institution to the degree to which Moore's poem fixed Santa Claus for all time to come.

Insofar as one can ascertain, Santa Claus' classic picture was drawn first by Thomas Nast, the famous political cartoonist, in 1863. Nast's drawing, duplicated thousands of times by flesh-and-blood Santa Clauses in American stores during the long Christmas season, is based on the description in Clement Moore's poem.

Moore, curiously enough, for a man whose reputation rests

almost exclusively on a children's poem-song, was professor of Oriental and Greek literature at New York's General Theological Seminary. An ordained divine, Moore gave the land on which the Seminary stands. One of America's finest linguists of the early era, he attained tremendous professional stature for *A Compendious Lexicon of the Hebrew Language*, published in 1809.*

Only slightly less viable are Scrooge and Tiny Tim, from Charles Dickens' (1812-1870) *A Christmas Carol*, published in 1843. At that time, the 31 year-old Dickens, father of six, was grappling with some problems attendant to the writing of his novel *Nicholas Nickleby*. Apparently, the idea for the *Carol* obsessed Dickens as he tramped London's cold streets late at night, trying to reconcile his difficulties with *Nickleby*.

Dickens seems to have been somewhat strapped for money in 1843, and he expected *A Christmas Carol* to sell well. The long, long story, now happily abridged of some of the superfluous ghosts and repetitive scenes, appeared, first in Dickens' magazine, *Household Words*; and even though the reception was warm, the book, itself, sold only 15,000 copies the first year it was circulated, at a shilling a copy, then equal to 12 pence, or 24 1/3 cents. (There is a sharp contrast with *Mugby Junction*, now generally forgotten, Dickens' Christmas offering of 1863, which sold 250,000 copies the first year.)

In the ensuing years *A Christmas Carol* has become an international legacy, and literature has few sheer exaltations superior to the picture of the transfigured Scrooge listening to the bells on Christmas morning.

---

*A parallel, somewhat similar, exists with Eugene Field (1850-1895), author of the aforementioned "Jess Afore Christmas." Field, remembered for such tongue-in-cheek sentimentalities as "Little Boy Blue," collaborated with his brother, Roswell, in 1893, on *Echoes from the Sabine Farm*, astonishingly good versions, and perversions, of Horace; and it was Eugene Field, a premier drama and music critic, who wrote of Creston Clarke, "He played the King as if under the apprehension someone else would place the ace."

Dickens, a consummate actor,* and one of the first authors to achieve international response from the reading of his own works, read the *Carol*, at Oxford, as early as 1853. His dramatic format, a small table lighted by a single candle, with a backdrop of dancing shadows, is yet emulated by American actors at Christmastime.

Scrooge, Tiny Tim, and Bob Crachett have had the same international personalities these past one hundred and thirty-three years as the folks down the street. And, indeed, it is the Charles Dickens of the *Carol*, of *Christmas Chimes*, the Dickens who wrote of Christmas in several successive issues of *Household Words*, who did so much to rejuvenate the season as an intelligent, rollicking, hedonistic festival of good will.

Dickens came at the propitious juncture in British and in American history. Christmas was still suffering the glum, doleful effects of Oliver Cromwell (1599-1658)** whose life-style was a flesh-and-blood anticipation of H.L. Mencken's observation that the zealot's abiding fear is that "somehow, somewhere, some poor bastard might have a little pleasure."

New England was still terrified, at least partially, by the baleful shadows cast by Jonathan Edwards (1703-1758) and Cotton Mather (1663-1728), Cromwell's New World counterparts. It was Dickens, more than any single person, who helped to restore and to revitalize the Christmas depicted in the sprig of holly, by the carollers, the festive board, the whole outgoing amalgam of robust fellowship, of giving and sharing.

*In company with Sinclair Lewis, the American who created George F. Babbitt et al, Dickens seems to have been a superb mimic. Like Lewis, Dickens leaped from his writing desk to run to a mirror to mimic characters whom he was writing about. Both Lewis and Dickens were skilled amateur actors, and each liked nothing better than appearing in what came to be known as "home talent plays," chiefly, innocuous ones of their own composition.

**In 1972, the late Glenn Tucker of Fairview, N.C., eminent historian revived the contention that Oliver Cromwell actually booked passage for the Massachusetts Bay Colony. Cromwell, according to this report, was actually aboard the ship, when he was detained. God only knows how the history of England and New England would have been altered had Cromwell's voyage to Massachusetts been consummated.

The shooting of firecrackers, the sounding of horns, the ringing of bells, and all the ebullient hullabaloo that now attends secular Christmas (and New Year's), inexplicable to many students, is fairly new, in substance, only. Festive hell-raising at Christmastime may be an outgrowth of the old *charivari*, usually spelled and pronounced "shivaree" in the American south. The original *charivari*, ("sha-ree-va-ree") was a French custom of hazing, and frequently it devolved upon a widow thought to have remarried too hastily, although during the so-called Middle Ages such outbursts were raised against political apostates, also. In either case, neighbors collected at night around the objectionable home to blow tin horns, to ring cow bells, to beat upon dish pans, to hiss and to chant. And, frequently, the crowd wore masks, or some sort of outrageous camouflage.

The couple, or individual, obtained an armistice by paying a ransom, usually in terms of food and drink. The French immigrants who settled in Louisiana brought the tempestuous *charivari* to America, but in the southern states the ancient volubility ascribed much more to married couples and to holiday festivals. (The tying of shoes, tin cans etc. to the honeymooners' automobile is a direct outgrowth.)

The *charivari*, tagged as a "calithump," rough music, in British English, fanned out from Louisiana to encompass weddings, Christmas, and New Year's celebrations, frequently in the form of improvised parades, but parades that were likely to be exuberant burlesques of regimented parades. (In Germany the *charivari* is called *Katzenmusk*, or cat's concert. "Hans and Fritz," the compulsive imps of the old comic strip, "Katzenjammer Kids," were household characters in America until World War II. *Katzenjammer*, or "cat's wailing," literally, means "hangover," figuratively.

In recent years "Christmas Is Coming," set to music by Edith Nesbitt, has attained the status of a Yuletide "in-thing." The lyrics, printed and sung almost endlessly during the

Christmas season, go:

Christmas is coming, the geese are getting fat,
Please to put a penny in the old man's hat;
If you haven't a penny, a ha'penny will do,
And if you haven't a ha'penny, why God bless you.

Apparently, the far better known lyrics are a take off from the ancient English children's Christmas begging chant:

The roads are very dirty,
My boots are very thin,
I have a little pocket
To put a penny in.
If you haven't got a penny
A ha'penny will do.
If you haven't got a ha'penny,
God bless you.

As is noted in the section on Time, Christmas used to be celebrated during the twelve days between December 25 and January 6, the Epiphany, the coming of the Magi or manifestation of divinity. Old Christmas is still celebrated on North Carolina's Outer Banks and at one or two places in the Kentucky mountains. One of the lyrical residues is the incredibly popular carol, "The Twelve Days of Christmas," with the magnetic refrain, "And a partridge in a pear tree."

This carol began as a singing game in which guests at a home had to repeat all of the various "gifts" enumerated in the song, in order, without mistake. Any guest who missed a "gift" had to pay some innocuous penalty, some of which were paid in the aforementioned "Yankee dimes."

In insular America, notably in rural sections, considerable lip-service attached to the myth that domesticated animals kneeled in their stalls on Old Christmas Day to pray and to talk, as tradition had the animals doing when Jesus was born in the manger in Bethlehem. The late Elizabeth Madox Roberts, author of the incomparable novel, *The Great Meadow* (1930), perpetuates the tradition in her exquisite poem, "Christmas Morning":

...I'd run out through the garden gate,
And down along the pasture walk;
And off beside the cattle barns
I'd hear a kind of gentle talk.

In several of the more sparsely-settled southern communities an animal – the same animal in a specific locality – was integral in the secular celebration of Old Christmas. According to local tradition, an animal, in the colonial or early republic era, had come to the settlement for the duration of the holiday as a viable spectator. This tradition was implemented by the presence of a simulated human under an animal's skin, at the annual Old Christmas Day ceremony.

The format, with slight topical variations, was: The villagers, most of whom were kinsmen, assembled in the community's common meeting place. Just before the exchange of gifts, "Old Buck," the local deer, ox, or whatever, walked in. (The animal had an enduring first name.) His appearance was the signal for a holiday from school, or for the commencement of the essence of the local celebration, be it a community deer or fox-hunt, a barn dance, visitation of the shut-ins, a community sing, athletic contests, a taffy-pull, or whatever. In some communities the Old Christmas animal's functions approximated those of Aaron's Biblical scapegoat: All of the community's bad luck of the preceding twelve months was deposited on the animal's person, and when it left the meeting place, it took the bad luck with it.

Beyond peradventure, the annual appearance of such a cherished animal relates to the animals that talked in the manger at Bethlehem, but here and there a specific creature had become a community talisman. It had spread the alarm in face of a forest fire, some natural calamity, or an Indian attack.

The late Roy Helton's "Old Christmas Morning," subtitled, "A Kentucky Mountain Ballad," carries on the tradition – "And critters kneel down in their straw "– brings in the supernatural elements often ascribed to the event –"Yes, elder bushes, they bloom Old Christmas"–in a poem that contains one of the most absorbing mystery stories in the language. It is doubtful if any of the ghost stories and dramas of Lord Dunsany, truly a master of the eerie, is so heightened by such successful dramatic suspensions as Helton's astonishingly effective ballad.

The Christmas carol, as it is sung in America, came from England. Some authorities relate the original carols to St. Francis of Assisi (1182-1226), who built a manger scene, about which he and his spiritual brothers chanted adorations. Carols are now almost universal: The French *noel*, the German *kristlieder*, and their counterpart in the Russian *kolyda*, until fairly recently. (One of the most enduringly popular, "O, Come, All Ye Faithful," is credited to John Francis Wade (1712-1786). Wade, a militant Catholic, is supposed to have written the present words and the original music during the turbulent 1740's when he was in exile, with other Stuart sympathizers near Dounay, France.)

(And there is this persistent paradox, predicated upon the faulty placement of a single comma: In one of the oldest Christmas songs, known only as "Carol," and of anonymous authorship, many of us sing, "God rest you merry gentlemen,/Let nothing you dismay." Commas come, properly, before and after "gentlemen": "God rest you merry, gentlemen,/Let nothing you dismay." This is not supposed to be sung as "merry gentlemen." Conversely, it means "God keep you happy, gentlemen.")

Sir Henry Cole, infused with a passionate desire to improve the public taste, is credited with the first Christmas card, in 1843. Undoubtedly, Cole was influenced by the custom in British schools whereby students sent their parents "Christmas pieces," to convey greetings and to demonstrate their penmanship. These "pieces" were large sheets, decorated with colored borders, on which students wrote copperplate Christmas greetings and wishes.

Cole instructed J.C. Horsley, R.A., to adopt the medieval form of triptych, or a set of three illustrations. In the Cole-Horsley production, the central piece shows a group of adults and children rejoicing with food and drink. (This brought the Temperance Society down on Cole for a testy inning.) Beneath the picture was "Merry Christmas And A Happy New Year," and the side panels depicted feeding the hungry and clothing the naked. Nonetheless, Cole's idea did not catch on with the British public until the 1860's, when his bright cards became big business.

Not just incidentally, Cole helped to modernize England's postal system, constructed Albert Hall, and he was vital in the arrangements of the Great Exhibition in 1851 and in the inauguration of the Victoria and Albert Museum.

The Christmas tree, first used by the Germans, may have been introduced into England by Prince Albert (1819-1861). Obviously, the tree's green foliage was associated with the winter solstice, and in Norse mythology the world tree's branches and roots joined heaven, earth, and hell. The tree, itself, symbolized renewal and the leaves symbolized immortality.

One German legend relates the Christmas tree to St. Boniface, who came from England to convert the heathen. In Getsmar, St. Boniface embittered and estranged the population by cutting down a revered oak tree. To show his faith, he replaced the oak by planting a fir, and the fir tree symbolized the Christian faith he preached. But, of course, another account gives the credit for the Christmas tree to Martin Luther (1483-1546), who cut down a fir from his garden, brought it into his home, and put candles on the branches to suggest the glory of God as Luther had seen it in the starry sky.

German immigrants and travelers, sailors and merchants, particularly took the concept of the Christmas tree with them across the civilized world. Albeit, the tree was slow taking root in England. The first public mention seems to have been at a children's Christmas party in 1821 at Queen Caroline's Court. Ironically, Charles Dickens castigated the Christmas tree as "the new German toy." But by 1841, two years prior to the publication of *A Christmas Carol*, the tree gained acceptance, undoubtedly because Albert, the Prince Consort, put one in Windsor Castle as a surprise for the young Prince of Wales, and as a nostalgic reminder of the German Christmases Albert had known as a youngster.

Of all the Yuletide traditions, none surpasses the innocent charm of kissing beneath the jaunty sprig of mistletoe. Curiously enough, mistletoe (*toe*, from the Anglo-Saxon *tan*, twig, and *mistel*, Anglo-Saxon diminutive of *mist*) seems to undergo complete mythological transformation. In Norse mythology, the evil Logi kills Balder, the beautiful sun-god, with an arrow fashioned from mistletoe. But by the time of the Druids, the oak tree and its mistletoe developed sacred properties. Mistletoe heals physical wounds, and its spiritual, magical implications are so magnetic that when warriors meet beneath it they throw down their weapons. To show their honorable intentions, they embrace prior to sitting beneath the oak tree in a blessed respite of peacefulness.

Because the Druids maintained proscriptions relative to written records, little is known of them. But they were priests, poets, and prophets among the ancient Celts in Gaul, Britain, and Ireland. Even if their rituals were committed to memory, only, the Druids are reputed to have been magicians and astrologers, and they were experts in the mysterious prowess ascribed to certain animals and plants, such as the mistletoe.

Some authorities reason that "druid" is derived from a forgotten Celt word that meant "oakmen."* Others derive "druid" from the Celtic *druidh*, men of learning, especially in the sense of a wizard or diviner. There is the legend that the Celts and their priesthood were the offspring of Japheth, Noah's son, and that they migrated to Europe from Asia around 2000 B.C., settling in Ireland first, and spreading out to Britain and to France. Druids still lived in Wales, and in parts of France, at the time of the Roman invasion. One of the best extant accounts of the Druids, in Julius Caesar's *Commentaries*, tells how they were divided into distinct orders, with distinctive, mystic functions.

Their resistance to the Romans, their attempts to incite others to repel the Romans, culminated in their expulsion from Britain. Their last home, apparently, was on the Island of Anglesey, off the coast of North Wales, in the Irish Sea. There, most of the surviving Druids were liquidated by a Roman force under Agricola. Although the modern opinion is that Stonehenge was constructed in prehistoric times, the Druids probably used Stonehenge, and other stone structures, to impress the populace with their mystic incantations.

---

*In his monumental *The Golden Bough*, the late Sir James Frazier wrote: "Among the Celts and Gauls, the druids esteemed nothing more sacred than the mistle toe and the oak on which it grew; they chose groves of oaks for the scene of their solemn service, and they performed none of their rites without oak leaves."

EPILOGUE

If few absolutes remain in our complex, contradictory society, one may be reasonably certain the most voluminous etymological argument of the bicentennial year pertains to the origin of "as clean as a whistle," but hardly anyone spoke with finality. But because this argument was waged across many pages of stationery and newsprint, we shall enumerate the theories we have heard and read, many of which are a part of our own folk-etymology.

The phrase is said to have come from the sounds of a tea-kettle, or from an old locomotive whistle. Many tie it to the process of stripping clean the bark from pussy-willow to make a penny-whistle. (This seems to be viable in relationship to the southernism, "As slick as a whistle.") The same derivation relates to the slickness and the shrill sound from a whistle fashioned from slippery elm. And, obviously, the phrase has to relate to the piercing, clean sound made by the whistle of a policeman, athletic referee, scout master et al. Some have opted for the boatswain's pipe, and others to the "dirty" and "clean" notes made by an orchestra, "when the flutes have no harmonics and give off a pure, clean sound." It is probable that the phrase ties to railroading because it became popular in the 1850's, when railroads were criss-crossing the nation. Locomotive whistles were operated by blasts of hot steam, and the whistle, perforce, was cleaned with every blast. This would certainly stand out since it was almost the only clean portion of the grimy locomotive.

Whether or not this informal study has run the gamut from A to Z, there is no prejudice against the letter "z" such as existed in England from around the time of the Normal Conquest (1066) into the Elizabethan era. During this period the British invoked numerous synonyms for "z,":– Zed, Zod,

Zard, Issod, Uzzard, and several others. Indeed, many Americans still say from "A to Izzard" to mean an entirety. The British thought "z" superfluous since it represents merely a voiced "s," and Elizabethans preferred to write "z" as "s."

In *King Lear*, Shakespeare flails out: "Thou whoreson Zed! thou unnecessary letter." And "whoreson" has been semantically devious. Prior to Shakespeare the word was deemed arrant indecency. Its written or spoken use was prohibited by law. Then when the legal restriction was removed, over-use made "whoreson" as meaningless as over-use made "bloody" later on.

In *Hamlet*, the gravedigger speaks of a "whoreson dead body," and the gravedigger calls poor Yorick, "a whoreson mad fellow." But "whoreson" became a term of endearment, and speedily. For Doll Tearsheet, in *Henry V*, compliments Falstaff with: "Thou whoreson little tidy Bartholomew bear-pig."

Finally, thousands of people are baffled by the inevitable use of the word "commencement" to mean the exercises with which school years terminate, the occasion of which diplomas are awarded.

During the medieval era virtually all higher education was under the aegis of the state, the principality, or some potentate, some sponsor. Those who enjoyed the privilege of higher education agreed to teach a specified period following graduation, as partial compensation for the privilege of higher education. These teaching tenures usually "commenced" immediately upon graduation. In other words, the graduate "commenced" his professional obligation.

Today's graduate usually receives a single sheet, sometimes of parchment. This used to be folded, from the Greek *diploma*, or folded sheet, from *diplous*, double. And the official bearer of such a sheet of folded parchment was a *diplomat*.

384